DISCRETION

DISCRETIONARY POWERS

A Legal Study of Official Discretion

D. J. GALLIGAN

*Professor of Law, University of
Southampton, formerly Fellow of
Jesus College, Oxford*

CLARENDON PRESS · OXFORD

*This book has been printed digitally and produced in a standard specification
in order to ensure its continuing availability*

OXFORD
UNIVERSITY PRESS

Great Clarendon Street, Oxford OX2 6DP

Oxford University Press is a department of the University of Oxford.
It furthers the University's objective of excellence in research, scholarship,
and education by publishing worldwide in

Oxford New York

Auckland   Cape Town Dar es Salaam   Hong Kong   Karachi
Kuala Lumpur Madrid Melbourne Mexico City   Nairobi
New Delhi Shanghai Taipei Toronto
With offices in
Argentina Austria Brazil Chile Czech Republic France Greece
Guatemala Hungary Italy Japan South Korea Poland Portugal
Singapore Switzerland Thailand Turkey Ukraine Vietnam

Oxford is a registered trade mark of Oxford University Press
in the UK and in certain other countries

Published in the United States
by Oxford University Press Inc., New York

ISBN 978-0-19-825652-6

Printed and bound in Great Britain by CPI Antony Rowe,
Chippenham and Eastbourne

TO THE MEMORY OF
JOHN FELIX GALLIGAN

Preface

THIS book is a study from a legal point of view of discretionary powers exercised by state officials. Some reference is made to discretion in the hands of the superior courts, but the emphasis is on the decisions and actions of other officials who may be referred to loosely as administrative. The primary aim of the book is to contribute to the expanding interest in administrative law, but at the same time I have attempted at various points to link issues that arise in administrative law to broader ideas, particularly in jurisprudence and occasionally in social and administrative theory. The scope of the book is set out in section 1.1; it is sufficient to say here that the object has been to examine in a general and thematic way some of the main issues that arise with respect to discretionary powers in the hands of administrative officials. It is not intended to be a legal treatise on the law relating to discretion, nor is it a substitute for detailed studies of particular areas of discretionary authority. The book is written within the framework of British law, but there is some reliance on American writers and materials. At various points use is made also of Australian law.

Since the question has often been put why anyone would try to write a book about discretion, I should perhaps make brief mention of some of the reasons for doing so. The first and rather trivial was a casual remark by K. C. Davis in his famous book *Discretionary Justice* that administrative law provided many areas of research, none of them more interesting than discretion. When first coming across that remark, I had little idea what it meant, but it became something of a challenge to find out. Whether or not, many years later, I agree with the implications of the remark, I think that at least I now know what was meant.

The second reason is more serious. It did seem, as I became more interested and involved in both administrative law and jurisprudence, that discretionary powers in the hands of officials provided the setting for an interesting intermingling of ideas in both areas. On the one hand administrative law seemed to be skirting around the central issues; it was concentrated on questions of jurisdiction, errors of law, natural justice, and remedies, each endlessly fascinating in its own way, but at the same time seeming to miss the most important question, namely just how administrative powers do get exercised and what constraints they are subject to. To raise those questions is to enter the realm of discretion. On the other hand, ideas in jurisprudence and social theory were on the move, with old traditions being challenged in a virtual explosion of new lines of enquiry. There was the famous Hart–Dworkin controversy over whether judges exercised discretion, followed by Dworkin's conception of rights, and what it means to take rights seriously; there was the neo-libertarian challenge to the ideals and workings of the welfare state, with its heavy reliance on bureaucratic authority and discretionary powers; there was also the critical legal studies movement, which could almost be regarded as a distinct school of jurisprudence, and which was to a large degree centred around the alleged passing away of traditional notions of legality, and their replacement by some conception of discretionary authority. This is to name but a few of the themes which have dominated modern jurisprudence, and which appeared to have implications for administrative law and the study of discretionary powers. It is for these sorts of reasons that a study of discretion seemed an interesting and challenging undertaking.

In the years that it has taken to gather together materials and write this book, things have changed dramatically. When I began, the field seemed wide open, with little to be found beyond the important but preliminary works of K. C. Davis, and scattered essays, articles, and small-scale studies. Now, however, there is almost an embarrassment of riches. The last several years have seen a flood of books, extensive studies, and penetrating analyses of discretionary power in its various guises and facets. This has meant a regular reassessment of my own ideas in order to take account of the many interesting and imaginative arguments and suggestions that have appeared. It will become clear in the following pages that I have relied heavily on a number of these, particularly, for example, Keith Hawkins's *Environment and Enforcement* and the equally important study by Genevra Richardson and others, called *Policing Pollution*. Many others will find ideas and suggestions that can be traced to their own writings, and my general debt to those many people studying discretion in one or other of its aspects is hereby acknowledged in full.

One criticism that might well be made, and which, looking back on it, I would to a certain degree accept, is that in the second part of the book too much emphasis is put on legal regulation through judicial scrutiny. The only defence I would offer is, first that it did seem important to examine judicial review closely because it is somewhat controversial, and because it has been the subject, in my view, of a certain amount of misconception. Secondly, other forms of legal regulation, such as those developed by ombudsmen, have been dealt with extremely thoroughly in recent publications, like *Law and Administration* by Carol Harlow and Richard Rawlings. It might also seem that I have ignored or underestimated many of the more practical problems in discretionary decision-making. Fortunately that omission has been remedied in another excellent recent publication to which the reader is referred, namely Ross Cranston's *Legal Foundations of the Welfare State.*

The book is well travelled. It began while I was teaching in Oxford and the development of my ideas owes much to colleagues and friends from those days, in particular Eric Barendt, Peter Cane, Hugh Collins, Paul Craig, and Joseph Raz, and most of all Jack Beatson who made many helpful and perceptive suggestions. The book was continued at the University of Florence where I spent a term on a Wolfson Research Fellowship awarded by the British Academy. My sincere thanks go to the British Academy for its generosity, and to Professors Antonio Cassesse and Giorgio Gaja of Florence University and Professor Terence Daintith of the European University Institute. Most of the book was written at the University of Melbourne, and I wish to thank David Wood who for a short period was a valuable research assistant. The final stages of publication were overseen from the University of Southampton. My final thanks are to my wife Martha who for many years has given much valued help and support to my publications.

D.J.G.

Southampton

Contents

Abbreviations

A JOURNALS AND REVIEWS

AdmLR	*Administrative Law Review*
AmPhilQ	*American Philosophical Quarterly*
AmPolSciR	*American Political Science Review*
ARSP	*Archiv fur Rechts und Sozialphilosophie*
ArizLR	*Arizona Law Review*
AJPA	*Australian Journal of Public Administration*
ALJ	*Australian Law Journal*
BritJCrim	*British Journal of Criminology*
BJLS	*British Journal of Law and Society*
BJSoc	*British Journal of Sociology*
BASLP	*Bulletin of the Australian Society of Legal Philosophy*
CalLR	*California Law Review*
CLJ	*Cambridge Law Journal*
CanBR	*Canadian Bar Review*
CanJSoc	*Canadian Journal of Sociology*
ClevStLR	*Cleveland State Law Review*
ColLR	*Columbia Law Review*
CompPolStud	*Comparative Political Studies*
CornLR	*Cornell Law Review*
CrimLR	*Criminal Law Review*
CLP	*Current Legal Problems*
DalLR	*Dalhousie Law Review*
DukeLJ	*Duke Law Journal*
FLR	*Federal Law Review*
GeoLJ	*Georgia Law Journal*
GaLR	*Georgia Law Review*
Govt&Opp	*Government and Opposition*
HarvLR	*Harvard Law Review*
HofstraLR	*Hofstra Law Review*
IntRevLaw&Econ	*International Review of Law and Economics*
JBL	*Journal of Business Law*
JLegEd	*Journal of Legal Education*
JLegStud	*Journal of Legal Studies*
JLibStud	*Journal of Libertarian Studies*
JPhil	*Journal of Philosophy*

JPL	*Journal of Public Law*
Law&CP	*Law and Contemporary Problems*
Law&Phil	*Law and Philosophy*
LSR	*Law and Society Review*
LQR	*Law Quarterly Review*
ManLR	*Manitoba Law Review*
McGillLJ	*McGill Law Journal*
MichLR	*Michigan Law Review*
MLR	*Modern Law Review*
MonLR	*Monash Law Review*
NYULR	*New York University Law Review*
NZLJ	*New Zealand Law Journal*
NZLR	*New Zealand Law Review*
OhioStLJ	*Ohio State Law Journal*
OsgoodeHLJ	*Osgoode Hall Law Journal*
OJLS	*Oxford Journal of Legal Studies*
PolQ	*Political Quarterly*
PolSci	*Political Science*
PAdR	*Public Administration Review*
PubInt	*Public Interest*
PL	*Public Law*
RutLR	*Rutgers Law Review*
SCLR	*Southern California Law Review*
StanLR	*Stanford Law Review*
SydLR	*Sydney Law Review*
TexasLR	*Texas Law Review*
UCLALR	*University of California at Los Angeles Law Review*
UChicLR	*University of Chicago Law Review*
UNSWLR	*University of New South Wales Law Review*
UPaLR	*University of Pennsylvania Law Review*
VaLR	*University of Virginia Law Review*
UWOLR	*University of Western Ontario Law Review*
VaLR	*Virginia Law Review*
WashULQ	*Washington University Law Quarterly*
WiscLR	*Wisconsin Law Review*
YLJ	*Yale Law Journal*

B   JUDICIAL DECISIONS

AER	All England Law Reports
ALD	Administrative Law Decisions
AC	Appeal Cases
ALJR	Australian Law Journal Reports

ALR	Australian Law Reports
Burrows	Burrows Reports
Ch	Chancery
CLR	Commonwealth Law Reports
CB (NS)	Common Bench, New Series
CoRep	Coke's Reports
FLR	Federal Law Reports
KB	King's Bench Reports
Law RepHL,Sc	Law Reports, House of Lords, Scotland
LGR	Local Government Reports
NSWR	New South Wales Reports
NY, NE	New York, North Eastern Law Reports
P&CR	Property and Conveyancing Reports
QB	Queen's Bench Reports
QdR	Queensland Reports
SCt	Supreme Court Reports
US	United States Reports
VR	Victorian Reports
WLR	Weekly Law Reports

Table of Cases

I

Senses of Discretion

I.I THE GENERAL INQUIRY

A NOTICEABLE feature of modern legal systems is the extent to which officials, whether they be judicial or administrative, make decisions in the absence of previously fixed, relatively clear, and binding legal standards. Frequently it appears that decisions are made and so power exercised according to considerations which vary from one area of state activity to another, from one type of institution to another, and even from one set of circumstances to another, in the absence of that pattern of normative standards and principles which generally is thought to be so central to the very notion of legal order.

And yet an analysis of discretionary power has not been a major concern of legal theory. Discretionary authority is generally thought of as peripheral to the core of settled rules in terms of which legal order is characterized. The vagaries of language, the diversity of circumstances, and the indeterminacy of official purposes are, as H. L. A. Hart has reminded us, considerations which guarantee discretion some continuing place in the legal order and make its elimination an impossible dream. But these characteristics of rules do not exhaust the notion of discretion for they do not accommodate its stronger and more central sense as an express grant of power conferred on officials where determination of the standards according to which power is to be exercised is left largely to them. Taking discretion in this sense, the attitude so often is encountered that, while its presence may be inevitable, it is at the same time slightly deviant. Accordingly, it is often suggested that the proper legal strategy is to keep it to a minimum, and to make efforts towards its regulation by fixed and certain rules. It is also the case that where more careful consideration has been given to the place of discretion in the legal order, attention has concentrated on the discretion exercised by superior court judges rather than by judicial officers of lesser rank or, more importantly, by the great variety of administrative officials. Thus the modern jurisprudential debate about judicial reasoning is centrally about discretion, but only judicial discretion and then only about certain of its aspects, in particular the way that judges justify their decisions when the legal standards are indeterminate and unsettled in meaning, or where there appear to be gaps in them.[1]

The combination of those two factors has had the effect of distracting from a more comprehensive analysis of the nature and place of discretion in the legal order. If legal order is characterized in terms of a system of rules, then one tends to see as 'legal' only those areas of activity that are clearly rule-governed, and thus to expel other, discretionary areas of official power from the concerns of law and legal analysis. In this way the interests and concerns of legal analysis are limited to those areas of official power governed by rules. And yet it has become commonplace amongst jurists that the expanded role of the modern state has brought with it, for reasons not always made clear, an increase in discretionary powers in the sense that control over a wide range of matters is delegated to officials with varying degrees of guidance as to the policy goals to be achieved or the standards by which they are to be achieved. In theory, accountability for such powers is primarily to the political system and its institutions, but as it becomes clear that such controls are variable in scope and unreliable in effectiveness, the issue arises as to what extent legal values and institutions can be put in service to influence and constrain their exercise. This is the question that lies at the centre of administrative law and with which this book is concerned.

The general approach taken here is that discretionary power is neither merely peripheral to the exercise of official authority, nor an undesirable deviation from an ideal of government through rules. It will be argued that discretionary powers are important in any system of authority, that there are good reasons for having discretion, and that discretionary powers are neither necessarily nor typically in some way arbitrary and beyond the law. Concentration will be on discretion not just as a side-effect of having rules, but as a positive way of conferring powers where it is important that officials have more freedom as to the way they are to be exercised than a detailed set of rules might allow. But care must be taken even in putting the approach in those terms, since it is no part of my argument that discretionary power is distinct in

---

[1] This debate owes much of its origin to the view of adjudication advanced in H. L. A. Hart, *The Concept of Law* (Oxford UP, 1961). Two of the most interesting later discussions are: R. M. Dworkin, *Taking Rights Seriously* (London, 1977), and Neil MacCormick, *Legal Reasoning and Legal Theory* (Oxford UP, 1978).

the sense that it can be contrasted with some other kind of authority; rather, a central sense of discretion will be offered, based on a number of variables which may pertain to a greater or lesser extent in any grant of official power. Thus, far from legal rules and standards being its antithesis, they are always present in constituting, defining, and constraining discretion.

As for the scope of the book, it may seem unduly ambitious to take up a concept which occurs in such diverse contexts throughout law and administration. In a sense, each area of discretion has its own characteristics and its own problems, and it may seem that little can be said about discretion in general. The really important thing, finally, is to analyse particular areas of discretion, whether it be the discretion of judges or policemen, welfare tribunals or ministers of state; and it is a recent and salutary development in legal writings that just such investigations are being made. But, important as these studies are, they do not remove the need for discussion at a more general level of some of the recurring features and problems of discretionary authority. Accordingly, the object of this book is to consider some of these general issues, on the premise that behind the most practical decision-making lie matters of theoretical interest. It is hoped that the discussion of those issues will not only be of interest in its own right, but that it may also be of practical interest in helping to identify some of the problems that are encountered in any area of discretionary authority. Obviously there will be issues which I only touch on, or which are neglected altogether; I hope, however, that I have said enough to indicate how such matters might be dealt with more fully.

Broadly the book divides into two parts: the first is concerned with identifying and analysing various senses of discretion, with uncovering some of the legal and constitutional ideas that are relevant to discretion, and with explaining why discretionary authority is so prevalent in modern legal systems. Then there is an attempt to see some of the problems discretion raises from the point of view of the official who has to translate a broad grant of power into specific courses of action. Finally in the first part, there is discussion of the relationship between discretionary powers and concepts like arbitrariness, fairness, rights, and personal liberty. The second part of the book is concerned more explicitly with the legal regulation of discretion, and in particular with the principles of review, substantive and procedural, that have been developed by the courts. An attempt is made to identify the constitutional assumptions on which judicial review is based, and to consider some of the more interesting themes that have emerged. One of the main themes in this regard is the basis and development of participatory procedures; this is dealt with in the final chapter.

1.2   RATIONALITY, PURPOSIVENESS, AND MORALITY

One of the ideas underlying this study is that any official exercising power does so within a framework of legal and political principles, and that these principles are important in the justification and legitimation of decisions. Just what the principles are may differ from one society to another and is often a matter of dispute; but in general one principle, of particular importance in democratic systems, is that officials to whom powers have been delegated must account for their actions to the community. The underlying assumption is that all government powers, whether the sovereign powers of legislatures or the delegated powers of administrative officials, are held on behalf of the community and therefore account must be made to it. Because of the difficulties in large and complex societies of requiring accountability in any direct or populist sense, a network of principles and practices develop which mediate between the exercise of powers by officials and the community, and thus provide accountability in a more indirect way. Just what these substantive principles and practices are must be determined according to the deeper values that provide the foundation of political society. In the context of delegated powers, accountability branches off in two directions, one towards the political process, the other towards the legal system. My main concern is with legal accountability, which should be seen not as self-contained and independent of political morality, but as constituting the application and working out of that morality within the context of relations between citizens and the state. The appropriate context and the scope of legal principles is a matter to be considered later; it may be accepted for the moment that legal principles are part of the overall basis of accountability for official actions, but that they do tend to develop within that context particular matters of interest.[2]

The most rudimentary requirements of political morality are that in

---

[2] For some of the background to this approach to political morality and its translation into legal principles, see: John Rawls, *A Theory of Justice* (Oxford UP, 1972); Dworkin, *Taking Rights Seriously*; B. Ackerman, *Social Justice in the Liberal State* (Yale UP, 1980); Philip Pettit, *Judging Justice: an Introduction to Contemporary Political Philosophy* (London, 1980); and MacCormick, *Legal Reasoning and Legal Theory*.

exercising discretionary powers, officials should comply with standards of rationality, purposiveness, and morality; from these, more specific legal principles of accountability can be developed. They are not, however, very precise concepts, nor are they easily separated from each other.[3] Rationality requires that decisions be made for reasons which are rational in terms of our understanding of the world. But of course rationality is an extremely complex notion; decisions can be more or less rational from different points of view, and indeed what constitutes a rational decision may itself depend upon the objects to be achieved and the means available. No complete account of rationality is offered, but it is a concept that recurs throughout the book and various of its aspects are examined in relation to discretionary decisions. Purposiveness is also a complex notion, and we shall see later on some of the difficulties in identifying purposes with any precision; we shall also examine some of the claims made for purpose as a central concept in regulating official powers. The point for the moment, however, is that powers are conferred in order to serve and achieve certain ends and goals, and no matter how difficult they may be to discern, or no matter how vaguely they may be stated, officials must seek them out and direct their actions towards them in ways which are rational and reasonable. General considerations of morality impose a third level of constraints, in that officials, in rationally pursuing the objects of their power, must be responsive to moral principles. These may be seen as part of the axioms of rational action, or as providing subsidiary goals to be achieved, or simply as constraints on the pursuit of goals. Perhaps the most basic moral principle in this context is that the rights and interests of individuals be treated with understanding and respect; from this more specific principles, including ideas of fairness, both in substance and procedure, and non-discrimination, may be generated. These concepts, taken together in their interdependent relationships, constitute the foundations of a political morality which can be developed into more specific principles and priorities; these provide guidance and constrain the exercise of discretion by officials, and they also provide the basis for scrutiny and review of decision-making by legislatures, courts, and other special authorities.

---

[3] Each of these concepts may seem to be hopelessly imprecise, but this does not undermine their usefulness in developing a foundation of legal and political principles. J. M. Keynes is said to have remarked that ideas and concepts are like balls of wool with no sharp edges and that rigorous attempts at conceptual precision are likely to inhibit original thought. See A. Cairncross, 'No Wonder Bertrand Russell Was Afraid of Him', *Guardian Weekly*, 19 June 1983, p. 20.

The precepts of rationality, purpose, and morality are fundamental to that development.[4] At a minimum they require: (*a*) that any exercise of powers be based on reasons, and that the reasons be applied consistently, fairly, and impartially; (*b*) that the reasons be intelligibly related to a framework of equally intelligible purposes, policies, principles, and rules (in general, standards) which can be seen fairly to fall within and be the basis of the delegated authority; (*c*) that in matters of procedure and substance there be compliance with general, critical considerations of morality. Around these foundations more detailed and specific principles can be created. Their significance is that they go towards regulating the relationship between citizens and the state by stipulating the processes and principles that must be satisfied if the exercise of official powers is to be considered justifiable and legitimate. In particular they eliminate decision-making by whim, caprice, chance, or ritual; they provide the basis for identifying and eliminating arbitrariness, for developing general standards in making decisions, and for extending the requirements of fair procedures; and they open the processes of decision-making to external public scrutiny. There is then a focal point from which the decision-maker can have a critical view of his own decisions, and there is a basis for legal and judicial controls.

We may now deal with two practical points that often arise. Let us assume for the moment that a central feature of discretion is a degree of autonomy, within a defined context, vested in the decision-maker. There is a view that within such an area of autonomy the power-holder may decide according to whatever reasons he thinks fit, or indeed without reasons, provided that he remains within the circumference of his power. This view seems to have once controlled the courts' approach to judicial review of administrative actions, but no longer does.[5] It should now be clear, in the light of the previous discussion,

---

[4] For some of the philosophical literature on the nature of rational decision-making, see: Kurt Baier, *The Moral Point of View* (New York, 1965); R. M. Hare, *The Language of Morals* (Oxford, 1971), Joseph Raz (ed.), *Practical Reasoning* (Oxford UP, 1978). For a point of view of a wider and more sociological kind the following collection is useful: Bryan Wilson (ed.), *Rationality* (Oxford, 1970). With regard to the more clearly jurisprudential literature the following stand out for special consideration: Dworkin, *Taking Rights Seriously*; MacCormick, *Legal Reasoning and Legal Theory*; W. D. Lamont, *Law and the Moral Order* (Aberdeen, 1981); and Ch. Perelman, *Justice, Law, and Argument* (Netherlands, 1980).

[5] For an example of this view see: *Weinberger* v. *Inglis* [1919] AC 606. For a more contemporary approach, see *Padfield* v. *Minister for Agriculture* [1968] AC 997 and *Secretary of State for Education and Science* v. *Tameside MBC* [1977] AC 1014. It is

that there is no reason for granting this immunity from the requirements of rational decision-making to bearers of even the widest discretion. The important element in discretion is the authority to settle upon the reasons for a decision, not to act either without reasons or according to reasons which fall below the requirements of rational decision-making. Similarly, there is normally no good reason for not making one's reasons known.[6]

There is another practical point to be cleared up. Discretionary power is often characterized in terms of the authority to choose amongst alternative courses of action. So the paradigm of discretion is the power-holder faced with a choice between actions X, Y, and Z; his discretion is said to be freedom of choice amongst those actions.[7] This is true but oversimplified if the above claims regarding the requirements of rational decision-making are accepted: on the assumption that one's choices must be reasoned, discretion consists not in the authority to choose amongst different actions, but to choose amongst different courses of action *for good reasons*. The course of action cannot be separated from the reasons, and therefore the standards on which it is based. If indeed the standards are settled in advance (and there are often good reasons why they should be), the decision must be made according to their terms and an appropriate course of action will follow. Once this has been done there is no further element of choice as to whether to adopt that course of action. To adopt standards that point to action X and then choose action Y is irrational, and therefore illegitimate. One could of course adopt different standards that lead to action Y, but that only shows that discretion pertains not just to final actions but also to standards of decision-making. If the minister has discretion to deport or not deport A, he must first decide what are good reasons for deporting anyone, and then determine whether A falls

arguable that the heightened scrutiny in recent years is in the nature of a revival of earlier judicial attitudes as manifested in such cases as *Dr. Askew's Case* (1768) 4 Burrows 2186, at p. 2189.

[6] Two points should be noted: (*a*) the requirements of rational decision-making apply to all officials, but this does not mean that all decisions should be subject to judicial review to ensure compliance; there may be other reasons for regarding some narrowly defined areas of decision-making as largely beyond review; (*b*) the same applies to the giving of reasons; there should be reasons, but there may sometimes be good reasons for not disclosing them.

[7] It is common to find discretion expressed in this way; see: K. C. Davis, *Discretionary Justice* (Louisiana, 1969), p. 4; J. L. Jowell, 'The Legal Control of Administrative Discretion' 1973 *PL* 178; J. H. Grey, 'Discretion in Administrative Law' (1979) 17 *Osgoode HLJ* 107.

within them. If *A* does, it would be rational to deport him and irrational not to.

In practical decision-making the distinction between the two aspects is often concealed or ignored; decisions are said to be made on the merits or circumstances of the case with the implication that these somehow speak for themselves. In so far as this calls attention to the fact that standards of decision-making are often open-ended and in conflict with each other until made concrete and specific for the purpose of making a particular decision, then the idea of deciding cases on their merits is harmless enough. But merits are merits only because they correspond to or fall within some set of perhaps unarticulated standards. No harm is done by expressing discretion in terms of choosing actions, provided it is recognized that in the exercise of powers by public authorities there must be good reasons for the choice.

1.3   THE IDEA OF DISCRETION AND TWO PRINCIPAL VARIABLES

According to its etymological origins, the idea of discretion is judgment, in particular good judgment. In its modern legal usage, however, discretion has come to connote, perhaps unfortunately, rather autonomy in judgment and decision. To have discretion is, then, in its broadest sense, to have a sphere of autonomy within which one's decisions are in some degree a matter of personal judgment and assessment. There may be in the course of a decision various points at which such elements of judgment and assessment do occur. But the sense of autonomy that tends to be associated with the idea of discretion usually depends not only on the fact that on analysis of the terms of power there is scope for judgment and assessment; the very idea of discretion suggests also that the judgments and assessments which one official makes will be regarded in a certain way by other officials. In the first place, the extent to which one official is considered to have scope for judgment and assessment may depend on the attitude of other officials who have some relationship to the former; in the second place, the extent to which such exercises of judgment and assessment are accepted as final and conclusive depends on the attitudes of other officials. The concept of discretion, it is suggested, as it occurs in legal contexts, is based around these two variables: the scope for personal assessments in the course of a decision, and the attitudes of other officials.

To begin with the first of these, the following issues occur in the course of a decision: there are findings of fact to be made, standards to be interpreted, sometimes standards to be created, and there is the application of the standards to the facts. It may be helpful to set this out in the following way:

On finding facts F, and on the existence of conditions XY, official O may/shall do Z [taking into account factors S, S_2, S_3].

This formulation suggests that there are three primary elements to the decision: (*a*) finding facts F, (*b*) settling the standards, (*c*) applying the standards to the facts. With respect to (*a*), we shall see in the course of the chapter the senses in which there can be discretion in finding facts. Similarly, we shall see in respect of (*c*) that an element of judgment, which might sometimes be characterized as discretionary, is required in applying a standard to the facts, even where the meaning of the standard is clear.

Discretion in its more central sense relates to (*b*), that is where judgments and assessments have to be made as to the standards themselves which explain and justify a decision. There is discretion in this sense, either because the standards leave room for variable interpretations, or because the official is left to create the standards for himself. The notion of interpretation is necessarily rather loose, but it includes questions about the meaning, content, and weight of given standards. In terms of the above formulation, these issues can occur in respect of XY, Z, and S. Each of these may be to a greater or lesser degree vague, unclear, ambiguous, or unsettled in meaning, so that in order to apply them, the official has to settle on more specific meanings, and thus exercise a certain degree of discretion in so doing. The possible variation is considerable; at the one extreme standards may be drawn with such clarity and precision that whatever element of judgment is involved would hardly be considered to amount to discretion, while in other cases the standards may be so open in meaning and require such a substantial exercise of assessment and judgment as to make them discretionary in a very real sense.

Now while we can talk sensibly about discretion arising in the interpretation of standards, this still falls short of what may seem discretionary in the clearest and most central sense. This occurs in respect of Z, where the official is required to do, or to refrain from doing, some action, or where there are various ways of performing a task, and in deciding how or whether to act the official has to determine for himself the reasons and therefore the standards which are to guide his decision. Discretion in this sense occurs in an unlimited variety of situations—whether to grant bail or parole, whether to make a welfare payment or in deciding how much, in selecting the site for a new road, or in excluding a piece of evidence. The reasons for thinking of those situations as discretionary in its real, strong, or central sense, are twofold: first, the discretionary decision pertains to a final action (to grant bail), rather than being merely one step or element in the course of a decision (what does XY mean?); secondly, in these situations the official often is given little if any guidance as to the standards to apply but is required to formulate them for himself. He may be told simply that he may do Z—grant parole, deport an alien, requisition property—without being instructed as to what would constitute good reasons for deciding one way or another.

It is useful to work from a central sense in analysing the implications of discretionary powers (an idea to be taken up later in this chapter), but it is important to understand that there are no clear or precise lines between one sense of discretion and another. This can be seen with respect to the two reasons above. As to the first, I shall concentrate on discretion in so far as the element of assessment is linked directly to the doing of, abstaining from, or performing in a certain way of, a course of action, but whether or not that is the case may be a matter of semantic formulation rather than substance. For example, the meaning of conditions XY can be taken as a preliminary step to be resolved before making the final decision about Z; but they might equally be expressed in such a way that the really discretionary element is deciding the meaning of XY. There is a difference only of emphasis and degree in terms of the discretionary assessments to be made between the following: when it is in the public interest (XY), the minister shall deport D; and the minister may deport D, taking into account the public interest (S_1).[8]

---

[8] The various elements of assessment that are required to be made in reaching a final decision can be expressed in either of two ways: (*a*) one might say that there are a number of separate decisions to be made in order to arrive at a final decision to do or not do Z: deciding what XY means, deciding what Z means (deciding what S_1, S_2, S_3 mean), and finally deciding on Z or not Z; (*b*) one might alternatively say that each of these is an element of the final decision to Z or not Z. Analytically either expression is correct, but there might be important differences when courts have to decide who has the final say; they are more likely to adopt (*a*) and infer that the discretionary element in the decisions

Similarly, with regard to the second factor mentioned above, the distinction between applying given standards and having to create one's own is an unsatisfactory basis for precise, analytical distinctions. Where he has discretion in doing Z, the official may be left entirely to devise his own standards; but it is just as likely that some guidance will be provided (S_1, S_2, S_3), and this may be more or less specific and detailed, or in need of balancing and weighting in terms of importance. We have seen that a similar process may be required when the official is left to apply an open standard. The factors common in both cases are the necessity for the official to determine to some degree, with respect to some element of his decision, the reasons and therefore the standards for it. At one end of the spectrum this task requires the interpretation of given standards in order to apply them, at the other end it is directed to creating standards where none are given.

Between the two poles there is endless variation in the degree to which the official's decision may be constrained by given standards. He might have nothing more than a vague idea of purposes, or he might have guiding standards which are loose, abstract, and unclear, so that they must be interpreted and elaborated, given content, meaning, and specificity, before they can be applied to actual situations. He might have to rank given standards according to importance, to decide whether or not to apply given standards, or whether to depart from them. The possible points at which elements of assessment might arise, and the nature of the assessments to be made, are considerable. But whatever the permutations and combinations, they involve one or other or a mixture of: (*a*) creating standards, (*b*) giving meaning to standards, and (*c*) ranking standards according to their relative importance. It is useful analytically to separate these elements, but in practice they are likely to be closely interwoven; the creation of standards may occur in giving meaning to existing standards and the weighting of standards may be another way of both interpreting and creating. Discretion may be used to refer simply to the fact that an official in reaching a decision has to make assessments of one or other of these kinds.

On this approach discretion is a function of standards and is always a matter of degree; it may be stronger or weaker, greater or lesser. It is hard to imagine a decision which does not involve some discretion, and yet clearly some instances of discretion are much wider than others.

leading up to whether to do Z or not Z is for them to settle rather than the administrative official. Other factors will, of course, also enter into their decision.

Such a loose and undifferentiated concept is clearly of limited use for analytical purposes, and this has led to various attempts to identify more specific senses which are reasonably distinct and which carry specific legal connotations. Before considering those attempts, we must introduce the second set of variables in decision-making.

The second set of variables which affect the extent of an official's discretion can best be expressed in terms of the institutional arrangements, and in particular the attitudes that officials have towards the exercise of power. In performing their functions, officials work within different institutions, each of which has within the legal and political order a unique position determined by a variety of factors such as the kinds of powers it exercises, its historical development, and its constitutional and political basis. The attitude generated amongst officials within different institutions, an attitude nicely captured in H. L. A. Hart's notion of an internal point of view, is of particular relevance in two ways: firstly, in the way officials approach their own powers; secondly, in the attitudes which one set of officials has towards other sets of officials when there is some relationship between the two. As to the first, the official's own attitudes to his powers, to the institutional framework within which he works, and to the place of both in the constitutional and political order, are important considerations in understanding how powers are exercised; in turn these attitudes reflexively shape the nature of the institution. Out of these various influences patterns develop as to how powers are to be exercised, and as to the sorts of reasons that will be thought appropriate in explaining and justifying decisions. Thus, each area of delegated power may be seen as a subsystem within which officials develop attitudes and strategies as to how they will approach their tasks. The legal form by which powers are conferred is important in indicating the initial existence of such a subsystem, but it may be of limited value in understanding the strategies applied and the variables thought to be important within the subsystem. An understanding of such matters can be gained only by considering the internal point of view of the officials themselves and, thus, the way in which they perceive their tasks. To give a simple example, if only the enabling legislation is considered, a grant of power may be highly discretionary, in that little guidance is provided by way of guiding standards; yet within that context the officials may have formulated comprehensive standards which they regard as binding. And what occurs in matters of strategy and procedure, applies also to matters of policy and substance. In short, what may be discretionary from an external, legal point of view, may be anything but discretionary from the internal point of view of officials within the system.

The institutional arrangements and the attitudes which they engender are particularly important with regard to the second matter mentioned, the relationship between sets of institutions, especially between the superior courts and other institutions, where the former have the authority to scrutinize the decisions of the latter. Because they have the final say in settling legal disputes, courts have a central importance in the constitutional order. In determining whether power has been exceeded or abused, courts must first decide how those powers are to be characterized; they fix the legal constraints upon the exercise of any power, and they decide whether those constraints have been exceeded; they have the final say as to how final the decisions of any subordinate authority are to be; they determine what reasons are good reasons for a decision; and they settle the procedures to be followed. In practice these questions are not addressed directly but arise in the context of judicial review or appeal, and are approached through a filter of legal concepts and doctrines. These concepts and doctrines provide the means whereby the courts can determine with respect to any grant of power the nature and extent of legal controls, and conversely the extent to which matters are to be left for final settlement by the authority itself. The courts' attitudes will in turn be shaped by a number of variables which include the form the delegated power takes, the nature of the powers conferred, and the position in the political order of the empowered authority. I have used as an example the relationship between the deciding officials and the courts, but a similar analysis could be made of the relationship between the former and other officials with whom there is some interrelationship.

We can now see how these two variables interact; the first suggests that discretion is a function of the absence or relative absence of binding standards, while the second suggests that the attitudes of officials will be an important consideration in classifying powers, or elements of powers, as discretionary. In other words an analysis of the context in which decisions are made will reveal the extent to which there are elements of choice and assessment in creating, ranking, or interpreting standards; discretion in one sense refers to those elements of choice. However, in order to assess the real as well as the legal significance of these elements, or to make distinctions between them, the officials' attitudes towards them must be taken into account. It is only when there is a significant freedom of choice in the officials, and when that choice is recognized and respected by the courts or other authoritative body, that we may talk of a reasonably discrete notion of discretionary power.

1.4 DWORKIN ON DISCRETION

Leaving aside for the moment the attitudes of officials to the characterization of powers, and concentrating on discretion as a function of the relative presence or absence of guiding standards, as a way of indicating that the deciding official has to make assessments in creating, weighting, or interpreting standards, the question arises whether any qualitative distinctions can be made between different senses of discretion. The most obvious and appealing view is that discretion is a matter of degree ranging from the wide assessments that may be involved in creating one's own standards to the relatively narrow margins open in applying a reasonably clear standard. If that is correct, virtually any decision-maker will have some discretion, but how much he has will depend on the degree of choice there is in applying, weighting, or creating standards.

The best-known and most enlightening attempt to make discretion a more precise concept is R. M. Dworkin's distinction between one sense of strong discretion and two senses of weak.[9] One weak sense means simply that a decision will be regarded as final and will not be reviewed by any other authority. This can be put aside for the present. The important distinction is between the discretion involved in creating one's own standards (strong), and that required in interpreting a given standard in order to apply it (weak). So, the sergeant instructed to choose five men from patrol without being given criteria upon which

---

[9] The main discussion of discretion is contained in Dworkin, *Taking Rights Seriously*, esp. pp. 31–9, 68–71. Dworkin's discussion of discretion and its implications for his analysis of adjudication generally has stimulated an enormous amount of literature. Of particular importance for the notion of discretion are: Kent Greenawalt, 'Discretion and Judicial Decision: the Elusive Quest for the Fetters that Bind Judges' (1975) 75 *ColLR* 359; Barry Hoffmaster, 'Understanding Judicial Discretion' (1982) 1 *Law&Phil* 21; G. MacCallum, 'Dworkin on Judicial Discretion' (1963) 60 *JPhil* 638; MacCormick, *Legal Reasoning and Legal Theory*, pp. 246–55; Joseph Raz, 'Legal Principles and the Limits of Law' (1972) 81 *YLJ* 823; R. Sartorius, 'Bayes' Theorem, Hard Cases, and Judicial Discretion' (1977) 11 *GaLR* 1269. For an earlier analysis see W. A. R. Leys, 'Ethics and Administrative Discretion' 1943 *PAdR* 10. For discussion of limitations on the scope of judicial discretion, see D. F. Dugdale, 'The Statutory Conferment of Judicial Discretion' 1972 *NZLJ* 556.

to make the choice has strong discretion; but if he is told to choose the five most experienced men, he has only weak discretion in the sense that he has to exercise judgment. For Dworkin, there is a qualitative distinction between the two cases because in the former the choice of criteria is left to the sergeant, while in the latter the criterion is provided and the sergeant's only task is to apply it.[10] In answer to the objection that the latter task may nevertheless require discretion in interpretation, Dworkin claims that there are always existing principles for deciding such matters and that there is always a right way of applying principles.[11] The right interpretation might not be easy to find, and mortals lesser than Hercules, the fictitious, all wise judge, will never be sure even if they have done so; but there is in principle a correct interpretation to be derived by finding the meaning that best fits into the system of legal rules and principles, taken as a whole. Since there is a right interpretation to given standards, even if they appear to be open or unsettled, there is no choice and so no discretion required in their application. An official has discretion in the strong or real sense only when he may choose the final standards for his decisions, and he has that choice only when it is clear from the terms of his power that there are no given standards to apply. Where there is a given standard to apply, no such choice arises.

This analysis of discretion was made in the course of a debate about how judges do and should make decisions in hard cases. The point of Dworkin's argument was to show that in such situations judges do not have discretion since there are always legal standards to apply. But if the analysis is sound, it may be applied in the administrative sphere as a way of distinguishing between those powers that are properly discretionary, and those which are discretionary only in the weaker sense that they require the interpretation of given standards. The former might properly be left to be settled by the delegated authority, while the latter involve the interpretation of legal principles, a matter which is suitable for final adjudication by the courts. In a general way Dworkin's distinction between these two situations does match the way in which courts are inclined to construe a grant of power.[12] If there are no standards laid down, it is left to the delegated authority to create its

[10] Dworkin, *Taking Rights Seriously*, pp. 31–6.
[11] This is the result of standards of argument contained in *Taking Rights Seriously*, chs. 2, 4 and 13, 'A Reply to Seven Critics' (1977) 11 *GaLR*, and 'No Right Answer?' in P. Hacker and J. Raz (eds.), *Law, Morality and Society* (Oxford UP, 1978).
[12] For further discussion, see R. M. Pattenden, *The Judge, Discretion and the Criminal Trial* (Oxford UP, 1982), ch. 1.

own, and that decision is likely to be regarded as final, provided that it is within the area of authority and does not breach any legal principles. If, however, a standard is laid down, no matter how vague, the courts may well take responsibility for its interpretation. Indeed, there are statements to be found from both judges and jurists which distinguish between 'discretion' and 'judgment' in terms similar to Dworkin's distinction between strong and weak discretion.[13] When judgment is required, rather than discretion, the matter is likely to be approached by the courts as if there were a correct answer to be found in the surrounding legal materials.

However, there are two difficulties: in the first place, courts do not always make such a clear distinction between discretion and non-discretion; they may read constraining standards into an apparently strong discretion, and in construing given standards they may accept that some elements of interpretation are best regarded as discretionary matters for the deciding authority. Secondly, where courts do make the distinction between discretion and non-discretion, it is not always on the sole basis of whether or not there are given standards to apply; other variables may also be taken into account. But if Dworkin's argument that there is a sharp conceptual distinction between the two situations is correct, then we would have a simpler and more compelling basis for identifying and handling discretion.

The question is whether the argument is sound. Its premises are twofold: firstly, that a significant distinction can be made between having authoritative standards to apply and having to create one's own; secondly, that there is a right answer to questions of interpretation of given legal standards. With regard to the first, the distinction between being ordered to choose the five most experienced men for patrol, and being ordered to choose five men for patrol without further criteria, may not be as sharp as Dworkin claims. In the first case there is clearly a standard to apply, but it need not be a clear one, and as we have noted, standards vary in the degree to which they are clear and settled in meaning. On the other hand, it may be claimed that whether or not standards are specified cannot be decisive since all powers are granted for some reasonably specific purposes, and that those purposes themselves constitute standards, or at least provide the basis for generating standards. It would be no answer to say that purposes are

---

[13] See, for example, Dixon CJ in *R.* v. *Cornelius* (1936) 55 CLR 246 and *McDermott* v. *R.* (1948) 76 CLR 501; also R. Cross and C. Tapper, *Evidence* (London, 1985, 6th edn.) p. 168.

often unclear and controversial since that very point may be made about many authoritative standards. It would follow also from the requirements of rational decision-making that the official has a duty to reflect upon the purposes for which powers have been conferred and to put those purposes into practice.[14]

The argument, therefore, depends finally on the second part, the right-answer thesis.[15] Why should one accept that there is a correct way of interpreting legal standards regardless of how indeterminate and open-ended they may appear to be? An adequate analysis of this would take us into deep waters; in the present context it is wise to confine our attention to the general nature of Dworkin's argument and the main criticisms that may be made. The argument is that if one were of herculean capacities, it would be possible to construct a complex political and legal theory that would make the best sense of the total legal system of the society; working within such a theory, and by extrapolation from related legal doctrines, one could then see that every legal standard can be slotted into the system and, thus, has one interpretation that fits better than any other. It would be the duty of an official charged with applying any such standard to seek out that correct interpretation.

The first line of criticism is that this image of law as a giant tapestry unfolding over time is an implausible way of depicting the totality of law and legal decisions; law, or rather areas and pockets of law, appear rather to stumble along in fits and starts at the hands of an uncoordinated body of officials on a piecemeal and incremental basis, patching and sewing as the need arises. In practice, there is no grand tapestry of principles, and it is difficult to imagine how there could be in a mature and complex legal system. Secondly, even if the theory which Dworkin envisages could be constructed, it would be hard to be

---

[14] One of the curious features of Dworkin's distinction between strong and weak discretion is that a qualitatively significant distinction is made to depend on the form that a delegation of power takes. This takes no account of the fortuities that may lead to power being delegated in one way rather than another, nor of the fact that there may be little difference between requiring an official to apply a very abstract and indeterminate standard, and requiring him to create his own standards. See on this matter Greenawalt, 'Discretion and Judicial Decision'.

[15] For reference to Dworkin's discussion of the right-answer thesis, see note 11 above. For commentary: J. Jansen, 'Some Formal Aspects of Dworkin's Right Answer Thesis' (1981) 11 *ManLR* 191; P. Munzer, 'Right Answer, Pre-existing Rights and Fairness' (1977) 11 *GaLR* 1055; K. Greenawalt, 'Policy, Rights and Judicial Decision' (1977) 11 *GaLR* 991; S. Levinson, 'Taking Rights Seriously: Reflections on "Thinking Like a Lawyer" ' (1977–8) 30 *StanLR* 1071 esp. pp. 1082–4.

persuaded that it might not on occasions allow scope for rival interpretations of legal materials, each of which might find substantial support within the total system. Where the existing legal materials, together with the background political principles, provide cogent reasons for two or more possible interpretations, then it is difficult to see that the choice between them is not dependent upon considerations of policy and an assessment of consequences.[16] But if such matters enter into the task of interpreting legal standards, then the official has discretion in Dworkin's strong sense: in other words, if there is not a right answer, the official has discretion, since the antithesis of the right-answer thesis is discretion.[17]

It might be argued that even though there is not always a right answer in interpreting standards, there is in most cases, and since there is no way of distinguishing right-answer cases from no-right-answer cases, courts should proceed in all cases as if there is a right-answer. Rolf Sartorious has argued that judges do in general proceed in this way, and that they ought to.[18] But while judges often approach their tasks on the assumption that there is a right answer, they do not always do so; and when they do, their decision is not based solely on the fact that there is a given standard to apply. Some questions of interpretation of standards are approached on the assumption that there is a right answer, but others are regarded as conferring discretionary choices to be settled by the administrative authority, or

[16] For discussion, see B. Faller, 'Does Dworkin's Rights Thesis Succeed in Solving the Problem of Judicial Discretion?' (1984) 22 *UWOLR* esp. pp. 27–31. J. M. Steiner, 'Judicial Discretion and the Concept of Law' (1976) 35 *CLJ* 135. See also MacCormick, *Legal Reasoning and Legal Theory*, pp. 246–55, where he makes a distinction between speculative and practical disagreements. A speculative disagreement is one in respect of which there is a right answer (the distance from Edinburgh to Glasgow), while a practical disagreement is one for which there is no right answer (whether to have red or white wine with a meal). His argument is that disagreements in interpreting standards may be practical so that there is not necessarily a right answer; it is not entirely clear, however, from MacCormick's argument why disagreements about the meaning of standards may not be speculative.

[17] This point is well brought out in Hoffmaster, 'Understanding Judicial Discretion'. A similar view of discretion (viz. that there is discretion when there is no right answer) appears to be the conclusion reached by others, although not expressed precisely in those terms: J. H. Grey, 'Discretion in Administrative Law' ('Discretion may best be defined as the power to make a decision that cannot be determined to be right or wrong in any objective way'); John Dickinson, 'Legal Rules: Their Function in the Process of Decision' (1931) 79 *UPaLR* 833; and 'Legal Rules: Their Application and Elaboration' (1931) 79 *UPaLR* 1052.

[18] See: R. Sartorious, 'Social Policy and Judicial Legislation' (1971) 8 *AmPhilQ* 151; 'The Justification of the Judicial Decision' (1968) 78 *Ethics* 171; 'Bayes' Theorem, Hard Cases, and Judicial Discretion'.

lower court, which is charged with exercising the power. The sergeant told to pick the most experienced men may be left to decide what 'experienced' means for this purpose. Conversely, where power is conferred without stipulating the standards to be followed, the courts may consider nevertheless that standards are to be read in; and in some cases the implied standards may be drawn tightly and a right-answer approach taken to them. In short, courts often do distinguish between right-answer and no-right-answer situations, between no discretion and discretion, and while the form which the grant of power takes will always be an important consideration, other factors also are taken into account. The courts' attitudes to these matters may be hard to predict since they depend upon complex and not always consistent considerations which go well beyond any clear distinction between having and not having standards to apply.

The implication is that if we are to settle upon a central sense of discretion, it is necessary to go beyond analytical distinctions and take into account the second major variable in decision-making, the attitudes of the officials themselves. But beforehand, two further points should be noted about Dworkin's analysis. First, suppose that I am wrong in my criticisms of the right-answer thesis, and that there is in principle a right way of interpreting legal standards. Does that mean that the interpretation of statutory standards is never a matter of discretion, and that accordingly there is only discretion when the official is told to create his own standards? A judge might accept the right-answer thesis in general but have a rather special attitude to situations involving the delegation of powers to administrative officials. He might recognize that the way powers are allocated, and in particular the form they take, are on occasions largely fortuitous. We know enough about the legislative process to realize that the form which any delegation of powers takes can be the result of varied and conflicting factors. In the light of such knowledge the courts might decide that what is in form merely the application of a statutory standard (whether a practice is a 'restrictive trade practice', what constitutes 'fitness for release on parole', or 'undesirability as a resident'), is in substance a delegation of powers to a particular subordinate authority. The courts might sensibly take the view that rather than seek to fit that standard into the jigsaw of legal materials in searching out the right interpretation, such matters should be regarded as discretionary to be settled by the authority to whom the power is delegated. A judge might justify this approach in terms of his wider legal and political theory; he might consider, as judges often do, that one might both subscribe generally to the right-answer thesis, and at the same time accept that, in matters of legislatively delegated powers, special considerations arise.

Secondly, the point of the distinction which Dworkin makes between weak and strong discretion is to show that, while questions under the former are settled by applying legal principles according to a special method of reasoning, matters of strong discretion are in a sense outside the law. The law defines the extent of the power and may require compliance with standards of rationality, fairness, and effectiveness;[19] but within these constraints, whose content is not elaborated, the substantive choices are discretionary and uncontrolled by legal standards. The implication of Dworkin's account is that discretionary powers do constitute a distinct species of legal power, one of the principal characteristics of which is substantial immunity from the control of legal principles and from scrutiny by the courts. The premise underlying this view of the distinctness and separateness of discretion should be questioned. Even though there are elements in the exercise of discretion that are left finally to official preferences, the discretionary process can be subjected to legal principles which are not purely formal. Any exercise of official power should be capable of being explained in terms of its purposes and within a framework of constraining principles. Rather than isolating areas of power as discretionary with the implication that they have a special status, it is preferable to consider with respect to each the methods by which and the extent to which it can be brought within the influence and control of legal principles.

1.5   A CENTRAL SENSE OF DISCRETIONARY POWER

In the preceding section I considered one particularly powerful attempt to identify a sense of strong or real discretion which can be defined with analytical precision. This attempt appears to me to fail, as any such attempt seems bound to fail. One conclusion that might be drawn is simply that discretion occurs at a variety of points within any exercise of power, that the extent of discretion will always vary in emphasis and degree, and that little more can be said. There is some force in this argument, but if the attitudes of officials are taken into

---

[19] *Taking Rights Seriously*, p. 33.

account, then it can be seen that they do distinguish between different senses of discretion, that they have developed various strategies for dealing with these different senses, and that a reasonably distinct and central sense of discretion can be identified. Here we may adopt a method of approach familiar to jurisprudence; it consists in developing a concept by outlining various characteristics which may in practice be present in varying degrees, and when present to a high degree may be taken to constitute the central or focal sense of that concept. The usefulness of the central sense of the concept is twofold: in the first place it highlights the features common to certain recurring phenomena by giving an abstract or theoretical significance to those patterns of regularity;[20] in the second place, the central sense of discretion can be used to demonstrate one particular focus in the ordering of the modern state, and thus to highlight the questions that are posed for the legal order by reliance on discretion in that sense. So here my concern is to outline a sense of discretion in terms of a number of characteristics which are recurring features of delegated powers, and of the attitudes officials have to them. In the light of this sense of discretion, it is also easier to understand divergent and less central usages. Since this is primarily a legal study, the perspective from which the pertinent phenomena are viewed is a legal point of view, and therefore naturally brings with it certain characteristically legal ideas and doctrines, and places some emphasis on the attitudes of courts.

A central sense of discretionary power may be put as follows: discretion, as a way of characterizing a type of power in respect of certain courses of action, is most at home in referring to powers delegated within a system of authority to an official or set of officials, where they have some significant scope for settling the reasons and standards according to which that power is to be exercised, and for applying them in the making of specific decisions. This process of settling the reasons and standards must be taken to include not just the

---

[20] For discussion and employment of this methodology in jurisprudence, see: Hart, *The Concept of Law*, pp. 3–17; J. M. Finnis, *Natural Law and Natural Rights* (Oxford UP, 1980), ch. 1. For more general discussion of his methodology in the social sciences, see Max Weber, *Methodology in the Social Science* (New York, 1949). It is also to be noted that by posing a central sense of discretion, the objection can be overcome that discretion is neither a useful nor sufficiently precise concept to form the basis of analysis. By the device of a focal or central sense, the significance for ideals of law and legal values can be seen most starkly; as powers depart from that central sense, that significance diminishes. Compare, Z. Bankowski and D. Nelken, 'Discretion as a Social Problem' in M. Adler and S. Asquith (eds.), *Discretion and Welfare* (London, 1981).

more obvious cases of creating standards where none are given, but also individualizing and interpreting loose standards, and assessing the relative importance of conflicting standards. Central to this sense of discretion is the idea that within a defined area of power the official must reflect upon its purposes, and then settle upon the policies and strategies for achieving them. There may be discretion in identifying and interpreting purposes; there may also be discretion as to the policies, standards, and procedures to be followed in achieving these purposes. This then is the core idea of discretion in an analytical sense; around this core, however, there are a number of other features which are characteristically present to a greater or lesser extent. Firstly, discretion occurs in a context of standards, and although in the strongest cases of discretion these standards may offer little guidance or discretion, there are usually some standards guiding, constraining, and influencing the way a discretionary decision is made. Secondly, discretionary powers may be thought of as subsystems of authority within which the official has some degree of freedom and autonomy in acting as he thinks best. This means that the official has to decide to some substantial degree what the policies and standards are to be, the strategies for achieving them, and their application in specific cases, subject to whatever guidance may derive from the surrounding network of constraining principles. The degree of autonomy allowed to the official varies from one context to another. Similarly, the extent to which other officials respect that autonomy and regard the initial exercise of discretion as final, also varies, although in the clearest cases of discretion the degree of finality accorded is likely to be substantial. Thirdly, there is a characteristic of discretion which is especially pertinent in the administrative context. Here the idea is that the official should not simply formulate rules of decision-making and then apply them rigorously to situations as they arise, but must maintain a special relationship between the general standard and the particular case. This is not in any sense a necessary or immanent feature of discretion, since discretion may be granted precisely for the purpose of formulating binding rules. In the administrative law context, however, it is considered to be important that the discretionary authority does not simply legislate, but maintains an attitude of reflective interaction between the policy choices made and the special features of particular cases. I shall now consider various aspects of this suggested characterization of discretionary powers.

1.51   *The identification of discretion*

Discretionary power in the sense that is of particular interest in this study is based around the two variables to which attention has been drawn: the scope for assessment and judgment left open to the decision-maker by the terms of his authority, and the surrounding attitudes of officials as to how the issues arising are to be resolved. When these two variables coincide so that there is both significant freedom for the decision-maker in exercising his powers and the courts recognize that freedom, then there is discretion in its central sense. So in identifying and understanding the discretionary nature of authority, we must consider these two variables. It is useful in doing this to use as the primary example the attitudes of the courts to the powers exercised by other authorities. A similar analysis could be made by taking the attitudes of other sets of officials; I have chosen to use the judicial attitudes, however, because there is ample material in which these attitudes are expressed, and because, from a legal point of view, it is often the courts that determine the meaning and scope to be given to discretionary authority.

With respect to the first, the areas of choice left to the decision-maker can be ascertained by considering the terms in which powers are conferred. Delegations of powers to officials, tribunals, even courts, abound with instances of the delegate being instructed directly to decide the policies and strategies for its exercise; alternatively, the same conclusion may be drawn by implication from the terms of the delegation. So, in the simplest case, there is discretionary power when, according to the terms by which power is conferred, there is a relative absence of guiding standards, accompanied by the inference, whether express or implied, that it is for the authority to establish its own. In practice the position may be more complicated; in a clear case the distinction between being told to create one's own standards and to apply a given standard is quite striking, but, for the reasons we have discussed, the reasoned application of a given standard may require the creation of more specific, individuating standards. Thus, even though the exercise of power may be expressed in terms of applying a given standard, that process may itself be characterized as discretionary.[21] Conversely even where there are no final standards laid down the

---

[21] For an example, see *Dowty Boulton Paul Ltd* v. *Wolverhampton Corporation (no. 2)* [1976] Ch 13.

official might be given exacting guidance as to how he is to proceed: there may be express factors to take into account, matters to set against each other; there might be standards implied from the objects and purposes of the power, or there might be principles derived from wider legal or political or moral sources. These might be drawn so tightly that the decision-maker could be said to have discretion only in an attenuated sense.

At this point the attitudes of officials, in particular the courts, become important. It is the courts that finally determine from a legal point of view whether an official has discretion, and, if so, how much. Indeed, from that point of view, the question of how much discretion an official has usually arises in the course of an argument seeking to persuade the courts to exert varying degrees of control over an exercise of power. In deciding that issue, the courts will not necessarily regard every element of openness that occurs in the course of decision-making as a delegation of discretionary powers. There is extensive leeway in determining the extent to which assessments and judgments are to be left for final determination by the authority itself, and various strategies have been developed by the courts as to how such matters are to be characterized and dealt with. Some of these strategies may be considered briefly.

The first relates to the finding of facts and the characterization of facts in terms of the categories contained within a given standard. We shall consider later the possible elements of discretion that may be involved in such questions; the point of present interest is that questions as to the meaning of standards may be subsumed under the general process of fact-finding. In this way, any element of uncertainty or ambiguity that requires discretionary judgment may be characterized as a question of fact, and so treated as a reasonably objective matter to be settled by the courts.[22]

The second strategy is where courts decide that elements of discretion are to be characterized as incidental to the application of binding standards and to be seen not as a delegation of authority to the subordinate official, but as matters of law and legal interpretation. Such matters will be seen to fall within the broad notion of legal questions for which it is assumed that there is a best, if not a right answer, to be settled by the courts. To take a simple example, in *Amon* v.

---

[22] It is arguable that this is the way the House of Lords approached the matter in *Secretary of State for Education and Science* v. *Tameside MBC* [1977] AC 1014. See also *Coleen Properties Ltd* v. *Minister of Housing and Local Government* [1971] I AER 1049.

Raphael Tuck,[23] the court was faced with interpretation of the requirement that before a party could be joined in an action it must be 'necessary' as a party. Whatever arguments there might have been as to possible interpretations of that requirement, the matter was treated not as one to be settled in the discretion of the court, but as one of law, with the implication that there is a right answer to be derived from settled legal doctrine. In any area of law there are countless cases of the kind, where because of imprecision, ambiguity, and uncertainty of language, interpretation is required. However, whatever elements of choice and assessment there may be in these cases, they are unlikely to be emphasized, but rather buried in legal doctrine and in the processes and methods of legal reasoning. Often the assumption is that the legal materials provide a right answer in a Dworkinian sense, or at least that matters of choice and assessment are to be approached by the courts according to the constraints of what Neil MacCormick has called second-order justification.[24] In such cases, the courts are concerned to close up the gaps, to resolve the uncertainties in the way most compatible with legal doctrine, and to establish authoritative rulings for the future. Courts typically take this approach where a relatively narrow question of interpretation is involved, but even where the given standards are open-ended and unsettled, they may consider that it is for them to settle questions of interpretation in an authoritative way.

This leads to a third and related strategy where power is conferred on a subordinate authority but without final, authoritative standards being laid down so that there appears to be discretion in its central sense, the courts may take the view that it is for them to construct a set of standards and to oversee their application. In *Campbell* v. *Pollak*,[25] Lord Sumner complained that, with respect to an issue regarding the costs of an action, the Court of Appeal had 'so copiously laid down limitations and directions for the exercise of a judge's discretion as to constitute a body of jurisprudence, which tends to destroy that free exercise of his statutory power, which the legislature conferred'.[26] Yet in *Ward* v. *James*,[27] Lord Denning readily accepted that the trial judge's discretion as to whether there was to be trial by jury should be closely controlled by legal standards laid down by the higher courts in the interests of consistency and justice. In this case the stipulated

---

[23] (1956] 1 QB 357. For a further example, see *Sutherland Shire Council* v. *Finch* (1969) 123 CLR 657.
[24] MacCormick, *Legal Reasoning and Legal Theory*, ch. v.
[25] [1927] AC 732.   [26] Ibid., p. 764.   [27] [1966] 1 QB 273.

standards in effect removed any discretion from the trial judge, other than the element of assessment involved in applying the standards to the facts. The overlaying of standards on an apparently discretionary power in this way may be by a process of accretion by specific decisions over time, or it may on occasions be achieved by legislative type formulation. In other situations, the courts may go some way towards formulating decision standards, but without removing all discretion in the original authority. In *Stafford Winfield Cook and Partners Ltd.* v. *Winfield*,[28] Vice-Chancellor Megarry had to consider whether the trial judge's discretion regarding the transfer of a case from one division to the other had been exercised properly. While stressing its discretionary nature, the Vice-Chancellor proceeded, nevertheless, to stipulate the standards to be applied. In still other situations, the courts may proceed in a more negative manner by stipulating matters that are not to be taken into account, while leaving to the deciding authority the decision as to what positive standards are to be applied.[29]

Clearly the courts exercise considerable discretion themselves in deciding how far they should go in settling and overseeing the application of the standards to be followed by a subordinate authority. The illustrations I have given show a progression from those cases where elements of discretion are characterized simply as facts, or treated as legal questions, to those where guiding or even final standards are laid down where none was provided originally. In each of those cases, whatever elements of discretion as to standards there may be in analytical terms, they are either characterized in such a way as to be denied or concealed, or they are rapidly translated into firm legal principles. These different strategies adopted by the court may be seen as a series of related techniques for constraining, reducing, and even removing the discretionary element in decision-making.

However, as those constraints become more background and less concerned with stipulating the final standards governing decisions, as it comes to be accepted, in other words, that decisions as to those standards and their application in particular cases are matters for final determination by the delegated authority itself, then there is a recognition of discretionary power in its central sense. Discretion in

---

[28] [1980] 3 AER 759. See also by way of example in the trusts area *Re Evers' Trust, Papps* v. *Evers* [1980] 3 AER 399.

[29] For example, it may be held that certain matters should be disregarded by the Secretary of State in exercising a discretion but without positively saying what factors should be taken into account. This negative approach is common in judicial review of powers exercised by administrative authorities.

this sense is recognized commonly in legal systems, and in particular is the kind of power that is often delegated to administrative officials; and it is discretion in this sense that is my main concern in this book. However, two notes of caution should be entered; first, as should be clear, this sense of discretion is not advanced as a precisely defined form of power; on the contrary, it depends on the synchronization of the two variables considered, and represents one end of a spectrum at which an official has substantial choices to make in exercising his power, and is in the main unconstrained in doing so. Actual powers approximate or fall short of this central sense to varying degrees, depending upon the extent to which the exercise of power requires choices, and on the degree of autonomy allowed to the official in making those choices. Secondly, it is not being suggested that discretionary powers even in their central sense are immune from any legal controls. Lord Selborne once suggested that judicial controls aspire to do little more than ensure that discretionary decisions are made by officials 'in the honest and bona fide exercise of their own judgement',[30] but such self-denial by the courts would nowadays be considered inappropriate. Even the strongest discretion is subject to a range of constraints, and these are outlined in section 1.53; moreover, there may be considerable potential for a more critical and penetrating system of legal controls upon discretionary powers in precisely this sense.

We may now return to the question of how courts reach the conclusion that powers are discretionary in the sense that the standards of decision-making are to be settled with relative finality by the empowered authority. Various considerations bear on this conclusion, but the principal criterion is likely to be the one mentioned: whether from the terms of the delegation together with the general background it is clear that the original authority is intended by the legislature or other delegating body to have substantial control over an area of power. Often this is a matter of implication from the form the delegation takes, and the terms in which it is expressed: where little guidance is provided by way of standards, the power is likely to be considered as approaching the discretionary end of the scale; but if the standards of decision-making are laid down with any particularity, it is likely that the courts will assume general control. However, as we have seen, this need not be conclusive. There are other factors which

---

[30] Lord Selborne in *Macbeth* v. *Ashby* Law Rep. 2 HL, Sc. 360.

influence the courts' attitudes in these matters: the nature and constitutional position of the authority may be significant; it is noticeable, for example, that the attitude to lower judicial authorities is often different from the attitude shown to executive ministers and other authorities of a more clearly political kind. Also, the nature of the tasks being performed may encourage different attitudes; some matters clearly are seen as within the traditional concerns of courts, while others might be regarded as involving specialized skills, or to be by nature inherently policy-based or even political. The relative importance of these factors and their relationship to each other can be determined only in the context of a particular power.

1.52 *The general rule and the particular case*

The discussion so far has concentrated on that aspect of discretionary power which is concerned with settling the standards of decision-making. This may be regarded as the legislative or policy-making aspect of discretionary power. Powers may be delegated for the express purpose of legislating, that is of formulating general rules which are binding on decision-makers. In the British system delegated legislative powers are regularly conferred on a variety of authorities, while in the American system a similar function is performed by administrative agencies in rule-making.

Whether a grant of discretionary power may be used in order to legislate is not always clear, but depends ultimately upon the terms of the delegation. The general principle is that a grant of authority may be exercised legislatively only if that is provided by the empowering statute expressly or by clear implication.[31] Where discretionary power does not include the power to legislate, then a complex relationship arises between, on the one hand, the policy-making aspect and the tendency of officials to formulate general criteria of decision-making, and, on the other hand, the merits and circumstances of particular cases. The official has to make some general policy choices as to how his powers are to be exercised, and this generally results in the formulation of a network of general standards at differing levels of abstraction. In addition to the tendency, which seems natural within any area of decision-making, towards developing a framework of

[31] For discussion of the distinction between legislative powers and discretionary administrative powers, see D. J. Galligan, 'The Nature and Function of Policies within Discretionary Powers' 1976 *PL*, esp. pp. 344–6. Also J. A. G. Griffith and H. Street, *Principles of Administrative Law* (London, 1973), ch. 2.

general standards, are the axioms of rational action which connote some level of consistency from one decision to another. At the same time, however, stress is placed upon the importance of discretion as a means of ensuring that particular situations can be dealt with on their merits in order to achieve the best result in the circumstances, unencumbered by strict and binding rules.

There is a clear tension between these two objectives:[32] the greater the emphasis placed on establishing general and settled standards of decision-making, the less room there is for approaching the particular case with a relatively open mind, and thus achieving the best result, all things considered. If the emphasis is reversed, the risk is that decision-making will become haphazard, uncoordinated, and easily influenced by extraneous considerations. In practice the object is to achieve some reasonable balance between these two considerations, but just how the balance is to be struck depends on a number of variables which are discussed more fully in chapters 3 and 4. For the moment it is sufficient to note the importance of this concern with the particular case, and the implications it has for consistency in decision-making. Concern for the particular case forms the substance of the doctrine that an official exercising discretion must retain to himself the power and the willingness to modify, extend, or make exceptions to any general standards he may have formulated, in order to take account of the merits of actual cases. This has two implications: first, that any standards formulated must not be regarded as binding and conclusive rules; and, second, that past exercises must not be regarded as generating binding precedents for the future.

These two ideas, which often are referred to as the no-fettering doctrine, are negative restraints on the exercise of discretion, and as such barely touch on the more substantive questions as to the extent to which discretion ought to be translated into standards, principles, and rules, nor on the extent to which past decisions ought to be regarded as guiding or binding precedents for the future. These questions also are taken-up in chapters 3 and 4, where the variables that affect the normative form of decision-making are considered. It is shown that there are generally strong reasons, if charges of arbitrariness are to be avoided, for developing general standards, either by express formulation or by extrapolation from precedents, and for applying them consistently from one case to another. It may be noted, however, that emphasis on

---

[32] For analysis of the legal doctrines relating to fettering, see Galligan, 'The Nature and Function of Policies within Discretionary Powers'.

the circumstances of the particular case is more important and appropriate in some contexts than in others. The assumption, which is most appropriate in the context of judicial discretion, that each situation calling for a decision is unique in some way does not fit easily with the widespread diffusion of powers amongst administrative authorities. In practice, delegates of discretion often are taken as opportunities for specialized agencies to devise subsystems of policies and standards in order to regulate a particular matter.

This does not of course mean that regulation through systems of tightly drawn rules should be seen as the ideal. On the contrary, one of the virtues of discretion is that it allows a reasonable balance to be struck between the general standard and the particular case. Indeed, it is mistaken to assume either that the immediate object is to translate all discretion into tight rules, or that all discretionary decisions are so unique and individualized that they are impervious to regulation by general standards. The no-fettering doctrine is a reminder that particular cases may raise special problems, and it acts as a final safeguard against the degeneration of administrative decision-making into the unreflective application of rules. Just how the no-fettering doctrine has been interpreted and developed is considered in chapter 6.

1.53   *Legal constraints on discretion*

Discretionary authority in its central sense connotes a degree of freedom and autonomy in officials in creating the decision standards and applying them; there are, nevertheless, various constraints on that process.[33] These may be in the nature of practical constraints, or they may be more value-based and normative. In chapter 3, some of the more important constraints and influences, such as effectiveness and efficiency, the limitations on resources, organizational structures, and the moral attitudes of officials, are considered in some detail. In this section I am concerned to outline the ways in which the various types of constraints are linked to the concept of discretion.

The basic duty on an official vested with discretion is to realize and advance the objects and purposes for which his powers have been granted. The primary sources of guidance in this regard are the terms of power. These may dictate the governing standards to which actions are to be directed; for example, the sergeant who is told to choose the

---

[33] See, for discussion, T. Eckhoff, 'Guiding Standards in Legal Reasoning' (1976) 29 *CLP* 205; G. Hughes, 'Rules, Policy and Decision-Making' (1968) 77 *YLJ* 411; J. F. Burrows, 'Statutes and Judicial Discretion' 1976 *NZLR* 1.

most 'experienced' men for patrol has the standard of 'experienced' to interpret and apply. On other occasions, the purposes and objects may be a matter of extrapolation and conjecture, and in effect become part of the discretionary assessment that has to be made. But although the decision standards are left in such cases to the official's discretion, there may be guiding and constraining factors which must be taken into consideration ('factors S_1, S_2, S_3 . . .'); the sergeant may be left to pick whichever men he thinks suitable, but be instructed to take into account the hours which each has already done on patrol. The statute may stipulate all the matters to be taken into account, or it may stipulate the matters that must be taken into account, leaving the official free also to consider others. The relative importance of different matters normally would be left to the official, but of course the statute may indicate that some are more important than others.

Guiding considerations of these kinds may derive from sources outside the statute or instrument of delegation. They may be matters which, over a course of decisions, come to be regarded by the officials themselves as necessary to take into account. Alternatively, they may be matters which will be insisted on by reviewing courts. A sentencing magistrate would be held to have acted wrongly if he did not consider the past record of the accused, even though there is often no statutory duty requiring it. Just what factors must be taken into account where there is no express requirement, and what exactly taking into account means, is one of the recurring problems in the legal regulation of discretion. Moreover, matters which at one time were considered optional may come to be regarded as imperative. Factors of these kinds normally do not point to a particular conclusion, but provide steps or signposts along the way; and failure to take one or other into account, or not to accord it sufficient account, is likely to make the decision invalid.[34]

There is another category of constraints which influences the reasoning process in rather more indirect or negative ways. We have seen how standards of rationality and purposiveness are fundamental to the exercise of any official powers, and we shall see later on how closely many of the heads of judicial review are related to the axioms of purposive rationality. We shall also see how officials are influenced by their moral outlooks. Standards based on moral principles may also be

---

[34] For further discussion of the consequences of not taking into account what are called 'discretionary principles', see C. F. H. Tapper, 'A Note on Principles' (1971) 34 *MLR* 628.

a source of external constraints on discretionary decision-making. The concept of most importance is, perhaps, fairness, especially in a procedural sense. It may also have substantive implications: discretionary decisions that are disadvantageous should not be retrospective; an authority should not go back on its undertaking;[35] a sentence should not be lengthened because of the alleged dangerousness of the offender.[36] Fairness is not the only moral standard that affects discretionary decisions; there may be prohibitions on discrimination on the grounds of race or sex. These may be regarded as general moral requirements, or as principles which have been incorporated into positive law. In short, there may be a range of considerations deriving from moral principles which, in exercising discretion, range from having argumentative appeal to being express, legal imperatives.

In a sense, the scope of discretion is whatever is left after these constraints, whether directed at reasons and substance or at procedures, have been satisfied. This idea is often expressed through Dworkin's metaphor of a doughnut: discretion is represented by the hole in the middle while the doughnut itself constitutes the surrounding standards and constraints. This image, however, can be misleading in suggesting such a clear division between the surrounding standards and discretion; in the clearest and strongest cases of discretion that division may be clear, but more typically the two are interwoven, with discretion occurring where there are gaps in the standards, or where the standards are vague, abstract, or in conflict. The extent to which those issues are regarded, within the relationship, as discretionary for the deciding authority depends to a large extent on the varying attitudes of reviewing courts; they may be more or less exacting in their scrutiny of the reasoning process, in extrapolating purposes, and in the application of procedural and substantive constraints. In some cases they might not go beyond requiring compliance with minimum standards, while in other areas the courts might be so exacting in stipulating the standards of decision-making that the officials are left with discretion only in the sense that they must decide what relative importance to give to the various considerations in the case before them. The practice of sentencing, for example, has developed in this way; the matters to be taken into account are usually clear, and yet the complexity and variability of their application leaves the sentencing judge with

---

[35] For recent judicial consideration, see *R.* v. *Inland Revenue Commissioners, ex parte Preston* [1983] 2 AER 300 and *In re Preston* [1985] 2 WLR 836.

[36] *R.* v. *Veen* (1979) 53 ALJR 305.

considerable discretion.[37] Moreover, it is not only the attitudes of courts that are important; those of the deciding officials themselves may determine the scope of discretion and the constraints on its exercise, so that what appears to be, from a legal point of view, an area of wide and unregulated discretion, may be in practice tightly governed by constraints set by the officials themselves.[38]

1.6 FACTS AND THE APPLICATION OF STANDARDS

The discussion so far has centred around discretion as a function of standards, as a way of indicating that the official must to some extent create his own in achieving his objectives. However, according to our earlier formulation of the elements of a decision, there are two other matters to settle: the finding of facts, and the application of settled standards to the facts. It is often remarked that the decision-maker has discretion in respect of these matters; what is meant is that even though the standards are settled and clear, the deciding authority has a sphere of autonomy in applying them to the facts. This may be referred to as discretion in application; it recognizes that the decision as to whether a given situation falls within an authoritative standard often involves elements of judgment, opinion, and appreciation, such that reasonable persons may sometimes come to different conclusions each of which is itself reasonable. The elements of this notion of application can be made clearer. (*a*) Findings of fact are a mixture of evidence of perceptions and understandings about the world, and the characterization of that evidence into concepts and categories which are themselves often imprecise. The drawing of factual inferences from the evidence is itself, therefore, an imprecise and variable process. (*b*) The decision whether primary facts fall within the terms of a given standard is also a matter of assessment and judgment, and again open to variable conclusions. Sometimes of course this decision is clear and indisputable, but in other cases there may be room for variation and difference of

---

[37] See D. A. Thomas, *Principles of Sentencing* (London, 2nd edn., 1979). For some discussion of the particular problems discretion raises in sentencing, see D. J. Galligan, 'Guidelines and Just Deserts: A Critique of Recent Trends in Sentencing Reform' 1983 *CrimLR* 297.

[38] One system of decision-making in which the attitudes of officials to their tasks and the resulting constraints on their discretion is of considerable interest is the British Supplementary Benefits System. For discussion, see M. Adler, and A. Bradley (eds.), *Law, Discretion and Poverty* (Professional, 1975); see also Adler and Asquith, *Discretion and Welfare*.

opinion. The similar-fact rule in the law of evidence provides a good
example: it is said that the judge in a criminal trial has a discretion to
exclude evidence of previous misconduct where its probative value is
outweighed by its prejudicial effect. This formulation is not strictly
accurate because, once the judge concludes that prejudicial effect does
outweigh probative value, he has a duty to exclude the evidence; his
only discretion pertains to deciding whether on the facts the prejudicial
effect does outweigh probative value.[39] Of course a question may arise
about the proper meaning of prejudicial and probative, but this is
regarded as a legal question to be settled authoritatively by the higher
courts.[40] The trial judge has discretion only in the sense that he has to
decide what the facts are and whether they fall within the legal
standards.

It might be considered inappropriate to describe as discretionary the
finding of facts and the application to them of given standards.
Dworkin's second sense of weak discretion is suitable in this context,
since there is discretion only in the sense that whatever decision is
made is likely to be regarded as final.[41] So the referee at a tennis match
has no discretion in deciding whether the serve was a fault; the rules to
apply are clear and his only task is to decide whether the serve falls
within them. His decision may be final, but it is not discretionary.
However, once again the attempt to draw a sharp distinction between
discretion and non-discretion seems to fail. Initially, it seems odd to
talk of discretion as to matters of fact; the decision-maker is not
entitled in any way to choose or select the facts since his primary duty
is to seek out and arrive at the truth. Nevertheless, the facts can be
ascertained only by imperfect means, relying on imperfect procedures
—the evidence of others, one's own perceptions and understandings,
and the classification of those perceptions; also, there are limits to the
time that may be spent in the quest for factual accuracy. It makes some
sense, therefore, to accept that any decision requires assessment and
judgment, both in fixing the methods for eliciting the facts and in

[39] See *Director of Public Prosecutions* v. *Boardman* [1975] AC 421.
[40] For example, in *R.* v. *Chee* [1980] VR 303 the question arose as to whether similar-
fact evidence had to be of some probative value or of higher probative value before it
could be weighed against its prejudicial effect. The court rightly treated this not as a
matter of discretion for the trial judge but as a question of law to be settled by the higher
courts. The court went on to hold that the evidence need have only some probative
value; in a more recent case the Australian High Court has made it clear that the test is
higher probative value: *Perry* v. *R.* (1983) 57 ALJR 110.
[41] *Taking Rights Seriously*, p. 32.

deciding how much evidence is sufficient. Understood in this special sense, there is some justification for talking of discretion in settling the facts.[42] Similarly, in applying a standard to the facts, the decision-maker has to settle both the meaning of the standard and the characterization of the facts in terms of that meaning. Clearly unreasonable, deviant, or eccentric conclusions can be detected without difficulty, but there remains an exercise of assessment and judgment which is ultimately irreducible into more basic components.[43] Again, it is not inapt to detect in this an element of discretion, just in the sense that there is finally no criterion of correctness other than the tutored judgment of reasonable persons. In both matters, finding facts and applying standards, the sense of discretion is somewhat specialized; it derives from characteristics inherent in decision-making, in the need to select and characterize evidence, and from our limited understanding of the cognitive processes involved. In so far as it is appropriate to talk of discretion here, it is discretion that results from the inherent qualities, and in a sense imperfections, of human decision-making, as well as the elements of subjective judgment and evaluation that are irremoveably part of the search for facts and the application of standards.

While it is useful for analytical purposes to divide decisions into their components—facts, standards, application of standards—in practice the divisions are neither so easy to make nor likely to be made with rigour and precision.[44] The standards might be settled to varying degrees of specificity, and, where left relatively open, the process of applying them to specific facts may be seen partly in terms of the concretization of standards, and partly as the finding and characterization of facts in terms of those standards. The more open the standards, then of course the more the process of concretization shades into discretion in our central sense. A reviewing authority may have variable

---

[42] For example, in *Zamir* v. *Secretary of State for the Home Department* [1980] 2 AER 768 the House of Lords held that the decision of an immigration officer to the effect that leave to enter Britain by the appellant had been vitiated by deception, although in one sense a question of fact, nevertheless involved complex matters of evidence, of verification of documents, of misunderstanding as to oral statements, attitudes and practices, and so left 'room for appreciation, even for discretion' (per Lord Wilberforce, p. 772).

[43] This evaluative task is often characterized by the courts as one of fact, or possibly fact and degree: see S. A. de Smith and J. M. Evans, *Judicial Review of Administrative Action* (Stevens, 4th edn., 1980), pp. 96–7, 126–41.

[44] For further discussion of the relationship between facts and the application of standards: E. Mureinik, 'The Application of Rules: Law or Fact?' (1982) 98 *LQR* 587.

attitudes towards dividing a decision into its elements; where the standards are laid down it might typically decide that questions of interpretation are for it to decide, but then recognize in the original authority some autonomy and finality in applying them to the facts, subject only to residual constraints, like the requirement that there be a foundation of evidence, and that gross and manifest errors of judgment be avoided. These constraints themselves leave a certain amount of room for manoeuvre, and in developing its attitudes to them, a reviewing court might be guided by a number of factors: firstly, there are the elements of imperfection and irreducible evaluation already considered; secondly, there is a limit to the degree to which authoritative standards can be reduced to more specific and precise meanings, and similarly there is a limit to the extent that particular decisions can be generalized to provide any guidance in other cases;[45] thirdly, it may be that the original authority is simply in a better position than the courts to make findings of fact and to apply settled standards to them. Again, the similar-fact doctrine in evidence provides a good example; similar-fact questions arise regularly in criminal trials, and yet in general the decision in one case provides little guidance in another. There are exceptions, however, so that on occasions the reasons for a particular ruling may be universalized to provide guidance in other cases,[46] but more often the trial judge has to have direct resort to the broad standard (probative value outweighing prejudicial effect) in order to deal with the situation before him. The rationale is that he is in the best position to assess the evidence and to decide how the standards apply to it.

Naturally, the reviewing court has considerable leeway in deciding how loosely or tightly the reins of control are to be drawn. It may scrutinize rigorously any finding of facts; it may also wish to ensure that the standards have been applied according to its own view of the matter. On the other hand, the autonomy of the original authority may be conceded and its decisions regarded as final, subject only to weak background constraints. Situations approaching the latter position are

---

[45] For discussion of this problem in the context of conflicts between the public interest in the free flow of information and the interests of justice, see *British Steel Corporation* v. *Granada Television Ltd* [1981] AC 1096, esp. the speeches of Lords Wilberforce and Fraser.

[46] In cases of similar-fact evidence, subgroups of cases may develop more specific tests which assist the trial judge in setting the balance between probative value and prejudicial effect: e.g. the striking-similarity test: see Cross and Tapper, *Evidence*, ch. x.

often described appropriately as discretionary, signifying that there are elements in the decision upon which reasonable views might differ, and that with respect to such matters the considered views of the deciding authority are to be regarded as final. But, as in the other areas we have considered, there may be more or less room for disagreement, and the courts may wish to exert more or less control. So while discretion may be a suitable way of referring to the trial judge's task in a similar-fact case, it would be less appropriate where the legal standards are easier to apply, or where the higher courts see the context as one more amenable to their own final determination.

1.7 JUDICIAL DISCRETION

My main concern is with discretionary powers exercised by administrative authorities, but since most of the debate and controversy in recent years has been about judicial discretion, and since the discretion that courts have should fit into the general analysis, three of its aspects will briefly be considered. What is distinctive about judicial discretion is not that there are special types of discretion that we may call judicial, but that the judges exercising discretion, or reviewing the decisions of other judges, are likely to have special attitudes towards their tasks. The first aspect to consider concerns the sense of judicial discretion that has been at the centre of jurisprudential discussion; here the debate has been about how judges do and should make decisions when the legal rules appear to be unclear or incomplete; the second aspect concerns the discretion of judges to change existing legal doctrine; and the third occurs when judges are given delegated powers expressly by statutes or regulation, or pursuant to common law doctrines.

1.71 *Discretion implied in deciding cases*

With respect to the first aspect, the hard case as it has come to be known (a descriptive rather than pejorative term), it is not intended to consider the debate in detail, since I have tried to take account in the earlier part of this chapter of any insights as to the nature of discretion that have resulted from the debate. But the briefest consideration reveals some points of significance. The controversy arose out of H. L. A. Hart's argument that, when a judge in the course of deciding a case finds that the meaning of legal rules is unclear or uncertain or that there are gaps in them, he must exercise discretion, that is make a

policy choice in settling the meaning or filling the gap.[47] Hart's
comments regarding discretion were made in the course of a wider
argument that law consists of and is limited to a system of primary and
secondary rules. This was contested by R. M. Dworkin who argued
that law is not limited to a set of rules made according to a settled
procedure.[48] With regard to the judicial function he argued firstly, that
law never runs out since underlying the rules are legal principles, and
secondly that there is always a right way of interpreting legal principles
in resolving a dispute, and that, accordingly, the judge has no
discretion. A substantial critical literature has developed around these
ideas, and we have already considered some of the arguments against
the right-answer thesis and the distinction between strong and weak
discretion. If those arguments are correct, then Hart is right in
contending that judges do sometimes have to make assessments and
judgments of a discretionary kind, because the law is unclear or
incomplete, ambiguous, or inconsistent. It is arguable that there are
always some legal standards which the judge is bound to apply, so that
discretion occurs in giving meaning to them rather than in devising
standards afresh. Whether this argument is sound, is, however, a
matter of controversy; but even if it is, the standards in issue may be
exceptionally open-textured, so that the judge's task in settling
questions of interpretation still involves a substantial element of
discretion.

   Dworkin's account remains important, however, in drawing attention
to the complex relationship between the judicial process and the legal
and political principles of a society. He has shown how judicial
decisions reach far into those underlying principles, and that it is
unsatisfactory to assume that once judges find themselves outside a
settled core of legal rules they have to exercise discretion, and that
nothing more can or need be said. It is in just such cases that different
theoretical accounts of the judicial process are important. Dworkin's
own analysis based on principles and rights is too narrow to take
adequate account of the variables in judicial decision-making, but it
has stimulated others to enter into consideration of the complex
constraints that operate. It thus may be recognized that, in the normal
course of deciding, judges have to make assessments which are
characterized properly as discretionary, and yet also accept that this is
not incompatible with the existence of a range of normative constraints

---

[47] *The Concept of Law*, ch. vii.   [48] *Taking Rights Seriously*, chs. 2 and 4.

which influence and shape decisions. The important task is to identify those constraints, to classify them and understand their legal status, and to relate them to more basic political principles. Some progress has been made in this direction, and, in particular, Neil MacCormick has given a highly illuminating account of the method of judicial reasoning in terms of second-order constraints which, he argues, are compatible with a rational, just, and democratic society.[49]

Perhaps the point of most importance for our present purposes is Dworkin's insistence that officials exercising authority should be able to explain and justify their actions in terms of political principles and constitutional doctrines. This applies to judges, but it also applies to officials exercising discretion in its strongest sense. Different officials have different institutional and political roles, and, as we have seen, each develops particular attitudes towards its position and its tasks. The common factor is that each must be able to link its role and its attitudes to the wider political system, and to underlying political values. Dworkin, together with many of his critics, has been mainly concerned with the judicial process, which he has tended to distinguish rather sharply from the administrative. That distinction, however, is not always so clear, since many of the issues which confront judges also occur in the administrative sphere. But the really significant point is not so much the similarities between judges and administrators, but the need to examine administrative decision-making with a view to explicating its place in the constitutional order, and to identifying the normative constraints put upon it.

1.72 *Discretion to change the law*

A second aspect of judicial discretion occurs where judges assume authority to overturn or depart from established legal doctrine. This may occur in one of two ways: firstly, the court may depart from settled doctrine in order to achieve an equitable result, or at least to avoid an absurd one, in a particular case. Here the legal rules remain settled, except that the departure may create a precedent for the future and perhaps facilitate further departures. The second method is to overturn in a more general way a particular doctrine in order to bring the law into line with prevailing attitudes or circumstances, or in order to initiate a legal development that seems desirable. The point of this method is to create a new body of doctrine, and this may be done in a

[49] *Legal Reasoning and Legal Theory*. For further discussion of judicial reasoning, see the references in notes 9 and 11.

variety of ways: by creating a new rule; or by creating a general guiding standard which must be individualized in specific decisions from which, in turn, more precise standards may develop; or by leaving it to the discretion of the courts to decide future cases as they think fit.

Although those two types of judicial activity have much in common, I shall consider them separately; the first is considered in section 1.8 where it is regarded as an instance of unauthorized or self-assumed discretion which regularly occurs in decision-making, not just by judges, but also by administrative authorities. In this section, I shall be concerned with the second technique whereby courts deliberately change the law. There are two stages; the first is the decision to overturn existing doctrine, the second is the determination of the normative approach that is to govern future decisions. There is nothing new about courts changing the law, but it has become of particular interest in recent years, since a number of jurists have detected a widespread tendency whereby existing legal doctrines are being replaced by rather loosely defined standards, which are to be applied according to the merits of particular cases. G. H. Treitel has provided a perceptive analysis of this trend in the law of contract,[50] and similar movements can be seen in various aspects of administrative law,[51] the law of evidence,[52] and, undoubtedly, in any area of modern law. This phenomenon sometimes is seen as part of a general progression within modern legal systems away from clear and certain rules, towards more discretionary decision-making.[53] Our concerns are not, for the moment, with that theme which is considered in chapter 2, but with the mechanics of judicial law-making.

The first stage is the court's decision to overturn an existing legal rule or body of rules. This can be achieved by outright rejection, or more typically by subtle methods of distinguishing, refining, or by-passing. Whatever methods are used, the effect is to change an existing legal rule or body of doctrine by what appears to be an exercise of judicial discretion. The important question then is whether the decision to overturn or modify existing law is left to the subjective

[50] G. H. Treitel, *Doctrine and Discretion in the Law of Contract* (Oxford UP, 1981).

[51] For discussion, see: de Smith and Evans, *Judicial Review of Administrative Action*, pp. 35–46; D. J. Galligan, 'Judicial Review and the Textbook Writers' (1982) 2 *OJLS* 257.

[52] For discussion generally, see: Cross and Tapper, *Evidences*; Pattenden, *The Judge, Discretion, and the Criminal Trial*.

[53] See P. S. Atiyah, *From Principles to Pragmatism: Changes in the Function of the Judicial Process and the Law* (Oxford, 1978).

assessment of each judge, or whether that decision is governed by principles and standards in a more objective way. This power to change the law in the course of deciding cases is an integral part of any general theory of adjudication. However, the main jurisprudential debate has been concerned more with 'filling in gaps' in the law, or deciding what to do when the law is unclear; it has not recognized in full that the issue often is whether or not to overturn law which is both clear and settled. Hard cases are often hard for that very reason, and when they are, the issues that arise may be complex: overturning existing law may have a retrospective effect on rights and duties, it may undermine legal stability, and it raises questions as to the justification for judges assuming legislative capacities. On the other hand, the case for not following existing law is likely to be based on arguments from justice in a more substantive sense; the existing law may work unjust results, or it may be out of step with changing ideas of justice in a more general way.

Now, while these issues have not been at the centre of jurisprudential discussion of adjudication, they have become the subject of an interesting subdiscipline, particularly in England where the doctrine of precedent has been a major premise of the common law, and where judicial attitudes to the doctrine have gone through significant changes in recent years.[54] These matters have been the subject of extensive study, but for our purposes it is sufficient to take as an example the issues that arise from the recent practice direction of the House of Lords. Traditionally the House of Lords in its judicial capacity has regarded itself as bound by its previous decisions. In practice, however, it has always been possible to avoid applying unwelcome precedents by various means of refining and distinguishing, although the judges differed in their views as to how freely and openly that should be done. In 1966, the position changed; by a practice direction, the Law Lords announced that they would in future have the power to depart from their own past decisions.

The question then to be resolved in practice was in what circumstances there would be such departures. A. A. Paterson has shown, in an interesting study of the Law Lords, that again judicial

[54] Some of the leading material is as follows: R. Cross, *Precedent in English Law* (Oxford, 1964); Robert Stevens, *Law and Politics: the House of Lords as a Judicial Body 1800–1976* (London, 1979); Louis Blom Cooper and Gavin Drewry, *Final Appeal: a Study of the House of Lords in Its Judicial Capacity* (Oxford, 1972); Alan Paterson, *The Law Lords* (Oxford, 1982).

attitudes varied: on the one hand, Lord Denning considered the matter to be one of judicial discretion, to be exercised as the judge saw fit in the circumstances; on the other hand, there were judges who, being aware of the wider implications of judicial law-making, were concerned to develop guide-lines as to how the discretion should be exercised, guide-lines which would take account of the problematic position of innovatory courts in a democratic society.[55] According to Paterson, the undoubted leader in this matter was Lord Reid who, in a series of cases after 1966, developed a set of criteria governing the exercise of discretion. These included the following considerations: the power should be used sparingly; legitimate expectations should not be disappointed; the future consequences of a ruling should be considered; the importance of certainty ought to be taken into account; but decisions were to be overruled should there be a sufficiently important principle of justice at stake.[56] It has also been found that these criteria have acquired substantial support amongst the Law Lords, and that a reasonably settled method of ranking according to relative weight and importance has been established.[57]

The approach of the Law Lords to the exercise of judicial discretion in changing existing law is an admirable model which might be followed in other contexts. An area of discretion is established; then the various constraints that must be accommodated are identified—the requirements of certainty and predictability, the demands of substantive justice, the inherent uncertainties as to the future consequences of a ruling, and as to changes in social and moral attitudes; then, finally, there is the special relationship between courts and the democratic process. Out of this mêlée of competing and overlapping factors, a set of guide-lines is forged which provides a reasonable accommodation of conflicting values in a reasonably settled manner, while still allowing some scope for individual assessment in particular cases, and leaving open the possibility of adjusting the guide-lines should that be thought necessary in the future. From the litigant's point of view, the law remains settled subject to the possibility of change according to the guide-lines; this seems a reasonable compromise between certainty and justice. From the broader political point of view, the court is making a conscientious attempt to establish a role that is justifiable in terms of constitutional and political theory. Parliament remains the primary source of law-making, but it is unrealistic to expect Parliament

---

[55] Paterson, *The Law Lords*, esp. ch. 6.   [56] Ibid., ch. 7.
[57] Ibid., ch. 7.

to foresee all problems, especially in a system which traditionally has left extensive powers to the courts. Indeed, it would be an odd system which allowed no scope for judicial innovation where the settled law pointed to an unconscionable result in the particular case. (The discussion here has centred on the courts overturning their own decisions, but there may also be a case for allowing departure from statute in certain very clear cases). In short, the Law Lords have worked out a theory of adjudication which in many respects portrays a high level of understanding of the complexities of the issue, and of the place of courts in a modern, democratic society.

The second stage in changing the law concerns the normative framework to be adopted in making decisions which previously would have been governed by the overturned rules. This might take the form of a new rule, but it appears to be more typical for an abstract principle to be formulated which is then given meaning and specificity by incremental development; that is, rather than attempt to formulate a new rule or set of rules, particular problems are resolved in the context of specific cases, within a framework of broadly defined standards. Gradually, by universalization of the reasons for each decision, patterns of more specific standards may emerge which crystallize over time into relatively settled rules, until some further adjustment needs to be made. What may begin as discretionary is likely to be translated in this way over a course of decision-making into settled rules, principles, and standards.[58] This process, which is the quintessence of the common law method, has its costs in terms of certainty; but it also has the considerable advantages of providing a way of handling complexity, of overcoming the perpetuation of unjust or outdated rules, and of ensuring against over-rigidity. To return, then, to the point concerning the trend from rules to discretion, or from principles to pragmatism as it has been described,[59] it is easy to mistake the process that is continually occurring in adjudication. What may appear to be a trend whereby existing rules are overturned and replaced by judicial discretion, is often an incomplete account of what is happening; the part omitted being that, haltingly, over time, there is likely to be a progression from that discretion back to rules and principles.

---

[58] See G. H. Treitel's discussion in the context of contract law: *Doctrine and Discretion in the Law of Contract.*

[59] Atiyah, *From Principles to Pragmatism.* For a counterbalance to Atiyah's argument, see: Julius Stone, 'From Principles to Principles' (1981) 97 *LQR* 224.

1.73   *Delegated discretion*

The sense of judicial discretion considered so far refers to the decisions which a judge must make in interpreting, applying, settling, and changing the law. However, quite apart from this, judges often have discretion in our central sense when they are required to exercise powers deriving from statute or common law, in the relative absence of binding standards. They have discretion in this explicit way in a variety of contexts, such as matters of procedure and evidence, questions of the costs of litigation, and in sentencing. In practice, grants of power will approach and fall short of that central sense in varying ways and degrees; as with any discretionary powers, the nature and extent of the discretion conferred on judges is dependant on the terms in which power is conferred, and on the attitudes of the higher courts to them.

Differences between delegated discretion exercised by judges compared with other officials are related less to conceptual variation than to the different attitudes that are held in relation to them, and to the particular institutional features of courts. The latter are not required normally to make policy decisions of the breadth that may be required of, say, a minister; nevertheless, discretionary decisions by courts may involve important issues of policy having wide implications. Of particular interest are the different attitudes that the higher courts are likely to take to the discretion of a lower judicial body compared with their attitudes towards more clearly administrative bodies. In reviewing the former, the higher courts are likely to be more positive in stipulating the considerations to be taken into account, even to the extent of laying down the final standards to be applied. In the law of evidence, for example, there are numerous discretions, such as the power to exclude probative evidence where it has been gained by improper or unlawful means; or where its reception would be unfair to the accused. Some courts, particularly in America and Australia, have been concerned in recent years to stipulate the standards that are to govern in such cases.[60] Reasonably clear guide-lines have been established for the reception or rejection of illegally obtained evidence, whereas there is still uncertainty as to what exactly is meant by the expression 'unfair to the accused'.[61] More precise guide-lines as to what constitutes unfairness undoubtedly will emerge in the future.

---

[60] For discussion in the Australian cases, see: *Bunning* v. *Cross* (1978–9) 141 CLR 54; *Collins* v. *R.* (1980) 31 ALR 257; *Cleland* v. *R.* (1983) 57 ALJR 15; compare the disappointing discussion in *R.* v. *Sang* [1980] AC 402.

[61] See *Collins* v. *R.* (1980) 31 ALR 257, and *Cleland* v. *R.* (1983) 57 ALJR 15.

Similarly, there is likely to be a greater concern on the part of courts exercising discretion to extrapolate from specific decisions general standards to be applied in future cases. It is common for standards to evolve on a case by case basis with the effect of substantially reducing the scope of discretion, or even, on occasions, removing it, as shown by some of the examples previously cited.

Reviewing courts always have to decide how tightly the controls around subordinate decision-makers are to be drawn, and the character of the decision-maker as more or less judicial in nature is only one relevant factor. But higher courts do appear to be particularly zealous in controlling the decisions of other judicial bodies. It is useful here to keep in mind the distinction between discretion as to what the standards are to be, and discretion in applying reasonably settled standards to be facts. Generally, the higher courts consider that it is proper for them to settle questions as to what standards are to apply and any questions of interpretation that may occur, but then to leave a degree of autonomy to the lower judicial body in deciding how those standards apply in the particular case. For this reason, judicial discretion often means simply a degree of autonomy to decide how standards, which may be reasonably settled but open-textured, are to apply in a particular case.

There are good reasons for this approach. In the first place, where there are issues of policy to be decided, it is generally more appropriate that they should be settled by higher courts rather than lower. In areas of discretion, such as those found in the law of evidence, it is clearly right that matters of such importance should be settled after argument and reflection by the highest courts, rather than left to the discretion of each trial judge to be handled as he sees fit. It is arguable of course that such matters should really be settled by the legislature, but in the absence of legislative action the most appropriate surrogates are the higher courts.

Secondly, there are also good reasons for not drawing too tightly the standards governing many areas of decision-making. Indeed, in judicial decision-making, the main justification for discretion is that it is important in certain situations if justice in the particular case is to be done. Even when the standards are settled and reasonably clear, the task of applying them to particular situations may be a complex matter requiring an irreducible element of assessment or judgment. Whether in a particular case the prejudicial effect of evidence outweighs its probative value, how the costs of an action are to be allocated amongst the parties, whether an extension of time should be granted for bringing an action—to name a few of countless examples—are all matters in respect of which the governing standards can be fairly clear, but which nevertheless require a considerable exercise of judgment in application. Judicial discretion is often used to refer to this fact, and to indicate that the decision of trial judges upon the matter will be regarded as final, subject only to evidence of gross error. It is also sensible that in such situations the standards should not be made too precise, but should remain relatively abstract and open-textured, so that particular regard can be had to the variations that may occur from case to case, and thus ensure an equitable result in each. Indeed, one of the main reasons for having some discretion in judicial decision-making is that rules which are too strict in their terms will lead to odd or inequitable results.

I.8   UNAUTHORIZED OR ASSUMED DISCRETION

In the circumstances so far considered discretion is conferred expressly or by implication, or it occurs as a factor inherent in decision-making. There is another set of circumstances where those having public powers assume, without express authorization, the discretion to depart from legal rules for reasons of justice, or from practical necessity or expediency. Departure here must be taken in a broad sense to include acting in direct violation of a legal standard; or acting in a more subtle and roundabout way with the practical consequence that the standard is not followed or only partly followed; or by adopting such a strained or distorted interpretation that the effect is substantially to alter the standard; or, finally, to apply the standard in a selective and piecemeal manner.

In a criminal trial, for example, it is for the judge to expound the legal principles, and for the jury to decide what facts have been proved, and whether they constitute an offence within the rules. In practice, juries may return a verdict which shows a deliberate disregard for the law laid down. This sovereign capacity in jurors to apply their own sense of justice, even if it means departing from the legal rules, is for some the ultimate justification for retaining the jury trial, while for others it is the strongest reason for its abolition.[62] It is not only the jury,

---

[62] For discussion, see: M. R. Kadish and S. H. Kadish, *Discretion to Disobey: a Study of Lawful Departures from Legal Rules* (Stanford UP, 1973), pp. 45–72; Patrick Devlin, *Trial by Jury* (London, 1956).

however, that on occasions assumes to itself the power to depart from the law; attention often is drawn to the unofficial discretions exercised by police officers and prosecutors in taking decisions whether to arrest, to bail, or to prosecute, and in respect of the procedures to be followed.[63] Discretion in these matters might be conferred officially, but more typically the police have a legal duty to arrest and prosecute offenders, and strict procedures are often laid down.[64] Similarly, in areas of government regulation, where the conduct outlawed is less clearly of a criminal kind, the levels of enforcement of legal norms may depend upon an intervening network of unauthorized discretions. What is common practice in these areas is likely to have some place in any context of official decisions, no matter how clear and unequivocal the rules may be, and no matter how lowly or exalted the officials. Even judges on occasions assume discretion to depart from a legal rule in order to avoid a result which is unjust or unacceptable;[65] although there are notable cases where judges, while expressing regret at the unjust or unmeritorious consequences of applying a law, have felt bound by it nevertheless.[66]

The distinction between discretion officially delegated and discretion unofficially assumed is not always easy to make. Where key terms within a binding rule are open to interpretation, or where decisions are governed by abstract standards, there is a degree of flexibility in stretching the law to avoid unacceptable results. But, as Lord Devlin has remarked in relation to the jury, justice may require a decision beyond the farthest point to which the law can be stretched.[67] Similarly, what might at first sight look like departure from a rule, may on further analysis be a modification or extension which can fairly be included within its terms. Again, however, while some decisions made within the periphery of rules and standards can be accommodated in one or other of those ways, there are others which can fairly be explained only as departures.

There are two kinds of explanations for the unauthorized assumption

---

[63] Davis, *Discretionary Justice*. See also J. Goldstein, 'Police Discretion not to Invoke the Criminal Process' (1960) 69 *YLJ* 543. Much of the widespread practice of plea-bargaining takes place pursuant to unauthorized discretionary powers; see: A. W. Alschuler, 'The Prosecutor's Role in Plea Bargaining' (1961) 36 *UChicLR* 50.

[64] A duty reconfirmed in recent years by the courts in *R.* v. *Metropolitan Police Commissioner, ex parte Blackburn* [1968] 2 WLR 893.

[65] See Kadish and Kadish, *Discretion to Disobey*, pp. 85–91.

[66] See for example *Nominal Defendant (Queensland)* v. *Taylor* (1982) 56 ALJR 698.

[67] Devlin, *Trial by Jury*, p. 154.

of discretion. The first relates to practical necessities in achieving the objects of regulation; the second to the official's sense of justice and moral probity. The result may be discretion assumed on an organized and systematic basis, or it may be manifested only in the individualized and personal decisions of particular officials. With regard to practical necessities, discretion to depart from clear rules and duties can be claimed in order to cope with limited resources, and to facilitate the objects of power. Police discretions relating to arrest, interrogation, search and seizure, and prosecution are explained in this way; for example the criminal justice system could not cope if all those found to have committed offences were arrested and prosecuted. As a result, unauthorized discretions have been woven into the system, partly through the decisions of individual officers, which are unlikely to be checked by a higher authority, and partly on an organized basis whereby senior officials stipulate how powers are to be exercised. Assumed discretion may in fact enhance the effectiveness of regulation; a study of the German prosecutorial system has shown that, despite a general duty to prosecute all crimes, some never are, and that this decision, together with other unauthorized modifications of the rules, appears to contribute to the system's general effectiveness.[68] It may be the case that when the requirements laid down by legal rules prove to be unworkable, or too costly, or inefficient in other ways, the capacity to modify them by assuming discretion can lead to beneficial results. Similar considerations apply when the rules are considered by officials to be unjust in themselves, or to result in unjust consequences. By assuming discretion to depart from the rules, either on a systematic basis or according to the judgment of individual officials, injustice may be avoided.

In seeking strategies that might be of use in regulating and reducing unofficial discretion, a distinction may be made between situations where it is ingrained in the system because of ineffective, unrealistic, or unjust rules, and those where the rules are generally acceptable, but where a residual discretion to depart from them is a necessary element of justice or morality. The lines between these situations are not always clear, but let us consider the first. Here the widespread reliance on unofficial discretion is likely to be a consequence of deep-seated structural or institutional factors; the only hope for change in such circumstances lies in major reforms. Moreover, some areas of

---

[68] J. Herrmann, 'The German Prosecutor' in K. C. Davis (ed.), *Discretionary Justice in Europe and America* (U. of Illinois, 1976).

regulation are so complex, and the circumstances so variable, that certain levels of assumed discretion are necessary. Attempts at complete elimination are likely to be unsuccessful, or to have the effect of transferring the discretion from one point in the system to another. For example, an unforseen consequence of trying to eliminate discretion in sentencing has been to increase the pressure on the prosecutorial and plea-bargaining processes, and thus to force a greater assumption of unofficial discretion by officials at those points.[69] In circumstances like these, the object need not be the elimination of discretion, but the provision of a legal framework which recognizes its existence, and which places some controls on its exercise. This may force the law-making institutions to recognize that it is for them, rather than officials operating at a level of low visibility, to make the important choices between conflicting values and policies, and to reflect those choices in a body of governing standards. For example, it may be necessary for the working of any criminal justice system that the police have some discretion whether or not to arrest; the real problem is that, while this remains an unofficial discretion, the important choices are left to the individual officer, or are made according to unofficial standards that prevail within the force. It would be preferable for those decisions to be made, if not by the legislature, at least by officials at a high level of responsibility, and in a way which is open to public scrutiny and subject to accountability.

The problem may, however, be more intractable. Unauthorized discretion can be the result of a deliberate decision to depart from legal standards, but in many contexts it is more likely to be the consequence of complex factors which shape and influence the official's very perception and evaluation of the tasks set, and the position of legal rules in relation to that task.[70] Taking as an example law-enforcement by the police, various studies have shown that the police see their primary task as maintaining order, so that their powers are understood in those terms, and their actions are accordingly based around that end.[71] At the same time, the police are part of a complex, social organization which generates particular institutional attitudes and

---

[69] See generally Symposium on Sentencing (1978–9) 7 *Hofstra LR* 1.

[70] For an excellent discussion of some of the background influences on the unauthorized assumption of discretion in areas of social welfare, see: Ross Cranston, *Legal Foundations of the Welfare State* (London, 1985), pp. 138–43.

[71] See J. H. Skolnick, *Justice Without Trial: Law Enforcement in Democratic Society* (London, 1966); P. K. Manning, *Police Work: the Social Organization of Policing* (Massachusetts, 1977).

informal norms and conventions, and which encourages and rewards particular conceptions of efficiency. These factors taken together exert considerable influence over the actions and attitudes of individual police officers. Moreover, between those influences, and legal rules and values which emphasize the rights of individuals, notions of fairness, and the maintenance of constraints on the powers of police, there is substantial tension. It is understandable that in such an environment, police attitudes to legal standards are bound to be complex and variable; the law clearly is an important factor affecting their attitudes, but it must compete with those other, often more powerful, forces. The levels of departure from the legal rules, as manifested in the assumption of unauthorized discretion, can be seen as the results of this tension. The resulting consequences then appear either in the interpretation given to the legal rules, or in direct departures from the rules where they cannot be reconciled with the other, more potent influences.

The conclusion to be drawn is simply that one should be cautious in dealing with any suggestion that unauthorized discretion is the sign of a wanton deviation from legal requirements, to be remedied by more and stricter laws. Because of the organizational factors, and often of the need for the institution to deal with conflicting ideologies, it may be very difficult to remove the higher levels of unauthorized discretion. It does not follow from this, however, that no measures should be taken, nor that authorities should be permitted to act according to their own standards, immune from the political values sought to be upheld by law. Every opportunity should be taken to enhance compliance with those values, and to increase the ways and levels of accountability. The point is only that such tasks are likely to be performed most success-fully if proper account is taken of the causes and explanations for unauthorized discretions.

In the second situation outlined above, unauthorized discretion is claimed in order to avoid an unjust or immoral result which might follow from applying the rules. Here again there may be different situations. One is that some discretion is always a necessary complement to rules, if justice is to be done; no matter how justifiable the rules in general are, situations may occur where an equitable result can be achieved only by departing from them.[72] In other cases, the rule itself may be unjust, or immoral, either in its own terms or because of

[72] See Roscoe Pound, 'Discretion, Dispensation and Mitigation: the Problem of the Individual Special Case' (1960) 35 *NYULR* 925.

the outcomes to which it leads; in such cases, departure from the rule, or refusal to apply it, strikes implicitly at the rule itself.

Assuming that some level of unauthorized discretion in this sense is an inevitable feature of a legal system, a number of questions arise. One concerns the assessment of its advantages and disadvantages. The advantages are clear enough; discretion to depart from the rules enables the official to reach the decisions which he considers to be correct and just in the circumstances. The disadvantages are also clear. The first is that the official assumes the power to depart from or modify laws which have been made according to constitutional procedures. The second disadvantage is that in avoiding results in individual cases which offend more basic values, unofficial discretion may create uncertainty and instability. A third disadvantage is that assumed discretion may mean depriving a party of his rights under the existing law. There are similarities between unofficial discretion in this situation and the troublesome problem that occurs, as we have already noted, when courts, in the exercise of judicial discretion, change the law by overruling precedents in the course of deciding a case. The solution sometimes offered there, that overruling should be prospective and not retrospective, cannot be applied where the point of unofficial discretion is to reach a just result in the immediate decision.

It is the first of these disadvantages that raises the most interesting issues, but a brief word should be said about the other two. The relative costs and benefits of stability in legal relationships compared with the importance of upholding a basic moral principle are always difficult to assess, and any attempt at assessment can take place only with respect to a specific matter. Stability is not necessarily the most important factor, and, anyhow, departure from the rules need not be haphazard and unexpected, but may develop its own patterns. Where departure has the effect of undermining rights, there is a heavier onus to be satisfied. But, it is clearly the case that rights, like Shylock's claim to a pound of flesh, may on occasions be unmeritorious and unjust, and, where they are, it is not obvious why it is necessary to take rights more seriously than other moral considerations which an official might find compelling.

The more problematical questions concern the basis on which an official may assume discretion to depart from the rules. From a moral point of view, there clearly are circumstances in which an official not only is justified in departing from the legal rules, but would be committing a serious moral wrong if he were to enforce them. Any undertaking that he may have given to uphold the rules is an important but not conclusive factor in assessing his moral duties. Now, although the moral questions cannot be separated in any clear way from the legal questions, our present concern is primarily with the latter. On a positivistic account of law, the state and its officials act legally only if they act in accordance with valid legal rules. Any deviation would seem, therefore, to be an illegal act. This difficulty might be overcome by appeal to more abstract principles, which may be valid and binding, and provide the basis for modifying the rules in special circumstances. Dworkin has shown it to be a common feature of a legal system that rules are read subject to abstract principles.[73] In his famous example, the succession rights of a beneficiary to a deceased's estate where the former murdered the latter, were trumped by the principle that no man should benefit from his own wrong. So what looks like an assumption of discretion in order to avoid the consequences of applying a rule, may turn out not to be a departure at all, but reliance on background principles. A legal system might incorporate some such principles, which would provide officials with the basis for modifying and departing from rules in specified circumstances. This could be done by positive adoption or by official recognition that principles of this kind are implicit in the legal theory and practice of that society.

The difficulty would be to express such background principles in anything but the most abstract terms, with the result that an official may feel that any departure from the rules can be brought within the scope of background principles. However, this need not be a conclusive objection. The discretion to depart from a binding rule, guided by abstract principles, need not be radically different from any other broad discretion; the risks of arbitrariness and eccentricity can be guarded against by an understanding that the discretion to depart from the rules should be assumed only in very clear cases, and supported by reasons which appeal to both principles and consequences, and by the provision of adequate review procedures.

An alternative approach to justifying the assumption of discretion lies in the notion of purpose. Nonet and Selznick, whose views are considered further in chapter 2, have suggested that powers are conferred on officials and institutions for specific purposes, and that, by extrapolation, purposes can provide guidance in formulating rules and settling practices, and in criticizing them.[74] So, for example, the

---

[73] Dworkin, *Taking Rights Seriously*, chs. 2 and 4.
[74] P. Nonet and P. Selznick, *Law and Society in Transition* (Berkeley, 1978).

criminal trial has certain purposes—ascertaining guilt, meting out just punishments, upholding certain values—which constitute the basis for specific rules and practices; those purposes may in turn be used to criticize specific rules and decisions, and to urge reforms. Nonet and Selznick envisage a continuing dialectic between general purposes on the one hand, and specific practices on the other.

An approach having some similarities has been suggested by Kadish and Kadish in dealing with official departures from the rules.[75] They argue that there are important differences between delegated discretion and deviational or assumed discretion, and that the latter has a positive, distinctive, and legitimate place in legal systems. In justifying that place, Kadish and Kadish invent the concept of 'legitimate interposition'; the main idea being that each set of officials has within the community particular roles, which can be expressed in terms of general objectives (or purposes) and values. Specific rules may get out of step with that role, and then the official is justified in upholding the ends of his role, even if it means departing from the rules. When the jury, in order to avoid an unjust result, acts contrary to the judge's instructions, it acts justifiably. It is argued that there is positive value to the community in rule departures which are legitimate in this way; the links between official action and fundamental values are enhanced, the limitations of rules are recognized, and a basis is provided for legal change.

The strength and attraction of approaches based on purposes, or on the ends and values of roles, is that they provide a basis from which to assess practices. The difficulties, however, are several and considerable. Perhaps the main one is in making such notions sufficiently firm and objective so that they can be invoked as common standards of guidance and criticism. It might be thought that if there could be such objectivity as to the roles and purposes of officials and institutions, there would be no need for detailed rules in the first place, no need, indeed, for reasonably clear distinctions between law and morals. And, even if purposes could be made objective at some fairly abstract level, there is still the process of translating them into practice, and in making the assessments, the balancing and weighting, and the compromises that are required. It may often be that purposes and roles can be arrived at only by reconstruction from rules and practices; they are then likely to be either highly abstract and of little guidance, or varied and in conflict

---

[75] Kadish and Kadish, *Discretion to Disobey*.

with each other. These are not necessarily insuperable difficulties, nor are they conclusive arguments against justifying rule departures on the basis of purposes and roles; they do suggest, however, that any such approach is beset with difficulties, and is unlikely to provide a satisfactory justification in anything but the clearest cases.

To conclude, there are many aspects to the issue of officials assuming discretion to depart from legal rules; in this discussion it has been possible to touch on only some of them. Part of the issue raises questions of political morality, and these in turn require an analysis of the roots of an official's obligation to the legal system, and of the relations between those obligations and more general moral duties. An important beginning has been made by Kadish and Kadish, but there are still themes to be explored. The other part of the issue concerns the relationships between officials and the organizations they work in on the one hand, and legal standards on the other hand. Resolution or alleviation of the problems that arise out of this relationship is likely to be achieved only by careful examination of different contexts by continued reassessment of the scope for reducing, channelling, and regulating the assumption and exercise of unauthorized discretion.

1.9   CONCLUSION

Drawing together the strands of argument of this chapter, the first point is that in a constitutional system, officials exercise their powers against a background of political values; these provide guidance and direction in the exercise of powers, in the discretionary context, while notions of rationality, purposiveness, and morality constitute basic constraints, and although these ideas are so far rather vague, they are developed in later chapters. Secondly, discretion is not a precise term of art, with a settled meaning, nor is it a concept which, when found to be present, leads to fixed consequences. Rather it is used in different ways, often for different purposes. The approach here has been to emphasize that the sense of discretion depends on the context in which it occurs, and the attitudes of the officials who are involved with it. These, it has been argued, constitute the two primary factors in understanding the meaning, scope, and significance of discretion. This approach has meant challenging attempts which try to make precise analytical distinctions between different senses of discretion. Thirdly, it is nevertheless useful to suggest a central sense of discretion based around a number of variables. The usefulness lies in providing a focal point from which various issues in the exercise of powers by administrative officials can be considered. Finally, I considered a number of more specific instances of discretions and the context in which each occurs. This led to a brief appraisal of some of the more interesting issues that arise in these contexts, especially different aspects of judicial discretion, and of assumed and unauthorized discretion.

2

Discretionary Powers in the Legal Order

Now that various senses of discretion have been considered and a standard case suggested, the next task is to consider the relationship between discretionary powers and ideas about law and legal systems. Such an undertaking is of interest in its own right, but it has a special importance because of the belief that discretionary powers are in some ways incompatible with notions of law. If legality connotes a system of authority centred around general and stable rules guiding citizens in their actions and enforceable in the courts, then discretionary powers may seem in various ways to be anathema to the very idea. The object of this chapter is to examine that relationship. It begins by considering how discretionary powers fit into a descriptive account of law; we then move to a particular conception of legal authority based around the ideals of the rule of law. This is referred to as the private law model. It is shown how discretionary powers depart from this model, and an attempt is made by considering the social background to explain the prevalence of discretion, and why it does not fit easily into the private law model. This leads to the formulation of an alternative public law model which takes fuller account of the significance of discretionary powers. Finally, different approaches to the development of legal principles regulating discretion are considered.

2.1 THE MODEL OF RULES AND DISCRETIONARY AUTHORITY

One image of law which has held a prominent position in theoretical analysis is that of a system of binding rules applied with final authority by distinct sets of officials. This image has had its detractors and its critics, whether realists who emphasize law in action rather than law in the books, Dworkinians who consider rules to be an inadequate way of expressing the normative basis of law, or more radical critics to whom the very idea of rules is a fetish. Nevertheless, the idea of law as a system of rules survives as a useful focus for theoretical discussion, particularly because it is that idea that seems to be challenged most directly by discretionary powers. The view of law as a system of rules has also been important in a number of different traditions which will be of use in the present analysis. In the sociological tradition, Max Weber has depicted as the very quintessence of law the existence and impartial application of formal, abstract rules; he also considered this to be the dominant mode of authority in modern societies.[1] In the different tradition of analytical jurisprudence, H. L. A. Hart has concluded that the union of primary and secondary rules, and the distinctive attitudes of officials to those rules is the hallmark of a mature legal system.[2] There is a third tradition, operating at the level of political or constitutional theory, which argues that a conception of legal order, usually expressed in terms of the rule of law, is for moral reasons the most desirable means of regulating society.[3]

Each of these traditions will be important in this chapter and at other points in this book, but we shall begin by drawing on Hart's analytical and descriptive theory.[4] After displaying the shortcomings of earlier accounts of law based on the external features of sovereignty, commands, and sanctions, Hart urges the adoption of a different, internal perspective by seeing law from the point of view of members of the system. From this perspective, law is seen as rule-governed activity. Both the citizens and the officials rely on rules in guiding their behaviour: the official in determining what powers he has and how they are to be exercised, the citizen in planning his life in such a way as to be able to do whatever is necessary to achieve his own purposes, and to minimize interference by officials. Also, according to Hart, it is the relationship between rules that gives law its systematic qualities: legal rules and the decisions made pursuant to them are valid if they derive from or are authorized by another legal rule which is itself valid. Finally, all legal rules can be traced to a rule of recognition, which is the fundamental rule of the system, and which owes its existence to the fact that officials accept it as binding.[5]

The rules which are of special importance in discussing discretionary powers are those which Hart refers to as secondary rules. Secondary

---

[1] In general, reference is to Max Weber, *Economy and Society* (G. Roth and C. Wittich eds.), (California UP, 1978), esp. vol. 1, part 1, ch. iii, and vol. 2, part 2, ch. viii.

[2] Hart, *The Concept of Law.*

[3] There is a variety of literature dealing with the rule of law. In particular, see: Lon Fuller, *The Morality of Law* (Yale UP, 1964); Joseph Raz, *The Authority of Law* (Oxford UP, 1979) ch. 11; Finnis, *Natural Law and Natural Rights*, pp. 270–6; David Lyons, *Ethics and the Rule of Law* (Cambridge UP, 1984).

[4] See *The Concept of Law*, ch. v.   [5] Ibid., pp. 97–107.

rules may empower individuals to do things, but they are particularly significant in conferring powers on officials to make, administer, and adjudicate upon the law. It is the use of secondary rules in creating legal institutions, and in conferring powers on them, that marks the transition to a mature and modern legal system.[6] There is little reference in Hart's analysis to official powers which might be classed loosely as administrative, in the sense that, primarily, they are neither legislative nor adjudicative; nor is there particular reference to discretionary powers other than the discretion that is an inevitable but peripheral part of adjudication. However, there is no difficulty in fitting the great variety of administrative bodies into Hart's account of a legal system: such bodies are created by secondary rules, and their powers are constituted and defined by secondary rules. So, the question whether a minister, tribunal, or official body of some other kind has the powers that it claims, can be resolved by considering whether there are rules deriving from a higher source of authority, and which confer those powers.

Moreover, the question whether an authority has discretion and the extent of any discretion depends also on examination of the governing rules. Here it is perhaps useful to distinguish within the general category of secondary rules between those which constitute particular authorities and define the scope of their powers, and others which direct the authorities as to how they are to use those powers. Rules of the second kind, which usually carry with them duties of compliance on the authority, may derive from and form part of the secondary rules. It is quite common, for example, for the same body of laws setting up an authority and defining its jurisdiction, to stipulate the rules it is to apply in making its decisions. Alternatively, decision rules may derive from other legal sources, and constitute constraints of the kinds considered in section 1.53.[7] Those constraints on official decision-making may be in the nature of clear rules, and it seems to be implied that judges would normally be expected to have reasonably clear rules governing their decisions; the constraints may, however, be of different normative force, and are often likely to be in the nature of standards and principles that are, in their application, more abstract and indeterminate than rules.

---

[6] Ibid., pp. 89–96.

[7] There are difficulties with Hart's division between primary and secondary rules, and it is not clear whether, in his terms, the decision rules directing officials how to exercise their powers are primary or secondary. See *The Concept of Law*, pp. 28–33 and ch. v.

On this descriptive account of law, whether an official has discretion, or perhaps more accurately, since all officials have some discretion, the extent of an official's discretion is assessed by examining the rules and other standards which are binding on him in the exercise of his powers. Hart does not concern himself with discretion as a specific concept, nor with the implications of discretionary authority, and indeed there is no obvious reason why a descriptive account of law of the kind offered should. However, at a very general level, there is an implicit contrast between a legal system based around a system of rules empowering, defining, and limiting the powers of officials, and a system, if it could be called one, that is totally discretionary. It is implicit that while there may be substantial pockets of discretion, it is characteristic of a legal system that they are only pockets, and that even they, in general, are circumscribed by rules.

The suggestion that in the very idea of a legal system there are implicit limitations on the scope and extent of discretionary powers is made more explicit in two respects. In the first place, it is part of the descriptive account not just that there are rules, but that rules have the specific function of guiding behaviour, both of officials and citizens. If law is to serve that function (which is clearly part of the reason for emphasizing rules as central to the descriptive account), there must be a reasonable foundation of stable rules setting out rights and duties, and governing official actions. Discretionary powers which are conferred without a reasonable level of standards stipula.ing the conditions for their exercise, fail to provide anything but the lowest level of guidance. This does not mean that they would cease to be legally valid powers, but only that they would defeat the very idea of law, which, on Hart's account, is tied closely to the provision of a reasonably stable system of guiding rules.[8] It is for this reason that the employment of officials of 'scorer's discretion', in the sense that powers are exercised according to the whim of the moment, is castigated.[9] It is for similar reasons that, while recognizing the limits inherent in our capacity to subject any activity to rules, it is Hart's argument that the resulting pockets of indeterminacy and discretion are incidental and peripheral to a corpus of rules, since 'both the

[8] For Hart's account of the functions of law, see *The Concept of Law*, pp. 38–41, 133–44, 238–9. For discussion of the complex question of the functions of law, and in particular the distinction between normative and social functions, see: J. Raz, 'On the Functions of Law' in A. W. B. Simpson (ed.), *Oxford Essays in Jurisprudence* (Oxford, 1973).
[9] *The Concept of Law*, pp. 139–44.

framework within which they [i.e. decisions settling elements of indeterminacy] take place and their chief end product is one of general rules. These are rules the application of which individuals can see for themselves in case after case, without further recourse to official direction or discretion.'[10]

A second source of restrictions on discretionary authority is implicit in Hart's notion of the minimum content of law; the idea here is that, although it is mistaken to think of legal systems as necessarily having any particular purposes, especially moral purposes, they are at least about providing minimum levels of regulation so that their members can survive in reasonable harmony, security, and tolerable affluence.[11] In order to achieve even such limited aims, it may be necessary to regulate the use of force and the exploitation of resources. It may also be necessary as part of this minimum requirement of legality to ensure that official powers, at least in the more important areas, are regulated by clear and settled rules, rather than left to untrammelled discretion.

So, although Hart's primary concern was to elucidate the concept of law in a descriptive sense, which he does by putting the idea of rules at its centre, we can see how description leads into consideration of the function of rules. And while many actual legal systems, each with its distinctive characteristics, are compatible with this analysis of law, and with the notion of a minimum requirement of legality, it is only another short step to begin considering the special virtues of legal systems, and to claim that above that minimum some particular modes of authority are more desirable than others. There are points in Hart's own account, and in his other writings about law, where he makes clear the virtues of state powers being exercised according to rules.[12] The guidance that rules give, especially in the relations between citizen and state, is important in enabling individuals to live and to plan their lives, knowing the circumstances in which state action may be taken against them. Hart's main object is to identify a concept of law in a descriptive sense, but there is a symmetry between that and a particular version of normative, political theory.

However, it is only when our interests move from identifying the very idea of law and legal systems to considering actual legal systems, and the constitutional theory on which they are based, that we become concerned with specific types or conceptions of legal authority, and, in

---

[10] Ibid., p. 133.   [11] Ibid., pp. 189–95.
[12] Ibid., pp. 153–63, and ch. vii. See also similar ideas expressed in: *Punishment and Responsibility* (Oxford UP, 1968).

turn, with the implications for them of discretionary powers. There is one conception of law that has been of special importance in the western tradition of constitutional theory, and which has been identified as the dominant mode of authority in both the practice and ideology of particular western legal systems: this is the rule of law model. As an ideal, the rule of law sets forth a model of authority which is morally commendable, and which ought to be achieved in the formation of legal systems.[13] As a characteristic of actual legal systems it has been claimed that the rule of law has flowered in liberal, capitalist societies; on some accounts, this is because such societies have made efforts to establish the system of authority that is morally most compelling, on other accounts because the rule of law served the material and economic forces within the society.[14] Whatever the final explanations, the central tenets of this version of legal authority is that state power, in so far as it affects individuals, is to be exercised according to binding general rules made and known in advance, and of sufficient specificity to allow individuals to know with tolerable certainty their rights, obligations, and liabilities. The powers of officials are to be closely circumscribed by rules, which are to be adjudicated by courts, which in turn are themselves in the main separate from and independent of the legislative and executive branches. Such a view of legal authority is most compatible with a state which is restrained in its degree of intervention in social and economic matters, and with a political outlook which emphasizes the acquisition and protection of private rights.

The rule of law can operate at different levels, and may be more or less exacting in its restrictions on official powers; normally, however, it connotes something substantially more demanding than Hart's minimum idea of legality, and, for our purposes, it is useful to take it in a reasonably strict sense. A major concern of constitutional theory has been, then, to identify the conditions under which such a stable environment of general rules may be preserved. Certain conditions have been of special importance: first, a separation of powers, and in particular a functional and institutional differentiation between rule-making and rule-application; secondly, a special and characteristically

---

[13] For discussion of the rule of law, see: Fuller, *The Morality of Law*; Raz, *The Authority of Law*, ch. i; Davis, *Discretionary Justice*, ch. i. For a more exacting version, see F. A. Hayek, *The Constitution of Liberty* (London, 1960).
[14] For discussion, see: R. M. Unger, *Law in Modern Society* (New York, 1976) pp. 66–86, 166–92; Nonet and Selznick, *Law and Society in Transition*.

judicial method for applying rules. The first is an attempt to delineate the division between political and legal spheres; it makes a distinction between the legislative process by which the rules are made, and the adjudicative process by which they are applied. At its simplest, the legislator or its delegates decide what the rules are to be, while other officials are responsible for their application and enforcement. Within its area of competence, the law-making authority acts on a range of considerations—political, social, and economic; but once its policies have been settled, they are to be rendered into rules, rules which provide guidance to the citizen, and which are applied and enforced according to their terms by the courts. The second idea is that there is a distinctive body of authorities whose concern is to apply the law, and who proceed according to a method of reasoning which has its roots in the interstices of the legal rules. Any dispute about the meaning and application of the rules is ultimately for those institutions, the courts, to settle. On this approach, the courts are not regarded as part of the primary policy-making branches of government, their task is to interpret and apply the rules according to their terms and to the corpus of doctrine that envelops them. So, while the legislator and its delegates may range across a variety of policy matters in settling and justifying what the rules are to be, the primary justification for judicial decisions lies in applying or extrapolating from existing rules.

This idea of a special method of judicial reasoning has been criticized on the ground that judges are policy-makers like any other arm of government. However, more moderate views try to show that while judges have to interpret the law, and on occasions to create new rules based on policy considerations, this is done around a core of settled rules, according to a process of reasoning which emphasizes continuity and consistency from one decision to another, and the extrapolation from precedents of general rules and principles.[15] The concern to show that the judicial process is distinctive and different from the policy-making process involved in rule-making reaches its apex in the writings of R. M. Dworkin,[16] who argues that judges do not have strong discretion, that there are always principles to apply, and that there is one right way of applying principles. His account of legal standards is wider than rules and includes principles, but the basic

---

[15] For discussion of the method of adjudication, see: Hart, *The Concept of Law*, ch. vii; MacCormick, *Legal Reasoning and Legal Theory*.

[16] *Taking Rights Seriously*, esp. ch. 4.

institutional and methodological divisions between law-maker and law-applier are made stronger and more significant.

It can be seen why law is sometimes described as autonomous, standing apart from the political system, having its own institutions, methods, and specialized profession. As a network of rules, law constitutes a bridge between political practice and its transformation into decisions binding on individuals, since, to be efficacious, political action must cross the bridge and emerge on the other side in the character of legal rules.[17]

The main issue for our present concerns is the implications of discretionary powers for this conception of legal authority. The most significant point is that discretionary powers are a hybrid of the legislative process and the adjudicative, a mixing of the political and the legal spheres. In one sense an authority with discretion is a surrogate legislator in that it must decide on policies and strategies in achieving social goals, that often are outlined only broadly in the grant of power. At the same time, it is responsible for applying those policies to particular situations where individuals are often affected in their lives and interests in an important and immediate way. However, within discretionary subsystems there is often neither the division of functions nor of institutions, nor the characteristically legal method, all of which are important to the view of law considered above. The emphasis in exercising discretion is not necessarily on producing general rules; it may be in achieving broadly defined policy goals in individual cases, with the result that the standards of decision-making remain relatively unformed or very abstract, to be settled only in the context and for the purpose of making a particular decision. Nor, for similar reasons, is there necessarily emphasis either on a division between those deciding policy and those applying it, or on the decisions of one official being scrutinized closely by another. In making discretionary decisions, there are other goals and objectives which may be important, for example reaching consensus or compromise, or retaining the flexibility to change and adjust decisions which have continuing effect; and these may compete with the ideal of general,

[17] See Unger, *Law in Modern Society*, pp. 176–181. For a study of the law of contract carried out against this understanding of legal authority, see: Patrick Atiyah, *The Rise and Fall of Freedom of Contract* (Oxford UP, 1979). However, most of the analysis and criticism of the legal autonomy thesis has come from the Marxian tradition which has tended to see law in capitalist societies as a way of obscuring the real social and economic relations. For example, see I. D. Balbus, 'Commodity Form and Legal Form: an Essay on the "Relative Autonomy" of the Law' (1977) 11 *LSR* 571.

abstract, and comprehensive rules. The attitudes of officials may contribute to this heterogeneity, this lack of differentiation, within discretionary authority: courts have reviewing powers, but traditionally they have assumed that it is for officials other than them to determine the policies and the strategies to be pursued. Accountability is primarily political and administrative, rather than legal, but often with the result that discretionary decisions fall between the two.

It is for reasons of this kind that discretionary powers are sometimes considered to undermine an important conception of legal authority: the lack of commitment to general decision rules, the consequential merging of political and legal processes, and the diminution in importance of adjudication. Of course, the contrast has been drawn between two theoretical models of authority, the legal and the discretionary, whereas in practice the degree of divergence is likely to vary considerably. However, the contrast is useful in pointing up two issues for further examination. One is to give account of why discretionary powers have become so prevalent in modern legal systems; this requires an analysis of some of the conflicting forces at work within discretionary authority, and then an explication of the links between these and the regulatory activities of modern states. The second line of enquiry is to examine the implications for legal and political values, and in particular to consider how law and its processes may be of use in regulating discretion. This requires further deliberation on the values underlying the notion of legality, and consideration of how they may be given effect within a system that relies extensively on official discretion.

2.2   THE SOCIAL CONTEXT OF DISCRETIONARY POWERS

In following the first of these lines of enquiry, the question of foremost importance is why are discretionary powers relied on so widely in contemporary legal systems? In order to suggest some answers to this question, we may turn to the sociological tradition and draw on Max Weber's concept of rational authority. This is useful for a number of reasons. First, it constitutes a theoretical model or ideal type of authority which Weber was able to construct after extensive comparative study.[18] Secondly, although it is based on sociological analysis of how

[18] For discussion of the relationship between Weber's ideal types of authority, and social and historical factors, see W. Mommsen, *The Age of Bureaucracy* (Oxford, 1974), ch. iv.

authority is exercised, formal rational authority has close parallels with the normative rule of law model of constitutional theory. So, by considering the exercise of state powers, we are able to see why any strict view of the rule of law needs to be modified and reformulated, if it is to represent a realistic normative basis for modern authority.

2.21 *Max Weber on legal authority*

Max Weber, the German sociologist and lawyer of the late nineteenth and early twentieth centuries, is acclaimed for his contribution through an analysis of legal and administrative institutions to the administrative and social sciences; it is not so well acknowledged that this same analysis has influenced the outlook of modern jurisprudence. There are two sides to Weber as legal theorist; on the one hand he defined law in terms of coercion, on the other hand his study of legal and administrative institutions led him to characterize the quintessence of legal authority in terms of a system of formal, abstract rules. It is the second of these that is of present interest.

Weber suggested that there are three main ideal types or models of political authority, that is to say modes or patterns according to which power is exercised, and which is regarded by those exercising it as legitimate: charismatic, traditional, and legal rational.[19] Elements of each type of authority may be present in any system, but Weber considered it characteristic of modern societies that the primary pattern of authority is legal rational. Legal rational authority may be contrasted with pre-modern societies where powers might be exercised at the personal will of officials, or according to the variable dictates of a charismatic leader, or by following custom and tradition.

Power is exercised according to legal rational principles when decisions are justified by considerations which transcend the particular case by being related to generalized standards.[20] In one sense, then,

---

[19] For Weber's discussion of the models of authority, see *Economy and Society*, vol. 1, part 1, ch. iii, and vol 2, pp. 654–8, 809–15. There are considerable difficulties and ambiguities in Weber's account of the types of legal authority; these are discussed and elucidated in A. T. Kronman, *Max Weber* (London, 1983), ch. 4. For further analysis of Weber's models of authority and in particular legal authority, the following are useful: R. Bendix, *Max Weber: an Intellectual Portrait* (London, 1966), chs. xii and xiii; and pp. 481–6; Alan Hunt, *The Sociological Movement in Law* (London, 1978), ch. 5; D. Trubeck, 'Max Weber on Law and the Rise of Capitalism' (1972) 3 *WiscLR* 720; Mommsen, *The Age of Bureaucracy*, ch. iv.

[20] *Economy and Society*, pp. 654–8. This is the important distinction between rational legal authority and substantively irrational authority: the latter proceeds on adjudication of a 'purely ad hoc sort in which cases are decided on an individual basis and in

legal rational authority means simply rule-governed authority. Within the category of decisions made according to rules and standards, a distinction is drawn between formal and substantive approaches. Formal legal authority appears to connote, firstly, a clear boundary between legal rules and ethical or political principles; and, secondly, the application of the rules according to logical analysis of their meaning, together with a highly systematic relationship between the rules. Each legal decision is made by application of the rules according to legal logic, and the system of rules is comprehensive in its coverage of legal situations.[21] Weber drew an analogy between the calculations involved in accounting and the application of formal rules; he also drew a parallel between formal rationality and the market system of capitalism with its emphasis on efficiency.[22] In the context of legal institutions, formal rationality similarly connotes efficiency of administration through the formulation and implementation of rules. On the other hand, substantive rationality assumes a framework of standards, but there is a diminution in the formal rationality of the system since the official is concerned to make the decision that best achieves the ends sought. Such an approach is rational, but there is not the same concern either to separate law from ethical, political, or religious ideas, nor to develop the system of abstract legal norms that characterizes formal authority. Because of the emphasis on achieving a particular goal or value, there is likely to be a tendency towards individualized decision-making, towards ensuring the maximum realization in each case of the desired ends. Rules may also of course be directed towards social objectives and values, but the point is that once they are formulated the official task is to apply them strictly according to their terms. The specific virtue of rules is that they increase legal calculability, and in turn the more clearly ethical values which result, in particular personal freedom in the sense that one is able to plan one's activities with clear knowledge of the legal rules. Decisions according to substantive rationality promote a direct correlation between the goals and purposes to be achieved in the

accordance with an indiscriminate mixture of legal, ethical, emotional ánd political considerations': Kronman, *Max Weber*, p. 77.

[21] For a fuller statement of the elements of formal rational authority, see: *Economy and Society*, pp. 657–8. As Kronman points out, Weber attributes various meanings to 'formal rational authority', but the one indicated in the text is the most compatible with his general principles and is of most interest for our present purposes: see *Max Weber*, ch. 4. I have benefited greatly from Kronman's lucid analysis.

[22] See *Economy and Society*, vol. 2, ch. xi.

resolution of specific cases. The virtue of substantive rationality is the realization of those goals and purposes even at the cost of legal calculability.

For Weber it was formal rather than substantive rational authority that dominated modern political systems. He saw a general cultural trend away from the traditional and charismatic modes towards the rational use of power, and in particular to the formal rational mode, a trend which was closely linked to the rise of capitalism, based as it is on the rationality of the market, and the need to maximize productivity and efficiency.[23] These forces permeate all spheres of social life, and nowhere are they more clearly manifested than in the administrative authorities of the state. Within government bureaucracies, the exercise of authority gravitates around formal rational principles; this implies the existence of a consistent system of abstract rules to which all officials owe obedience, to be applied impartially to particular cases; in addition there are rules which define the areas of competence and expertise within which officials operate. The development of bureaucracies towards this form of organization is attributed to its purely technical superiority over any other form of organization.[24]

Formal rational authority constitutes a theoretical model rather than the description of any actual society; it is interesting to consider, however, the implications for discretionary powers of a system of decision-making based on formal rational authority. Firstly, there would be no need for a sharp functional differentiation between administrative authorities and courts since both would be concerned with the rational application of rules, or, especially in the case of the former, with the formulation of rules in accordance with legislative policy. Secondly, there would be no problem of administrative discretion since the concern of the bureaucratic institutions would be to find the most rational and efficient means for implementing legislative policies. On Weber's account, it is the internal workings of administrative bodies that best mirror the ideal type of formal rational authority; this could be done according to processes of logical reasoning which would not require the administrator to make policy or value choices. One reason, according to Weber, for the growth of

---

[23] *Economy and Society*, pp. 1393–5; also *The Protestant Ethic and the Spirit of Capitalism* (London, 1930), p. 25. For discussion, see: Hunt, *The Sociological Movement in Law*, pp. 118–22; Tom Bottomore, *Theories of Modern Capitalism* (London, 1985), ch. 2.

[24] For discussion of formal legal rationality within bureaucracies: Weber, *Economy and Society*, vol. 2, ch. xi; Bendix, *Max Weber: an Intellectual Portrait*, pp. 423–30.

bureaucracies is increased specialization, with the result that officials could be given wider powers to be exercised according to their specialized knowledge.[25] Any dangers that there might be in delegating wide powers to officials would be balanced by the belief that their knowledge could be applied scientifically and objectively. Thirdly, because of the rule-governed and scientific nature of administration, problems of accountability and legitimacy would easily be resolved. Even when invested with wide powers, officials would operate within a hierarchy of rules which would be based on implementing legislative policy, and even where the officials might have to create the more specific rules for themselves, they would be guided by formal rational principles. Any exercise of power could be linked directly to legislative policy, and in this way ensure compatibility with democratic principles.[26] Considerations of legitimacy would be further buttressed by appeals to the certainty and predictability of official actions, and to the even-handed application of the rules that such a system would encourage.

2.22   *Tensions within formal rational authority*

Such a view of officials, hierarchically ordered, applying rules according to an analysis of their meaning and without direct reference to purpose or consequence, captures one side of the state and its institutions familiar enough, whether through the literary satires of Kafka and Balzac, or from personal experience; yet it is not surprising that the idea of formal rational authority has been subject to criticism and readily discarded as bearing little resemblance to the way powers actually are exercised in modern societies. Criticisms of this nature are in some respects well-founded, but it must be kept in mind that one of the important uses for Weber of the model of formal rational authority was to demonstrate the contrast between the charismatic and traditional modes of authority of earlier societies, and the movement of modern societies towards a more impersonal rationality. Put to that use, formal rational authority can be seen as a powerful method of explicating one fundamental characteristic of modern societies. However, its inadequacy as a complete account of authority in contemporary societies can be seen by identifying points of tension within the model, and then by considering how those tensions manifest themselves in modern legal systems.

---

[25] See M. Albrow, *Bureaucracy* (London, 1970), pp. 43 ff.
[26] On the relationship, within Weber's account, between the vesting of wide powers in officials and democratic principles, see: Albrow, *Bureaucracy*, pp. 106–19.

The first point concerns the distinction between formal and substantive rationality.[27] The assumption of formal rationality is that the official's primary concern is to apply the given rules, or to create new rules that are logically consistent with higher rules; substantive rationality on the other hand urges officials to consider the substantive merits and the value implications of their decisions in a way that might not be compatible with precise, general rules. Around this distinction a number of related problems arise. Firstly, there is only a thin line, if indeed there is any line, between seeking the logical meaning of a rule and reasoning about its purpose, and therefore about the principles, policies, and values that support it. There may be a settled core of meaning, but one is soon in the penumbra where reasoning about the purpose of the rule is inevitable;[28] even the distinction between core and penumbra may be artificial, with the consequence that rule-application almost always reaches into underlying principles and policies. The line then between rules as self-contained meaning-contents, and as specific instances of a deeper system of values and principles, is precarious and easily obliterated; this is even more so when rules are cast in terms of broad and open standards, and external pressures are brought to bear to achieve specified social goals in individual cases.

Secondly, rules by nature impose restrictions on the considerations that may be taken into account in decision-making. To formulate a rule is to select in advance the relatively few factors that are relevant to the decision; the greater the number and complexity of these, the less clearly rule-governed the decision becomes. Accordingly, rules narrowly drawn and strictly applied impose a rigidity and an inability to accommodate new, unforeseen, complex, or unusual situations. The benefits of rules are consistency and predictability in the way powers are exercised; they also provide a system of controls upon officials which, by requiring adherence to the rules, minimizes the opportunity for arbitrary or unpredictable exercises of power. But their costs are equally clear: rules restrict consideration of wider factors, and may prevent the making of decisions in a way which provides the best accommodation of values and purposes, and which achieves the best

---

[27] Weber was fully aware of the tensions between the two modes of rational legal authority. See *Economy and Society*, pp. 812–13 and Kronman's excellent analysis in *Max Weber*, pp. 92–5.

[28] For the distinction between core and penumbra, see Hart, *The Concept of Law*, ch. vii.

result in the particular case. Nonet and Selznick talk of the tension between openness and fidelity:[29] openness in the sense of being able to mould decisions according to an underlying framework of broad principles relatively free of the restrictions of rules; fidelity in the sense that the existing rules are applied consistently and even-handedly. Within any actual system of authority there will be a constant tension between the two, between having rules and applying them faithfully, and making decisions according to the merits of the case and within a broader framework of goals and values. These two focal points correspond to Weber's ideal types of formal and substantive authority, but there is no precise line between them, and any area of decision-making will involve a mixture of the two. An important factor for the present is that divergence from the more formal end of the spectrum towards substantive rationality increases the discretionary aspect of decision-making.

The second main point of tension within the formal rational model concerns the delegation of powers to administrative officials. According to that model, discretionary powers create no special problems since officials give effect to legislative policies by a combination of logical reasoning and technical expertise. This may seem unrealistic, although it is salutary to note that beliefs not greatly different lay behind the proliferation of administrative powers in the present century, and in particular had a central place in the ideals of the American New Deal. But, as both observers and participants in that great social experiment came to realize, logic and science have their place, but they complement, not supplant, the value judgments and policy preferences required in regulation, whether in welfare, planning, or anything else.[30] The exercise of discretionary powers by officials requires decisions about the purposes of the power, and about the means for translating those purposes into concrete acts and decisions. But once it is recognized that acts and decisions must encounter the shifting grounds of moral and political values, that they necessitate choices about the pursuit of social policies, then further problems arise. It was a common theme of the realist and sociological schools of jurisprudence that a wider view of the legal domain ought to be taken by casting aside formal, rule-based constraints, so that issues of social policy and social

---

[29] Nonet and Selznick, *Law and Society in Transition*, p. 76.
[30] For discussion of this matter in the American context: J. M. Landis, *The Administrative Process* (New Haven, 1938); L. L. Jaffe, 'The Illusion of the Ideal Administrator' (1973) 86 *HarvLR* 1183.

justice could be confronted by legal institutions and, with assistance from the social sciences, be resolved.[31] The delegation of tasks to specialized administrative authorities appeared to answer that call exactly; but it soon became clear that the precepts of social justice may be more difficult to determine, communities more divided in their interests and values than might have been expected, and the contribution of the social sciences more limited.

We can see from this brief analysis how the ideal types of formal and substantive rationality provide an outline of the tensions that occur in any system of authority. Above the threshold of rational action, there are various configurations or strategies of decision-making which might be adopted; Weber's ideal types serve as focal points around which those strategies are centred, with each exerting a pull and influence on that process, so that in practice decision-making is likely to be a complex mixture of the two. Whatever the pressures towards a substantive rationality, there are likely to be equally strong countervailing pressures towards formalism. The pull towards substantive rationality is both a force contributing to the grant of discretionary powers, and a factor influencing their exercise; but equally there are strong reasons for conferring powers according to clear and unequivocal rules, and, within bureaucratic organizations, there are considerable forces pulling towards the model of formal rules. This understanding of the scope of rational action, and the tensions within it, has two implications for discretionary powers. In the first place, part of the explanation for the expansion of discretionary powers can be seen in terms of the limitations of formal rationality in achieving the goals that are undertaken by the modern state. This theme, which suggests a distinct shift towards substantive rationality, will be taken up in the next section. The second implication is that in the exercise of discretion a central issue is to discover the configurations of formal and substantive rationality that are most suitable in achieving specified goals, and at the same time meeting the constraints imposed by other values.

There is one further and significant point about the exercise of authority in the modern state: Weber's ideal types, and the configurations in which they occur, are not a sufficiently comprehensive basis for analysing the forms that authority takes, especially in modern, complex societies. The limitations inherent in formal rational authority may to some extent be met by shifting to a more substantive basis for

---

[31] For the flavour of the realist and sociological schools of jurisprudence, see D. Lloyd, *Introduction to Jurisprudence* (London, 4th edn., 1979), ch. 7.

decisions; this allows greater freedom and adaptability in achieving the objects of power. This in turn depends on those objects being clear and objective enough for officials to justify their actions according to them, and for it to be recognized that the objects have been achieved. It may be, however, that powers are given without clear definition of purposes, either because there is no clear way of dealing with a problem, such as might occur in planning, the use of resources, or industrial relations, or because it might be preferable to leave the working-out in practice of abstract purposes to be influenced by those most directly affected. The legitimacy of discretionary decisions may then come to depend neither on compliance with fixed rules nor on achieving specified goals, but in providing institutions and procedures to enable different groups to bring their interests to bear on the decision process. There are of course various types of participatory procedures that might be employed, depending on the context, the interests at issue, and the outcome that is sought. These will be considered further in this chapter and in chapter 7. It is sufficient for the moment to recognize that in order to have a full view of the modes of state authority, the concepts of formal and substantive rationality need to be supplemented by this further sense which is sometimes referred to as an aspect of reflexive rationality.

2.23 *Discretionary powers in the modern state*

We can now consider how these points of tension around the ideal type of formal rational authority are manifested in the modern state. It has become commonplace that a notable characteristic of the modern legal system is the prevalence of discretionary powers vested in a wide variety of officials and authorities. A glance through the statute book shows how wide-ranging are the activities of the state in matters of social welfare, public order, land use and resources planning, economic affairs, and licensing. It is not just that the state has increased its regulation of these matters, but also that the method of doing so involves heavy reliance on delegating powers to officials to be exercised at their discretion. Similarly, within areas that have long been the subject of state control, like criminal justice and the penal system, there are signs of a trend towards greater discretion. Of course, discretionary powers are not an innovation of the modern state since any system of authority relies on discretion in varying ways and degrees; the argument is only that in recent decades the quantity of discretion has increased to make it a more significant facet of state authority. This expansion can be seen not only in powers expressly delegated, but also in the levels of unauthorized discretion, in the sense that officials assume to themselves the power to depart from, change, or selectively enforce authoritative legal standards.[32]

The extended reliance upon discretionary powers has accompanied and to a large extent been a product of the growth of state regulation.[33] There is ample evidence of that expansion in the later part of the nineteenth century and the major part of the twentieth as the state has extended its activities into a wide range of social and economic affairs. An adequate explanation of this extension would be a complex undertaking; it can clearly be linked to changing ideas about the nature of society, and about the proper role of the state in achieving ideals of social justice and welfare; it can also be related to the extended franchise. It can be linked to the increased necessity for state intervention and regulation of the economy, partly in order to achieve those social ideals, and partly in order to maintain and protect the basic structure of capitalist economies.[34]

The more immediate issue is why increased state activity should lead to a wider delegation of discretionary authority to subordinate officials. Here we must distinguish two sets of questions: one set requires a distinction between the factors which may influence the legislature or other authority in delegating powers in a discretionary form, and the extent to which those powers in the hands of the subordinate authority remain discretionary in the way they are exercised. There are always these two aspects to an enquiry into discretion: why power took a discretionary form when delegated, and how it is exercised by officials in practice. More will be made of this distinction in chapter 3, when we consider the strategies that an

---

[32] See the discussion in section 1.8. For a study of one aspect of assumed discretion, see: Kadish and Kadish, *Discretion to Disobey*. Some of the factors that contribute to the assumption by officials of assumed discretion can be seen in: Davis, *Discretionary Justice in Europe and America*, esp. ch. 2. See also section 2.1 above.

[33] The literature on this theme is voluminous; in general see: E. Freund, *The Growth of American Administrative Law* (New York, 1923); J. Dickinson, *Administrative Justice and the Supremacy of Law* (Harvard UP, 1927); J. Wilson, 'The Rise of the Bureaucratic State' (1975) 41 *PublInt* 77; Unger, *Law in Modern Society*, ch. 3; G. Poggi, *The Development of the Modern State* (London, 1980); Atiyah, *The Rise and Fall of Freedom of Contract*.

[34] For an analysis of the nature of modern welfare states, see: J. Habermas, *Legitimation Crisis* (London, 1976); C. Offe, *Contradictions of the Welfare State* (London, 1984); I. Gough, *Political Economy of the Welfare State* (London, 1979); M. Brice, *Coming of the Welfare State* (London, 1968, 4th edn.); for more specifically legal aspects, see Cranston, *Legal Foundations of the Welfare State*.

authority might adopt in exercising its powers; in the following discussion, I shall allow this distinction to be blurred by considering in a general way the factors that contribute to the growth of discretionary powers. A second set of questions requires a distinction to be made between factors that have as a matter of history contributed to the discretionary nature of authority, and the possibility that there is some more fundamental, conceptual link between the nature of modern societies and the role of the state, and the rise of discretionary powers.

To begin, it is possible to identify some of the general historical factors contributing to the increase of discretionary powers. In order to effect comprehensive controls in areas of welfare, the economy, and the environment, it has been necessary to vest in a variety of officials and agencies a wide range of powers. At one level of explanation, this diffusion of powers itself provides part of the explanation for the increase in administrative discretion; the very magnitude of the task of regulation has encouraged legislatures to delegate authority to subordinate bodies, and to allow more specialized policies and strategies to be devised by them. This is not to suggest that all delegations are made in discretionary forms, but only that, with growth in the size, diversity, and complexity of regulation, it is inevitable that the legislature, itself having limited capacities and resources, should delegate specific problems and undertakings to subordinate and specially created authorities.

A second and closely related factor in the expansion of discretionary powers has been the belief that many regulatory undertakings are to be approached as technical or scientific matters to be settled by specialist authorities. Once problems are characterized in·this way, there are good reasons for leaving them to the discretion of the expert agencies with only minimum guidance from the legislature. Here we encounter the shades of the Weberian idea that administration is a matter of logical reasoning and scientific application. There is, however, no clear line between matters which can be resolved by the application of technical skills, and matters which require decisions of policy and value. Subordinate authorities, even those with specialist skills, are often required not only to make judgments based upon technical expertise, but also to make decisions about the allocation of resources, about the goals to be achieved, and about the distribution of burdens and benefits among groups and interests.[35] A striking example of both

---

[35] For discussion of some of the problems associated with the exercise of discretion by professionals, see: Adler and Asquith, *Discretion and Welfare*, especially the essays by

the inseparability of matters of expertise and matters of policy, and the way that issues may be characterized in terms of the former, thereby obscuring the latter, is the treatment and control of offenders within the penal system. For a large part of the present century questions of rehabilitation and deterrence have been seen as matters to be resolved in accordance with the social and medical sciences; on this basis, extensive controls over offenders have been taken in order to allow scope for the diagnosis and treatment of each according to his own peculiarities.[36] In this and in many other areas of social order and welfare (mental health, child care, juvenile crime), the claims of science and the readiness to classify problems as scientific have justified an increase in the discretionary powers of agencies and experts. Only in recent years has it come to be realized that each claim must be examined closely, and that, within areas like the penal system, discretionary powers must be reduced and restrained according to firm legal standards.[37] Similar concern has begun slowly to penetrate other areas where discretionary assessments over matters of the most value-based kind are made in the name of science.[38]

A third matter which signals a tendency away from formal to substantive authority, and thus to greater reliance on discretion, relates to the nature of the tasks undertaken by the state. Most of the activities of the state can be grouped in two broad categories: those related to individual and social welfare, and those related to social order. These categories naturally overlap, but within the first are matters like the alleviation of poverty, the provision of sound housing, education, medical care, and a clean environment; the second includes regulation

Adler and Asquith, G. Smith, H. Giller and A. Morris, T. McGlew and A. Robertson. See also the essays in N. Timms and D. Watson (eds.), *Philosophy in Social Work* (London, 1978).

[36] For a general discussion of these ideas in the penal system, see P. Bean, *Rehabilitation and Deviance* (London, 1976). For a related issue, see C. Slobogin, 'Dangerousness and Expertise' (1984) 133 *UPaLR* 97.

[37] For some of the background to the way views began to change, see: American Friends' Service Committee, *Struggle for Justice* (New York, 1971); A. von Hirsch, *Doing Justice* (New York, 1976). The response has been all too often a return to narrow formalism, see: Galligan, 'Guidelines and Just Deserts: a Critique of Recent Reform Movements in Sentencing'.

[38] There is, however, a growing literature directed towards showing the interconnection between science and policy, and the consequences for discretionary powers. For example: L. Gostin, *A Human Condition* (London, 1976); Ian Kennedy, *The Unmasking of Medicine* (London, 1978). For discussion from a more specifically legal point of view, see M. Shapiro, 'Administrative Discretion: the Next Stage' (1983) 92 *YLJ* 1487; C. S. Diver, 'Policymaking Paradigms in Administrative Law' (1981) 95 *HarvLR* 393.

of the economy, control of business practices, regulation of interest groups, law and order, and the reduction of crime. The tasks undertaken by the state within each category are the products partly of political ideals, and partly of practical necessity; but typically in each area broad policy goals are set—an unpolluted environment, alleviation of poverty, a balanced plan for urban development, industrial harmony, fair competition, reduction in crime rates—and powers are delegated to achieve them. In doing so, there are two kinds of factors which have an important bearing on the movement away from formal rules to a more substantive rationality. In the first place, decision-making is purposive in the sense that, however abstract the goals may be, the whole rationale for conferring powers is to achieve those goals to the highest degree possible. It is understandable that there should be among officials a concern to relate individual decisions directly to those goals, and a natural impatience with formal, complex, and possibly unsatisfactory, mediating rules: the mother in need must be helped, the offender must be rehabilitated, the factory polluting the river must be stopped, and, if an oversupply of public houses is contributing to local disorder, the number of licences must be reduced. The test of success, and to a large extent the legitimacy of official decisions, is how well they realize specified goals, not whether they have been made by the impartial application of fixed rules. Of course, there are likely to be pressures towards formalism, so that the end result will reflect an accommodation of the two; the point of importance, however, is the natural tendency for purposive, goal-based decisions to veer towards substantive rationality, and therefore towards discretionary authority.

Another type of constraint which adds to the substantive nature of decision-making has two components: one is the complexity of the matter, the other the variability of the problems encountered. With regard to the first, complexity is a function of the nature and variety of the interests involved or affected, the degree of real or potential conflict between them, the range of solutions that might be open, and the consequences of any particular solution for other areas of social or economic activity. In many areas of state regulation the level of complexity in achieving a particular social goal is likely to be extremely high. To take an example, the control of pollution levels may seem a relatively simple matter of setting firm standards and then ensuring their enforcement. But soon the complexities appear: what, after all, is an acceptable level of pollution in a world heavily reliant on industrial enterprise; what trade-offs are to be made between reduced pollution and more expensive goods; to what extent are the consequences to be taken into account of pollution controls upon the capacities of the manufacturer, in terms of expense, reduced output, and perhaps redundancies; how much, if at all, do the interests of anglers and swimmers in having clean rivers and streams count? Factors like those give some indication of the complexities that may arise in achieving broadly defined social objectives. Indeed, as we shall see, the concept of complexity itself has become important in understanding modern legal systems; the point for the moment is simply that any resolution of complexity might best be attained by a broad grant of power to an administrative authority, allowing it considerable discretionary freedom in settling upon courses of action.

Considerations of variability are closely related; in achieving objectives broadly defined, there may be such differences from one situation to another that it is hard to find a sufficiently common basis for comparisons and generalizations. Each instance may present its own special and peculiar problems, and so provide little guidance for the future. An example commonly used is the notion of personal need in social welfare; but examples abound in other areas—the potential of an offender to be rehabilitated, the settlement of a particular industrial dispute, a specific conflict between the use of resources and the interests of ecology, or the construction of a development plan for one city rather than another. The relevant factors are likely to be closely locked into that specific case in a way which may not recur in quite the same way in any other case. Variability has the effect, therefore, of directing both the form in which power is conferred, and the methods by which it is exercised, towards the discretionary end of the scale.

These three sets of factors emphasize different aspects of the overall problems of pervasive state regulation, and taken together they help to explain the discretionary trend both in the allocation and the exercise of authority. The concern of the state to attain through its instrumentalities specific social goals results in a strong tendency to substantive rationality. This does not mean, however, that substantive rationality provides a complete or adequate picture of authority; on the contrary, the very tensions identified at the theoretical level can be seen in play at the practical level; the currents flowing towards substantive rationality are opposed by a concern for the formality of clear and general rules mediating between the general goal and decision-making in specific cases. Just how these conflicts are to be resolved can only be determined in the context of specific powers, where the various considerations can be assessed in settling upon a suitable strategy for making decisions.

There is a fourth, important factor contributing to the discretionary nature of authority, and this can be related to shifts in the power structure of modern states. The extension of state activities is to some extent a product of and at the same time contributes to the formation of interest groups—employers, employees, corporations, consumers, conservationists, professions, etc.—who are able to exert influence upon the legislative and administrative processes.[39] It is characteristic of interest groups of this kind that they are highly organized, usually with a core of permanent professional staff, able to command a high level of loyalty from their members, often organized on democratic principles, and sometimes financially powerful. The protection and advancement of their members' interests is their primary aim, although the interest group as an entity might acquire substantial independence of its rank-and-file members, and become powerful in its own right.

It is sometimes said that interest groups and corporate bodies of this kind constitute the really important centres of power in modern societies; whether or not there is sufficient evidence for that claim, it is clear that they have had considerable impact on the exercise of political power. One sign of this can be seen in the fact that matters of political importance are sometimes settled within those institutions themselves; another sign is the shift away from the chambers of the legislature as the most important focus of power. Corporate groups can pursue their aims in the ministry and the department, the party room, the boardroom, and in the administrative agencies. Parliament remains juridically sovereign, but many problems are in practice settled elsewhere, within the administrative organizations for example, with the result that parliament's role may be merely to give its formal approval, and to provide the necessary legal authority. The result is a greater diffusion of powers amongst subordinate authorities, and politicization of the administrative process. Where problems are left to be resolved and the strategies settled in the exercise of administrative discretion, it is inevitable that groups should try to bring pressure to

[39] For discussion of this shift in power from the state to interest groups, see: Poggi, *The Development of the Modern State*, ch. vi; J. Winkler, 'Law, State, and Economy' (1975) 2 *BJLS* 103, and 'The Political Economy of Administrative Discretion' in Adler and Asquith *Discretion and Welfare*; Unger *Law in Modern Society*, pp. 200–3; Leo Panitch, 'Recent Theorizations of Corporatism: Reflections on a Growth Industry' (1980) 31 *BJSoc* 159.

bear in order to achieve results satisfactory to themselves. In these circumstances, it is more difficult to formulate general decision rules; and in any event the reasons for doing so are weakened. It may be that there is no clear sense of the public interest, so that decision-making becomes a matter of seeking compromises and adjustments amongst the groups and interests that will be affected. If we add to these considerations the growing complexity and variability of the matters sought to be regulated, then the pull of general rules is further weakened.

Interest group politics are an old phenomenon and, provided that there are controls on their internal organization and their activities, they are a legitimately democratic form. But while interest groups and corporate structures are important in understanding the political organization of modern societies, this does not mean that the state has become a kind of neutral umpire in the contests between groups. Indeed, the existence of such groups may increase the need for the state to exert direction over them, and thus create a tendency towards a highly regulated, state corporatism. An illustration of this occurs in regulation of the economy.[40] Western capitalist economies are organized primarily on principles of private ownership and rely heavily on market forces; but, because of economic crises on the one hand and the state's commitment to social goals such as welfare and increased prosperity on the other, it is necessary for it both to support private economic organization and at the same time to direct it towards public goals.[41] Economic activity becomes mingled with political and social activity, the public and the private spheres become substantially merged; in order to maintain this 'corporate' character, whereby the state 'directs and controls predominantly privately owned businesses towards four goals: unity, order, nationalism and success',[42] the state may need to be able to act quickly, to change policy abruptly as circumstances change, and to use economic incentives as a way of achieving social goals.[43] It is important in this environment that the

[40] See, generally: J. Winkler, 'Law, State, and Economy'; T. Daintith, 'Public Law and Economic Policy' 1974 *JBL* 9; G. Ganz, 'The Control of Industry by Administrative Process' 1967 *PL* 93.

[41] For discussion of the British government's attempts to control private enterprise in the 1970s and the implications for law, see J. Winkler, 'Law, State and Economy'.

[42] Ibid., p. 106.

[43] The reliance by the government on discretionary authority to achieve counter-inflation measures is discussed in V. Korah, 'Counter-Inflation Legislation: Whither Parliamentary Sovereignty?' (1976) 92 *LQR* 42; see, also, T. Daintith, 'The Functions of Law in the Field of Short-Term Economic Policy' (1976) 92 *LQR* 62.

legal structure be sufficiently open and malleable to accommodate the state's needs. This encourages a weakening of the concern for general legal rules and for a division of institutions; it also creates a greater reliance on discretion. What occurs in economic matters may also be detected in other areas of state regulation.

Each of the four factors considered, when viewed against the background of Weber's modes of authority, goes some way towards explaining why legal authority is so often of a discretionary kind. It is sometimes suggested, however, that there are more fundamental connections between the activities of the modern state in providing social welfare and maintaining social order, and the discretionary mode of authority employed. R. M. Unger has argued that welfare and corporatist tendencies have substantially eroded the idea of legality, meaning something like a mixture between formal rational authority and the rule of law, in favour of a pervasive substantive rationality based on notions of equity and communal solidarity.[44] Unger's account of types of authority in many respects parallels Weber's, but while Weber, at the time he wrote, detected only limited elements of substantive rationality in modern law, Unger sees these elements as dominant. He appears undecided, however, whether this is simply a normal cycle in the life of a society, or the signs of a more fundamental transformation of the nature of legal authority.[45] P. S. Atiyah has identified a similar shift from formal authority to substantive, or as he prefers to put it, from principles to pragmatism. He has found evidence for these trends in various areas of law, and in contract law in particular, and has offered an explanation which also relies heavily on the interventionist nature of the modern state.[46] His view seems to be in general to deprecate the consequential erosion of the certainty and formality which he considers central to the notion of law. Similar views appear in the writings of E. Kamenka and A. E. S. Tay who have identified three legal paradigms: *gemeinschaft, gesellschaft*, and

---

[44] This change in the nature of legal authority is one of Unger's principal themes in *Law in Modern Society*; the idea may also be seen in Hayek, *The Constitution of Liberty*. There is also a tradition of Marxist theory which detects, at a deeper theoretical level, a similar theme in the transition from a capitalist to a communist society: E. Pashukanis, *General Theory of Marxism and Law*, C. Arthur (ed.) (London, 1978). For discussion, see P. Hirst, *On Law and Ideology* (London, 1979), ch. 5.

[45] Unger, *Law in Modern Society*, pp. 213–4.

[46] This is how the change has been expressed by Atiyah in *From Principles to Pragmatism*; it is also one of the themes of his *The Rise and Fall of Freedom of Contract*.

bureaucratic-administrative.[47] Modern societies contain elements of each; but just as capitalist, liberal societies signified a move from the organic, communal society of *gemeinschaft*, to the individualistic, exchange relationships of *gesellschaft*, so there is in modern societies a shift to a system in which the individual right-bearer is no longer at the centre of the stage. Here the dominant mode is bureaucratic rationality, which is the mode of authority most suited to achieving the goals of public policy.

Whether there has been a qualitative change in the nature of legal authority is rather hard to assess. It is clear that the activities of the state and the political environment are conducive to substantial reliance on discretionary authority; it is equally clear, however, that in respect of many matters, state power proceeds according to the tenets of formal rationality. Any claim that there is a predominant tendency towards discretionary authority must depend on careful examination of the many areas of state regulation, and this has not yet been done in a systematic way. It is sufficient to recognize that authority centres around the focal points of formal, substantive, and reflexive rationality, and that the patterns that emerge are not constant but ever grouping and regrouping. And in any event, the interesting task is to see what place law has in respect of any particular pattern.

There is, however, a related argument which needs to be considered in more detail. Here the ideas of complexity and variability are taken up, and given greater importance in understanding the nature of authority. A recurring idea in the views of those who see a turning away from formal authority is that the objects, which the state is trying to achieve through regulation, are so complex (and here complexity may be taken to include variability) that they cannot be realized effectively by a system of authority based on the formulation and application of general rules. Any attempt, then, either to understand the structure of the state in terms of that model, or to use it as a practical guide in allocating and exercising powers, is likely to result in distortion of the way power is exercised in practice, and to hinder the achievement of its objectives. It is important to Unger's account that the modern state, in its concern to regulate the economy, to control the use of resources,

[47] These paradigms have been discussed in various writings of E. Kamenka and A. E. S. Tay; see, for example: 'Social Traditions, Legal Relations', and '"Transforming" the Law, "Steering Society"' in E. Kamenka and A. E. S. Tay (eds.), *Law and Social Control* (London, 1980) and 'Beyond Bourgeois Individualism—the Contemporary Crisis in Law and Legal Ideology' in E. Kamenka and R. S. Neale (eds.), *Feudalism, Capitalism and Beyond* (London, 1975).

and to achieve ideals of social welfare and justice, has to deal with
matters which are too complex to allow for the generalizations
characteristic of rules. The best that can be done is to provide broad
policy goals to be achieved through the discretionary choices of
officials.[48]

This approach has been pushed to heights of great sophistication
and abstraction by other social theorists. One of the most interesting of
these is Niklas Luhmann who has made complexity a key concept in
his analysis of modern societies.[49] Luhmann has developed the theory
that modern societies are exceptionally complex; this results from the
great diversity of interests, groups, and values within them, from the
possibilities that are made available by science and technology, and
from the nature and interrelatedness of economic systems. Societies
are unable to assimilate the full range of possibilities that are opened
up by such complexity, and so the main function of social activity is to
reduce complexity; this is done by selecting aspects of the environment
and thereby simplifying it. Subsystems within society develop in this
way; they simplify or reduce the complexity of the total system, and yet
at the same time they match or correspond to the total environment.
Thus, modern society becomes characterized by the proliferation of
subsystems, whether economic or political, cultural or educational,
each of which performs certain functions within society. The
proliferation of subsystems has the effect of reducing complexity and
making social life possible, but, at the same time, the 'functional
differentiation', or splitting of society into a mass of subsystems, also
increases complexity. And modern society, argues Luhmann, is
characterized by functional differentiation.[50]

This has important implications for law. One of the effects of the
positivization of law, and the putting aside of natural law constraints, is
that the law is whatever the lawmaker decrees. This has enabled legal
regulation to be extended over any area of activity for whatever reasons

[48] *Law in Modern Society*, ch. 3.
[49] Much of Luhmann's writing is not available in English translation but the following
provide an introduction to his views: Niklas Luhmann, *Trust and Power* (London, 1969);
'Differentiation of Society' (1977) 11 *CanJSoc* 29; 'Generalized Media and the
Problem of Contingency' in J. Loubser *et al.* (eds.), *Explorations in General Theory in the
Social Sciences: Essays in Honour of Talcott Parsons* (New York, 1978). Useful discussions
in English of Luhmann's work are Poggi, *Trust and Power* (introduction), and 'Two
Themes from N. Luhmann's Contribution to the Sociology of Law' 1981 *BASLP*; also
W. T. Murphy, 'Modern Times: Niklas Luhmann on Law, Politics and Social Theory'
(1984) 47 *MLR* 603.
[50] 'Differentiation of Society', pp. 35 ff.

seem fit. However, the increasing complexity of other social subsystems, and their differentiation from the total environment and from each other, make it correspondingly difficult for legal systems to formulate abstract norms capable of accommodating the complexity and variability of the situations sought to be regulated. This affects not only the model of formal but also substantive rationality; since, even if the goals and values are stated, there is no guarantee, because of functional differentiation, that they can be achieved simply by the decrees or decisions of one set of officials. Legal regulation is then at risk either of distorting reality by imposing formal rules, or of being forced to rely on extremely abstract statements of purposes. In either case, instead of being an integrating force, law may add to the conflicts amongst subsystems; this may hamper efficient regulation and undermine social stability.

The question, then, is whether there are avenues open for the development of legal regulation in modern societies. Luhmann makes clear that no one centralized system or structure—whether legal, moral, or economic—is capable of providing overall social integration and regulation. It is necessary, therefore, to concentrate on the relationships between sub-systems, and to create mechanisms which make possible a certain compatibility or harmony amongst them. Here the idea of reflexion is important: each subsystem must develop the capacity to limit its own actions, so that it may co-exist with other subsystems. This process of reflexion becomes a primary method in modern societies for integrating subsystems.[51] Within the legal context, this means that with respect to certain issues, perhaps industrial relations or economic regulation, the capacity for comprehensive legal rules is limited; instead, an assessment of the subsystems affected and the conflicts between them may show that other techniques are suitable, perhaps mediatory procedures for the first, and greater reliance on market forces for the second. Put more simply, the legal system must approach each problem with a view to solving it in the best way possible, recognizing that techniques other than simply formulating general norms may be required. Thus law becomes concerned with providing institutions and procedures within which conflicts between subsystems can be resolved, rather than attempting to provide comprehensive social control.[52] So Jurgen Habermas, who,

---

[51] See G. Tuebner, 'Substantive and Reflexive Elements in Modern Law' (1983) 17 *LSR* 239 at pp. 272 ff. I have relied heavily on this analysis.
[52] An example can be taken from American constitutional law; on one approach to the

from a different perspective, has been concerned with similar issues, has concluded that 'since ultimate grounds can no longer be made plausible, the formal conditions of justification themselves obtain legitimating force'.[53] Connections can be seen between these theoretical conclusions and the popular call for greater representation and participation in public decisions.

It has been possible to give only the barest outline of theories which are highly suggestive in demonstrating the scope for legal regulation. They advance a number of hypotheses which can be verified only by extensive empirical analysis of different areas of legal control. Nevertheless, a number of implications for discretionary authority may be suggested. In the first place, the complexity and functional differentiation of society provides an important part of the explanation for the expansion of discretionary authority. Differentiation generates conflict between subsystems, and it falls to the state to be involved in its resolution. This often takes the form of delegation to specialized bodies on the understanding that they may have the capacity to develop suitable and innovatory techniques of dispute resolution. Secondly, however, there is always the question of the most suitable balance between precise normative direction by way of legal standards, and the delegation of discretionary authority with its emphasis on flexibility and capacity to adjust. Legal regulation is undertaken to achieve goals which are considered desirable for moral and political reasons, or out of the necessities of preserving order; the difficult question always is to know how far regulation may go in achieving those goals without creating intolerable levels of conflicts or consequences which undermine the very point of the regulation. Thirdly, if one of the consequences of complexity is increased reliance on reflexive techniques, then issues about decision strategies and participatory procedures become increasingly important. Greater attention should then be devoted to developing different techniques suited to different tasks, to understanding the implications of those techniques in terms of legal and political values, and in developing an adequate framework of accountability and legal regulation.

constitution which seems to be increasing in popularity, judicial review is not directed towards the substantive ends of law in a democratic society, but only towards the conditions which must be satisfied if an outcome is to be considered democratic. See J. H. Ely, *Democracy and Distrust* (Harvard UP, 1981).

   [53] Jurgen Habermas, 'Towards a Reconstruction of Historical Materialism' 1975 *Theory and Society* 287. See also: *Legitimation Crisis*. For discussion see: Tuebner, 'Substantive and Reflexive Elements in Modern Law'.

2.3   LEGAL APPROACHES TO DISCRETIONARY POWERS

The object of the analysis so far has been to identify at an abstract level the factors which contribute to the reliance by the state on discretionary powers. The extent to which these factors are actually at work is an empirical question to be settled with respect to particular legal systems, in the context of specific issues within them; the extent to which they are present is related to the degree of state intervention, whether for welfare purposes or in order to preserve order and stability. It is reasonable to claim that in fact these characteristics are present to a significant degree in modern, welfare state systems, and that, therefore, discretionary authority is not simply a passing phenomenon, but is linked securely to the social structure. If that is the case, then the question arises as to the implications for law: what consequences follow for traditional notions of legality and what scope is there for legal regulation?

If legality implies the exercise of authority through general rules, together with a functional and institutional division of law-makers and adjudicators, then the implications are clear: that mode of law is in various respects incompatible with discretionary authority. A central aspect of that mode of authority is legal formalism, but the earlier discussion has shown this to be an inadequate basis for authority, and needs to be supplemented by notions of substantive and reflexive rationality. If there are incompatibilities between the exercise of state authority and the more exacting sense of legal order, then it is insufficient simply to urge legislators and administrators to be more conscientious in formulating rules, and to be more vigilant in preserving a separation of institutions and functions. Some areas of regulation might, without loss, be made to conform more precisely to the model of general rules, but there are others where the incompatibilities are deep-seated. This might suggest the alternative argument that, since the objects of regulation cannot be achieved without undermining legality, the state's spheres of regulation should be reduced. The underlying premise is then that the values of the rule of law, in particular a version of negative liberty, are of such importance that the state should concern itself only with matters which can be pursued in harmony with them. Views of this kind, which have had substantial influence in the case for deregulation, depend on the rule of law being more important than the objects and values achieved by discretionary regulation. That might sometimes be the case, but it is clearly not always so; the positive objects of regulation may represent values upon which great importance is placed, and there is no justification for conferring automatic priority upon the rule of law. It is preferable to proceed on the alternative assumption that the state is likely for good reasons to continue its regulatory activities, and that within them discretionary powers are likely to continue to be prevalent. The issue then is to consider whether ideas of legality may, nevertheless, have some role in restraining and directing the exercise of discretion.

2.31   *Two images of legal authority*

It has been useful in the discussion so far to postulate a model of legal authority, which will be referred to as the private law model, and then to show the implications for it of extensive reliance by the state on discretionary powers. It is now appropriate to suggest a second image of authority, the public law model, within which those implications can be incorporated, and which can be contrasted with the private law model. It is to be emphasized that these are models rather than descriptions, and while there are obviously substantial elements of both in the arrangements of any modern legal system, the extent to which actual areas of legal regulation can be fitted into one or the other is a matter of empirical assessment. The two models may be expressed in terms of a number of attributes divided into three groups: the first is concerned with functions, the second with the institutional structure, and the third with the relationship between individuals and the state (see table 1).

Table 1. Two images of legal authority

	Private law model	Public law model
Functions	(a) Social order	Social order requires more positive, interventionist measures
	(b) Provision of stable facilities for private relations	Provision of welfare requires pursuit of positive objectives
Institutional structure	(a) Legislature: makes general rules	: sets social goals and provides legal framework : delegates realization of goals to executive and administration

	Private law model	Public law model
	(b) Executive and Administration : implement rules	: achieve policy goals : exercise discretion in doing so
	(c) Courts: adjudicate disputes about the rules and their application	: are concerned to set limits and constraints on discretion rather than adjudicate substantive merits
Citizen–state relationships	(a) Primacy of rights: citizen has spheres of privacy and autonomy defined and protected by rights	Rights lose their primacy: become subject to policy goals : emphasis shifts to person's interests : interests conflict and compete
	(b) State intervention in private actions is effected through rules : state intervention is likely to be restrained	State intervention through discretion where object is to attain policy goals : state intervention is likely to be pervasive
	(c) Disputes about rights resolved by adjudicative procedures : emphasis on applying the law	Disputes about interests occur when administrative agencies are deciding on courses of action : emphasis on influencing outcome : appeal to policy goals : conflict amongst private interests, and between private interests and public interests
	(d) Participatory procedures : separation of political and adjudicative : political participation occurs at macro-political level : distinctive participation in adjudication	: mixing of political and adjudicative : political type participation extends to discretionary decisions : elements of adjudicative procedures also relevant in discretionary decisions

This brief characterization is sufficient to create images of two types of legal authority, each with a markedly different emphasis. The private law model is based around a firm separation of powers, both in terms of functions and institutions, with the definition and protection of private rights at the centre of the stage. The state is likely to have a limited role, but, when intervention is necessary, it is done through rules which are adjudicated by the courts. The emphasis of the public law model is quite different: the predominant concern is with the achievement of policy goals, whether of public order or social welfare, and thus private rights and interests are subordinate to notions of public interest. But what constitutes the public interest is likely to depend partly on the way political activity at the broadest level is translated into legislative standards, and partly on the more precise working-out of those standards in the course of discretionary assessment by administrative officials. The consequences are that the normative structure has to remain reasonably open and adaptable, rather than concentrated on the formulation of rules, and the particular conceptions of public interest are likely to be constituted in part by some compromise between conflicting private interests.

Within the private law model, the separation of powers and the emphasis on general rules means that the judicial trial is the focal point of law. In the public law model, however, the mixing of functions, the displacement of private rights, and the emphasis on purposive reasoning in pursuing policy goals mean that the main concerns of law and legal institutions are less clear. A number of fairly specific issues arise: is discretionary authority impervious to being governed by general standards; what place is there for traditional ideas which extol the virtues of certainty and predictability in law; does the displacement of private rights mean that rights have no place in the face of discretionary powers, or is it possible to develop a more suitable concept of rights; and with the mixing of adjudicative and policy-making elements in the same decision, what basis is there for participatory procedures? These are some of the issues that are to be considered; first, however, it is necessary to formulate some more general ideas as to the object and scope of legal regulation of discretionary authority.

2.32   *Accountability and the diversity of legal values*

Are there legal values, or are there legal points of view, which exist independently of the goals to which specific laws might be directed, and which provide the basis for controlling official actions? There is the minimum sense of legality that we have noted in Hart's account, but his interests were descriptive and sociological, and so provide little guidance of a normative kind. Similarly, the ambitious attempt by E. B. Pashukanis, the post-revolutionary Soviet jurist, to characterize the quintessence of law in the contractual relationship between right-holders, offers little normative guidance.[54] According to this view, law reaches its apogee under capitalism, and degenerates as societies move towards communism, where the emphasis is not on law but on what is described as the administration of things. Accounts of this kind are highly selective in what they describe as law, and, in any event, are descriptive rather than normative. Similar attempts have been made at the normative or constitutional level to identify fundamental legal values. F. A. Hayek has argued for a strict version of the model of law as general rules adjudicated by courts; on this view, an exercise of authority over individuals by means other than general rules is a corruption of law.[55] But this view depends, as we have noticed, on the special importance attached to stability in legal relationships, which in turn depends on the primacy ascribed to the negative liberty that rules protect over the other values and purposes that might be achieved by discretionary regulation.

It is not clear why we should expect there to be one central idea of what law is, or of the tasks it is meant to perform, or of the values it is supposed to serve. Some level of regulation through rules may be necessary from a sociological point of view, if there is to be any order at all, and it may be desirable from a moral point of view, if life within any system of authority is to be tolerable. But, above such thresholds, law and its institutions serve diverse social objectives and moral values. The primary objective within the private law model may be the provision of certainty and stability in legal relations, and so one may be led to regard those as the pre-eminent, if not exclusive legal values. But, while certainty and stability have an important and secure place within the public law model, they are not the only or even necessarily the most important objectives in the allocation of tasks and the exercise of powers. Thus, within the public law model, the question as to what are the values and objectives to be sought through legal standards and institutions, becomes acute. The view taken here is that there is no fundamental and irreducible legal ideal or principle, but rather that law and legal institutions are part of the political and social composition of a society, and that they can be made instrumental in upholding values

---

[54] Pashukanis, *General Theory of Law and Marxism.*
[55] F. A. Hayek, *The Constitution of Liberty,* and *Law, Legislation and Liberty* (London, 1973–9).

several and diverse. What those values are depends on the political theory and practice of a society, and once any particular value had been identified as important in this way, consideration can then be given as to how it is to be achieved effectively, and as to its relationship with other, possibly conflicting values. This may be contrary to an influential view, best represented in the work of L. L. Fuller, that the overall concern of law is governance through general rules, and that this task entails both a certain logic and a certain moral outlook.[56] Fuller's analysis is of considerable value in so far as it is concerned to show that governance is a complicated business, and that certain procedures have to be followed if the decrees of an authority are to be effective in their aims. But in so far as that analysis suggests that there is a distinctively legal aspect of political endeavour, then it is unjustifiably narrow, as is manifest when one considers the role of law and legal institutions within the public law model.

If we accept the plurality of legal values and the instrumental nature of law and legal institutions, then the question arises as to what are the goals of legal regulation in relation to discretionary powers; which political values are to be made the basis for influencing and regulating the exercise of discretion, for developing legal principles and procedures?[57] Any answer to this question must depend on a certain degree of personal preference, both as to the values selected and the importance of each; but reflection on the political theories that underlie modern, democratic, liberal societies would tend to suggest that the following have a position of importance, and that each provides scope for the development of more specific legal principles. The four basic values suggested are: stability in legal relations, rationality in decision-making, fair procedures, and finally a rather loose, residual category of moral and political principles.

With regard to the first of these, *stability in legal relationships* is the value most closely associated traditionally with the rule of law. Stability is dependent upon various factors but primarily on official actions being governed by a system of reasonably clear, settled, and binding standards. Standards may derive from various sources, whether by statutory decree, by judicial law-making, or self-regulation by ad-

---

[56] Fuller, *The Morality of Law*; also David Lyons, *Ethics and the Rule of Law*.
[57] For discussion of legal values, see: P. Stein and J. Shand, *Legal Values in Western Society* (Edinburgh UP, 1974); P. Verkuil, 'The Emerging Concept of Administrative Procedure' (1978) 78 *ColLR*. 258; R. C. Cramton, 'Comment on Trial-Type Hearings in Nuclear Power Plant Siting' (1972) 58 *VaLR*. 585; J. M. Sellers, 'Regulatory Values and the Exceptions Process' (1984) 93 *YLJ* 938.

ministrative authorities. The level of stability naturally varies, being more important in some circumstances than others. Moreover, since stability is not the only value of importance, it may have to compete with other considerations. Such potential conflicts are most pronounced in discretionary contexts. It may be necessary, in order to achieve certain social objectives, whether based on ideals of political justice or stemming from practical necessity in maintaining order and efficiency, to compromise the levels of certainty and predictability. The most satisfactory compromise can be settled only in specific contexts, guided by the nature of the interests at issue and the objectives being sought. In some situations, for example, areas of personal liberty, the nature of the interests may be so important that certainty and predictability are given high priority, at the expense perhaps of a more efficient or effective achievement of goals; in other situations the reverse might be true.

On this approach, stability in legal relations is important in dealing with discretionary powers, but it is not the only matter to be considered. It is understandable, however, that, within stricter versions of the rule of law, maximum certainty and predictability in legal relations should have come to be regarded as the dominating concern. Such views of the rule of law are associated with the historical development of particular western societies, and with the ideologies that have accompanied and added to their legitimacy. It is linked to the development of capitalism, and to political ideals which emphasize the protection of private rights, freedom and security of contracts, equality before the law, a limited state, and a firm division between political and civil society. For these reasons, the rule of law has been a powerful basis for condemning the use of discretionary powers, and so for limiting the activities of the state.[58] To the critics of liberal, capitalist systems, the rule of law is regarded, for similar reasons, as providing powerful ideological support for the social and economic inequalities that such systems produce. Indeed, to more radical critics the rule of law has no importance beyond its ideological functions, and would cease to be important with the demise of capitalism.[59]

It is necessary, however, to distinguish between the rule of law as

[58] Hayek, *The Constitution of Liberty*.
[59] Critics of the rule of law writing from a Marxist viewpoint have been inclined to regard it in this way. For example, see Pashukanis, *General Theory of Law and Marxism*. Some criticism of this may be seen in E. P. Thompson, *Whigs and Hunters* (London, 1977), pp. 258–65.

part of a wider ideological framework, and the importance of rules in guiding citizens in any system of social organization. By providing stability, which includes guidance, rules contribute to elementary notions of individuality and autonomy; these can be accepted as important without a further commitment to any general system of ideologies about the proper objects of state regulation. More specifically, the provision of reasonable guidance through rules may be valued without one being committed to strict versions of the rule of law, and without denying that there may be other social objectives with which guidance may have to compete.

Once guidance and the resulting stability in legal relations is recognized as an important, but not the exclusive value served by law, the scope for other values can be assessed. The second factor suggested is *rationality in decision-making*; legal principles may be employed in enhancing the rational basis of decisions, and hence reducing arbitrariness. Philip Selznick has suggested that '[T]he essential element in the rule of law is the restraint of official power by rational principles of civic order.'[60] He then goes on: '. . . the proper aim of the legal order, and the special contribution of legal scholarship, is to minimize the arbitrary element in legal norms and decisions'.[61] It is not entirely clear why this should be seen as the 'essential' element of law when clearly there are other values served by law. We might hesitate also in thinking of law as pre-eminent amongst various ways of raising the level of rationality.

Selznick also appears to assume rather too readily that law necessarily heightens rationality; and that the rule of law is the most effective means for doing so. We shall see later on that the relationship between law and rationality is in fact more complex. Nevertheless, we may accept the implicit Weberian claim that the tendency towards greater rationality in the exercise of authority is a mark of modern societies, and that law and legal institutions have been a significant part of that movement. We saw in section 1.2 that rationality in attaining the objects of power is a background constraint on officials exercising discretion; various aspects of rationality and arbitrariness are taken up in chapters 3 and 4. We shall see that arbitrariness is a complex notion, and that there may be competing models of rationality and different levels of attainment. However, it may be accepted that while final conceptions of rationality and the ultimate rationality of a particular

---

[60] P. Selznick, *Law, Society and Industrial Justice* (New York, 1969), p. 11.
[61] Ibid., p. 13.

course of action are to some degree matters of disagreement, the general requirement of rationality is fundamental, and that law and legal institutions have significant potential in that general enterprise. That potential may be developed in different directions; for example in requiring that decisions be reasoned, that the reasons be good reasons within the objects of power, and that extraneous or personal factors be eliminated from consideration. The idea of rational decision-making may be extended further to require that there be evidence for findings of fact, and perhaps that there be some framework of general standards, applied with reasonable consistency, and changed or departed from only for good reasons.

The third basis for the development of legal principles lies in matters of *procedure*. It is in this area that the law might be thought to have made its distinctive contribution; the idea of good procedures, of which due process is one aspect, is often taken as very central to the legal enterprise. However, the basis of good procedures is mixed: the primary concern is to achieve satisfactory outcomes in an efficient manner, while considerations of fairness may restrain or supplement that object. The criminal trial, for example, is primarily concerned to reach an accurate outcome, but it is also concerned to uphold, as side constraints, values considered to be important. Connections can be drawn between issues of procedure and our earlier discussion of complexity and reflexive rationality; law may have a useful role to play in devising procedural frameworks within which the conflicts between subsystems can be resolved. Moreover, in considering procedures in discretionary contexts, it is necessary to go beyond traditional ideas of due process, to develop a wider understanding of the basis of good procedures, and to identify the connections with underlying political values. Procedures are to be seen as having their place within a wider political framework, and the concept of participation is of undoubted importance. Participation takes various forms, ranging from voting in elections to that mode familiar in a court of law. Again, the basis of participation is not only fairness, but efficiency and effectiveness; nevertheless, fairness might be seen as an important aspect of the relationship of interaction and reciprocity between officials and citizens, as Lon Fuller has expressed it.[62] Since this relationship is increasingly important in the discretionary context, especially when policy decisions have to be made in the course of settling a specific

[62] Fuller, *The Morality of Law.*

issue, it is necessary to consider the development of different modes of participation. Many issues dealt with in the context of discretion are not of the state-versus-individual kind, but concern decisions about the public interest, and have consequences of a continuing and positive nature for many interests, groups, and individuals; it is important, then, to develop procedures which extend participatory procedures into discretionary decision-making. Participatory procedures may also add to the rational basis of decisions by allowing individuals and groups to bring information and arguments to bear on the matter in issue.

In addition to stability, rationality, and fair procedures, as the bases for legal principles, there is a *residual category of moral and political principles* which might be used to generate constraints on discretionary decisions. Ideas of fairness are important not only in matters of procedure, but extend also into other aspects of decisions. It may be unfair, for example, in respect of important interests of personal liberty to act without reasonably clear standards, or to depart from settled standards, or to go back on an undertaking that has been given.[63] Other moral values may also be important; a framework of legal standards has been built around the injustice of discrimination whether on the grounds of race, national origins, or gender. In general, there is always scope for the development of moral concepts and general ideas of justice and equity which become constraints on the exercise of discretion. These constraints might be the creation of statute or common law, or they might become accepted by administrative officials themselves as binding principles. At a certain point, a particular principle may come to be recognized to be of such importance that it becomes a legal constraint on the exercise of power.

One further question that arises is whether there is any unifying basis underlying the suggested directions for the development of legal principles. If the matter is appraised in consequentialist terms, the emphasis would be on settling for whatever combinations contribute most to the maximization of utilities – in short to the best consequences, all things considered. More interesting is the possibility that at the foundation of legal principles is a notion of respect for persons; this then would provide not only the inspiration for developing legal principles, but also the basis for rights. The question of rights is taken up in section 4.2, and it is there suggested that there is scope

---

[63] For judicial application of this idea, see: *R. v. Inland Revenue Commissioners ex p. Preston* [1983] 2 AER 300, but note *In re Preston* [1985] 2 WLR 836.

for notions of substantive as well as process rights. In more general terms, however, while each of the values identified can be linked to respect for persons, and while the relationship between citizen and state is of major importance in exercising discretion, it is not clear that this is the only basis on which those values rest. For example, questions of legal stability may be related not only to respect for persons, but also to social order and efficiency; similarly, we have noted that questions of procedure involve a mixture of efficiency and fairness. It seems preferable, therefore, to accept that the values underlying legal principles, while clearly related to respect for persons, may also serve other ends.

Now that certain political values have been identified, we may go on to consider two further issues. The first concerns the translation of these values into legal principles; this requires some explanation as to what is meant by legal principles. The second issue concerns the division of tasks amongst the different governmental authorities, in particular the legislature, the administration, and the courts. And, as we shall see, these issues are closely interwoven. To begin, a useful contrast can be drawn between the private and public law models. In the private law model, the division of functions and institutions marks out the way different tasks are to be performed; the legislature has primary responsibility for making the law, the executive and administration for implementing it, and the courts for resolving any disputes that arise. Legislative accountability lies to the political process, and administrative accountability lies to the legislature. The courts are required to apply the law, and although that does not prevent occasional policy innovation, the judicial function is tied securely to the idea of impartial application of the rules. In the public law model, such neat divisions disappear. The legal and formal links between legislature and administration are retained, since the latter derives its powers from the former, and is accountable to it for the way they are used. But the legal and formal relationship provides an inadequate account of the workings in practice. In the first place, the delegation of discretionary powers connotes a certain autonomy in the administrative authority in deciding on the courses of action to be taken, the standards to be adopted, and the strategies to be followed. The legislature may in the terms of delegation direct and instruct the authority as to how it should act, but in practice that is done only to a limited extent. Accountability for a discretionary decision after it has been taken may be effective in some cases, but again, in practice, it is bound to be piecemeal and, in many cases, too late to alter the outcome of particular decisions.

For these reasons, the accountability, within the public law model, of officials for their discretionary decisions has to be extended. This may take two general directions, one political, the other legal, in the senses to be explained. The chain linking the legislature and the administrative authorities remains the primary basis of accountability, the guiding principle being that an authority acts properly, if it acts within the terms and in accordance with the conditions set by the legislature. But this needs to be supplemented by other devices which increase accountability for the way discretion actually is exercised. Those may consist in checks of one authority by another, appeals from one to another, or by a division and balancing of powers between authorities; there may also be scope for a more direct accountability to those groups and individuals whose interests are affected by extended representation and participation in the political process. The diversity of those devices and techniques can be matched by equally diverse sets of institutions, ranging from Parliament and committees of Parliament, to administrative tribunals and officials like the Ombudsman, and to the courts.

Now while the overall level of accountability is to be assessed in terms of those devices and institutions, the question is whether some of the techniques can be considered as distinctively legal, and thus suited to application and development by the courts. This problem is particularly acute within the public law model where any sharp differentiation between institutions and between functions has been lost. It is unclear in this model what particular place there is for the courts in regulating the exercise of discretion; if they become active in placing constraints on the actions of authorities which are accountable to the democratic, political process, then questions may arise about the accountability and legitimacy of the courts themselves. In the private law model, these issues raise little difficulty; the official accounts for his actions by showing he has acted in accordance with the rules set by the legislature; the task of the courts is to ensure that he has, but this is a matter of objective adjudication, and so no problems arise about judicial accountability.

Opinions undoubtedly may differ about the nature of principles regulating discretion and about the place of the different institutions. The following approach is suggested, however, on the grounds that it has considerable support in terms of constitutional principles and institutional history. In explaining, first, the idea of principles regulating the exercise of discretion, a useful distinction may be drawn between those aspects of a decision which are left to the assessment and judgment of the empowered authority, and those aspects which in a sense are fixed in advance and which constitute constraints on the decision-maker. The former are usually matters of substance and content, or policy and merits, and for those matters primary accountability usually lies to the more clearly political aspects of government. The latter, which may be referred to as legal principles, are concerned in shaping, guiding, and regulating the discretionary process; they are not concerned directly with final outcomes, nor with the merits of the policies and strategies followed. Procedural principles are a good example: they stipulate the procedures to be followed without necessarily affecting the outcome. But we must be careful not to put the distinction simply in terms of substance and procedure; even procedures may affect outcomes by requiring certain matters to be taken into account and interests to be heard or consulted. And, as we move from procedural matters to principles based on those other values suggested, like rationality, stability, or fairness, the distinction between substance and procedure become increasingly difficult to maintain. Perhaps the idea of 'process' comes close to capturing the nature of legal principles: process suggests a range of constraints on the way decisions are made, on the reasoning process, and on the sort of outcomes that are permissible, while recognizing that there is some final element of substance which is for determination by the authority itself.[64] Principles of process are not aimed directly at outcomes, but nevertheless unavoidably influence and shape outcomes.[65]

Principles of process, or legal principles, are the basis of legal accountability. They have their origins in political ideals and values about the way government ought to be conducted, and they constitute some of the conditions that are to be satisfied if official actions are to be considered justifiable and legitimate. Compliance with legal principles would not normally be a sufficient justification for the decision made, since such principles may be complied with and yet the

---

[64] For an illuminating study of the concept of process in constitutional law, see Ely, *Democracy and Distrust*. Ely is mistaken, however, in so far as he argues that matters of process do not involve decisions about substantive moral and political values. For further discussion: D. J. Galligan, 'Judicial Review and Democratic Principles: Two Theories' (1983) 57 *ALJ* 69.

[65] For further discussion of this sense of process, see D. J. Galligan, 'Judicial Review and the Textbook Writers'.

decision be quite unjustifiable. Moreover, compliance may sometimes be perfunctory, a matter of form, with no real effect on the substantive outcome. Nevertheless, conscientious compliance with legal principles in making discretionary decisions is a demonstration by officials of their concern to justify and account for their actions, not only to other political institutions and in substantive political terms, but also in accordance with more generalized and enduring political values. In other words, it is not only final outcomes that matter, but also the processes whereby those outcomes are reached. Good government means more than good results in terms of one or other set of political goals; it depends partly on consideration of and compliance with a range of values and ideals in arriving at those results.

The selection of the values that are to be translated into legal principles may be made by a number of institutions within the framework of government; they may stem from legislative enactment, judicial decision, or from one or other of a range of special administrative tribunals and authorities. For example, efforts are made by legislative enactment to ensure fair procedures and to enhance the rational basis of decisions; special administrative tribunals may be established to develop principles of good administration in exercising discretion; further principles might stem from special bodies like the ombudsman. However, in practice the courts also have an important role either in applying rather loose statutory standards or in developing principles of their own. Indeed, in Anglo-American systems substantial responsibility to devise legal principles has been left with the courts. Some of the more specific issues about judicial review are dealt with in later chapters, but a few remarks should be made now about the judicial role.

In developing legal principles which regulate discretionary powers exercised by other authorities, the courts are required inevitably to make their own political choices, and to take a stand on moral and political principles. They may try to be as neutral as possible between different political ideologies, but the very performance of their task makes it impossible for them to avoid political and moral choices. And, since courts are not linked into the democratic process, the question arises as to their own accountability, and the justification for the role they serve. These issues are considered further in chapter 5, but two very brief lines of answer may be suggested: firstly, it is not clear why it should be thought that the only basis of legitimacy of official actions is the democratic process, since there are many other values which are prized by societies, and which may be advanced by judicial decisions; secondly, in justifying legal principles which regulate discretion, the courts must appeal to values and ideals that are in a sense pre-constitutional, part of the political and moral infrastructure of the society. If they lose touch with these ideals, there are procedures available for overruling their decisions. We shall see that questions about the proper division between political and legal accountability are themselves aspects of a wider sense of political accountability; but courts do try to work out their own spheres of special concern, and these tend to be based in the way explained around processes rather than final outcomes.

To sum up, we have been considering the issue of accountability, and the basis and scope of legal principles which regulate discretion. If discretionary authority is a central and permanent part of modern government, and if the object of discretion is to achieve social and economic goals considered to be desirable, then the question is whether law has any role in this public law model. I have suggested that there are certain values which are important in any system of good government, and that these may be the basis for creating a framework of legal principles, or principles of process, which constitute constraints on the exercise of discretionary authority. Such principles complement rather than compete with more direct methods of political accountability by contributing to the overall justifiability and legitimacy of discretionary decisions.

2.33 *Responsive law*

The approach suggested here for the legal regulation of discretionary powers proceeds on the basis that legal techniques and legal institutions have an important but limited role in the management of modern societies. These techniques and institutions are important in providing a framework of principles which influence and constrain the exercise of powers, and which provide a bridge between political values and official decision-making; they are limited in the sense that not all questions arising in the regulation of society are suitable for final determination by legal procedures and institutions. This approach recognizes that many of the issues occurring in the course of the multifarious activities of the modern state are best resolved by institutions other than courts, according to strategies that do not necessarily centre around rules and adjudication.

This may appear to be inadequate legal response to discretionary

powers. The risk is that discretionary powers fall between the two
poles of accountability: on the one side political checks may be
ineffective, while on the other side legal regulation is confined to
process constraints upon decision-making, rather than directed at final
outcomes. For this reason it might be argued that law should have
greater involvement in the discretionary process. Just such a case has
been put in recent years by the American legal sociologists Nonet and
Selznick,[66] who suggest developing what they call responsive law. The
main point of their argument is that formal, rule-based authority is
unable to cope with the tasks undertaken by the modern state, and so
some new direction for law has to be found which moves away from the
ideal of rules, without however abandoning government regulation to
the discretion of administrative agencies.

Their solution to the integration of legal authority and discretionary
power is responsive law, and the key concept of responsive law is
purpose. The basic idea is that all powers are conferred upon
institutions for specific purposes, and that these can be made objective
enough to provide guidance, both in designing the institutions and
procedures for decision-making, and in determining the substantive
ends to which decisions are to be directed. The emphasis on purpose
has two particular virtues. The first is that it provides an objective basis
for making decisions, and for their external scrutiny. Even where
purposes are not specified in the grant of power, or are left unclear,
they may be extrapolated by reflecting upon the nature and terms of
power in the light of community values. Purposes provide the basis for
policy choices, and for settling standards and strategies for giving
effect to them. But, while purpose is always the touchstone of action, it
is not static and constant; it must be shaped and reshaped in response
to the influences that wider participation creates. So participation by
citizens in the decision-process is also an important aspect of
responsive law.[67] The purpose behind any grant of power will then be
moulded and remoulded in response to the arguments and ideas of
diverse groups, it will take account of changing ideas and values, of
empirical research, policy analysis, and the methods of social science.[68]

The second virtue of purpose as the dominant concept in both
administrative decision-making and legal control is that constant
reflection upon the purposes of power and the standards they generate

[66] Nonet and Selznick, *Law and Society in Transition*, ch. iv in particular.
[67] Ibid., pp. 95–103.   [68] Ibid., pp. 80–5.

provides a basis for criticizing existing practices and patterns of decision-making; it also gives positive guidance as to what methods are employed most suitably in making decisions. A constant concern with purpose also creates a way of tempering the tendency of institutions to develop rules of decision-making, which then are applied blindly as ends in themselves, and so become separated from both the principles which support them and the underlying purposes. Concern with purpose and the principles that may be derived from it thus provides a basis for developing a normative structure of standards, guide-lines, and rules according to which decisions are to be made, but it also provides a basis for critically assessing that structure to ensure congruence between the two.[69]

This is a brief outline of a complex and imaginative attempt to develop a strategy for law in modern societies. It envisages the administrative system as the fourth branch of government, in the sense that power is decentralized and diffused among a wide range of authorities, which in turn become centres of political activity. But the politicizing of the administrative process is not to be seen as an abandonment of law; on the contrary, the legal process remains the dominant organizing principle, but now with a different emphasis. Instead of being based on rules, its new focus is regulation, which is taken to mean the process of elaborating and concretizing the policies, and extrapolating the principles, required for the realization of a legal purpose. Legal order based around the sovereignty of purpose will embrace all areas of state regulation.

The approach taken by Nonet and Selznick can be seen as part of a wider movement towards establishing a rational and morally justifiable basis for the exercise of state powers by administrative authorities. But, while the claim can be accepted that discretionary decisions should be intelligibly and rationally related to the purposes for which powers have been conferred, that the rational pursuit of purposes is a central facet of the justifiable use of official powers, it is another matter to assert that purposes are necessarily sufficiently objective to attract a high level of consensus. The definition and application of purposes may be highly discretionary matters, being dependent on the way that officials at different levels of authority are able to link their powers to political objectives and values. The derivation and concretization of purpose may be included amongst those matters that are most suitably

---

[69] Ibid., pp. 82–4.

left for officials to settle, and for which account is to be made to the political process. On this approach, the courts would be concerned primarily with ensuring that officials do adopt a rational and coherent view of purpose, rather than dictate what it is to be, and how it is to be realized.

Nonet and Selznick have much more ambitious plans for purpose. They consider that purposes can be made sufficiently objective and consensual to allow individuals and institutions, whether administrative officials or courts, to agree on the specification of purposes and the policies for translating them into action. Although there are hints of ambivalence, Nonet and Selznick take the view that the courts should be fully involved in and finally responsible for substantive questions about purpose. Amongst the numerous difficulties with this approach, there are two of special importance: the first concerns the problem of objectivity of purposes; the second relates to the division of powers and the capacities of the legal process.

Regarding the first, there are difficulties in making specific in an objective way the purpose or purposes for which powers have been granted, and in translating them into more detailed policies and standards, again in an objective and consensual way. An initial problem is in ascertaining what the purposes of power are; Nonet and Selznick offer little guidance, but the idea seems to be to look at whatever indications there are in the legislative grant of powers and supporting materials, and then to try rationally to reconstruct purposes in that light and under the general guidance of political and legal values. But given the diversity and complexity of society, and the widely different concerns and values of its members, it is hard to see why it should be assumed that rational reconstruction will lead to one consistent set of purposes and policies, rather than two or more which are incompatible with each other, but each of which might be consistent in its own terms and with background materials; indeed, reflection upon purpose may lead simply to a confused mixture of goals and values.[70] Even if, at an abstract level, purpose can be settled objectively, there is still the difficulty of translating it into specific policies. We may well agree that the object of official powers is to produce industrial harmony, to increase manufacturing output, to have an efficient transport system,

[70] Nonet and Selznick's approach to purpose follows a similar pattern to that advanced by Dworkin in adjudication (see note 16). The irony is that the many difficulties which such an approach faces in the limited sphere of adjudication are compounded when the approach is applied to the total society.

to reduce crime—and yet have very different views about how each object is to be achieved in practice. At each level of specification, there are decisions to be made which reach into economic calculations, political factors, social perceptions, and value assessments, in a way so complex that there is likely to be room for diverse and conflicting conclusions. The problem is likely to increase if, as Nonet and Selznick suggest, a greater range of issues are to be brought within legal regulation, since this would transfer to the legal system those deep conflicts which presently occur at the economic, social, and political levels. In short, under the cover of purpose Nonet and Selznick have put forward an holistic view of society which assumes, finally, a right order of things, and a set of political values on which all rational persons will come to agree. They offer little argument or evidence, however, to show why the harmony which is always elusive at these other levels should be available when the issues are characterized as legal.

A further source of difficulty is the uncertain relationship between the objectivity of purposes and policies, and the participation of individuals and interest groups in influencing the courses of action adopted. Nonet and Selznick clearly consider that popular participation is to be a central aspect of the new legal order. This fits in with their pluralist views, according to which diverse interests are brought to bear on an issue, and then a consensual solution is achieved. But there is a certain tension between the idea that purposes and policies can be settled according to objective considerations of public interest, and the importance attached to diverse interests participating in order to find a solution to a particular problem. The latter image suggests that there is no sense of public interest beyond whatever accommodation may be reached amongst conflicting interests. Even if consensus can be reached with respect to each matter that arises, there is no reason to expect that there will be the nice consistency that Nonet and Selznick seem to expect over all areas of regulation. Indeed, in other contexts, the basis for politicizing the legal process, and opening it to popular participation, stems partly from the belief that there is no objective basis for settling social issues, and that the only course open is to accept whatever accommodation amongst conflicting interests can be achieved. Moreover, the consensual assumptions of the account are themselves open to doubt. Whatever elements of consensus there may be in modern societies, there are also deeply ingrained conflicts based on economic and social inequalities, on different value systems, and on a range of other variables. Two of the familiar criticisms of pluralist, consensus theories of political science are equally applicable here: in the first place, there are such deep conflicts between interests and values that there is often little scope for consensual accommodation; in the second place, pluralism is biased towards the more powerful and better organized interests, so that what appears to be consensus may be effective domination.[71] Some of these issues are taken up in chapter 7, but Nonet and Selznick offer little advice as to how the difficulties could be overcome; the obvious answer is to fall back on purpose as a way of correcting interest group bias, but that line is at least partly blocked since the definition of purpose is in the first place dependent to a great extent on the influence of private interests.

The second general difficulty with Nonet and Selznick's approach relates to the division of powers, and to the capacities of the legal process and the courts. Few reasons are given, and indeed are hard to find, for entrusting to the legal process the responsibility for creating a normative structure, capable of resolving fundamental issues and conflicts at every level of state regulation, whether in the economic, social, or political spheres. Courts do not have the technical capacities or resources to conduct the comprehensive research, nor to make the policy assessments that are envisaged by responsive law. They might be able to acquire it, but the costs would be high, since it would require substantial changes to both institutions and procedures. It is of course difficult to describe with precision what it is that is distinctive about courts, but it would seem to be the combination of elements of relative detachment from the political process, specialized institutions whose members are generalists, and whose main skills are in resolving carefully defined disputes in response to the issues put before them by the parties and their legal advisers, and according to existing standards. The tasks contemplated by responsive law would seem to require institutions of a quite different kind. Moreover, the rational extrapolation of purposes and policies, and the building up of appropriate standards and strategies for achieving them in practice, are often matters of considerable complexity and controversy; decisions about them are accordingly discretionary in the most clear and central sense, and it remains unclear what gains would be made in terms of legitimacy by entrusting them to courts. Other institutions and

---

[71] For basic criticisms of pluralism, see W. Connolly, *The Bias of Pluralism* (New York, 1969).

processes may be both more effective in performing these tasks, and more appropriate in terms of political responsibility.

These reservations about responsive law in controlling discretionary powers can be linked to the ideas in social theory that have already been considered. Both Luhmann and Habermas have argued that the potential for legal control in the modern state is limited, and certainly more limited than responsive law suggests. We have noted Luhmann's argument that modern society is characterized by a complex of overlapping and potentially conflicting subsystems, and that the legal system does not have the capacity to integrate and resolve the total conflicts within society. On that approach, the most suitable strategy for law as an integrative social force is to nurture the growth of institutions and procedures which regulate the methods of conflict resolution rather than stipulate their outcomes. Nonet and Selznick do not advert to these difficulties, although some tacit acceptance of the limitations of legal order seems implicit in the emphasis they put on the politicization of the administrative process. But, in the end, they adopt a position in sharp contrast to reflexive rationality by insisting that the goal of participatory procedures is to arrive at objective standards.

The relative merits of the competing views of society can be tested, finally, only in the context of specific areas of state regulation. Within some areas, the development of a notion of reflexive rationality may be the most satisfactory approach to resolving conflicts. But, even in such matters, there is likely to be a complex relationship between allowing individuals and groups to reach a solution acceptable to them, and the importance of the state through its institutions having general powers to guide and direct decision-making towards goals, and in accordance with values, which are deeply based in the community. One of the important aspects of responsive law is the emphasis it places on the continuing interaction between these two considerations. It recognizes that procedures and outcomes are not totally separable, and that the very process of fixing the procedures of decision-making involves reflection upon the implications of democratic principles, upon fairness, and upon a variety of political values. And to make decisions about these matters is to begin to develop a set of substantive principles to be applied if power is to be exercised legitimately. Final courses of action may be left to the discretion of the administrative authority, or to the outcomes achieved by negotiation and compromise, but the legal system still has a significant role in settling the framework of values within which it takes place, and thus indirectly influencing final outcomes.

Responsive law, it may be concluded, proposes an excessively ambitious programme for the legal process; it underestimates the complexity of purpose, and gives little importance to a division of powers. This is not to argue that purpose has no place in legal development, but only that issues of purpose and policy may be controversial, and that for reasons of accountability and competence they may be better left to the discretionary choices of administrative officials. At one point, Nonet and Selznick distinguish between purpose as a critical basis for reviewing decisions, and purpose as an affirmative basis for settling policy matters.[72] The emphasis in the first is towards setting the boundaries within which there may still be room for different policy assessments, and in devising constraints on the way that such assessments are to be made; the second concerns the more positive task of stipulating with particularity the objects of power and the policies for achieving them. It is the first of those that is the more clearly justifiable object of the legal process and judicial review.

2.4 CONCLUSION

The object of this chapter has been to understand why discretionary authority has become such a prominent part of modern government, and to consider the implications for ideas of law, legality, or the rule of law. The first of these tasks was approached at two levels. By analysis of Weber's ideal types of legal authority, it was shown at an abstract level why formal rational authority is an inadequate model of authority in a modern society. Various factors could be identified which lead to substantive rationality, and to the more recent concept of reflexive rationality. I then moved on to consider at a more practical level some of the factors within the modern state which have contributed to the increased reliance on substantive and reflexive rationality. Then suggestions in social theory that there are certain fundamental links between the activities of the modern state and discretionary authority, were considered.

The second main issue concerned the legal approach to discretionary authority. This question was approached by proposing two models or images of legal authority, the private law model and the public law

---

[72] *Law and Society in Transition*, ch. iv.

model. It was shown how discretionary authority undermines important features of the private law model, and fits more readily into the public law model. The task then was to consider the scope for legal principles and institutions in regulating the exercise of discretion. A number of political values and goals were identified, and it was suggested that those constitute the basis for a framework of principles and standards to be developed by various government institutions, including the courts. It was accepted that those principles are inevitably concerned more with process than with final outcomes, but it was shown that there are important relationships between the two. Reasons were given for preferring this diversified process approach to a more comprehensive, substantive regulation as envisaged in the idea of responsive law.

3
The Exercise of Discretionary Powers I

THE discussion so far has been concerned with the nature of discretionary powers and their relationship with models of legal authority. Discretionary powers have been characterized as relatively autonomous subsystems of authority, where the emphasis is neither on decision-making according to pre-established general rules nor upon a separation, institutionally and methodologically, of the policy-making and policy-application functions. By considering the activities of modern government, we have identified the reasons for delegating powers to diverse administrative authorities, and explanations have been suggested as to why these are likely to be in discretionary form. Two models of legal authority were proposed, one of which might be thought of as a private law model, the other public; the widespread reliance on discretionary powers suggests the suitability of the latter in analysing questions of legal regulation.

The strategies of legal regulation of discretionary authority may be divided into two broad categories: one is concerned with participatory procedures to ensure the representation of groups and interests; the other concentrates on developing a framework of legal principles which shape and influence discretionary decisions. But before going on to consider the basis and principles of legal regulation, it is desirable to examine more closely the anatomy of discretionary decisions and the way decisions are made, to identify some of the primary influences and constraints affecting the decision process, and to suggest different types of decisions that can occur within discretion. This leads into a brief survey of administrative theory and its implications for legal regulation. The final task in this chapter is to consider the place within discretionary contexts of a number of critical concepts, in particular rationality, arbitrariness, fairness, and guidance.

3.1 THE ANATOMY OF DISCRETIONARY DECISIONS

Once there is discretion in something approaching the central sense previously outlined, the main discretionary issues arise: is the prisoner to get parole, what policies are to be laid down for the guidance of welfare officers, which site is to be selected for the road, is the licence to be granted, or the offender prosecuted or otherwise penalized? Amongst these issues there is enormous variation as to the objects and degree of discretion, as to the constraints on its exercise, as to the procedures and strategies that are suitable. Each, however, presents similar kinds of questions for the official or authority: the objects and purposes for which powers have been conferred must be clarified; intermediate goals and standards guiding the course of specific decisions must be devised; and the strategies or modes of proceeding must be settled. These three aspects of discretionary decisions involve matters of substance in the sense of interpretation and implementation, and matters of procedure and strategy. These are convenient labels but care must be taken not to exaggerate the extent to which they represent distinct processes, since they are in many respects overlapping and interconnected, and each often is subject to and influenced by the same factors. So the interpretation of vaguely stated legislative objects may be influenced by the official's appraisal of the resources available and the most effective way of using them, or by the official's moral understandings in an area of moral ambiguity. Those same factors may also shape the procedures and strategies adopted; limited resources, for example, may encourage negotiation and compromise between an authority and its clients or subjects, and discourage unilateral action. With this qualification, we may use these divisions in examining the substance and procedure of discretionary decisions, and in identifying some of the influences and constraints that operate.

3.11 *The substance of discretion*

The legislative statement of objects and purposes is of clear and central importance in exercising delegated powers. By that means the content and scope of powers are defined, and guidance is provided to the official in making decisions; moreover, it is in terms of those objects that any assessment or evaluation of a decision is to be made. And yet we adverted previously to the difficulties arising when the reform of legal regulation is made to depend on the objectivity of purposes; later we shall encounter further difficulties in the judicial interpretation of purposes in defining the legality of discretionary decisions. The general point is that while the statement of objects and purposes may sometimes be clear, there is more often considerable scope for interpretation and assessment—interpretive discretion as it has been called—which increases as the precision of statutory formulation decreases.

Nevertheless, the official or authority must form some view about the task to be performed, the job to be done.[1] That view then becomes the focal point around which official activity is based in devising policies, settling strategies, and making decisions. In the formation of an official's view of his tasks, the rational reconstruction of legislative intention is an important element; but where the terms of power are stated vaguely, the official is unlikely to be concerned with more precise definition beyond adopting a working conception of the objects to be achieved. The greater concern is likely to be with the more specific goals, policies, and procedures for achieving those objects. In other words, while courts, in exercising review, may have to reconstruct statutory purposes to a high level of precision, with precise lines being drawn between what is authorized and what is not, the administrative official is more likely to be concerned with the operational policies and procedures for getting his job done in a reasonably acceptable way. For these reasons, the administrator may be surprised to be told that he has taken into account an irrelevant factor or pursued an improper purpose, since the definition of such matters is bound to appear somewhat arbitrary and irrelevant to his task. Even where the statutory objects, or directions for their implementation, are stated with precision, it does not follow that the administrator's working conceptions will not deviate from what is specified, and he may even see it as necessary deliberately to modify, embellish, or depart from those objects or directions in order to accommodate influences upon him, or to satisfy his own perceptions of the problem and its solution. We have already considered some of the issues that occur when discretion is assumed in this way in the absence of clear authorization or even contrary to clear directions.

Assuming that some working conception of statutory objectives has been settled, the task then is to decide on more specific policies and strategies. This is the very heart of the discretionary process, and the overall guiding concern is to achieve those statutory objectives efficiently and effectively. But what counts as effectiveness depends to

[1] Two recent studies which have been of great assistance in understanding the exercise of discretion and to which reference is made at many points in the following discussion are: Keith Hawkins, *Environment and Enforcement: Regulation and the Social Definition of Pollution* (Oxford, 1984) and Genevra Richardson, with A. Ogus and P. Burrows, *Policing Pollution: a Study of Regulation and Enforcement* (Oxford, 1982).

a substantial degree on the subsidiary goals that are set and the extent to which they are achieved. In settling that matter, the official may be required to make important choices about political and economic objectives; about, for example, the relationship between environmental protection and unrestrained economic activity, or between equity and deserts and the forward-looking goals of criminal justice, or about the distribution of scarce resources. Such issues may provide ample opportunity to pursue a particular political theory, such as the principles of just distribution of resources, about criminal offenders, or how aliens are to be treated, the future shape of urban development, or the educational system that is to be achieved. There may be scope in deciding such matters for the official's own policy preferences, even political commitments; a minister may have a very specific theory of distributive justice which guides the exercise of his discretionary powers; similarly the prison governor may have a definite penal policy which he takes every opportunity to implement in the exercise of his various discretions.

On the other hand, there are bound to be restrictions on the extent to which any official or authority is able to propagate his or its own policies and theories; the minister may be instructed by Cabinet to give preference to certain policies, the prison governor may have to curb his own penal theory in order to meet directions from the Home Secretary, and the national corporation may have to comply with the economic theory of the government of the day. The more important issues of policy are settled, naturally, within the higher echelons of an authority exercising discretionary powers, but similar if lesser decisions have to be made at every level down to the officials performing the most modest tasks. Whether it be the field officer in an environmental protection authority, the prison warder, the listing clerk, the social welfare official, or the sentencing magistrate, each within his limited sphere of autonomy has to make decisions which require resort to policy preferences, to political leanings, and to moral outlooks. The scope for such choices at the lower levels of decision making can be restricted by clear and binding policy directions from above, but the specificity of such directives is bound to vary according to a multitude of factors, including the impossibility of comprehensive rules and the very need to allow considerable scope for individual initiative in achieving goals. And even where clear directives are given, it is difficult to rule out the familiar phenomenon whereby officials depart from, ignore, or selectively apply even the clearest instructions.

While the statutory objectives provide the central focus of an official's actions, it would be misleading to think that the effective achievement of objectives is a simple matter of finding suitable means to a given end. The relationship between means and ends can be direct and simple, but it is more likely to be influenced and modified by a host of factors which bear on the means and strategies employed, the substantive policies pursued, and even the level of achievement that can reasonably be expected. So, for example, it has been shown how the field officer in controlling levels of water pollution has to take account of the need for co-operation and agreement by the polluters themselves, and so must rely heavily on negotiating procedures rather than simple rule-enforcement; those, together with other factors like the economic capacities of the polluters, the moral ambivalence of the community towards pollution as a criminal activity, and the resources of the authority, in turn affect the levels of control that can be attained.[2] It may be maintained that the field officer's actions are still directed towards the rational achievement of statutory goals; this may be true, provided it is recognized that indirect and apparently tangential means may have to be adopted in order to attain even reasonable levels of success. The different positions are illustrated in figures 1 and 2.

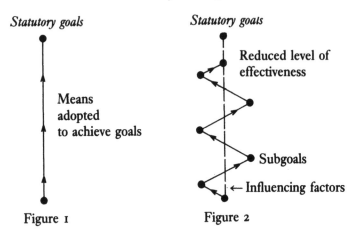

Achievement of Statutory Goals

Figure 1

Figure 2

---

[2] See Hawkins, *Environment and Enforcement*, for examples, pp. 12, 30–4, 42, 56, 73–5, 100, 196; Richardson, *Policing Pollution*, pp. 95–7, 108 ff, 124–32.

Figure 1 depicts a clear and direct relationship between the specified goals and the means adopted for its achievement. This is an idealized picture which assumes the relationship to be essentially technical and mechanical. Figure 2 seeks to show the relationship more realistically; the means adopted are shaped by a range of constraints; subgoals have to be set and attained in order to accommodate the constraints, and the final outcome is likely to be a more modest level of achievement of the overall statutory goals.

The factors influencing discretionary decisions are many and varied, but perhaps they can be grouped broadly into the following categories. (*a*) The nature of the task being performed, and hence the need to consider generally the most effective and efficient ways of execution. (*b*) The political and social environment within which the powers are to be exercised. It may be necessary, for example, to consult a variety of interest groups, and, in the light of the views expressed, modify policies and practices that otherwise would be followed. The minister dealing with immigration matters may have to bow to views entrenched in the community; the parole board may formulate its policies in awareness that the community's toleration of parole is slight. (*c*) The moral background, including community views as well as those of the deciding officials. Moral positions firmly held by either are bound to have a material effect on the shape of discretionary actions, since officials are naturally loath to act contrary to their own moral outlook, and they recognize that prudence demands attention to the moral views of those interested or affected. (*d*) Economic considerations are also of substantial influence in various ways. The resources available to an authority are obviously relevant to the levels of achievement set and the means adopted. Similarly, the economic consequences for those affected by official actions may be a material constraint on the decisions that are made. Again, we may point to the way in which those two factors have been shown to affect the levels of compliance with water pollution standards and the strategies adopted in gaining compliance.[3] (*e*) Finally, the organizational structure within which decisions are made may have complex effects on both policies and procedures at the various levels, ranging from the highest policy-makers to the lowliest enforcement-officers.

There are undoubtedly other factors affecting the exercise of discretion which do not fit readily into these categories; the point,

---

[3] See Hawkins, *Environment and Enforcement*, p. 73 and Richardson, *Policing Pollution*, p. 162 ff.

however, is not to give an exhaustive list, but to illustrate the effects that such diverse matters can have on content and procedure. The impact of such matters is important in understanding discretionary decision-making, and later in this chapter more detailed consideration is given to their effects and to the implications for legal regulation.

3.12   *Types of decisions and strategies*

It is the outcomes of decisions that finally are most important, but procedures also matter both for their relationship to outcomes and because they serve certain values independently of outcomes. Issues of procedure and the place of notions of representation and participation are considered in chapter 7. Also, in that chapter, different types of participatory procedures, whether adjudicative, consultative, or mediatory, are examined and their suitability in different types of discretionary decisions are explained. In this section, however, my concern is to suggest various types of decisions, in terms of a number of variables. Within the range of discretionary powers, four recurring and reasonably distinct types can be identified (see table 2).

Table 2.   Classification of Decisions

Classification	Nature of issue	Normative framework	Interests affected
Adjudication	Individualized: determination of rights and duties	Standards settled with reasonable precision	Parties whose rights-duties are in issue
Modified Adjudication	Individualized: how person or situation to be treated	Standards less settled: some discretion in deciding	The party subject to the decision, but also may affect other interests less directly
Specific Policy Issue	Individualized: how to act, what to do	Some standards but substantial discretion	A range of interests affected
General Policy Issue	Formulation of general standards for application in individual cases	Some abstract standards but substantial discretion	A range of interests affected

The *first* is the paradigm of adjudication which is represented best in criminal and civil trials; it is also the procedure followed by many administrative authorities and tribunals, although the more closely decisions approach this mode, the less scope there is for discretion. Where there is discretion, it is discretion in the senses that occur in interpreting and applying given standards, and in finding facts. The *second*, modified adjudication, represents a large portion of decisions entrusted to administrative officials: examples are many and include sentencing and other decisions in the penal process, social welfare, immigration, and deportation. This category is distinguished by the combination of adjudicative and discretionary elements; it is adjudicative in that it is individualized, being a decision about a person or his situation, and there are usually some guiding standards; but it is discretionary in the stronger sense that, within whatever guiding standards there are, matters of policy and preference have to be considered and decided. Moreover, similar issues are likely to recur so that patterns of a generalized kind may develop. The room for variation within this category, between settled standards and open discretion, is considerable; and often it is left to the official to decide on how firmly fixed the standards are to be, and how readily they may be departed from or changed. The *third* category is also concerned with a specific, individualized decision, but here the object is to settle a matter of wide public interest and consequences: whether to build a motorway and, if so, what route it is to follow; whether to declare an urban area for slum clearance, or to allow a new airline to enter into service. Cases of modified adjudication naturally overlap with specific policy decisions, since in determining how to treat a person or situation, it may be necessary to decide a matter of public interest; but usually particular cases fall squarely into one category or the other. Within this third category, there are typically some guiding standards, but these are likely to be abstract and in conflict so that a degree of weighting and balancing of goals must be undertaken. The *fourth* category consists of decisions of general policy, the object normally being to formulate general standards of varying degrees of specificity for application in future cases. Where there is delegation of legislative power, the result is legislative rules; in the case of administrative discretion, a similar task may be performed on a more informal basis by a minister, his departmental officials, or by other officials and authorities. The Supplementary Benefits Commission, for example, has detailed and extensive rules governing the grant of benefits; similarly, comprehensive guide-lines have been formulated within a discretionary context for the payment of compensation to the victims of crime.[4] Issues of general policy are sometimes settled as a preliminary

---

[4] For discussion and examples, see M. Adler and A. Bradley (eds.), *Justice, Discretion and Poverty* (London, 1975).

to individualized decisions, at other times the two are merged, so that general policy matters are resolved or made more concrete in the course of individualized decision-making. It would be unusual for an authority not to formulate some general standards, especially in recurring situations, regardless of whether there is express statutory authorization or directive, and apart from whether or not the standards are made public.

Discretionary decisions generally fall into one or other of a combination of these types of decisions; the categories overlap and the lines between them cannot be drawn too precisely. They are useful, however, in showing that discretionary decisions do not take one standard form, and that different considerations arise within the different categories. We shall see in chapter 7 the relationship between these categories and different modes of participation. Adjudication attracts a specific mode which emphasizes the application of set rules to particular issues; however, as decisions become more discretionary, adjudication gives way to other modes of participatory procedures, especially consultation and to a lesser degree negotiation and mediation with interested parties. Links also can be seen between the nature of the issue and the normative framework; the nature of the former may suggest that one type of framework is more appropriate than another. For example, where the issue is about how to treat a person, there is an initial case for reasonably clear and settled standards, subject to the possibility of slight modification in the light of the circumstances. It normally would be inappropriate to leave issues of wide public concern to be settled in the course of modified adjudication; the more suitable decision mode in such cases would be the specific, or general policy decision where the wider public and private interests can be represented.

A final point may be made about the classification of discretionary decisions according to the general object sought. Generally, discretionary actions are concerned primarily with one or other of the following: future planning, conferring benefits, enforcing regulation. Future planning normally would come within a general policy decision, where the emphasis is on the wide representation of interests, and where the object is to formulate general standards for individualized decisions in the future. Similarly, a specific policy decision, although individualized, is also primarily concerned with future planning; for example, where to site the new airport or power station, or whether to grant a licence to operate a new air passenger service. Other individualized decisions, however, which fall more clearly within modified adjudication may contain an element of planning, but the emphasis in such cases is on dealing with a specific problem within reasonably settled and specific standards: for example, is the benefit to be granted in this case, or how is the regulatory standard to be enforced? Cases of modified adjudication would not normally be expected to raise wide issues of public policy, but there may, nevertheless, be considerable variation as to the most appropriate strategy to adopt in coming to a decision. Studies of regulatory decision-making, for example, have shown that compliance with a given standard may best be achieved by negotiation and compromise, rather than by the threat of more punitive consequences.[5] Similarly, the conferring of benefits need not be a single, unilateral action, but may be of a continuing nature, involving an element of bargaining, and being concerned to meet the exigencies of the particular case as well as maintaining relevant elements of public policy.

It can be seen from this analysis that discretionary decision-making can be classified in various ways, according to a number of variables; it can also be seen that both the substantive outcomes of discretionary decisions and the procedures followed are influenced and shaped by a range of matters, which may themselves be a mixture of substance and procedure. My general concern has been to emphasize two points: firstly, that discretionary decisions occur in a social and political environment, so that there exists a complex interrelationship between the two; secondly, that within the general category of discretionary decisions, there are reasonably distinct modes of decision-making, each with a certain inherent logic and each having a complex relationship with surrounding considerations. Against this background, we may now consider some more specific aspects of discretionary decision-making, beginning with the theoretical basis of administration, and examining more closely some of the constraints already mentioned.

3.2 THEORIES OF THE ADMINISTRATIVE PROCESS

Just as jurisprudential writers have been concerned to understand the process of judicial decision-making, other theorists have sought to identify the variables of administrative decision-making and to postulate theories about the process. And just as there is a range of

[5] For examples, see Hawkins, *Environment and Enforcement*, pp. 30–2, 42, 99, 196; Richardson, *Policing Pollution*, pp. 97, 109.

theories about adjudication, which might be seen as one small part of the total administrative process, it is not surprising that theories of administration are numerous and enormously diverse. The administrative process is not a single, discrete phenomenon, but is itself made up of a range of organizations and functions, and while there are theories that are directed specifically at government administration, it is more often a matter of applying to administration, theories which have been developed in other contexts, whether psychology, organizations, systems, rational choice, or economics. Nevertheless, it is worth considering the general purport of certain theoretical themes and their implications for discretionary authority. Space permits only the briefest survey, but it is hoped that some idea will be conveyed of the objects of administrative theory, using that term in the broadest sense, and its connections with administrative law.

At the most general level, the objects of administrative theory are to understand the workings of official institutions and the process of decision-making, and on that basis to postulate general principles of administration. A leading figure in the development of modern approaches is Max Weber, whose notion of formal rational authority was developed in the context of bureaucratic organizations.[6] Formal legal authority, with its emphasis on the impersonal application of general laws, operates within such institutions depending on the extent to which they are routinized, specialized, hierarchical, expert, corporate, inappropriable, and documented.[7] The resulting image is of an organization which is self-contained and independent of the political environment, and which operates according to objective rules, assisted where appropriate by technical expertise.

These two characteristics—the separation of administration from politics, and objectivity in decision-making—can be linked to a wider approach, commonly referred to as scientific management.[8] One major theorist in this extensive category is F. W. Taylor, who sought to show that management could be a true science with clearly defined laws,

---

[6] For discussion of Weber's approach to administrative theory, see Martin Albrow, *Bureaucracy*. See also C. J. Friedrich, 'Some Observations on Weber's Analysis of Bureaucracy', and F. S. Burin, 'Bureaucracy and National Socialism: a Reconsideration of Weberian Theory' in R. K. Merton (ed.), *Reader in Bureaucracy* (New York, 1952).

[7] Summarized in this way in A. Dunsire, *Administration: the Word and the Science* (London, 1973), p. 84.

[8] The following provide useful discussions of theories of scientific management: Dunsire, *Administration*, ch. 6; P. Self, *Administrative Theories and Politics* (Toronto UP, 1973), ch. 1.

rules, and principles, and that the science of management could be applied to all organizations.[9] These ideas were expressed around the turn of the century, and the approach that they signify appears for many years to have influenced theoretical studies of government administration. The emphasis lay on efficiency of operation which was thought to be gained by clear lines of command and allocation of responsibility, by close co-ordination of activities, and by specialization. The search for scientific principles of administration was an important backdrop to ideas which informed the New Deal and the general expansion of government activities.[10]

Two of the main lines of criticism of scientific management are of present interest. Firstly, there is scepticism about the existence of any clear division between policy and administration. Where there is discretion, there is the making of policy, and modern administration is shot through with discretion.[11] Administration also involves more than the application of technical skills and logic, and it has come to be recognized that issues of policy and value are unavoidable. Secondly, scientific theories overestimated the extent to which administration can be organized around clear and precise rules, since many tasks are dealt with better in a more informal and adaptable environment. The capacity to tailor decisions and strategies to the circumstances of endlessly variable situations may produce better results and still be efficient in terms of time and resources; similarly, when more attention is paid to personal relationships and the quality of the work environment, the administrators themselves may perform more effectively.[12]

It does not follow from these criticisms that any attempt at developing scientific principles of administration had to be abandoned; the suggestion is rather that the underlying assumptions of the scientific approach had to be reconsidered to accommodate the complexities of organizational behaviour, and theoretical approaches had to be broadened. More emphasis had to be put on the human and

[9] For an example of Taylor's work, see *Principles and Methods of Scientific Management* (New York, 1911).

[10] Other works of importance are: L. Gulick and L. F. Urwick (eds.), *Papers on the Science of Administration* (New York, 1937); H. Fayol, *Industrial and General Administration* (London, 1949).

[11] See D. Waldo, *The Administrative State: a Study of the Political Theory of American Public Administration* (New York, 1948) and P. Appleby, *Policy and Administration* (Alabama UP, 1949).

[12] For discussion, see Self, *Administrative Theories and Politics*, ch. 1 (I have found the discussion here particularly helpful).

psychological factors in order to explain the workings of subgroups, the relations between groups, and the behaviour of individuals within groups. Another direction to be explored was the variety of institutions and the differences between them; this required empirical evidence and analysis. It also stimulated a burgeoning of systems theory, within which organizations are taken to comprise groups of interdependent units forming a whole for the purpose of achieving particular objectives. Organizations and even subunits within organizations acquire a certain autonomy and inner dynamic, which have significant implications in understanding how decisions are made and the effectiveness of external controls.[13]

While those various strands of theory have shown the complexities of organizations, there are other strands of theory which have attempted to assimilate those complexities in developing distinctive approaches to decision-making. If decision-making is to be rational and effective, it must take account of the constraints and influences at work both within organizations and from without. An important approach of this kind is based around the work of Herbert Simon who developed the notion of bounded rationality.[14] Assuming that administrative authorities 'are formed with the intention and design of accomplishing goals',[15] Simon argued that, although administration could not be understood in terms of a few scientific principles, the process can still be rational, at least in respect of factual matters. It would come closest to being perfectly rational if administrators, taking into account the organizational constraints, were able to examine all possible courses open to them, trace through the consequences of each alternative, and then separately evaluate the benefits and costs in each situation.[16] But there are limitations on that process: firstly, there is

[13] For discussion of the various directions theories have taken, see Dunsire, *Administration*, ch. 7 and Self, *Administrative Theories and Politics* ch. 1.
[14] Herbert Simon, *Administrative Behaviour* (New York, 1945).
[15] Ibid., p. 96.
[16] See Self, *Administrative Theories and Politics* pp. 29–30. The position is in fact rather more complex than suggested in the text; see Alfred Schutz, 'The Problem of Rationality to the Social World' (1943) 10 *Economica* 134. There it is said that in order to achieve a reasonable level of rationality in pursuing given goals, the following are necessary:
(a) Knowledge of the place of the end to be realized within the framework of the plans of the actor (which must be known by him, too).
(b) Knowledge of its interrelations with other ends and its compatibility or incompatibility with them.
(c) Knowledge of the desirable and undesirable consequences which may arise as by-products of the realization of the main end.

neither the time nor the facilities for the administrator to search out the perfectly rational decision, and even if there were, there might not be the resources necessary to achieve it. Secondly, there is the more fundamental fact that the decision-maker cannot know all the options open to him, nor the full consequences of any action, nor how future events and consequences will be evaluated. So, by its very nature, the administrative process operates within a bounded or limited environment; the decision-maker must 'satisfice'[17] that is accept certain constraints and choose his course of action from the options open to him, relying on his limited knowledge and choosing between alternatives as best he is able. The administrator cannot achieve perfect, purposive rationality in his decisions, nor is he able relentlessly to pursue one broadly defined goal; rather he must seek the course of action which, subject to all the various constraints and limitations, leads to a reasonable accomplishment of the objectives for which his powers have been conferred. This may mean, on occasions, being content with relatively modest levels of achievement.

Simon's work is important in bringing out both the complexity of decision-making and its policy-making sides. Policy is inherently evaluative, and even issues of fact may not be merely matters of objective evidence and assessment; but, nevertheless, the realization of a given policy can still be based on reasonably rational principles. An administrative authority trying to follow Simon's idea of rational decision-making would consider, as comprehensively as possible, the goals to be achieved, the options open to him, the constraints on him, the relative consequences and the trade-offs that must be made, and then settle on an appropriate set of policies, together with the means of realizing them. Once a comprehensive plan of action had been formulated, its various parts could be implemented down the administrative line. This approach recognizes that choices have to be made in formulating the overall plan, and possibly that further choices have to be made at various points along the line. Nevertheless, the plan should provide extensive guidance whenever decisions have to be

(d) Knowledge of the different chains of means which technically or even ontologically are suitable for the accomplishment of this end, regardless of whether the actor has control of all or several of their elements.

(e) Knowledge of the interference of such means with other ends or chains of means including all of their secondary effects and incidental consequences.

(f) Knowledge of the accessibility of those means for the actor, picking out the means which are within his reach and which he can and may set going.

[17] Simon, *Administrative Behaviour*, pp. 38–41, 80–1, 240–4, 272.

made. By way of illustration, we might think of a statute which confers powers on an authority to establish and conduct a system of pre-school centres; the authority would reflect on the terms of the statute and perhaps on the circumstances that led to it, and thereby formulate a set of general goals to be achieved. It would then formulate the more specific operational goals and methods, taking into account all relevant matters like the resources available, and the varying needs in different districts for pre-school centres; it might be influenced by various interest groups, and it would seek whatever guidance the educational and psychological sciences might have to offer. Further decisions of policy may have to be made at various times and at various points within the authority, but these can be taken within a structured framework, which both guides the making of further decisions, and places limits on the sorts of decisions that may justifiably be made.[18]

This view of decision-making, which is sometimes referred to as comprehensive planning, offers one view of rational action in administrative decisions. However, it has been the subject of criticism for being Utopian and unrealistic, and for being insufficiently responsive to the complexities of decision-making. An alternative which has been proposed as a more realistic account of how decision-making works, and as having greater legitimacy, has become known as incrementalism.[19] On this approach, Simon's notion of bounded rationality is given a much-reduced interpretation, on the grounds that in practice institutional decisions proceed according to policy choices made within a narrowly confined context, and that each decision makes only marginal adjustments to what went before. Here the emphasis is on finding a solution to an actual problem, and this is done by trying to accommodate conflicting interests and considerations so far as possible within a developed pattern of decision-making. Policy-making is confined to whatever is necessary for this purpose, rather than aimed at a comprehensive plan of action. Incrementalism stresses that decision-making is typically decentralized, with authorities and officials at different levels having their own special problems to solve. There may be intervention on occasions from a higher level, for example by a

[18] For discussion of Simon's work, see: Dunsire, *Administration*, ch. 7; Self, *Administrative Theories and Politics*, ch. 1.

[19] Two of the classic accounts of incrementalism are R. Cyert and J. March, *A Behavioural Theory of the Firm* (New Jersey, 1963), and D. Braybrooke and C. Lindblom, *A Strategy of Decision: Policy Evaluation as a Social Process* (New York 1963). See also C. Lindblom, *The Intelligence of Democracy: Decision Making Through Mutual Adjustment* (New York, 1965) and 'The Science of Muddling Through' (1959) 19 *PAdR.* 79.

senior official or the legislature, but even this will tend to concern itself with a particular problem or to adjust a line of decisions, rather than to offer an overall plan.

The claims for this approach to decision-making are twofold. Firstly, there is evidence to suggest that administrative decisions tend to be made in accordance with the incremental model.[20] Its particular virtues are a capacity to deal in a flexible way with new situations and unforseen events, and, by emphasizing adaptability and decentralization, it enables wider interests to be considered at each level of decision-making. Connections can be made between the claims for incrementalism and the earlier analysis of the rise of discretion, and particularly the idea of reflexive rationality. The second claim is that incrementalism is to be preferred to attempts at comprehensive planning, partly because the very idea of comprehensive planning means that choices are made which may turn out to be wrong, but hard to reverse; comprehensive planning is said also to connote an over-reliance on state planning and a certain authoritarianism. It is claimed that incrementalism is more in accordance with the democratic idea that any relevant interest should be able to have some influence at each level of decision-making.

What then are the implications of this brief survey of administrative theories for discretionary decisions? The various theories are concerned primarily with understanding the structures of organizations, the forces at work within them, and the external influences on them. These factors are of great importance simply in understanding how discretionary decisions are made, and in determining the scope and methods of legal regulation. Here again it is useful to take up the earlier contrast between two images of administrative decision-making: on the one hand, a rather simplified Weberian model within which power is directed towards the rational and effective achievement of legally specified goals by officials hierarchically ordered; on the other hand, a model within which powers are diffused amongst a number of subunits operating at different levels of responsibility, each acquiring a degree of independence and distinctiveness, and each subject to a variety of influences.[21] It is the second image that better

[20] For a recent study which reaches that conclusion, see M. C. Harper, 'The Exercise of Executive Discretion: a Study of a Regional Office of the Department of Labour' (1982) 34 *AdmLR* 559. Hawkins, *Environment and Enforcement*, also shows how pervasive elements of incrementalism are in the fixing and enforcement of anti-pollution standards.

[21] For discussion, see J. L. Mashaw, 'Mirrored Ambivalence: a Sometimes Curmudgeonly Comment on the Relationship Between Organisation Theory and Law'

represents the way administrative bodies really work, and which lies behind modern theories of organizations and decision-making. The factors that operate within this image and affect outcomes are various; firstly, the final decision should be understood not only as the rational application of a legal norm, but also as the product of processes and interactions amongst officials and influences; secondly, the factors that carry influence are not just those formally and legally authorized, but include a range of considerations, formal and informal, deriving from within the organization and outside it.[22]

It may be useful at this point to offer some remarks about the dynamics of decision-making. Accepting that the decision process is subject to a host of factors, many questions remain: in what ways does the influence of each manifest itself; how is the role and importance of each to be calculated and conflicts settled; in what sense can decisions, subject to the apparently chaotic effects of such constraints, be considered rational? The preceding discussion should suggest some answers to these questions, but perhaps the matter can be taken a little further with the following. The image of a framework or perspective through which problems are seen and decisions are approached provides a starting-point. This framework is composed of a range of factors of the kind we have noted. One central element is the legal context, meaning the legislative goals, the legal rules and directives; another is the organization, meaning the structure of the institution and the arrangement of its personnel, its attitudes as passed down by higher officials, and as developed by expertise and practical experience. There are of course other factors, but how does each of them rank in influencing decisions, both as to procedure and outcome? Clearly the legal elements are vital; they are likely to provide the parameters and some guidance for decisions; they are likely to be reasonably constant, and they may be subject to consideration and enforcement by outside bodies.

Nevertheless, some accommodation must be achieved between the

1983 *JLegEd* 24. For the outlines of a research programme into the working of administrative bodies, see W. A. Magat and S. Estomin, 'The Behaviour of Regulatory Agencies' in A. R. Ferguson (ed.), *Attacking Regulatory Problems* (United States, 1981).

[22] See further P. H. Shuck, 'Organization Theory and the Teaching of Administrative Law' 1983 *JLegEd* 13. For an excellent study of the influences, formal and informal, on the exercise of discretions relating to the enforcement of standards regulating water pollution, see Richardson, *Policing Pollution*, and Hawkins, *Environment and Enforcement*. For another useful account of organizational influences on officials and decisions, see P. Selznick, 'A Theory of Organizational Commitments' in Merton, *Reader in Bureaucracy*.

legal components and other factors. The former are subject to characterizations and interpretations which derive from those other factors comprising the perceptual framework. The relationship is clearly reflexive and reciprocal; environmental factors shape the official's understanding of the legal requirements, but the latter in turn may influence and modify the former, so that, for example, the official may be led to reassess his conceptions of what is practical and feasible in order to accommodate legal constraints. The relationship, therefore, is one of interaction and mutual adjustment. Moreover, the framework through which issues are viewed need not be constant, but may change with circumstances, and as the official's perceptions and understandings change. This phenomenon of perspective and context operates not only in relation to interpretation and policy, but also in settling the facts, since what counts as relevant, and what is considered adequate to establish a relevant fact is itself partly dependent on one's perspective and criteria of selection.[23]

Another vital aspect of decision-making is the way in which different factors acquire relative weight and importance. Decisions are not typically made in isolation, with a host of factors competing for attention, as if each case requires a fresh start, a reassessment of all that has gone before. Rather, there tends to be sufficient continuity, even in areas of decisions that seem disparate, for selections to be made from all that might be relevant, so that certain factors come to be recognized as the important ones. A certain ranking and ordering occurs so that decision-making follows recognizable patterns, based around relatively fixed points, each of which may have, however, soft edges and a degree of open texture. It is from this very process of selection, continuity, and ordering that standards—meaning rules, principles, and norms—begin to emerge. At one end of the spectrum, rules that are clear and binding may be stipulated; but as one moves away from that position, it is noticeable that standards derive from a range of sources and are enormously variable as to their normative qualities. As to sources, standards may derive not only from outside legal authorities, but also from various points within an institution, ranging from the official centres of policy-making to the most modest

---

[23] For discussion of decision-making, the following are especially helpful: A. V. Cicourel, *The Social Organization of Juvenile Justice*, (New York, 1968) esp. chs. 1 and 2; H. Garfinkel, 'Studies of the Routine Grounds of Everyday Actions' (1964) 11 *Social Problems* 225 and 'The Rational Properties of Scientific and Common Sense Activities' (1960) 5 *Behavioural Science* 72.

official who is likely to develop within his sphere of discretion a complex pattern of normative standards. The possible variations in normative qualities can be seen by noting that what characterizes a standard is the degree of protection that a given reason has in the making of a decision; this may range from a clear and binding rule which must be applied, to reasons which carry some weight in the decision, and which must be given some degree of protection, but which may have to compete with other factors. Between these two points, there may be variations of great subtlety, and there may be cases where the normative quality of a given factor is extremely difficult to assess. The important point to note, however, is that one is likely to find within any actual area of decision-making a highly structured and patterned system in the sense that at any time the factors which figure in the decision are identifiable and their normative qualities, in the reasoning process of the official, roughly quantifiable.

Let us now consider the significance of this discussion for legal regulation. The important general point is that greater understanding of how organizations work may assist in the design and structure of appropriate institutions for specific tasks. The theoretical and practical understanding of decision-making within organizations does not necessarily lead to precise consequences in these matters; but, without proper concern with issues such as the possible modes of decision-making, the inner dynamics of organizations, and the problems of rational action, the design of governmental authorities and the suitability of powers allocated to them, must remain a matter of chance. It is only by the reciprocal testing of theory against practice, and practice against theory, that knowledge in these matters can be advanced. Secondly, unless there is some understanding of the factors influencing decisions, it is difficult to assess the accuracy and validity of the reasons that may be advanced for decisions. Thirdly, it is important to recognize that the bare fact that a legal standard or value is imposed does not guarantee that it will be upheld effectively in decisions. Legal stipulations must compete with the other institutional forces at work, and may indeed be modified by them in the ways we have noted. This conflict may occur with respect either to procedures or to matters of substance. Compliance with and the effectiveness of procedures may depend on there being adequate harmony between procedures and other influences on the decision-making unit. Also, substantive legal requirements, such as the standard regulating the treatment of suspects in custody, may depend on the prevailing ethos, the mores and ideology of the police force and its institutions. Finally, it must not be assumed, however, that there is a body of theory about how institutions work which can be taken up by legal institutions and used to enhance the effectiveness of legal regulation. There are many and varied theories, but they are often themselves open to question, sometimes in conflict, and frequently lacking empirical support. Moreover, the relationship between legal standards and other factors that influence decisions is itself an aspect of the theory of organizations that is still in its early stages.

Of particular importance in the study of discretionary powers is the theoretical analysis of the specific decision strategies of comprehensive planning and incrementalism. In the New Deal years, it has been said, the decisions of American administrative agencies fitted the incrementalist model, while more recently the emphasis has come around to comprehensive planning through more detailed legislative standards, and greater rule-making by the agencies.[24] Similar shifts may occur within the common law which is traditionally incremental, emphasizing the specific case, and maintaining a special relationship between the case to be settled and what has gone before, and avoiding attempts at comprehensive planning.[25] This piecemeal approach may be interrupted from time to time by legislative intervention in order to impose comprehensive standards; but then, in the very process of applying them, in giving meaning to abstract terms and in resolving conflicts and overlaps between standards, incrementalism is likely to reappear.

The relationship between the two approaches to decisions can be put in this way: incrementalism is an attempt to characterize the type of process that emerges most naturally within administrative organizations; it is cautious, proceeding step by step, solving problems as they arise, relying on past wisdom to approach new issues, and so is the natural strategy for decision-makers of limited capacity and knowledge in a world of complexity. On the other hand, comprehensive planning represents a loftier ideal of rational action; it seeks to bridle the environment by understanding all factors and difficulties, and then providing a comprehensive and co-ordinated plan. We have here at a practical level the same problem encountered in the previous chapter: comprehensive planning encourages the laying down of general rules

<hr />

[24] C. S. Diver, 'Policymaking Paradigms in Administrative Law' (1981) 95 *HarvLR* 393.
[25] For an analysis of incrementalism in judicial decision-making, see Martin Shapiro, *The Supreme Court and Administrative Agencies* (New York, 1968), pp. 73–103.

and standards, and thus leans towards formal and substantive legal rationality; incrementalism, however, suggests that problems should be solved as they occur, and so is directed more clearly towards substantive and reflexive rationality. There are also differences in accountability: comprehensive planning allows outside scrutiny of stated standards and policies, and tends to assume that they have been settled in the political domain; incrementalism, however, makes external scrutiny more difficult, and is dependent on the different sense of accountability that occurs when interested parties are able to participate directly in the decision.

However, it is neither wise nor necessary to draw too starkly the contrasts between the two. In order to solve problems, policy choices have to be made, and these should provide some direction for future decisions; moreover, problems are not solved in a vacuum so that there must be some background standards that guide the process. The chief virtue of incrementalism is its capacity to respond to complexity and diversity, and to allow wider participation and influence in decisions. On the other hand, the ideal of comprehensive planning is of great attraction in a society that seeks to regulate the activities of its members in accordance with social and political goals. Moreover, what begins on an incremental basis may develop into a set of fixed standards, and even the most comprehensive plan may allow room for elements of incrementalism. All that can perhaps finally be said is that administrative theorists have been able to demonstrate some of the strengths and weaknesses of each, and that the final form in which the two are mixed has to be settled according to an assessment within specific areas of decision-making.

3.3 CONSTRAINTS ON THE EXERCISE OF DISCRETION: (*a*) THOSE OF A MORE PRACTICAL KIND

Following this account of administrative theories and their relationship with issues that arise in exercising and regulating discretionary powers, we may now consider, again briefly, some of the main influences and considerations that bear on both the substantive outcomes and the decision strategies adopted. This is of interest not only in providing illustrations of the preceding discussion of administrative theories, but also in understanding better the exercise of discretion.

3.31   *Efficiency and effectiveness*

Efficiency is a concept which is most at home in the mechanical sciences, and which can be transplanted only with difficulty to government administration.[26] Within business organizations, the concept of efficiency refers to the relationship between the resources used and the returns that result; the mediating notion is profit, and a business is operating most efficiently when the greatest profit is produced by the least use of resources. Although simple to state, this relationship might be highly complex in practice since the firm must take into account matters like capital expansion, re-investment, and worker satisfaction. Nevertheless, there is within business a reasonably clear framework within which to make assessments of efficiency.

The position is different in an administrative agency. Here the primary object is not to profit from some marketable commodity, but to achieve stated goals—to relieve poverty, to provide a tolerable environment, or to regulate public houses. The overall test of success in such cases is the extent to which the respective goals have been achieved. It is useful then to distinguish between efficiency and effectiveness; efficiency pertains to the relationship between resources and outcomes, while effectiveness refers to realization of goals.[27] Effectiveness is of vital importance in the exercise of discretionary powers, but is not itself an easy test to apply. The goals may themselves be unclear, or they may be interconnected so closely with other programmes and with wider notions of social welfare that judgments of effectiveness are hard to make. In any event, rationality and purposiveness would seem to require that the discretionary authority sets for itself, within the terms of its authority, some goals against which effectiveness may then be tested.

Within the general concern to achieve goals effectively, efficiency has an important role. Administrative decisions involve costs and resources, and it is possible to make some appraisal of the relationship between expenditure and results. Appraisals can be made at different levels; it may be a matter of technical assessment, whether mechanical equipment might perform some of the tasks that are otherwise labour

[26] For discussion of this issue see Self, *Administrative Theories and Politics* pp. 261–77 (of special importance); also D. Keeling, *Management in Government* (London, 1972); P. P. Craig, *Administrative Law* (London, 1983), pp. 235 ff.

[27] The distinction is made in Self, *Administrative Theories and Politics* p. 264. For a study of the notions of effectiveness and efficiency in the regulation of natural resources, see O. R. Young, *Natural Resources and the State* (University of California, 1981), esp. ch. 4.

intensive, or whether re-organization of an institution would enable more work to be produced, and perhaps bolster staff morale. The concern in such cases is to determine whether the same or better results could be achieved, in terms of goals, by a lesser dissipation of resources; for this purpose, efficiency is a natural and useful concept to employ.

Difficulties may arise, however, when assessments of this kind extend beyond reasonably clear technical matters, and attempts are made to calculate the costs and benefits of broader policy goals. A noticeable aspect of the current scepticism towards regulation is the demand that administrative programmes be subjected to rigorous analysis, to make clear the goals being sought, the wider consequences, the costs and benefits, and in some cases the net benefits to society. In America, President Reagan has issued executive orders requiring agencies to prepare, with respect to all major rules they adopt, an analysis of their impact, including the costs and benefits, and in particular the net gains to society.[28] There are undoubted virtues in generally raising the rational basis of discretionary decisions, in being clear about alternative courses of action and their respective costs, and in seeking the maximum benefits from official actions. There are considerable dangers, however, in extending the techniques of cost-benefit analysis into the assessment of the overall social advantages of particular programmes. Regulatory action may be prompted by a range of values and intangible considerations which cannot easily be assessed in economic terms; moreover, it is often difficult to separate the costs and benefits of any one programme from a wider assessment of government action.

The notion of effectiveness in realizing given goals is a basic concept, both in the exercise of discretion and in its legal regulation. It is important for this reason to modify the suggestion that might derive from an hierarchical and instrumental view of authority, that effectiveness is achieved simply by finding the most suitable means to a given goal.

[28] Executive Order No. 12, 291, Sections 2 and 3(d), 46 Fed. Reg. 13, 193, 13, 194 (1981) quoted in Diver, 'Policymaking Paradigms in Administrative Law', p. 417. For a study of the many aspects of cost-benefit analysis in relation to environmental regulations, see D. Swartzman, R. A. Liroff, and K. G. Croke, *Cost-Benefit Analysis and Environmental Regulations: Politics, Ethics and Methods* (United States, 1982). For discussion of how economic efficiency might be accommodated with other goals and values, see B. Ackerman and W. Hassler, *Clean Coal/Dirty Air* (Yale UP, 1981) and R. Stewart, 'Regulation, Innovation and Administrative Law: a Conceptual Framework' (1981) 69 *CalLR* 1259.

In the first place, the goals may themselves be various and conflicting so that the advancement of one goal may be to the detriment of another. The assessment of effectiveness then depends on how the goals are ranked in relation to each other. In the second place, effectiveness may also depend partly on satisfying certain subsidiary goals, or recognizing certain values in the process of reaching a final outcome. In complex matters, for example, effectiveness may be judged according to how well disputes amongst interest groups are resolved and participatory procedures applied.

Apart from these general considerations regarding efficiency and effectiveness, an authority with discretion may have to decide the more specific issue as to what strategies of decision-making are to be adopted. Various factors, as we have noted, will be influential; but the different decision strategies may themselves contribute in different ways to effectiveness. The range available is between comprehensive planning, with a clear statement of goals and heavy reliance on clear standards, and incrementalism, with a loose framework of standards to be developed in a piecemeal manner. Rules which are formulated carefully to achieve stated goals might be expected to attain a high level of effectiveness; they have the obvious advantages of guiding officials in making decisions, and enabling citizens to know how decisions are likely to be made. Rules also generally simplify decision-making by representing a distillation of knowledge and experience gained in the past, and thus limiting the range of considerations to be taken into account in dealing with specific circumstances.[29]

Rules have costs, however, and these may be grouped in three categories. Firstly, because of complexity and variability, rules are not always the most rational means for achieving purposes. The cost of rules in such circumstances is to impose a selective and possibly oversimplified view of purpose; as a result, the gains in certainty might not be sufficient to compensate for the costs in reduced effectiveness. Secondly, there is the problem of overinclusion and underinclusion; Ehrlich and Posner have noted a 'necessarily imperfect fit between the convergence of a rule and the conduct sought to be regulated';[30] sometimes a rule will have results which are not the best in terms of

[29] In this section I am following the analysis of rules by I. Ehrlich and R. A. Posner in 'An Economic Analysis of Legal Rulemaking' (1974) 4 *JLegStud* 257. See also W. Hirsch, 'Reducing Law's Uncertainty and Complexity' (1974) 21 *UCLALR* 1233, and A. I. Ogus, 'Quantitative Rules and Judicial Decision-Making' in P. Burrows and C. G. Veljanovski (eds.), *The Economic Approach to Law* (London, 1981).

[30] Ehrlich and Posner, 'An Economic Analysis of Legal Rulemaking', p. 268.

purpose, while other situations which should come within the rule may be excluded. The extent to which either of these situations occurs is a function of the precision of rules on the one hand, and complexity and variability on the other hand, or, as Ehrlich and Posner put it, heterogeneity. The difficulties of heterogeneity can be overcome to some extent by allowing the decision-maker to depart from the rules by invoking broader purposive standards of interpretation, and by relating particular circumstances directly to purposes. But this has obvious costs, since the higher the incidence of departure from the rules, the less useful they are as guides to outcomes, and the more opportunity there is for officials to make mistakes. Decision-making then becomes increasingly incremental, until a point may be reached at which rules give little indication of how decisions are in fact being made. Thirdly, in any assessment of effectiveness two different standpoints should be considered; that of the officials regulating, and that of the citizens being regulated. From the citizen's standpoint, efficiency in regulation is likely to be closely connected to precision in rules; but from the regulator's point of view, the precision of rules may seem an insupportable obstacle in a more precise achievement of purposes. Discretionary powers are not concerned always with regulating behaviour, but, where they are, a compromise may have to be sought between the importance of rules and the virtues they engender, and the need for close correlation between action and purpose. Finally, there is a wide variety of surrounding transaction costs which relate to any decision strategy: for example, the relative costs of setting up procedures and institutions to formulate rules, compared to the equivalent costs of incremental processes. Costs of this kind must be assessed and balanced in relation to particular tasks.

3.32 *Political considerations*

Although the primary concern of a discretionary authority is to achieve given objects, this requires policy choices and assessments which are subject to a range of influences. These may flow from superior officials or from interest groups pursuant to formal participatory procedures; alternatively, such influences may derive from a multitude of informal sources, and produce effects of a subtle, variable, and intractable kind. Also of interest are the perceptions of the authority itself as to its place in the political system, and the values and goals that warrant its support.[31]

[31] For useful discussion of examples and case studies, see Schuck, 'Organization Theory and the Teaching of Administrative Law'.

Influences stemming from the political system in this way can affect not only substantive outcomes, but also the formal strategies that are employed. An example can be seen in the workings of the parole system: it is characteristic of parole that in both Britain and elsewhere legislators, executives, and parole boards are reluctant to stipulate with any precision the criteria by which parole decisions are to be made. One reason for this is the belief that the early release of offenders is such a sensitive political issue that the emphasis must be on exercising great caution to ensure release of only the best risks, and to prevent any suggestion that parole is a matter of right rather than privilege. Decision-making tends then to be incremental, with emphasis on the unique features of each case, and with little effort being made, at least publicly, to develop patterns of consistency.[32] Similarly, within the welfare system efforts are made in certain areas to retain powers in a highly discretionary form in order to avoid or conceal the necessity for difficult policy choices about the distribution of resources. For example, a discretionary format may allow reduction in expenditure without appearing to make changes to the system; alternatively, a discretionary structure facilitates inaction on the part of the authority, and this may itself be a useful way of satisfying political pressures.[33]

3.33 *Organizational factors*

We have seen at some length the importance of the organizational structure of administrative authorities in affecting the substance and strategies of decision-making, so my remarks here may be short. The general point is that the way an authority is organized, in terms of the authority structure and so the degree of power which one official has over another, the extent to which it is hierarchical, the degree of autonomy particular officials have to act as they think best, the position regarding promotion—each of these factors, together with a range of others, has some effect on the way discretionary powers are exercised. To give just one example, Keith Hawkins in his study of the enforcement of standards regulating the pollution of water has noted the conflicts that occur between the organizational structure and the control exercised over field officers on the one hand, and the need for

[32] For discussion of parole decision-making, see: Parole Board Annual Reports (London); F. Beverley and P. Morris, *On Licence: a Study of Parole* (London, 1975); P. Cavadine, *Parole: the Case for Change* (London, 1977).

[33] For a discussion of political constraints in the British welfare system, see Tony Prosser, 'The Politics of Discretion: Aspects of Discretionary Power in the Supplementary Benefits Scheme', in Adler and Asquith, *Discretion and Welfare*.

the field officer to have substantial discretion in negotiating and bargaining with polluters on the other. Compliance with anti-pollution standards is gained most effectively by these tactics rather than the immediate threat of prosecution; but the field officer may experience considerable conflict between the need for such flexibility and the control deriving from the superior officials within the water authority.[34]

According to the Weberian approach, decision-making within large organizations tends towards the ideal of formal rational authority; but there are other factors as well, some of which may pull in other directions. The level at which decisions are made, the competence of staff, the complexity of the tasks, the extent to which powers are diffused and decentralized, the effects of outside influences: these are some of the factors that may bear upon the approach taken within any organization towards decision-making.[35] To take another example that might occur within a welfare agency: the relatively low competence of officials at the front desk deciding individual cases is likely to influence officials at higher levels to formulate rules of a fairly strict kind. Yet, ironically, it is often at the front desk that an incrementalist approach is most appropriate in dealing with individual cases. In practice, the result is likely to be a compromise between the strict application of rules, and the freedom to depart from them in specific cases, subject to various mechanisms at higher levels for monitoring anomalies.[36] By contrast, the fact that the members of parole boards do not form part of a highly structured organization, but are laymen who meet to decide specific cases, and that each comes with some professional expertise, adds to the incremental nature of parole decision-making. Similarly, where authority is diffused amongst small units, the members of which are highly motivated and who hold shared values, decisions may be made most effectively in the relative absence of detailed rules.[37]

[34] See Hawkins, *Environment and Enforcement*, pp. 70–1.

[35] For a detailed study of organizational influences on the exercise of discretion, see Richardson, *Policing Pollution*. There are other factors which might be included under this broad heading, such as highly personal considerations which have affected the strategies adopted in exercising discretion. For a study which deals with such personal considerations, see Austin Lovegrove, 'The Listing of Criminal Cases in the Crown Court as an Administrative Discretion' 1984 *CrimLR* 738. For studies of the variables that operate within police forces, see J. H. Skolnick, *Justice Without Trial: Law Enforcement in Democratic Society* (London, 1966), and P. K. Manning, *Police Work: the Social Organization of Policing* (Massachusettes, 1977).

[36] For discussion of how this compromise has worked out in practice in the British welfare system, see Adler and Bradley, *Justice, Discretion and Poverty*.

[37] For a case study of decision-making in such an environment, see Lars Busck, 'The

3.34   *Economic factors*

Administrative agencies are concerned unavoidably with issues of resource use and allocation. All agencies must be concerned to use their resources efficiently and effectively in achieving goals; some agencies also are concerned with the direct allocation of resources to others. The resources available to any agency are limited, and, consequently, it is hardly necessary to note that economic considerations affect both the substantive decisions made, and the form which decision-making follows.[38]

As to substance, the limitation on resources is a significant factor in deciding the courses of action to be followed. It is usual for an authority to have to make choices as to which amongst possible goals is to be sought, or the methods to be employed in doing so, and in this way the discretionary nature of decisions is increased. We have noticed before the selectivity used in arresting, prosecuting, and trying offenders, and how limited resources may lead to the non-enforcement of legal duties. In a different context, the inevitable selectivity required in deciding to advance one goal rather than another, because of limited resources, has been described as 'emphatic' discretion, the suggestion being that this is the most highly discretionary aspect of decisions.[39] Emphatic discretion in the use and allocation of resources gives the agency an increased control over parties whose interests are affected, by making the grant of concessions or benefits depend upon compliance with certain standards or conditions. This position of control in the allocation of resources may even enable the agency to achieve goals which are not strictly within its powers.[40]

The level of effectiveness in achieving goals may itself be affected significantly by scarcity of resources. In one study of water pollution

Family Guidance Centre in Copenhagen', in Davis, *Discretionary Justice in Europe and America*.

[38] For an excellent study which considers the economic constraints on the exercise of discretionary powers, see M. C. Harper, 'The Exercise of Executive Discretion: a Study of a Regional Office of the Department of Labour' 1982 *AdmLR* 559.

[39] Ibid., p. 566.

[40] In a study of the exercise of discretion by regional officials implementing the comprehensive Employment and Training Act, it was found that the scarcity of resources, was a most significant variable affecting decisions. See Harper, 'The Exercise of Executive Discretion'. A study of pollution regulation in Britain has revealed the way in which discretion in allocating resources for enforcement are used to encourage goals which may not be required by law: Hawkins, *Environment and Enforcement*. See also K. Carson, 'White Collar Crime and the Enforcement of Factory Legislation' (1970) 10 *BritJCrim* 383.

control, it was found that this factor resulted in paucity of research and
a backward state of scientific knowledge; this meant in turn that the
standards of control imposed were somewhat arbitrary.[41] The same
studies have emphasized the effects which limited resources have on
the methods employed to secure compliance with standards. Because
the water authorities could not maintain a system of strict detection
and enforcement through prosecution and the threat of it, they are
forced to negotiate, bargain, and strike compromises with polluting
firms.[42] Thus, there appears to be a direct connection between the
resources and capacities of an authority, and the tactics it employs in
achieving its goals. It is also interesting to note the significance of the
economic position of the polluting firm in the field officer's decision
whether any action, and if so what, should be taken against breach of
the standards. Indeed, this factor was an important component in the
formation of an officer's moral evaluation of particular cases of
pollution.[43]

Economic factors may also influence the selection of a position
between comprehensive planning and incrementalism, but there is no
set correlation between the two. Where limited resources are being
distributed, comprehensive planning with rules governing allocation
may seem the most effective way of accommodating economic
limitations. However, rules can become rigid and give rise to
expectations which, it may turn out, cannot be met. A more
incremental approach has the virtue of allowing flexibility in accommodating decisions within economic constraints, especially if the latter
are themselves likely to change; the resulting costs are a relative lack of
planning and co-ordination in the way resources are allocated.[44]

3.35 *The nature of the task*

Attention has been drawn to the connection between the growth in
discretionary powers and the kinds of tasks that the modern state has
undertaken; we saw in particular how the ideas of complexity and
variability help to explain both the initial delegation of discretionary

[41] See Richardson, *Policing Pollution*.
[42] See Hawkins, *Environment and Enforcement*, pp. 42 ff; 99; Richardson, *Policing Pollution*, pp. 97, 124.
[43] Hawkins, *Environment and Enforcement*, pp. 73–5.
[44] For a study of the effect of economic constraints as one of several influences in the change of decision strategy from being rule-governed to discretionary, see David Noble, 'From Rules to Discretion? The Housing Corporation', in Adler and Asquith, *Discretion and Welfare*.

powers, and the strategies adopted by the delegate in exercising them. It may be helpful now to see further how these concepts affect the decision strategies. Where to site a new airport, for example, is clearly a matter of considerable complexity, involving many interests, and so is suited to an incremental approach which allows consideration of various possibilities, and ensures the maximum representation of interests. Where, however, decisions of a highly complex kind are made regularly, there are countervailing forces pulling towards more comprehensive planning. For example, the grant of licences to conduct public houses might be considered complex in terms of the interests and factors involved; but decisions on these matters have to be made regularly, and thus tend to be governed by relatively settled, if oversimplified standards. In such cases, complexity is compromised in order to gain in efficiency and consistency. On the other hand, being responsive to complexity and variability may be of primary concern, especially in economic regulation. It has been remarked that regulation of economic affairs requires quick and informal adaptability, and for this reason is often dealt with most suitably towards the incremental end of the scale.[45] Similarly, where there is a high level of variability from one case to another, a relatively loose framework of guiding standards may lead to more satisfactory solutions. It has been found, for example, that the provision of financial assistance to families experiencing a period of temporary difficulty was made in a most effective and responsive manner when the emphasis was on a case-by-case approach with few controlling rules.[46] However, its success was partly due to other factors; the organization was small, it was not overworked, and its members shared a common set of values and ideals; without these factors, the position might have been different.[47] So, while complexity and variability have natural affinities with incrementalism, they may have to compete with other factors which point to greater reliance on advance planning and general standards.

[45] For general discussion of discretionary powers concerned with the regulation of economic activity, see J. Winkler, 'The Political Economy of Administrative Discretion', in Adler and Asquith, *Discretion and Welfare*.

[46] See Lars Busck, 'The Family Guidance Centre in Copenhagen'.

[47] Notice, however, that as administrative units increase in size, decision-making tends to be subjected to greater control by rules; see: A. A. M. F. Staatsn, 'General Assistance in the Netherlands' in Davis, *Discretionary Justice in Europe and America*. Compare J. F. Handler and E. J. Hollingworth, *The Deserving Poor* (United States, 1971).

3.4   CONSTRAINTS ON THE EXERCISE OF
DISCRETION: (*b*) THOSE OF A MORE VALUE-BASED
KIND

It is not only practical matters of the kind considered that affect both the substance and form of discretionary decisions. Other considerations are of a more clearly value-based kind, and include not only the personal moral views of officials, but also the background of moral and political values. These divide into two broad but connected categories, the first being the political values that are linked to rational decision-making, the second being the implications drawn from moral principles, in particular from ideas of fairness. It can now be shown how these matters affect discretionary decisions by taking a number of specific topics: the moral attitudes of officials, the implications of rational action, the concept of arbitrariness and the principles of consistency, considerations of fairness, and the importance of guidance.

3.41   *The moral attitudes of officials*
It has been shown in earlier discussion how the moral attitudes of officials are likely to be important factors in assuming discretion to depart from, modify, or selectively enforce binding legal rules. These same moral attitudes are of significance in the exercise of discretion generally. They are likely to affect the official's perceptions of the statutory purposes, and to influence the interpretation put on them; such moral attitudes will also influence the formation of subsidiary and instrumental goals that are set in achieving overall purposes; and, finally, those attitudes will be of importance in shaping the methods of enforcement. This is not to suggest that an official will simply apply his own moral policy; the position is more complex. It has been shown that sentencing judges have ample scope for giving effect to their own penal philosophy, but they may have to modify that philosophy in order to comply with clear legislative directions or rulings from higher courts.[48] Similarly, a judge's philosophy may have to be modified and compromised in order to fit into existing institutional structures and practices. These various factors may in turn cause the sentencing judge to adjust his penal outlook.

There is clearly a close and complex relationship between an official's moral views, his practical actions, and the environment in

---

[48] The classic study is J. Hogarth, *Sentencing as a Human Process* (University of Toronto Press, 1971).

which he works. The image, then, is not of an official with clear and rigid views which he brings to bear in performing his duties; it is rather of an official with a range of views, some more firmly held than others, some more important than others, which influence the tasks he is required to perform, but which also are influenced by these same tasks. There is also a close interrelation between the views an official has and the wider community morality. Indeed, the official's perceptions of the community morality may be a major component of his own views. It has been shown in studies of regulatory enforcement that officials are highly sensitive to community morality, and that their actions and interpretations are much affected by it.[49] The police, for example, derive reinforcement for their attitudes to crime control because there is usually little doubt that they have the support of the community; on the other hand, other areas of regulation may employ the devices of the criminal law without, however, removing community doubts as to the 'real' criminality of such matters. This moral ambiguity may create serious tensions in the role of officials and influence their approach to enforcement. Officials charged with regulating water pollution experience this moral ambiguity, the result being a more moderate approach to enforcement, with the emphasis on securing compliance by negotiation, at least in the early stages, rather than positive sanctions.[50]

At the more particular level, an official's moral outlook is bound to be influential at each point in his decision. Examples may again be taken from studies of pollution control. In deciding whether there has been pollution of a sufficiently serious kind to warrant enforcement action, it appears that a major consideration is the field officer's moral judgment about the case. This in turn depends largely on whether the pollution was accidental or deliberate, and the company's economic capacity to take the necessary precautions.[51] Hawkins has shown how important is the component of moral disreputability, meaning wilful or negligent rule-breaking or persistent disregard for an officer's authority.[52] Conversely, a complementary study of pollution control has pointed to the disgust shown by field officers when a genuinely accidental spillage was prosecuted.[53] Examples could be multiplied,

[49] For useful discussion of the relationship with community morality, see Hawkins, *Environment and Enforcement*, pp. 7–15; K. Carson, 'Some Sociological Aspects of Strict Liability and the Enforcement of Factory Legislation' (1970) 33 *MLR* 396.
[50] Hawkins, *Environment and Enforcement*.
[51] Ibid., pp. 28–30.
[52] Ibid., pp. 35–6.   [53] Richardson, *Policing Pollution*, p. 177.

but for our present concerns it is enough to be aware of the real and complex relationship between moral attitudes and discretionary actions.

3.42   *The implications of rational action*

Accepting that officials exercising discretion are under a duty of the most basic kind to comply with the canons of rationality, subject to the inevitable boundaries and limits explained, what does this mean in practical terms? At its most elementary it has the effect, as we have noted, firstly of eliminating decision-making according to whim, caprice, or ritual, and it requires that decisions be reached by reasoning which is intelligible and reasonable. Secondly, the reasons must be directed towards and related intelligibly to the purposes of the power. In order to meet this latter requirement, officials must develop reasonably clear views as to what those purposes are, and must settle upon more specific policies and strategies for achieving them. This does not mean necessarily the formulation of precise rules, but only that a framework of goals and standards be established to provide guidance and perspective in making specific decisions. Even where the emphasis is on an incremental approach, it is still necessary to settle on some general standards to provide the framework for specific decisions. Thirdly, the official is expected to act impartially in the sense that he should have no personal interest either in the outcome of his official actions, or in the circumstances of any party subject to his decisions. Fourthly, the principles of rational action require that there be, in the sense to be explained, a certain continuity and consistency in making decisions. These canons of rationality raise a number of issues which are examined in the following pages.

The general point is that the canons of rational action constitute constraints on discretionary decisions, but they are in the nature of threshold constraints above which there remains room for official judgment and choice both as to substantive and procedural matters. In other words, within the bounds of such constraints, different modes of decision-making may be employed. This is well illustrated by taking examples of the four types of decisions noted in 3.12: general policy issue, specific policy issue, modified adjudication, and adjudication. (*a*) An authority with discretion normally has to make some decisions of general policy. When the Supplementary Benefits Commission formulates general criteria for the distribution of welfare benefits, it tries to reach some balance between government policy, the interests advanced by pressure groups, and its own views about just distribution. It tries to ensure that its standards are as effective as possible in achieving the overall good or relieving poverty, that the standards are compatible with each other, and that they are revised from time to time to take account of change or to remove abuse. (*b*) The official deciding on the site for a new school may proceed by basing his findings on evidence and sound knowledge and opinion; he should ensure that he has a full view of the factors in issue by listening to interested parties; he should base his decision on guiding standards which are both reasonable in themselves and serve the objects of his authority, and by reaching a final outcome that is reasonable all things considered. (*c*) A parole board is likely to proceed somewhat differently in so far as it is involved in a course of recurring decisions; it is likely, therefore, to develop general standards of decision-making, although it may revise them from time to time, and it may wish to retain substantial freedom in dealing with each case. The result is likely to be some balance between incrementalism dealing with each case on its merits, and a system of standards which ensure some continuity and consistency from one case to another. (*d*) The final example is judicial decision-making within the common law tradition; this is not always exactly a matter of rule-based decisions, but it places considerable emphasis on continuity and consistency from one case to another, and that rulings made in the past are extrapolated and applied in the future; there is also concern to gain an overall coherence in the application of more basic principles and values. So, where judges do not have clear rules to apply, they may follow, nevertheless, a highly structured method of second-order reasoning.

These modes of decision-making differ in important ways, and yet each may be a reasonable working out of the canons of rational action. It might be asked, however, whether there is not some ideal mode of decision-making, which maximizes rationality and constitutes a model for all discretionary decisions. It might seem, for example, that the judicial mode is a fine model of how decisions ought to be made, and so is a mode that ought to be emulated so far as possible in discretionary contexts. The judicial concern to develop general standards governing decisions, to rely extensively on second-order reasoning and the principles of coherence and consistency, and to foster continuity and stability by extrapolation from one precedent to the next, is defended on occasions as a highly rational and just manner of decision-making.[54] There are certainly considerable virtues in the judicial manner of approach, and it is in many areas of discretionary decisions an instructive model.

There are, however, some points of reservation to be noted. In the first place, the method of the common-law courts has developed for a range of historical and institutional reasons which are to do with the evolution of courts as separate, independent, and hierarchical institutions, with the autonomy-of-law idea, and with the importance placed on stability in legal relationships, especially where personal and property rights have been in issue. For these reasons, it would be misleading to see the judicial method as the fruits of an unrelenting concern with rationality, justice, or other specific values. The second reservation is that the judicial method represents a specific and particular view as to the importance of consistency and continuity, and in turn as to stability in legal relationships. The same concern is not always warranted in discretionary contexts where importance may be placed on adaptability, and on achieving substantive goals more directly, with less concern with what has been before or whether two cases have been treated in exactly the same way. Finally, rather than seek one dominant model, it is preferable to recognize that there are different modes of decision-making, each of which has certain characteristics which make it suitable for the most rational and effective realization of goals and purposes in an appropriate context. Moreover, what counts as rational and effective is, as we have seen throughout this chapter, not a simple, mechanical matter of finding a suitable means to a given end. The means may themselves be important, even hard to separate from ends; notions of fairness, participation, and representation, for example, may affect our evaluation of what constitutes the desired goals. Moreover, it would be mistaken anyhow to understand decision procedures just in terms of rationality and effectiveness, since they are connected intimately to other values like fairness and equity. These last points are taken-up in chapter 7, but we should conclude for the present that different kinds of tasks can be performed most effectively by different modes of decision-making, and that there are links between such modes and other values of importance in discretionary contexts.

3.43 *Arbitrariness*

There is a long tradition of criticism of discretionary powers on the

---

[54] In his highly illuminating account, MacCormick sees those as central to the judicial process; see *Legal Reasoning and Legal Theory*.

grounds that they are inherently tainted with arbitrariness. Many have echoed Dicey's famous contrast between a system of authority where the powers of officials are governed by general legal rules, and one in which powers are 'wide, arbitrary or discretionary'.[55] Dicey may not have meant discretion as a synonym for arbitrariness, but he certainly suggested that where there is discretion there is a high risk of arbitrariness. In this section, I shall consider the substance of such criticisms by outlining a number of senses of arbitrariness and their significance for discretionary powers.[56]

In its clearest sense, arbitrariness relates to the reasoning process by which decisions are made, and is a way of criticizing certain kinds of defects or omissions in that process. Arbitrariness in this sense is the antithesis of rationality, the basic requirements of which are noted in the preceding section. An action is rational if it is believed by the actor to be a means to a given end; it is arbitrary if he does not have that belief. In the exercise of public powers, there is a further restriction in that rationality must be given a certain objectivity, so that an action must not only be believed to be a means to a required end, but there must be objective, empirical reasons for the belief. For example, one of the recurring criticisms of the rehabilitation of offenders as a purpose of sentencing is that no adequate knowledge exists as. to how that purpose is to be achieved. There is neither empirical knowledge for deciding in general what is necessary for rehabilitation, nor in deciding what is necessary in respect of particular offenders.[57] It may be difficult to set the threshold of knowledge that is required before an action can be considered as sufficiently related to purposes, but it is nevertheless important to have such a test. Moreover, once that threshold is satisfied, actions may be more or less rational depending on how

[55] A. V. Dicey, *The Law of the Constitution* (London, 1961), p. 188. An even stronger association between discretion and arbitrariness can be seen in Lord Hewart, *The New Despotism* (London, 1929), ch. iv.

[56] The issue is discussed more fully in D. J. Galligan, 'Arbitrariness and Formal Justice in Discretionary Decisions' in D. J. Galligan (ed.), *Essays in Legal Theory* (Melbourne UP, 1984). The present section follows that discussion with some modifications. There does not appear to be a comprehensive analysis of the concept of arbitrariness, but each of the following gives some attention to it: J. L. Jowell, 'The Legal Control of Administrative Discretion' 1973 *PL*, pp. 186–92; MacCormick, *Legal Reasoning and Legal Theory*, pp. 76, 100–1, 268; G. Marshall, *Constitutional Theory* (Oxford UP, 1968), p. 143; Raz, *The Authority of Law*, pp. 219–20; Selznick, *Law, Society and Industrial Justice*, pp. 12–16.

[57] See, for example, M. E. Frankel, *Criminal Sentences: Law Without Order* (New York, 1972). For discussion: M. Davis 'Sentencing: Must Justice Be Even-Handed?' (1982) 1 *Law&Phil* 77.

closely they achieve an optimum realization of purpose. The difficulties of achieving a perfectly rational action led administrative theorists to talk of 'bounded rationality',[58] but within the bounds there may be a number of courses which are reasonably economical and effective means to given ends, so that any one might be chosen as a rational course to take.[59]

Although one action might be more rational than another, it is characteristic of common and legal usage to confine the ascription of arbitrariness to actions which fail to meet a threshold of rationality. Arbitrariness connotes not just that an action is less rational than it might be, but that it falls below or violates a minimum threshold of rationality. The charge of arbitrariness is avoided if those choices can be seen to be related in a reasonably objective way to the purposes of particular powers. When we come to consider judicial review, we shall see that various doctrines are based around this sense of arbitrariness; judges do not often talk in terms of arbitrariness, but their concern that power should not be exercised arbitrarily is revealed in doctrines of irrelevant considerations, improper purposes, and unreasonableness. Similarly, it must be shown not only that relevant matters have been taken into account, but also that results are produced which are related in a sufficiently rational way to the objects of power.[60] Also, matters of fact and evidence are related to this sense of arbitrariness; a decision may be arbitrary unless the facts upon which it is based are established with some reasonable level of certainty and reliability. Connections can be drawn between the principle against arbitrary action, and doctrines relating to insufficient evidence.[61] Judicial review under any of these heads will be more or less stringent depending on how far judges are concerned to raise the level of rationality in decision-making.[62]

[58] See Simon, *Administrative Behaviour.*
[59] For discussion, see J. Ladd, 'The Place of Practical Reason in Judicial Decisions' in C. J. Friedrich (ed.), *Rational Decision* (New York, 1964), p. 126.
[60] For an example, see *Green* v. *Daniels* (1977) 51 ALJR 463.
[61] For an account of this doctrine, see H. W. R. Wade, *Administrative Law* (Oxford UP, 4th ed., 1977), pp. 274–86. For an account of the American approach, see B. Schwartz and H. W. R. Wade, *The Legal Control of Government*, (Oxford UP, 1972). See section 6.2 below.
[62] It is interesting to note that the American Administrative Procedure Act criterion for judicial review of agency discretion which is expressed in terms of 'arbitrary or capricious' has been interpreted as requiring a threshold standard of reasonableness: see B. Schwartz, *Administrative Law* (New York, 1976), pp. 452, 604–5. The more stringent test that has been developed in recent years is expressed not in terms of arbitrariness, but as the requirement that there be 'reasoned decision-making'. See P. R. Verkuil, 'Judicial Review of Informal Rule Making' (1974) 60 *VaLR* 185.

There are two further points of explanation. Firstly, although the reasoned pursuit of purpose is the basis of rational action in the exercise of discretionary powers, and therefore, conversely, the criterion for assessing arbitrariness, the purposes sought may themselves be open to criticism as irrational or arbitrary. An arbitrary purpose may be implemented in a rational manner; for example, a decision by an education authority that children wear black shoes on Thursdays appears unrelated to any rational, educational purpose, and yet it may be implemented in a perfectly rational manner. But here the links between rationality and arbitrariness become less clear; it might be conceded that actions taken in application of that decision are instrumentally rational, but nevertheless arbitrary since no good reasons can be given for them other than furtherance of an arbitrary policy. Generally, however, a purpose would be considered arbitrary only if it fell below a basic threshold of rational justification. Secondly, arbitrariness should not be confused with reasonableness, nor with moral approval. Moreover, arbitrariness should be kept distinct from other terms of disapprobation, in particular unfairness or injustice. An arbitrary act may be unfair and unjust, but not all unfair or unjust actions are necessarily arbitrary, nor arbitrary actions unjust or unfair.

Discretionary decisions can be arbitrary, but there is no reason so far for assuming a natural link between the two. Not only Dicey, but others, of whom F. A. Hayek has been the most influential, have argued that just such a link exists.[63] The argument, in Weberian terms, is that movement away from formal to substantive rationality brings with it a sense of arbitrariness. At first sight this seems odd; the impartial application of abstract rules may overcome the arbitrariness associated with pre-modern societies, that is the arbitrariness that goes with patronage and self-interest in the disposal and exercise of office. But the impartial application of abstract rules is itself arbitrary in another sense of the term: here the arbitrariness arises by limiting the factors that are taken into account in decision-making, and thereby reducing the level of congruence between particular decisions and underlying purposes. The movement towards substantive rationality, and hence discretionary authority, is an attempt to achieve and maintain that congruence; and this would appear to raise rather than lower the rationality of decisions.[64]

The claim linking substantive rationality and arbitrariness may take

[63] Hayek, *The Constitution of Liberty*.
[64] For discussion, see Selznick, *Law, Society and Industrial Justice*, ch. 3.

a stronger or weaker form. The weaker claim is that rules have the effect of reducing arbitrariness, partly by providing an objective and public basis against which decisions can be measured, and partly because rules reduce the opportunity which an official has for introducing into his decisions factors which are personal or otherwise extraneous. The most conscientious official may find it difficult in making a discretionary decision to confine himself to clearly relevant considerations, and to maintain the high level of argumentation and reflection required by rational decision-making. And, even where the official does meet these demands, it might still be difficult in the absence of clear rules to convince those directly affected of the legitimacy of the decision and its supporting reasons. Rules provide comfort not just for the decision-maker, but also on occasion for those to whom the decision is directed. This is part of the rationale for K. C. Davis's sustained advocacy of rules to govern 'low visibility' discretions, such as police decisions to arrest or caution, since they are prone to being influenced by improper considerations and are hard to control.[65] Similar concerns lie behind many of the arguments for detailed codes governing sentencing and parole.[66]

Now, while rules clearly do help to reduce arbitrariness in these ways, they are only one of a variety of techniques for ensuring the propriety of decisions, and other methods of scrutiny and control can be equally effective. Moreover, since rules carry with them the sense of arbitrariness noted above, it is necessary to assess their merits and demerits in relation to other considerations in settling a strategy which, all things considered, produces the most rational and least arbitrary decisions. There is no reason to think that the outcome will always be in favour of general and comprehensive rules.

There is a second claim which suggests a stronger link between the failure to make decisions according to rules, and arbitrariness. Here the argument is that rules and discretion are incompatible with each other, so that where there is discretion there is necessarily an absence of rules guiding citizens and controlling officials. The consequence is that where power is exercised in the absence of rules, the official has a choice between different courses of action, and this creates a state of

---

[65] Davis, *Discretionary Justice*. For a fuller study of discretionary powers in American Criminal Justice systems, see P. E. Dow, *Discretionary Justice: a Critical Inquiry* (United States, 1981).

[66] For discussion, see D. J. Galligan, 'The Return to Retribution in Penal Theory' in C. F. H. Tapper (ed.), *Crime, Proof and Punishment: Essays in Memory of Rupert Cross* (London, 1981).

uncertainty and unpredictability, which itself constitutes a sense of arbitrariness.

With regard to the first part of this claim, there clearly is no incompatibility between having discretionary powers, and at the same time developing clear and reasonably comprehensive standards governing their exercise. The concept of discretion is not precise enough to require any stringent limitations on the decision strategies that are to be adopted; it means only that, within a defined area of authority, the official has some scope in fixing the decision standards and in applying them to specific cases. It is usually in the interests of good decision-making that the official should formulate standards, although just how precise and binding they are to be depends on a variety of factors, some deriving from the nature of the task, others from organizational considerations. There are also constitutional constraints on the way discretion is used; but these typically require only that standards laid down should not have the status of binding rules.[67] Provided that the official retains the capacity to depart from, extend, or reformulate the standards, constitutional constraints would be satisfied. Subject to these limitations, there may even be a positive duty to formulate standards.[68]

The second part of the claim proceeds on the basis that it is characteristic of discretionary authority that in fact officials often do not lay down standards; or that the standards are loosely drawn; or, even where they are reasonably precise, the official is able, indeed, sometimes is required, to depart from them if it seems desirable in the particular case. The result is an element of uncertainty and unpredictability, with the further consequence that individuals, who may be affected by discretionary decisions, are unable to direct their own actions, or to arrange their affairs in ways that avoid official interference. It is the element of unpredictability that is said to constitute a sense of arbitrariness which can be removed only by clear and certain rules.[69]

What, then, is the relationship between rational decision-making and general standards? My decisions are not arbitrary merely because I

---

[67] For discussion, see D. J. Galligan, 'The Nature and Function of Policies within Discretionary Power' (1976) *PL* 332.

[68] K. C. Davis has argued for the existence of such a duty; see his *1982 Supplement to Administrative Law Treatise* (St. Paul, 1982), ch. 7.

[69] Arbitrariness is often confused with unfairness; but while they may coincide, they are not the same. For brief consideration of the relationship between the two, see J. R. Lucas, *On Justice* (Oxford UP, 1978), p. 11; Marshall, *Constitutional Theory*, p. 143.

do not formulate in advance a set of firm standards which I then follow. I may prefer to take situations as they occur, and then consider how to deal with them; I then may give sound reasons for acting in one way rather than another, and it is difficult to see why this is not a perfectly rational approach to decision-making. There might be good reasons for setting down standards or rules in advance, and it might be desirable over a course of decisions to develop patterns of standards based on precedents. However, the reasons for acting in this way are not inherent in the very idea of rational action, but derive from a number of factors: it is easier and time-saving to have rules of thumb, or it is desirable to give those likely to be affected by my decision notice of how I intend to act. These reasons, as well as others, apply to officials: rules are likely to enhance accountability; they are also likely to help overcome some of the organizational difficulties within bureaucracies; or where rights are in issue, it might be thought that they are best protected by settled standards. It may be highly rational, and typical, to proceed according to settled standards even at the cost of a certain flexibility, but it is not a requirement of the very idea of rationality to do so; and whatever configuration of rules, principles, and looser standards is most suitable, is a matter to be settled in each set of circumstances.

Officials approaching the question of how they should exercise their discretion must form some view about the objects of their powers, and how they are to be realized. Similarly, each time a decision is made it contains within it a commitment to one or more universal or generic standards which are linked to purposes, and which could be appealed to in justifying the decision.[70] In this sense, any rational decision is made within some framework of standards and in turn generates further standards. But these properties of rational action impose only minimal constraints which can be satisfied by standards of an abstract and open-textured kind; all they require is that there be some standards to which the particular decision can intelligibly be related. This is compatible with substantial discretion in dealing with particular cases, and it certainly does not make the existence of precise rules and principles in advance of individualized decisions a condition of rationality. Nor does it follow, as we shall see, that, because a standard

---

[70] For discussion, see MacCormick, *Legal Reasoning and Legal Theory*, pp. 73–6, 97, 124, 273, and Z. Bankowski and D. Nelken, 'Discretion as a Social Problem' in Adler and Asquith, *Discretion and Welfare*.

has been relied on in the past or is inherent in a previous decision, there is an obligation to apply it in the future.

There is another argument from rationality which makes stronger claims about the need for specific standards in order to reduce unpredictability. J. A. Passmore has drawn a distinction between two (official) brutes, one who decides according to specific principles, the other whose actions are entirely arbitrary. They are arbitrary because 'not to have any idea where one stands, to be wholly subject to the changing whims of autocracy, this is destructive of all human dignity'.[71] If 'whim' is meant to indicate a lack of rational reasons, then by definition the second brute is acting arbitrarily. The more pertinent contrast is between two different sorts of brutes; one who lays down explicit and reasonably precise standards, and another who works within a loose framework with the result that his actions are fairly unpredictable. But unpredictability is not the same as arbitrariness, since within those loose standards he may have perfectly rational reasons for acting as he does. Passmore goes on to accept that discretionary decisions are usually subject to some guiding standards; and in any event the real criticism contained in his example is not one of arbitrariness, but the lack of respect for individuals that is demonstrated, supposedly, in unpredictable decisions. Arbitrariness might be extended to include unpredictability, but that would be to sever it from its connections with lack of reason. Moreover, we shall see that unpredictability is not necessarily a sound basis for criticizing discretionary decisions.

There usually are good reasons for settling in advance with reasonable particularity the standards of decision-making. The present argument is concerned only with the limited point that to fail to do so is to act arbitrarily. It is normally important that those affected by official decisions should know the governing criteria; the chief virtue of the rule of law, as Joseph Raz has pointed out, is, after all, guidance,[72] and in the hands of other writers, guidance is linked to deeper values—for Fuller the reciprocity between rulers and ruled,[73] and for Selznick the maintenance of civic principles of rational action.[74] But guidance is not the only consideration: the nature and complexity of the task, the

---

[71] J. A. Passmore, 'Civil Justice and Its Rivals' in E. Kamenka and A. E. S. Tay (eds.), *Justice* (London, 1979), p. 34.
[72] Raz, *The Authority of Law*, ch. 11.
[73] Fuller, *The Morality of Law*, pp. 38–51.
[74] Selznick, *Law, Society and Industrial Justice*, ch. 1.

expertise of officials, and the opportunity for participation by individuals and groups, are all factors that bear on the final structure of decision-making; whatever strategy finally is used is likely to be a compromise, an illustration from another point of view of Simon's notion of bounded rationality.

Another potential constraint on discretionary authority which is sometimes claimed to stem from rationality, and at other times from justice, is the principle of consistency. In its more obvious sense, consistency, as a requirement of rationality, means simply that the reasons for an action are compatible with each other. In the jurisprudential literature, however, consistency has been extended to mean that when a decision has been made in one set of circumstances, a similar decision should be made in similar circumstances. This can be expressed in terms of reasons: once a decision has been made for reason *r*, future cases should be decided in accordance with *r*.

If consistency is a requirement of rationality, it would amount to a significant constraint on the exercise of discretion, in that an official would be obliged to ensure consistency from one decision to another, and to develop a system of precedents similar to that normally associated with judicial decisions. However, there are reservations to be made about the argument from rationality, which may be brought out by considering MacCormick's account of legal reasoning. There are three main steps. The first is that the doctrine of precedent is an example of the application of the principles of formal justice, that is to treat like cases alike and to give everyone his due; in other words, to act consistently. In turn, formal justice and consistency are components of rationality.[75] To act without regard for consistency is to act arbitrarily.[76] Secondly, whenever a court decides a point of law in a case, it commits itself to one or more universal or generic reasons. This explains how judicial decisions become precedents for the future: each case represents not only a specific decision, but also a general rule or principle.[77] The third step is that formal justice requires courts to make decisions that are consistent with existing rulings. In this way the doctrine of precedent is linked directly to the idea of formal justice, and so to the requirements of rationality.[78]

The difficulty in this argument turns, however, on the interpretation given to the idea of consistency. In the first place, to treat cases or

---

[75] See the discussion in *Legal Reasoning and Legal Theory*, ch. iv.
[76] The strongest assertion of this seems to be ibid., pp. 268–9.
[77] For the development of this argument, ibid., pp. 74–99.   [78] Ibid., ch. v.

people consistently is not necessarily to treat them justly or rationally.[79] A rule of sentencing, for example, which requires the imprisonment of all first offenders could be applied consistently, but it would be difficult to show that it is just or rational. Secondly, and more importantly, the interpretation that is given to the principle of consistency to move from step two to step three is unwarranted. It clearly is not necessarily irrational and arbitrary for a judge to depart from, reject, or change a past ruling in deciding the present case. He might do so for a variety of reasons: he might change his mind about its wisdom or its justice; he might have been mistaken or have acted on wrong or inadequate information; he might now simply be able to think of better reasons for ruling differently; or the past ruling might lead in the present case to an unacceptable outcome. In any of these circumstances, it is rational not only not to apply the earlier ruling, but it would be irrational to do so *unless* such a course of action could be justified for other kinds of reasons. Those other reasons can be of various types: they can be the same sorts of reasons we have noted for having settled standards of decision-making; or they might derive from institutional and constitutional factors. The lower court judge, for example, follows the rulings of higher courts, no matter how much he thinks he could improve on them, because it is accepted that higher courts should have the final say in laying down the law.

It is for reasons of these kinds that courts follow the doctrine of precedent, not because to do otherwise would be to act inconsistently and arbitrarily. This can be understood more clearly if we consider why, in the absence of such further reasons, a person might follow in case *b* the reasons *r* which he had for deciding case *a* as he did: he does so not only because he has relied on *r* in the past, but also and *primarily* because he still regards *r* as good reasons for deciding case *b*. This is not to say that the doctrine of precedent is misconceived; there are indeed usually very good reasons for extrapolating standards from past decisions for application in future cases, whether it is judges or administrative officials who are deciding. It is also desirable, generally, that where past decisions are not followed, reasons ought to be available to explain why. The present argument is concerned only to show why officials might adopt a strong version of consistency and the doctrine of precedent; there may be various reasons, such as the importance of providing guidance and stability in legal relations, or

---

[79] For discussion of this point, see L. Chipman, 'Formal Justice and Rational Individualism' (1978) 67 *ARSP* at p. 51.

because of the limited capacities of individual officials to make rational and justifiable decisions, or because rights are in issue.[80] But the force of considerations such as these, and questions as to how rigorously the principle of consistency is to apply, have to be assessed within the parameters and according to the circumstances of each area of discretionary power.

To sum up: (*a*) The notion of arbitrariness has various aspects, but its primary reference is to rationality in decision-making, and it is a useful, negative concept for critically assessing defects in decisions. (*b*) One aspect of this assessment relates to the formulation of standards; some level of general standards normally enhances the rational basis of decisions and eliminates arbitrariness, but just how precise and exacting the standards ought to be depends on a number of factors centred around the effective realization of the objects of power. (*c*) Consistency from case to case has a place in enhancing rationality, in the sense that once a set of reasons has been relied on, they ought to be followed, unless further reasons are given for not so doing. Consistency in that sense should not be taken, however, as an overriding requirement of rationality.

3.44 *Fairness*

Many instances of discretionary power do not raise directly issues of fairness; the decision to establish a new town, to paint road signs orange, or to increase the number of buses at peak hour, do not obviously do so. Yet in other contexts discretionary powers do raise questions of fairness or justice in one or other of its senses. Fairness in a substantive sense concerns the principles upon which benefits and burdens are distributed amongst the members of society. In this sense, fairness or justice (the terms being used interchangeably) is often an important factor in the legislature's decision to regulate a particular area of activity; and, accordingly, where such tasks are entrusted to the discretion of administrative officials, they in turn are faced with questions of substantive fairness or justice. Questions about the distribution of economic resources, the grant or revocation of licences or franchises or privileges, the imposition of penalties or the conferring of benefits, all in some way raise questions of fairness. The rational administrator, like the rational legislator, is expected to subscribe to some political principles to guide and justify his decisions in these

---

[80] See, for example, Dworkin, *Taking Rights Seriously*, ch. iv.

matters. The more reflective officials might have noticed the range of general theories to be found in contemporary political philosophy, and, from one or other or some combination of these, might form views as to how they should approach their own tasks. A second sense of fairness with which the administrator is frequently confronted is procedural; in the western tradition, emphasis has been placed on the importance in public affairs of procedures, not only because they lead to good results, but also because a notion of fairness is involved. This sense of fairness is considered in later chapters.

It is suggested on occasions that there is a third sense of fairness closely linked to but distinguishable from substantive fairness; this third sense I shall refer to as formal fairness. The very concept of justice or fairness has been expressed in the maxim 'treat like cases alike and different cases differently'.[81] This maxim, it has been said, has two parts: one concerns the substantive principles as to what constitutes for a particular purpose justifiable categories of likeness and difference; the other concerns the even-handed application of those principles to specific situations. Compliance with the second is then taken to constitute a distinct sense of fairness, quite apart from whether the substantive principles are themselves justifiable. Adjudication within the legal system exemplifies this sense of fairness, since a judge's primary duty is to apply the legal rules as he finds them quite apart from their substantive merits. Now it is not easy to see how this 'primitive equity', as it has been called,[82] in applying the rules just because they are rules, constitutes a sense of fairness. However, the issue is important in the context of discretionary powers, since often it is said that fairness in some sense is violated by the very idea of discretion. This then is used to support the case for adopting rules in the exercise of discretion, since rules remove the sense of unfairness.

There is, however, considerable ambiguity about the very idea of formal fairness: what does the maxim requiring like treatment of like cases mean; does it divide into two components so that substantive principles of fairness can be separated from their formal application? Indeed, what senses of fairness are at stake in the exercise of discretion? In order to unravel these issues, we may begin with K. C.

[81] For discussion of this maxim of equal treatment, see: Hart, *The Concept of Law*, pp. 153–63; MacCormick, *Legal Reasoning and Legal Theory*, ch. iv; Dworkin, *Taking Rights Seriously*, pp. 86–8, 112–14; A. M. Honoré, 'Social Justice' in R. M. Summers (ed), *Essays in Legal Philosophy* (Oxford, 1970); Brian Barry, *Political Argument* (London, 1965), pp. 97–106; Rawls, *A Theory of Justice*, pp. 58–60, 235–43.
[82] The expression is Brian Barry's in *Political Argument*, p. 100.

Davis's famous critique of discretion.[83] His central claim is that in exercising discretion it is unfair, whether imposing burdens or granting benefits, to treat persons and situations differently where the relevant circumstances are substantially similar. A striking example is the attitude of police officers in deciding whether to arrest and charge, or simply to caution juvenile offenders who are caught committing an offence.[84] In exercising discretion, the police may base their judgment not just on the nature and seriousness of the crime, but also on their assessment of whether a caution would be sufficient to ensure against future repetition. That assessment may be influenced by the young offender's home background, which in turn is often linked to socio-economic and class considerations. The result is that those from better backgrounds have a good chance of being released with a caution, while those from poorer, or ethnic, or disturbed backgrounds, bear the brunt of the law. The criminal justice system provides many such examples, whether the context be bail, sentencing, or parole. Similarly, various aspects of social welfare raise the same questions: is it unfair to treat differently two applicants for a similar welfare benefit where there is no significant difference between their positions?

Arguments such as these tend to confuse a number of issues. One issue concerns the substantive principles of fairness that ought to govern any area of decision-making, whether it be sentencing, parole, or social welfare. Another is whether there is some formal notion of fairness which affects the manner by which substantive principles are put into practice. The second of these would appear to raise two different issues; one is whether fairness requires the translation of discretionary powers into clear and settled standards, the other is the relationship between fairness and consistency from one decision to another. Each is considered in turn.

Does fairness require the translation of discretion into clear and settled standards? The adoption of precise and binding rules is the solution commonly offered to problems of unfairness within the criminal justice system,[85] and a similar proposal has been made by K. C. Davis for discretionary powers in general.[86] This solution must be examined more closely. Unfairness may occur when there is a high

[83] Davis, *Discretionary Justice*, ch. vi and *Discretionary Justice in America and Europe*, introduction.
[84] Davis, *Discretionary Justice*, ch. vi.
[85] For a discussion of these matters in the context of sentencing, see Galligan, 'The Return to Retribution in Penal Theory'.
[86] See, generally, Davis, *Discretionary Justice*.

likelihood that different considerations will be taken into account by
different officials, or even by the same official, in similar cases. In some
areas of discretion, such as decisions to arrest, prosecute, or parole,
there is a high risk that extraneous matters will be taken into account,
that not all relevant matters will be considered, or that they will be
considered differently in similar cases in areas where important
personal interests are at stake, or the risk of abuse is high. Rules can be
important in reducing not only arbitrariness, but also unfairness in this
sense. Unfairness may occur also because the objects are multiple and
individual circumstances so variable that similar cases appear to be
treated in ways that are substantially different. Sentencing again
provides a good example; where there are two similar cases of
fraudulent passing of cheques and one offender receives a sentence of,
say, ten years and the other a few months, there is inevitably the
appearance of unfairness and inequality of treatment. On further
investigation, the disparity might be explicable in terms of legitimate
penal policies and variable personal circumstances, but the appearance
of unfairness, once created, may be hard to dispel. At the cost of
reducing the degree of individualized attention to the circumstances of
each case, it may be necessary, in order to remove any hint of
unfairness in the sense of unequal treatment, to specify reasonably
clear and objective standards against which decisions may be judged.[87]

Another strand of argument linking discretion and unfairness is
based on predictability: by not enabling individuals to build up
expectations about how decisions are to be made, discretion, it has
been said, creates unfairness. A principal argument for settled rules is
that people are able to form, and have satisfied, expectations about the
exercise of authority. A. M. Honoré has argued that each member of
society has a claim that the rules of the society should be observed as a
matter of justice.[88] The injustice, where this is not done, stems partly
from a right to equal treatment and partly from the concern not to
disappoint the expectations that rules create.[89] Considering the case
based on expectations, there are differences between disappointing
expectations and not allowing them to arise in the first place; there
seems to be sufficient similarity between the two, however, for the
main arguments for the former to apply to the latter. It may be just as
serious an affront to a person's dignity not to allow expectations to

[87] For a good discussion of these issues in regard to sentencing, see M. Davis,
'Sentencing: Must Justice Be Even-Handed?'
[88] Honoré, 'Social Justice', pp. 66–7.   [89] Ibid., p. 70.

develop, as to disappoint those that have. The argument is that the ability to plan one's affairs with reasonable security is an important part of individuality and autonomy, and since valuable personal interests may be affected by discretionary powers, there is a strong case for settled standards governing their exercise, whether laid down by the legislature in the original delegation of powers, or by the authority itself in deciding how to proceed.

The general claim that fairness requires the formulation and notification of the standards to be used may be accepted. The difficulty is in knowing how exacting that requirement is, since other factors bear on the overall assessment of whether decisions are fair. In the first place, there may be tension between the predictability that rules create, and the realization of goals of substantive justice. Rules operate as rules by selecting a narrow range of facts as relevant, and excluding others as irrelevant. The nature of the task may be such that it can be performed more clearly in accordance with its underlying objectives if decisions are made on a more discretionary basis, so enabling account to be taken of a wider spectrum of circumstances than rules would allow. Assuming that those objectives are justified in terms of a substantive theory of justice, then a certain unpredictability may be an unavoidable cost in achieving them; in other words, in order to satisfy principles of substantive justice, it may be necessary to sacrifice or curtail the sense of fairness that is served by predictability. Normally, a satisfactory compromise can be reached between the two, between the predictability that goes with settled rules, and the need to make decisions that are most in accordance with underlying objectives. In any case, there is no reason for assuming, when the two are in conflict, that predictability is necessarily more important than substantive outcomes.

Much depends on the circumstances.in which powers are exercised. For example, the case for sentencing codes turns partly on the difficulty of preventing arbitrariness and unfairness in the sense of extraneous matters being taken into account; it also makes an appeal to fairness in the sense that derives from predictability.[90] This in turn is its major weakness; fairness in this sense may be gained at the cost of unfairness in a more substantive sense, because of the limitations that sentencing rules inevitably place on the sentencer's capacity to deal subtly with the circumstances of each case. In short, it may be that

[90] See, for example, von Hirsch, *Doing Justice*.

some interests ought to be protected by rules rather than a looser belt of standards, but that conclusion follows, if it does, not solely from the fact that rules remove unpredictability, but from an assessment that, all things considered, a system of firm standards will produce the fairest and best results.

A second reason for qualifying the assumption that unpredictability connotes unfairness is that in some contexts of discretion, where it is difficult or undesirable to formulate precise legal norms, it may be important to have strategies based on the representation of interests, and the participation of individuals and groups in ways which would be excluded, if decision-making were according to rules. It may be desirable to find, through mediatory procedures, a consensus between parties as to how discretion ought to be exercised; alternatively, the discretionary authority may wish to consult interested groups by allowing them to present evidence and arguments as to how a particular problem ought to be resolved.[91] Both methods are employed extensively, and each assumes that a certain unpredictability as to outcomes is countered by the greater capacity of the parties to participate and influence those outcomes.[92]

So, while total unpredictability in discretionary decisions can give rise to a sense of unfairness, that must be considered as part of a general assessment which takes account of substantive outcomes and substantive senses of fairness. Secondly, since the unfairness that can be created by unpredictability is based on a lack of respect for persons, there may be alternative procedures which, by allowing more extensive modes of participation, restore the shortfall.

Formal fairness in another of its guises is associated with the notion of consistency. The argument goes as follows: consistency derives from the principle of treating like cases alike (and possibly different cases differently), and this is a fundamental principle of justice. This argument is relevant to discretionary decisions in two ways: it may be necessary, in order to ensure consistency, to have a set of rules governing decisions; it may also mean that once a decision has been made to treat a situation in one way, there is a commitment to treating similar situations in similar ways. So, the consistency principle has

[91] For discussion of mediation and consultation, see L. L. Fuller, 'Mediation: Its Forms, and Functions' (1971) 44 *SCLR* 305; M. Eisenberg, 'Private Ordering Through Negotiation, Dispute Settlement and Rule-Making' (1976) 89 *HarvLR* 637.
[92] See the discussion in section 2.23 and G. Tuebner, 'Substantive and Reflexive Elements in Modern Law' (1983) 17 *LSR* 239.

been invoked to explain the doctrine of precedent in judicial decisions, and to show its connections with justice.[93]

The principal basis for assessing whether or not the treatment of situations in similar or different ways is just or unjust is some substantive theory of justice. When K. C. Davis criticizes the police practices to which I have referred, or when H. L. A. Hart comments adversely on sentencing systems which allow rehabilitation to override deserts,[94] each is relying primarily upon substantive moral principles as to how individuals within those systems ought to be treated. Equal treatment and consistency then are satisfied by the even-handed application of those substantive principles.

It is asserted often enough, however, that the precept of treating like cases alike and the notion of consistency are requirements of justice which are in some sense independent of the justice of substantive outcomes. Rules may foster equal treatment but, if they do, it is for the contingent reasons which we have considered—their capacity to reduce consideration of extraneous matters—rather than because of any conceptual link with justice. What counts as equal treatment is to be determined according to the tenets of one or other substantive conception of justice, and whether rules are instrumentally advantageous in that regard depends on a variety of factors. Similarly, the justification in terms of justice for following precedents is primarily that they are in harmony with substantive principles; if they are out of step with substantive principles, it would be unjust to follow them, and resulting decisions would be a departure from the requirement of equal treatment.[95] The confusing factor is that there is a sense in which following precedents, even bad ones, amounts to equal treatment: X is treated equally if he is treated in the same way as Y before him. But unless the reasons for treating Y in that way are just, there is no reason in justice for treating X in the same way. The most that can be said is that there is a primitive sense of equity in treating X in the same way as Y, but that would not normally be a sufficient reason for perpetuating injustice. Again, there may be other reasons for continuing to apply a bad precedent, but these are separate from and should not be confused with reasons of justice.

[93] See, MacCormick, *Legal Reasoning and Legal Theory*.

[94] Hart, *Punishment and Responsibility*, pp. 24–7.

[95] Dworkin uses the idea of 'articulate consistency', but by this he appears to mean that particular decisions should be in accordance with substantive principles; if a decision is made which is out of step, it should be isolated by not allowing it to have gravitational weight: *Taking Rights Seriously*, ch. iv.

It might be objected that this argument takes inadequate account of the importance that officials in their decisions place on notions of fairness in its various senses. Recent studies of discretion have found this sense of fairness to be a recurring and substantial factor in the attitudes of officials; and while fairness may be used in its substantive and procedural senses, it is often taken to mean simply that there ought to be consistency from one case to another.[96] This does not mean that such officials are labouring under a false sense of fairness, as might seem to be the inference from my earlier analysis. Rather the explanation is that in practical decision-making it is often the case that no distinction is drawn between some underlying, substantive principles of fairness and the decisions that are made in particular cases. Instead, notions of fairness are developed in deciding particular cases, and once a decision has been made in one way, that becomes the yardstick for future cases. The official must still have some background sense of what is fair treatment, but that may remain unarticulated, being made manifest only when a stark conflict arises in a particular case between the underlying substantive principle and what has been done in past cases. Indeed, it might be seen as an advantage of such an incremental approach that the official does not have to try to formulate a general theory, but is able rather to develop as he goes a set of working standards as to what is fair. If questioned about the fairness of a particular way of doing things, the official may refer to the fact that it is in accordance with previous decisions and actions; but if taxed further, he is likely to be able to offer some sort of general principle which underlies his actions. The mere fact that officials tend to develop incrementally their working conceptions of fairness, rather than by explicit deduction from given principles, should not mislead us into thinking that their sense of fairness is based simply on consistency, on repeating what has been done before.

To return to the alleged unfairness in disappointing expectations, little need be added to the earlier discussion. If expectations have been created on the basis of settled standards or precedents, and then are disappointed as a result of their not being followed, there may be a consequential sense of unfairness. But the unfairness is not a necessary consequence of not following standards or precedents; it depends rather on various contingencies such as the reasons for departure, the level of expectations, the interests at stake, and the

[96] See Hawkins, *Environment and Enforcement*, pp. 24–5, 70, 181–2; Richardson, *Policing Pollution*, pp. 96–105.

substantive fairness of the result. The frustration of expectations is one element only in the total assessment of whether a fair outcome has been achieved.

The relationship between formal justice or fairness and some substantive theory of justice has been a source of enduring difficulty. Much of this stems from the idea, neatly expressed by H. L. A. Hart, that justice consists of two parts: 'a uniform or constant feature summarized in the precept "Treat like cases alike" and a shifting or varying criterion used in determining when, for any given purpose, cases are alike or different'.[97] The simple point is that once the substantive requirements of a theory of justice have been applied, there is no remainder to which the idea of formal justice refers. It is the substantive principles of the particular theory that regulate the distribution of benefits and burdens, and so determine how individuals are to be treated. For example, if the substantive principles were that persons should not be discriminated against on the grounds of national origins, and if those principles were applied rationally, anyone subject to the decisions would be treated equally and consistently in accordance with the substantive theory. The precept to treat like cases alike is satisfied by the rational application of a substantive theory of justice.[98]

The discussion of fairness in discretionary decisions may be summed up as follows: (*a*) Like arbitrariness, fairness has various facets; one facet that is pertinent in discretionary contexts is based on the risk of unequal treatment. (*b*) General standards help to reduce the risk of similar cases being treated differently in the sense that extraneous matters are considered. (*c*) For similar reasons, there is a case for acting consistently by extrapolating standards from precedents. (*d*) In assessing how exacting the standards are to be and how rigorously consistency is to be maintained, it is necessary to see that equality of treatment, and hence fairness, is to be judged finally on how well substantive principles of fairness are achieved. (*e*) In attaining acceptable levels of substantive fairness in specific cases, it may be necessary to maintain open standards and not to apply consistency too strictly. (*f*) another aspect of fairness relates to predictability; but while

[97] *The Concept of Law*, p. 156.
[98] For one of the most illuminating accounts of this relationship between formal justice, rationality, and substantive principles, see L. Chipman, 'Formal Justice and Rational Individualism' (1981) 67 *ARSP*. See also Peter Westen, 'The Empty Idea of Equality' (1982) 95 *HarvLR* 537.

some level of predictability may be a requirement of fairness, it may again be necessary to maintain substantial unpredictability in order to allow scope for achieving substantively fair outcomes.

3.45   Guidance

Stability in the relations between citizens and the state is a virtue that lies at the core of the legal tradition, and one which has a prominent place in the exercise of discretionary powers. Stability depends on official powers being exercised according to standards and procedures which are sufficiently settled and precise for individuals to be able to predict, with reasonable accuracy, the nature and extent of state action, in so far as it affects their affairs. It is the importance of stability in legal relations that provides the main case for settled rules and principles, for systems of precedent, and for formalized procedures. Since discretionary powers leave to officials scope in devising policies and strategies of decision-making, the issue arises as to what steps they should take towards creating stability by translating their powers into guiding standards, either through planning in advance or by incremental development. How important, in other words, is it to provide guidance and thus to create stability in the exercise of discretion? This can be approached by considering firstly the methods by which guidance is provided, and secondly how guidance is to be measured against other values.

Guidance is provided most directly and completely by a system of precise rules which are stable, applied consistently, not changed too often, known publicly, and not unduly complex. Guidance can never be complete because of the inherent uncertainties and ambiguities in even the clearest rules. Nevertheless, the primary virtue of rules is guidance, and in some circumstances it might appear to officials that the objects of power can be achieved most satisfactorily by a set of rules that are relatively detailed and precise, because, perhaps, the objects are relatively simple and the circumstances constant and predictable. It might be desirable in cases of that kind to formulate a set of rules, subject only to being prepared to make changes which from time to time might seem opportune, and subject to the proviso, as Roscoe Pound has noted,[99] that in any system of decision-making it is advisable to retain some discretion to deal equitably with the novel, unforeseen, or unusual case. The point of conferring discretion on a

---

[99] Roscoe Pound, 'Discretion, Dispensation and Mitigation: the Problem of the Individual Special Case' (1960) 35 *NYULR* 925.

particular authority may simply be to allow it, perhaps because of its special expertise, to settle the governing rules.

While it is not uncommon to find behind the facade of discretion a system of informal rules, it is perhaps more typically the case that discretion is exercised within a context of mixed standards, some firm and precise, others of varying particularity and conclusiveness. Moreover, guidance is not an all-or-nothing matter; standards that are less specific and binding than rules, nevertheless, provide some guidance. Statements of policy, the issuing of guidelines and directions, even an enumeration of the matters to be taken into account—all these offer guidance and create some degree of predictability. Decisions normally occur within a context of some general standards, and, over a course of decisions, there are usually strong reasons for translating those standards into reasonably clear and settled guidelines, to ensure continuity and consistency from one decision to another. It is a mistake to think that there is some deep incompatibility between discretion and guiding standards, as if the very point of having discretion were to enable each decision to be fashioned according to its own special circumstances. Indeed, situations may sometimes be so variable that there is insufficient common ground between one circumstance and another for anything but the most abstract standards to be established. It is more likely to be the case, however, that situations differ only in marginal ways, leaving a common core around which standards can be developed; and standards may be reasonably settled and instructive, while allowing variations to be accommodated within their terms, or by incremental extension and modification. There is always a certain tension, which we have noticed at various points, between the general standard and the particular case, so that ultimately the decision-maker must hold in his mind's eye some particular but variable balance between responsiveness to individual circumstances and the need to relate decisions to a continuing framework of rational and purposive activity.

Discretionary decisions appear on occasions to be unpredictable not because they are made without standards, but for the more mundane reason that officials are not required to articulate and make public the standards on which they are relying. Nevertheless, there are some factors which contribute to the image of instability and unpredictability in the exercise of discretion. Policy decisions may be made, or existing standards changed or made the subject of exceptions in the course of a particular decision; sometimes the settled standards may be so indeterminate and so much in the background that they offer little guidance; and sometimes the context may be such that little by way of generalization can be made from one case to another. Added to this is the relative lack of political and legal controls over the way discretion is exercised, so that both the initiative and responsibility for developing standards is left to the authority itself.

So while in principle there are always some general standards governing discretion, and while guidance is a matter of degree depending on the firmness and specificity of standards, the question remains as to how important it is to provide guidance in the discretionary context. Some level of guidance in the form of general standards is required if decisions are to avoid the charge of arbitrariness, or at least the appearance of arbitrariness. Fairness also has a place in support of guidance: it may be unfair not to provide the basis upon which expectations can be built; similarly, once expectations have been created, it may be unfair to thwart them. These factors make up a case for threshold levels of stability in relation to discretion; above the threshold the claims for guidance and stability may be offset by the importance of ensuring substantively fair and rational outcomes in particular cases, and of allowing scope for interested parties to participate and influence those outcomes.

To conclude, the point of this section has been to examine the requirements in discretionary contexts of rational action and the related notions of arbitrariness, fairness, and guidance. We have seen how each of these concepts has different senses and connotations, and while each provides both guidance and constraints in discretionary decisions, the application of each and the relationships between them must be settled in the particular circumstances. It is rather difficult to say in the abstract that any particular decision strategy is the most justifiable or the most satisfactory; but we must now go on to consider whether any more specific guidance can be suggested to assist in that process.

4

The Exercise of Discretionary Powers, II

IN the light of the various influences, practical and normative, discussed in the preceding chapter, my first concern is to consider whether any guidance can be suggested in the design of decision procedures; or, in other words, whether there is any right balance of discretion, of comprehensive planning with an emphasis on rules and standards, and incrementalism, with its emphasis on the particular problem. The remainder of the chapter deals with two issues, firstly, with the concept of rights—their relationship to discretion and their place in the public law model; secondly, the relationship between personal liberty and discretionary authority in relation to A. V. Dicey and F. A. Hayek.

4.1 THE RIGHT BALANCE OF DISCRETION

Within the parameters set by considerations of rationality and purpose, any decision strategy is bound to constitute some balance of comprehensive planning and incrementalism—of formal, substantive, and reflexive rationality—and the balance is found by reaching some compromise amongst the various practical and normative constraints of the kinds considered in the previous chapter. Indeed, much of the discussion of the last two chapters is about the limitations of rules, the variables that enter into discretionary decisions, the relative merits of comprehensive planning and incrementalism, and the types of decision-procedures that may be suitable. The question often arises, however, whether any more precise guidance can be given as to the relative virtues of different strategies in formulating, allocating, and exercising powers. The issue is likely to occur in a number of contexts: in the design and allocation of powers by the legislature or other delegating body; when the authority itself is deciding how to deal with the powers it has been given; the matter may also arise for the courts in developing principles of review. Sometimes this issue is put in terms of the right balance of rules and discretion, at other times in terms of structuring. It may be somewhat oversimplified to express the matter in terms of one general problem, since there are in fact a number of rather more specific matters to resolve: should an attempt be made in the first instance to formulate a comprehensive set of rules; should the deciding authority begin incrementally but rapidly develop a set of precise rules through extrapolation of precedents; where rules are laid down, in what circumstances should departure in particular cases be accepted? These are questions of policy and strategy, and it is difficult to conceive of any master plan as to how they are to be resolved. My earlier discussion has shown some of the variables to be accommodated and matters to be considered; all I shall try to do now is set out more precisely some of the practical issues to be resolved in dealing with the general question of the best balance of discretion.

The first point to notice is that the issue is not simply whether to have rules or discretion, in the sense of strict decision rules on the one hand, or discretion where anything goes on the other hand. All discretionary decisions are directed towards goals from which it is possible to derive some general, guiding standards. Moreover, it is to be concluded from earlier discussion that some attempt to formulate general standards, either by stipulation or by extrapolation from specific standards, is tied closely to the very idea of rational decision-making. In practice, there is likely to be, as a result, a mixture of standards of varying normative weight and of varying degrees of specificity. These might point out the conclusion to be reached, or provide guidance in reaching that conclusion; they might sometimes require, at other times prohibit, things being done, steps taken, or matters to be taken into account or weighed against each other.[1] Such standards might be imposed by a superior legal authority, be deduced from stipulated legal standards, or be adopted informally by the administrative authority itself. Different aspects of a decision can be dealt with according to different approaches, and an approach initially selected may be modified over a course of decisions. Moreover, even where there are clear and precise rules there may be extensive room for assessment and judgment in applying them, or in establishing the presence of the pertinent facts; or in deciding whether to depart from the rules. Considering these factors and the variations that occur, it is necessary to be wary of any question which is put simply in terms of the merits of choosing between rules and discretion. All that can be attempted is to offer some rather general guidance as to the right

[1] For an attempt to identify different kinds of 'decision referents', see D. J. Gifford, 'Decisions, Decisional Referents, and Administrative Justice' (1972) 37 *Law&CP* 3.

balance between formal rules and adjudicative procedures on the one hand, contrasted with looser standards and an incrementalist approach on the other hand, bearing in mind that around this issue there is considerable room for shades and shifts of emphasis.

Secondly, notice must be taken of the relationship between this issue and the categories of decision strategies suggested—adjudication, modified adjudication, specific policy decision, general policy decision. Within these categories, the question is to what extent decision-making ought to be based on general but detailed rules made in the exercise of a general policy decision, followed by the application in particular cases of those rules in an adjudicative manner. The question really is about the reasons for retaining the categories of specific policy decision and modified adjudication, rather than forcing all decisions into the rule-making (legislative), rule application (adjudicative) dichotomy. For example, why not lay down rules for parole decisions, welfare payments, the prosecution of offenders, and for selecting the route a new road is to take? Many of the reasons have been discussed in chapters 2 and 3, where it is shown that the different considerations are often in conflict and may be interpreted in different ways. What we are now concerned with is whether, considering those reasons, any firm, general conclusions can be drawn about the desirability of different strategies in different situations. Obviously, the question as to whether powers should be translated into rules makes no sense with respect to the very power to make rules in the first place, although even rule-making may be guided by abstract standards. Similarly, it is clear that there are many occasions on which decisions of a very basic policy kind have to be made in the context of a specific problem which is unlikely to recur. Such decisions might be guided by broad, purposive standards, but it would make little sense to talk about the policy issue being itself governed by rules. Any question about the right balance of discretion is most at home in respect of individualized decisions which are likely to recur, and where it is unlikely that each case will raise new and basic issues of policy. It is here that questions about rules and structuring are most pertinent.

A third point to be mentioned now and elaborated in the following discussion is that any answers to the right balance of formal, substantive, and reflexive rationality are complex and inevitably somewhat controversial for two reasons. Firstly, much depends on the point of view taken and what is considered within that point of view to be most important. One approach might stress the efficient and effective realization of goals as the dominant consideration, while another might emphasize stability in legal relationships, or procedural fairness, or extensive participation by interested parties. Those of course are interrelated, but the emphasis given to one will affect the strategy selected. Secondly, even within a particular point of view, there may be different factors which cannot easily or uncontentiously be assessed. Assuming, for example, that the effective realization of goals is taken to be most important, it may be necessary to assess the problem of overinclusion and underinclusion in considering the virtues of rules.[2] Bearing in mind these complications, we may now consider some of the approaches towards decision making that might be adopted.

4.11 *K. C. Davis and structuring discretion*

The unrivalled pioneer in this field is K. C. Davis, who has argued that the regulation of discretionary authority is one of the most pressing issues of modern law.[3] Davis saw a number of values under threat from discretionary powers, but it is increasing unfairness and arbitrariness that concern him most; unfairness in the sense that similar situations are treated differently, arbitrariness in the sense that extraneous matters are taken into account. Davis offers three reasons for the growth of discretion in government: (*a*) tasks are undertaken in respect of which no one is able to prepare advance rules; (*b*) even where officials are able to formulate rules, discretion is often desirable for individualized justice; (*c*) habits have developed of allowing discretionary powers to grow in areas where they are unnecessary and where controls are inadequate.[4] The task he sets is to remedy (*c*), that is to eliminate discretion which is not necessary in terms of (*a*) or (*b*), and to regulate that which is necessary. The task of elimination and regulation is to be achieved by confining, structuring and checking: discretion is confined by specifying with particularity the scope of powers, and by stipulating whenever possible clear decision rules; it is

[2] See the discussion in section 3.31.

[3] The principal work is Davis, *Discretionary Justice*; see also *Administrative Law Treatise* (St Paul, 2nd edn., 1979), vol. 2, section 8:1. For critical discussion, see H. T. Wilson, ' "Discretion" in the Analysis of Administrative Process' (1972) 10 *Osgoode HLJ* 117; J. Skelly Wright, 'Beyond Discretionary Justice' (1971–2) 81 *YLJ* 575; Richard Stewart, 'The Reformation of Administrative Law' (1974–5) 88 *HarvLR* 1667, esp. pp. 1698–1702; D. J. Gifford, 'Discretionary Decisionmaking in the Regulatory Agencies: A Conceptual Framework' (1983) 57 *SCLR* 101; R. Baldwin and K. Hawkins, 'Discretionary Justice: Davis Reconsidered' 1985 *PL* 570.

[4] *Discretionary Justice*, p. 20.

checked by one official's actions being scrutinized by another official; and it is structured by a variety of normative standards which may range from fairly tight decision rules to standards of a broader kind.[5]

We need not dwell on the first and second of these techniques, but the third, the idea of structuring discretion, raises a number of points. In the first place, it seems that structuring may be achieved by one or other of two broad approaches: one of these, which Americans somewhat loosely call adjudication, is in the nature of an incremental approach, proceeding case by case, and developing a framework of standards by generalizing the reasons from one case to the next; the other, directed more clearly towards comprehensive planning by formulating general standards, is referred to by Davis, also rather loosely, as rule-making. This may take the form of plans, policy statements, rules, or guide-lines. Davis has no doubt that comprehensive planning is the superior technique, and urges its much greater employment by administrative authorities. Its principal virtues are claimed to be that it is more efficient in identifying a sense of the public interest; it is fairer because rules operate prospectively rather than retrospectively; and it is more democratic because interested parties may be given easy access to the policy-making process.[6] Incrementalism, or policy-making through specific decisions, is seen as a much less satisfactory way of developing general standards; fewer parties are likely to be represented, the view of the public interest is likely to be more limited, and there is an inevitable element of retrospectivity. Those assertions have not gone without challenge, but we must be content to note that clearly any assessment depends more on the circumstances of different situations than Davis allows.[7] Nevertheless, Davis concedes that incrementalism may be necessary in dealing with complex matters (and so would be suited to (a) above),

[5] Ibid., chs. iii, iv and v for further explanation of these terms.
[6] Ibid., pp. 65–8.
[7] Ibid., pp. 97–116, 225–6. For criticism of Davis's claims, see G. O. Robinson, 'The Making of Administrative Policy: Another Look at Rulemaking and Adjudication and Administrative Procedure Reform' (1970) 118*UPaLR* 485. Robinson argues that an incremental approach is an effective way of developing standards, and is sometimes more effective than attempts at comprehensive planning. The real difficulties with incremental decision-making are the practical ones of encouraging officials to link decisions together and to extract general standards from them. See further: L. Hector, 'Problems of the C.A.B. and the Independent Regulatory Commissions' (1969) 69 *YLJ* 931 (where a strong argument is made against policy-making through adjudication); C. Auerbach, 'Some Thoughts on the Hector Memorandum' 1960 *WiscLR* 183 (where a counter is offered to Hector's criticisms); C. S. Diver, 'Policy-making Paradigms in Administrative Law' (1981) 95 *HarvLR* 393 (where a balanced discussion is offered).

and indeed he sees structuring as the outcome of rule-making and incrementalism working in combination.

The second point that arises from Davis's idea of structuring discretion concerns the right balance between settled standards and the particular case. He talks of achieving an optimum balance between the two, and emphasizes the importance of having some discretion, and the creative opportunities it offers to the official in dealing with particular circumstances: he also recognizes that in respect of some tasks it may be very difficult to formulate rules in advance. This gives rise to a number of comments. While emphasis is placed on rule-making as the primary technique for structuring discretion, there is a certain ambiguity about the notion: according to American administrative law, rule-making refers rather generally to the formulation of standards which may vary in terms of weight and specificity. Discretion occurs then within the framework of those standards, and varies in degree according to how closely the standards are drawn. This is the image of discretion suggested in the present work, and is the one implicit in much of Davis's work. Sometimes, however, his emphasis is such as to suggest that rule-making refers to rules in the sense of precise standards that eliminate discretion; rules and discretion are then contrasted, as if each were the antithesis of the other. While rules in that sense do have their place in respect of some aspects of decisions, the more useful image of discretion is the former, where the question is how open or closed the framework of standards is to be.

4.12 *The optimum balance of settled standards*

The more important issue concerning the structuring of discretion is the idea of an optimum balance between settled standards, whether they be stipulated in advance or developed incrementally, and the particular case. The importance of some standards in exercising discretion is obvious,[8] but it is more difficult to find any clear indication of how precise they are to be, or how the optimum balance is to be discovered. Davis points out the problem, but offers no clear guidance for its solution other than an assessment of different situations according to their circumstances; in so far as there is an emphasis, it tends to be on the need for greater specificity of standards,

---

[8] For further discussion of the need for standards, see H. J. Friendly, *The Federal Administrative Agencies* (Harvard UP, 1962). In Davis's later works, there is greater recognition of these complexities, and of the factors that weigh against rules.

for piling rules on rules in order to enhance consistency and a sense of formal justice.[9]

The work of K. C. Davis has been a landmark in the development of public law, and much of the modern interest in discretionary authority is owed to him. However, there are aspects of his approach which need to be modified. The theme running throughout his work is that powers are likely to be used with greater fairness and less arbitrariness if standards are formulated in fairly precise terms, and then applied even-handedly in particular cases. This does not mean that Davis neglects the policy side of discretion; rather he envisages that primary matters of policy will be resolved at the rule-making stage. His view appears to be that it is preferable, where possible, for policy to be settled according to the procedures that accompany rule-making, rather than in the course of individualized decisions. Indeed, it is individualized decisions, decisions about how to treat a person or situation, and the consequential questions of personalized justice that are the focus of his interest. Even in these terms we must be a little wary of accepting the claims made for rules, since it has been shown in earlier discussion that fairness and arbitrariness are rather complex concepts, and that they are not necessarily or completely eliminated by rules. Moreover, there are other difficulties and shortcomings arising from a deep commitment to rules as the principle means for regulating discretion.

Before considering these other aspects of the debate over structuring discretion, it may be useful to state in more general terms the issues that have to be faced in settling the balance of discretion.[10] Following the earlier analysis of discretionary decisions, it is reasonable to accept that the general object is to achieve effectively and efficiently the goals for which powers have been conferred. The first step is to decide what those goals are, the second is to set about achieving them by intermediary standards and strategies. The governing standards might initially be set at an abstract level by direction of the administrative

---

[9] For an interesting analysis pointing out some of the drawbacks of rules at a broader, cultural level, see S. Toulmin, 'Equity and Principles' (1982) 20 *Osgoode HLJ* 1.

[10] See K. C. Davis, *Discretionary Justice in Europe and America* and *Administrative Law of the Seventies* (Illinois UP, 1976.) For further discussion generally, see: D. R. Shulman, 'Nonincremental Policymaking: Notes Towards an Alternative Paradigm' (1975) 69 *AmPolSciR* 1354; I. Ehrlich and R. Posner, 'An Economic Analysis of Legal Rulemaking' (1974) 3 *JLegStud* 257; R. Archibald, 'Three Views of the Expert's Role in Policymaking' (1950) 1 *PolSci* 73; I. Lustick, 'Explaining the Variable Utility of Disjointed Incrementalism' (1980) 74 *AmPolSciR* 342.

authority, and possibly after consultation with interest groups. Within this framework of standards, specific decisions are made. Where the specific decision involves a matter of policy that is unlikely to recur, the final outcome may be reached after considering the circumstances and after listening to the arguments of interest groups. Where similar situations are likely to recur, the issue is whether those broad standards should be translated into more precise and detailed standards, even rules, and to what extent efforts should be made to generate precedents for guidance in the future.

The principal criterion throughout this process is the effective and efficient realization of objects. This can be formulated more specifically: the net effectiveness of a decision strategy is determined by the level of realization of objects, set against both the resources used in making a decision, and the adverse side-effects of the strategy.[11] The primary goal then is to find the strategies that are most effective in this sense. The goal of effectiveness is subject, however, to two factors. One is the point noted previously as to the difficulties inherent in the notion of effectiveness; it may be misleading to see the task as simply a matter of finding the most rationally instrumental means for achieving a given object, since the objects can be diverse, and the achievement of one may depend on the realization of others; successful achievement may consist partially in finding reasonable compromises between conflicting interests, or in providing a stable environment within which decisions are made.[12] The other point is that there may be side-constraints on the pursuit of rational effectiveness, which derive from other values; again stability in legal relations might be one, moral principles, especially notions of fairness, might be another, and factors relating to accountability a third. Whether such factors are considered within the general notion of effectiveness or as side-constraints does not matter, provided it is recognized that they carry weight in settling decision procedures.

The virtues of rules are that they constitute a clear and certain basis

---

[11] See D. J. Gifford, 'Discretionary Decisionmaking in the Regulatory Agencies: a Conceptual Framework' (1983) 57 *SCLR* 101; see further R. Posner, 'The Behaviour of Administrative Agencies' (1972) 1 *JLegStud* 305.

[12] It might be argued that the importance of discretionary decisions in instrumentally realizing goals is an excessively rationalistic view and that other, more diversified approaches might be taken, based on a different characterization of the process. For a suggestive account of other models of the discretionary process, see J. L. Mashaw, 'Conflict and Compromise Among Models of Administrative Justice' (1981) *DukeLJ* and *Bureaucratic Justice* (Yale UP, 1983).

for official action, and they may be effective and efficient in achieving goals. They provide a good level of stability in legal relationships, they ensure a certain level of procedural fairness, and they constitute a firm basis for outside scrutiny. For these reasons, there would seem to be a strong case for reasonably clear and certain standards governing discretion. There are, however, a number of considerations which cause complications and which need to be accommodated; these can be divided into two categories, those which derive from the very character of rules, and those which concern the suitability of rules for certain tasks.

In the first place, the relationship between rules and effectiveness may be complex. By selecting and restricting the factors to be taken into account, rules are, as we have noted, over-inclusive and under-inclusive. As a result, rules may in matters of complexity provide a low level of achievement in terms of goals. This can be overcome to some extent by constant review of the rules, and by encouraging departure or modification where the circumstances require. Whether this is a realistic counter depends on the attitudes of officials, who may adopt legalistic attitudes towards the rules.[13] Other considerations arise when the issues are complex, and it is necessary to consider the net consequences of, say, stipulating a rule, compared with the consequences of a procedure which aims at extensive consultation with affected interests wherever the issue arises. A rule might achieve its goals only modestly, it might aggravate conflict between subsystems, and be expensive to enforce; a consultative procedure, on the other hand, might be less costly, and it might produce harmony between the more important subsystems. It might be a major cost, however, that smaller groups are disadvantaged in influencing outcomes. There is some evidence to show that a greater level of compliance with regulatory standards may be gained by negotiation, consultation, and compromise between the parties, rather than by stipulating a rule and attempting to enforce it by sanctions.[14]

A second factor in calculating the effectiveness of precise standards

[13] For discussion, see R. M. Titmuss, 'Welfare "Rights," Law and Discretion' (1971) 42 *PolQ* 113; E. Bondach and R. A. Ragan, *Going by the Book: the Problem of Regulatory Unreasonableness* (United States, 1982); A. C. Aman, 'Administrative Equity: an Analysis of Exceptions to Administrative Rules' 1982 *DukeLJ* 277; P. H. Schuck, 'When the Exception Becomes the Rule: Regulatory Equity and the Formulation of Energy Policy Through an Exceptions Process' 1984 *DukeLJ* 163; J. M. Sellers, 'Regulatory Values and the Exceptions Process' (1984) 93 *YLJ* 938.

[14] See Hawkins, *Environment and Enforcement*, pp. 96 ff.

relates to the changes that may occur in an area of continuing decisions, and to the variability of the situations that arise. It is tempting to think of discretion as a space or gap waiting to be filled up with rules; indeed, it is often assumed that, over a course of decisions, standards and policies will emerge so that decision-making naturally progresses towards the adjudicative rule-based model. This is, of course, true to a degree, but two important qualifications should be noted. Firstly, provision must be made for changing circumstances and for changing official attitudes, and these might best be accommodated in an environment of open standards rather than precise rules. Secondly, in areas of complexity, account must be taken of variability. It is mistaken to think that patterns of factual situations will rapidly form, and that all situations will neatly be encompassed. D. J. Gifford has made a sophisticated analysis of the importance of variability, or, as he expresses it, the recurrence of similar situations.[15] Rules and precedents are more effective in circumstances that recur with a high level of similarity. A rule or precedent may be efficacious in influencing the behaviour of those who are likely to be affected adversely by decisions, and in facilitating decision-making by officials. So, to over-simplify Gifford's analysis, decisions which are important and recurring are likely to be highly suitable for determination by general rules and by developing precedents. Now, situations are more or less variable or recurring, so that there is always some degree of over-inclusion and under-inclusion; but the point may be reached where standards of a looser nature than rules, by allowing a degree of flexibility, are more efficacious in achieving goals.

A third factor of substantial importance to the assessment of rules and effectiveness is the relationship between rules and other constraints. We have examined the influences that stem from organizational, political, moral, and economic factors; I have also given some indication of their relationship with normative legal standards. The consequence may be that a rule which is formulated without adequate regard for those factors will be largely disregarded or at least modified; unauthorized discretion then is created, and decision-making may depart substantially from the stipulated rules. This does not mean that normative standards can be effective only subject to those other factors; the relationship is more complex, with the various components interacting, and it is by no means the case that legal rules are inevitably ineffective in controlling other variables. The point is only that those

[15] Gifford, 'Discretionary Decisionmaking'.

factors are important and cannot be ignored; nor can they be removed simply by stipulating a rule. The design of decision procedures must take account of those matters, and it is only by carefully assessing their force that the capacities of normative standards in that context can be assessed.

In considering the other category mentioned above, the suitability of rules for certain tasks, there are two matters of special importance; one concerns the general functional limitations of rules, the other deals with the question of professional and technical expertise. As for the first, J. L. Jowell, in an important study of discretion, has suggested that there are strategic and functional limits to the capacities of standards, particularly rules.[16] Strategic factors have been considered; functional limitations are twofold: the first is where it is not meaningful to refer to a general community consensus, while the second applies where situations cannot be compared with each other, because they are so different, or because they depend on a set of unique or non-recurring circumstances.[17] Jowell illustrates these limitations by considering the concept of 'need' in social welfare legislation,[18] where the distribution of certain welfare benefits depends upon the needs of each applicant. The argument is that beyond certain of the most basic requirements of survival, the variety of personal needs is unlimited, and that there are no clear or agreed community standards for differentiating between them. Any attempt to assign an objective value to particular needs or to rank them according to importance is said to be arbitrary; ideally, then, the assessment of needs should be left to unstructured discretion so that proper provision can be made for each applicant's personal situation. The same argument might be applied to the regulation of a wide range of matters.

When this argument is assessed in terms of net effectiveness in achieving goals, a number of qualifications needs to be made. Since resources are limited, some choices amongst needs have to be made and priorities established. The question is how this is to be decided, and it is not at all clear that the choice should be left to each official to do as he thinks best. It would be more in line with considerations both of effectiveness and accountability that choices about such matters be made at some level of generality, and rendered into standards for the guidance of each official. Secondly, while needs are partly private they are not entirely so, and it may be possible to develop relatively clear

---

[16] J. L. Jowell, 'The Legal Control of Administrative Discretion' 1973 *PL* 178.
[17] Ibid., pp. 204–6.   [18] See Jowell's discussion, ibid., pp. 207 ff.

standards about specific aspects or kinds of needs that would be recognized as essential, according to the values of the society. The decision to cater for personal needs has been taken for a purpose, which is presumably to allow each citizen to have a certain level of physical, psychological, and cultural well-being, so that he or she may share in the life of the society. It may not be too difficult to sacrifice the longings of the erstwhile millionaire for the thrills that only a Rolls-Royce can provide, in favour of a mother's desire to have her children shod. So, although precise standards necessarily curtail the conceptions of need that will be met, the result may be, nevertheless, that the level of achievement is higher than would result from any alternative strategy. Thirdly, this does not mean that a set of criteria should be laid down in advance and applied inexorably in case after case. There are important differences between trying comprehensively to stipulate the needs to be met, and a more incremental approach which deals with new or unforeseen situations as they arise, while at the same time making reference to what has been done in the past, and establishing patterns of guidance for the future. Much can be done to settle standards as to minimum needs, while leaving some residual discretion for dealing with new and special circumstances. Finally, it is not intended to question the general point that there are many matters subject to state regulation which are not suitable for resolution through precise standards. The point is simply that in respect of virtually any matter subject to regulation, there has to be some reconciliation of the urge to achieve a perfect fit between goal and achievement with the need to make choices about the allocation of limited resources, and to decide priorities between conflicting values.

In urging the structuring of discretion through standards, Davis appears to have concentrated on areas of decision-making where the objectives and the means for reaching them are clear enough; police discretions, sentencing decisions, licensing, and the distribution of welfare seemed to fall into that category, and to raise issues of fair and equal treatment that could be managed reasonably well by rules together with occasional exceptions. There are many areas of regulation, however, where the goals may be clear, but the means for achieving them are dependent on evaluations requiring technical or expert knowledge and experience.[19] Those areas may range widely,

---

[19] See the discussion in section 4.2. Other materials of importance are: A. J. Reiss Jr., Book Review of Discretionary Justice (1970) 69 *MichLR* 794; G. E. Frug, 'The Ideology of Bureaucracy in American Law' (1984) 97 *HarvLR* 1276, esp. pp. 1318–33.

from matters obviously requiring scientific or technical skills to those based on the human, social, and psychological sciences. Indeed, some of those matters thought suitable for regulation by rules prove, on closer examination, to involve judgments based implicitly on some theory about human nature or human society. Thus, the need for expert knowledge in wide areas of regulation has been, as we saw in chapter 2, a major factor in the expansion of discretionary authority.

It may seem at first sight that standards have little place in structuring those aspects of discretion which depend on expert knowledge and judgment; the whole point being that each situation requires evaluation according to its peculiar features, and that the evaluation depends on the application of expert knowledge which, by definition, the non-expert does not have. Regulation of discretionary decisions based on expertise may be achieved by checking and confining rather than structuring, and we shall see later how judicial review has gone some way towards developing a basis for external scrutiny. There are, however, two general points to be made about standards in relation to expertise. One relates to the natural tendency to exaggerate both the need for expertise in particular contexts and its existence. A close investigation may show that part at least of what is claimed as expertise is in fact a matter of policy and values; it may also become clear that even where expertise is required, there is still scope for guide-lines. For one thing, areas of claimed expertise differ in their development and complexity; matters of mechanical technology, for example, tend to be more firmly established than areas of social science. Those areas which are more tentative in their methods and conclusions are open to guide-lines governing their use in a way that matters of engineering science may not be. Moreover, it would appear to be the practice in many areas of decision-making by experts that there are extensive guide-lines and accepted conventions as to how issues are to be handled; there may be well-established guide-lines as to how to build a bridge, just as there may be detailed codes of practice about when a child should be taken into care.

The point, then, is not to doubt the importance of expertise, or to underestimate the difficulties in structuring decisions requiring expertise. The argument is only that the claims made for expertise should be examined closely and that there may often be more scope for standards than generally is allowed. Those need not be precise, conclusive rules, but standards of differing levels of specificity which reduce and regulate the arbitrary elements in discretion just in the way K. C. Davis has envisaged.

It must by now be clear that the design and development of decision procedures is a complex undertaking, involving an element of speculation as to how different factors will relate to each other in a given context, and requiring that matters largely incommensurable be weighed against each other. Where the decision to be made is substantially one of policy, then the primary consideration is for a procedure which provides the maximum information and opinion, and which allows a broad representation of interests. Where decisions are more clearly about how to treat a person or his circumstances, and where similar situations are likely to recur, then questions about how specific the standards are to be become highly pertinent. It has been shown that various factors affect that issue, so that no firm conclusion of a general kind can be drawn. If this seems rather lame, then I would go a little further and agree with Davis's general argument that there is a strong, initial case in contexts of individualized, recurring decisions for reasonably clear and settled standards. Imperfect and over-simplifying though they may be, the existence of such standards satisfies important values; it also provides a tangible basis for argument, criticism, and reconsideration in the light of other values and goals, which in particular circumstances may lead to modification of the initial case for settled standards. To conclude, I consider briefly two kinds of circumstances which may be taken as examples of some aspects of the preceding discussion. One is the likelihood that powers will be misused, another relates to the nature of the interests, whether public or private, that are at stake.

4.13   *The risk of misuse*

One claim made for fixed and precise standards is that they reduce arbitrariness, in the sense of officials using their powers for improper ends or according to the wrong factors. The more strictly standards are drawn, the fewer the considerations that are relevant to the decision; so, standards which have the particularity of rules facilitate the scrutiny of decisions and provide a surer basis of accountability. On the other hand, the more indeterminate and unsettled standards are, the wider the spectrum of matters that may be taken into account. There may be less certainty as to the final criteria for decisions, but, by way of compensation, the parties interested in the decision have greater scope for influencing outcomes. Similarly, the official has greater opportunity to be influenced by the considerations put before him, as well as by his own conception of the public interest. This open and incremental approach has various advantages, some of which we have considered; but its very openness creates a risk that decisions may be made according to matters which, if not actually extraneous, are likely to be influenced by considerations other than a concern to achieve the best result in the circumstances. It may also be difficult to maintain even the most basic levels of consistency, either within the decisions of the same authority, or more particularly from one set of officials to another where both are exercising similar powers. Whatever the advantages of an incremental approach, there may in some circumstances be countervailing disadvantages which constitute strong reasons for reasonably precise standards.

One such situation is where the parties have little capacity or opportunity to bring their interests to bear on decision-making, so that one of the principal constraints on incrementalism is absent. There is a risk that those interests will not be considered properly, and that extraneous factors will be taken into account. It is desirable in such circumstances that standards be formulated in advance, leaving some scope only for the unforeseen situation. In this way, the risk of arbitrariness in the particular case can be reduced. A further advantage of settling standards in advance is that the policy issues are resolved in a public manner, allowing for interest groups to advance their arguments. Whereas the individual member of an interest group may have little capacity to influence the particular decision affecting him, the group as a whole may be able to exert influence over the choice of policies at the rule-making stage.

A second situation in which the risk of arbitrariness is high is where powers are exercised by officials whose expertise and training are limited, and whose decisions are unlikely to be reviewed or checked in a systematic way by other officials. In such areas of low-level, but relatively final, discretionary decisions, there is a risk of extraneous matters entering into the decision, either because the matter involves complex considerations, or because it is the type of matter that lends itself to widely different approaches and assessments. Many of the decisions in social welfare provide examples of the first, while numerous instances of the second occur in the criminal justice system. The most rational course in such circumstances may be the stipulation of relatively firm standards.

Firm standards do of course have their own costs: they limit the extent to which the particular case may be dealt with sympathetically, and by forcing decision-making into a uniform pattern they create in their own way a certain degree of arbitrariness. If standards are given the status of strict and inflexible rules, it may be difficult to determine which of the two senses of arbitrariness is greater—the arbitrariness that an absence of standards is likely to create, or the arbitrariness engendered by rules. The choice, however, is not usually so stark, and the potential of each may be exploited to different degrees and in different ways. Parts of the decision can be subject to clear rules while other parts are left for more flexible assessment. For example, it may be desirable in social welfare to have firm rules governing thresholds of entitlement, to have looser standards controlling matters arising over and above those thresholds, and, finally, to leave a largely unconstrained element of assessment to be invoked in the highly unusual case. Similarly, rules may be important in a negative way to prevent certain matters being taken into account, rather than positively requiring what actions are to be taken or what matters are to be considered. For example, various of the low-level discretions in the criminal justice system, such as the power to arrest or to prosecute, might be brought under control to a more acceptable degree by the use of firm but negative rules.

4.14 *The significance of public interests*

Another set of considerations which may affect decision procedures derives from the nature of the interests in issue. C. S. Diver has suggested that while incrementalism is normally a desirable strategy in environments which are relatively unstable because of novelty, technical uncertainty, or changing conditions, a firm stipulation of standards is to be preferred when 'small errors in policy can cause irreversible or even catastrophic harm'.[20] Suggested examples are the regulation of safety in nuclear power plants, carcinogenic substances in food, consumer products, and aspects of the environment and the work place.[21] The argument for precise standards is that in such circumstances the risks in allowing decisions to be made on a more incremental basis are too great, considering the damage that may result from the smallest errors. So in the production of nuclear power there are good grounds for requiring that minimum safety standards be

---

[20] For further discussion see Diver, 'Policymaking Paradigms in Administrative Law', p. 431.
[21] Ibid.

formulated on the basis of the knowledge and expertise that is available, and then rigorously enforced. The costs of safety are likely to be very high, but they are the conditions that must be met if nuclear power is to be produced at all. In other, less striking areas, such as consumer products, there is likely to be more room for balancing the costs of safety against the value of the product, and, accordingly, there may be scope for incremental procedures.[22]

4.15   *The significance of private interests*

Considerations of private interests may also bear on decision procedures. Here the argument is that some personal interests are so important that they should be surrounded and protected by stable and precise standards. The claim has a negative and a positive side: negative in the sense of protecting private interests in the face of official interference; positive in the sense that fulfilment of an interest depends on official action. The point is that because of the importance of the interests at stake, stability in the sense of certainty and predictability is of such importance that firm and precise standards ought to be laid down and followed, even if this has costs in terms of reduced margins of effectiveness. The difficulty is to identify the interests that warrant the special protection provided by precise standards. Any selection is bound to be to some extent a matter of personal preference, taking its support partly from the values of the particular society, for instance those of social democracy, and partly from normative political theory, for instance the theory that may be offered in defence of a social democracy. The following is one possible approach which derives support from both sources, the main point being, however, not whether everyone would agree that those interests are in fact the most significant, but rather to demonstrate the relations between important interests and decision procedures. Let it be assumed, then, that the most basic interests are personal liberty, especially freedom from bodily constraint, and threshold levels of welfare.

With regard to the first of these, the argument is that in areas where official powers may be directed towards control over one's person, matters typically within the criminal justice and penal system, there is a good case for clear and certain standards. The negative sense of liberty

---

[22] See further: J. Yellin, 'High Technology and the Courts: Nuclear Power and the Need for Institutional Reform' (1981) 94 *HarvLR* 489; R. R. Merrill, 'Regulating Carcinogens in Food' (1978) 77 *MichLR* 171.

at stake is one of the liberties traditionally claimed as vital to personal autonomy; on that basis, there is a strong case for standards stipulating with precision the circumstances under which there may be official interference with personal liberty. Other liberties, such as those associated with free speech, are more likely to require balancing against each other, and against other values and notions of public interest, and are regulated in many circumstances more suitably by standards of a looser kind. But where the object of official power is the direct constraint of one's person, there is an interest of great immediacy in having the nature and scope of official interference specified with precision.

Welfare refers to those attributes of personal need the satisfaction of which is a necessary condition of a tolerable existence; it includes social welfare, the capacity to earn one's living, and threshold entitlements to property. In each case, the individual's interests are sufficiently important to be guaranteed and protected by firm standards. This is not directly an argument for substantive rights to welfare; its claims are only that, if welfare is to be provided by the state, then there is a case for the basic requirements being allocated according to firm standards. Above minimum thresholds, there may be scope for adjustments of an incremental kind. The same argument applies to the capacity to earn one's livelihood; the practice of trades and professions is often dependent on the initial issue of a licence, and its renewal from time to time in a way which is discretionary. Leaving aside questions as to the extent that regulation in such areas is justified, there are good reasons for having fairly precise criteria for the grant of licences. Similar arguments apply in respect of goods such as shelter, food, clothing, and minimum items of an educational and cultural kind. Again, this is not an argument for private property as such, but for the protection of certain attributes that might normally accompany property, such as security of housing.

The claim is that, whenever there are relevant official powers, these interests are too important to be left to piecemeal, incremental appraisal, but should be protected by clear standards. This can sometimes be justified as the most effective way of achieving desired objects; so it has been claimed in recent years that welfare is best guaranteed through rules rather than left on a more discretionary basis. It is often the case, however, that such a synoptic approach in fact reduces the level of effectiveness. In licensing, the advantages to those seeking or holding licences of having the criteria laid down with particularity may be in conflict with the advantages of being able to deny, revoke, or fail to renew a licence for reasons pertaining to the public interest, where those reasons are not defined easily with precision. Assuming that precise standards do result in net losses in the effectiveness of licensing systems, those losses must be justified in terms of other values—here, the gains in guaranteed levels of welfare without the risk of discretionary reduction; in cases of police powers, the gain in security of personal liberty.

The difficulty is to find any basis on which these conflicting factors can be compared and assessed. If it could be claimed that those applying for licences to pursue such activities have rights that the conditions be clear and precise, then that would be sufficient to warrant some consequential loss to the general community interest in effective licensing systems. But we have seen how rights have been pushed from the centre of the stage in the public law model; and although the scope for rights in this context is examined later in this chapter, there are difficulties in establishing claims to rights, and in any event some calculation still has to be made as to the relative importance of the right, compared with the relative importance of the public interest. But apart from claims of right, another approach is to assess the relative importance attached to those welfare interests within the political theory of the society. That level of importance can then be made commensurable with the relative importance of marginal gains in licensing control. So, unless there is substantial gain in effective licensing by maintaining open and unstructured discretion, the importance of the interest in being able to practice a profession warrants the formulation of firm standards. The calculation may not be easy to make, but it is suggested in chapter 7, where the point is considered again, that it is in principle possible; and the fact that such basic welfare interests are in issue might be taken to indicate that they carry substantial weight in any such calculation. Again, it is not necessary to make a simple choice between settled standards and no standards, and, by careful design of decision procedures, it may be possible to achieve high levels of licensing effectiveness, as well as satisfying welfare requirements.

To conclude, an attempt has been made in this section to consider the difficulties that occur and the variables that must be accommodated in designing decision procedures, and, in particular, in achieving the best balance of discretion. The fact that the most suitable balance has to be worked out in each specific context does not mean that the process need be haphazard or impervious to rational scrutiny. The argument suggested here is that the primary criterion in settling procedures is net effectiveness in achieving objects, subject to side-constraints like stability and fairness. Around this central concern, complex calculations have to be made both in balancing conflicting factors against each other, and in speculating on the effects which different directions might have; it is also necessary to have a view about the relative importance of different interests. But the design of institutions and procedures is not a purely technical matter; like any area of social activity, it involves decisions about values and assessments of consequences. Once this is accepted, questions about the right balance of discretion lose much of their mystery.

4.2   RIGHTS AND DISCRETIONARY POWERS

To an age which has invested much faith in the notion of rights, it is not surprising to find efforts being made to demonstrate the potential capacities of rights as a way of replacing or restricting discretionary powers. We have seen how within the public law model of authority, traditional ideas of rights have been pushed aside to make way for considerations both of welfare and public order; the question now is whether rights may reappear, perhaps in slightly different guise, as a useful way of mediating relations between the citizen and the state. In suggesting some answers to this question, a number of matters are to be considered: the background to the modern interest in rights, the basis of rights, the functions which they would have in the modern state, and the appropriateness of rights in the context of discretionary powers.[23]

4.21   *The background to rights*

The great interest in rights must be seen as part of a widespread revival of interest in political theory, and, particularly, in providing justifications for the political and economic ordering of society. Discussion of rights forms one part of this wider concern, the assumption being that the concept of rights may be the key to understanding and shaping relationships amongst the members of society, and between individuals and the state. Within rights theories, there is considerable variation both as to their theoretical basis, the consequences that follow from

[23] Generally, see I. Markovits, 'Socialist vs Bourgeois Rights' (1978) 45 *UChicLR* 612.

rights, and the substantive rights that we have or ought to have.[24] If there is any unifying theme, it is perhaps a common dissatisfaction with utilitarianism; at a theoretical level utilitarianism appears to take inadequate account of the status and autonomy of individuals, while at a practical level it seems to justify some of the unacceptable practices that occur within welfare systems.[25]

Those matters have special significance in the context of modern state regulation and discretionary powers. The expanded role of the state in so many areas—social welfare, planning, taxation, franchise, public order, and licensing—means that individuals are dependent in a great range of their activities on official action or approval. It has been said that individual wealth in the modern state depends upon one's relationship to government, and that all live to a greater or lesser extent on government largess.[26] It might be added that it is not only wealth that is determined in this manner, but also personal liberties, achievements, and satisfaction. However, it is not the accumulation of wealth and power in the state that is itself the problem, but that the dispensing of wealth and the deployment of power occurs through the discretionary actions of state officials. The reasons why this has occurred need not be repeated; the upshot is that the modern state, through the decisions of its officials, often is concerned to pursue objects based on notions of public interest, and that while the interests of individuals are important factors to consider, they are not the only ones. There are various ways by which the actions of officials may be regulated through political and legal controls; the question is whether a notion of rights may add to them in a significant way.

One approach, which appears in recent years to have been gaining ground, argues that there is a fundamental incompatibility between private rights and the welfare, social-engineering activities of the modern state. The solution, on this view, which we have already

---

[24] A selection of contemporary works of interest is: Dworkin, *Taking Rights Seriously*; Richard Flathman, *The Practice of Rights* (Cambridge UP, 1976); R. G. Frey, *Interests and Rights* (Oxford UP, 1980); Joel Feinberg, *Social Philosophy* (New Jersey, 1973); A. R. White, *Rights* (Oxford UP, 1984); J. Waldron (ed.), *Theories of Rights* (Oxford UP, 1984); J. Raz, 'On the Nature of Rights' (1984) xciii *Mind* 194 and 'Legal Rights' (1984) 4 *OJLS*.

[25] See further: Rawls, *A Theory of Justice*; Dworkin, *Taking Rights Seriously*, ch. iv; H. L. A. Hart, 'Between Utility and Rights' in *Essays in Philosophy and Jurisprudence* (Oxford UP, 1983).

[26] Charles Reich, 'The New Property' (1964) 73 *YLJ* 733 and 'Individual Rights and Social Welfare: the Emerging Legal Issues' (1965) 74 *YLJ* 1245.

encountered in the writings of F. A. Hayek,[27] is to curtail and confine the activities of the state to basic matters of order and the adjudication of private disputes. The objectives of social justice are seen as illusory, and the employment of officials and resources to such ends leads inevitably to a transgression of individual rights and liberties. Arguments of this kind, which have been given a firmer basis in recent years,[28] invoke rights as a basis for rejecting the economic and social regulation commonly practised by the modern state. Such arguments usually are joined with a belief that greater trust should be placed in market forces, which would result in general welfare being enhanced and problems of social order alleviated. We need not go into these claims, each of which is contestable; we may proceed rather on the basis, noted earlier, that the state is likely to continue its regulatory and welfare activities so that the place of rights within it remains an important issue.

4.22 The basis of rights against the state

In the relationship between the citizen and the state within the public law model, rights may be relevant in a number of ways. They may be a procedural kind, requiring that certain procedures be followed in making decisions that affect one's interests in substantive ways; here the right is not to any specific outcome but to the procedures for achieving outcomes. Rights in this sense are considered in section 4.24. Rights may also be of a substantive kind, which in turn may operate in two ways; one requiring officials to take certain actions or to provide certain goods or services, the other preventing certain actions being taken. The first and more positive task occurs in a variety of situations, which includes claims to welfare, but which may extend beyond welfare to such matters as the grant of a licence in one or other of its many forms, thus enabling the pursuit of activities which otherwise would be prohibited. In the second and more negative sense, rights may prevent officials from acting contrary to certain of one's interests, for example to resist a sentence of imprisonment being increased for reasons of social protection, or to prevent the requisition of one's house to make way for a road. Rights in both roles exhibit common properties, but a further word needs to be said about rights in the more positive sense.

---

[27] *The Constitution of Liberty.*
[28] The most important work is Robert Nozick, *Anarchy, State and Utopia* (Oxford, 1974).

What positive legal rights one has against the state depends upon the laws of the particular society. We may take a legal right in its clearest sense to be an interest 'protected or furthered by the existence or non-existence of a rule, law or understanding requiring action or inaction in ways which are designed to have a bearing on the right-holder; obligations, under those rules, are owed to the right-holder because they are obligations to further or protect [his] interests.'[29] There is considerable debate as to whether this 'interest theory' approach adequately captures the standard case of a right; we need not enter into that debate here, except to note that the concept of right, as expressed above, constitutes a useful and commonly adopted way of showing the special protections given by law to particular personal interests. Rights in respect of an interest demonstrate that that interest is considered within a given legal system to be sufficiently important to warrant special protections. The reasons for such recognition depend on some more basic legal and perhaps political principles. But once the special importance of an interest has been recognized, the basis is established for providing the necessary legal protection. As Joseph Raz has written, rights are grounds for duties; they are 'intermediate conclusions in arguments from ultimate values to duties'.[30] At a practical level, the legal recognition and protection of such an interest is likely to be effected by a mixture of Hohfeldian claim-rights, duties, privileges, no-rights, powers and liabilities, immunities and disabilities with respect to the claim, waiver, and enforcement of the right.[31] Normally, but not invariably, the person whose interests are protected by the right enjoys some control over those processes of claim, waiver, and enforcement.[32]

There is no difficulty in general in fitting into this conception of rights a citizen's rights against the state, or its officials or instrumentalities. The law may and often does create legal rights to welfare in its various forms; these may include rights to social welfare, to medical

[29] Tom Campbell, *The Left and Rights* (London, 1983), p. 92. For the interest theory of rights, see: Neil MacCormick, 'Rights in Legislation' in A. W. B. Simpson (ed.), *Oxford Essays in Jurisprudence* (Oxford UP, 1973); Tom Campbell, 'The Socialist Concept of Rights' (1982) 23 *BASLP* 82. Compare H. L. A. Hart, 'Bentham on Rights' in Simpson, *Oxford Essays in Jurisprudence*.

[30] 'On the Nature of Rights' (1984) xciii *Mind* 208.

[31] For an approach along those lines to welfare rights, see Carl Wellman, *Welfare Rights* (New York, 1982), esp. ch. 1.

[32] For discussion of the relationship between the interest and will theories of rights, see MacCormick, 'Rights in Legislation'. For an excellent discussion of rights generally, see Finnis, *Natural Law and Natural Rights*, ch. viii.

care, and to educational facilities. Similarly, there may be legal rights to the less tangible but nevertheless important personal liberties, such as freedom from bodily constraint and freedom of speech and association. But, while it is common for modern legal systems to provide rights to welfare—using welfare in the broad sense of basic needs—concern has been expressed at the very idea of rights to welfare. There have been two stumbling blocks; one is the suggestion of conceptual incoherence in rights to welfare, the other is the difficulty to providing the justification for such rights. The first claim has little substance; there is no difficulty in giving interests in welfare the status of rights, as indeed often occurs in modern legal systems.[33] As for the second, the case for rights to welfare usually begins with those fundamental interests, often put in terms of needs, or course-of-life needs, which must be satisfied as conditions necessary to a tolerable existence. These include needs of the kind listed in the previous section, such as food, clothing, shelter, educational and cultural opportunities, and perhaps certain attributes of property.[34] What is included is to some extent to be determined according to the possibilities offered within particular societies; it also depends on the arguments used to justify giving certain interests the special status of rights.

Attempts at justification for particular rights to welfare may take various courses. The principle of equal concern and respect might appear to be a powerful principle, although according to one of its main exponents, R. M. Dworkin, it does not yield welfare rights but requires only that each individual's interests be considered in allocating resources.[35] Arguments from utility, or from theories of justice or other ethical principles, may provide the moral basis for rights to welfare, although each does encounter difficulties which have not yet been resolved entirely satisfactorily.[36] The enquiry into the foundation of welfare rights is far from complete, but finally it may be necessary to appeal to a view of society not just as a collection of possessive, competing individuals, but also as a co-operative endeavour

---

[33] See Wellman, *Welfare Rights*, pp. 31–41, and R. Plant, H. Lesser and P. Taylor-Goodby, *Political Philosophy and Social Welfare* (London, 1980) esp. ch. 4.

[34] See Campbell, *The Left and Rights*, pp. 132 ff.; F. Michelman, 'Welfare Rights in a Constitutional Democracy' (1979) *WashULQ* 659 and 'Process and Property in Constitutional Theory' (1981) 30 *ClevStLR* 577.

[35] *Taking Rights Seriously*, ch. iv and 'Principle, Policy, Procedure' in C. F. H. Tapper (ed.), *Crime, Proof and Punishment* (London, 1981).

[36] For extensive discussion, see Wellman, *Welfare Rights*.

concerned to advance certain goods and values. The case for guaranteeing certain levels of welfare to those members of the society in need may then be made, partly in order to enable them to join in the common enterprise, as well as engage in private pursuits, and partly on the grounds that each is entitled to some share in the fruits of the common enterprise. Just what that share is, or, in other words, how exacting rights to welfare are, may vary from one society to another.

4.23 *Substantive rights and discretionary powers*

Accepting that there is a sound moral basis for welfare in the sense of sharing in the communal wealth, and that this is likely to require positive action by the state, the issue then is the most appropriate legal means for doing so.[37] C. B. Macpherson has drawn an analogy between rights to share in the common wealth, and rights in private property which traditionally have enjoyed a special kind of legal protection.[38] His arguments, based on a principle of equality, urge that such rights to welfare ought to be given the legal status of private property rights. Charles Reich, in suggesting that individuals have claims to shares in government largess, has made similar claims.[39] There is some controversy as to what exactly are the special characteristics of property rights,[40] but it is sufficient for our purposes, without entering that issue, to note the general approach within which those claims occur. That approach has two features: that important aspects of the relationship between the citizen and the state ought to be expressed in terms of individual rights, and that rights can be protected only by a certain type of legal authority. The basis for the first part of the claim is that the concept of rights gives a special status to personal interests in welfare, and carries with it correlative obligations on officials to further those interests. The second part of the claim suggests that those obligations ought to be specified in legal rules rather than left to the discretion of officials. It is the second aspect that

[37] See C. B. Macpherson, 'Capitalism and the Changing Concept of Property' in E. Kamenka and Neale (eds.), *Feudalism, Capitalism and Beyond* (London, 1975) and 'The Meaning of Property' in C. B. Macpherson (ed.), *Property* (Oxford, 1978); Michelman, 'Welfare Rights in a Constitutional Democracy' and 'Process and Property in Constitutional Theory'; Charles Reich, 'The New Property'. Also: M. MacNeil, 'Property in the Welfare State' (1984) 7 *DalLR* 343.
[38] 'Capitalism and the Changing Concept of Property'.
[39] 'The New Property'.
[40] See Ronald Sackville, 'Property Rights and Social Security' (1973–8) 2 *UNSWLR* 246; Michael Crommelin, 'Economic Analysis of Property' in Galligan, *Essays in Legal Theory*.

is of particular interest, since it requires consideration of the relationship between rights in the sense of positive claims to goods, advantages, or welfare, and discretionary authority.

At first sight there may seem to be an incompatibility between individual rights and discretionary powers that is both deep and unbridgeable. If rights are taken in the sense of benefits or advantages legally defined and guaranteed to individuals, then it would seem necessary that there be clear rules stipulating the nature and extent of the rights, together with the necessary legal institutions for their enforcement. Discretionary powers might be seen, correspondingly, to be directed towards social goals which extend over and beyond, and which are potentially in conflict with the interests of individuals. It might seem, therefore, that rights require a normative structure based around clear and conclusive rules conferring benefits on individuals, while the regulatory functions of the state, concerned as they are with achieving through discretionary powers varied concepts of the public interest, require a framework which has no space for personal rights.

In order to test the apparent incompatibility between rights and discretion, a distinction must be made between two ways in which discretion can operate: sometimes discretion is directed towards objects which include, but extend beyond, consideration of the individual interests that might be affected; in other cases the objects of discretion may be the realization of an individual interest. In the first case, the public interest includes but is not exhausted by consideration of private interests, while in the second case the public interest consists in giving effect to a private interest. An example of the first is the licensing of public houses; whether a licence is granted depends on consideration of a number of social goals; these may include not only a concern to provide the community with adequate amenities, but also to ensure that public order is not endangered by over-supply, and even, perhaps, that the activity remains reasonably remunerative for licensees. In maintaining such concerns with the public interest, the licensing authority must have a degree of discretion in dealing with each application; standards may emerge as to what constitutes the public interest, subject to discretion to modify or depart from them when the public interest so requires. The considerations that count are not just those pertaining to the merits of the applicant, but include matters of a quite independent kind. In such cases, there is a clear incompatibility between a notion of rights and discretion, since any claim of rights is defeasible for reasons of public interest.

In the second situation, discretion operates differently. Its object is to determine how or the extent to which a personal interest is to be advanced or satisfied. An example might be a claim to social security; once certain conditions are satisfied, there is a right to some benefits, the only question for discretion being how much. In addition to the restraints that stem from limited resources, considerations of public interest may enter into the determination of amount, but not as reasons for defeating the claim. The concept of rights is at home in this context, and may be a forceful reminder to officials that their task is to give meaning and specificity to individual interests, not to consider what course of action might best be taken in the public interest. This can be made clearer by specifying the notion of rights being used: A (the citizen) has a right to X against S (the state), if S has a legal duty to give or make available X to A.[41] Two questions arise; whether S has such a duty and what is included within X. Whether or not the duty exists depends on interpretation of the relevant legal materials; if there is a power but no duty, then S has discretion whether or not to make X available and A has no right. But there may be a duty with respect to X, even though there is some discretion in determining the content or extent of X; in that case, A has a right to X, subject to the official's discretion in that sense. There may be that kind of discretion because the standards defining X have to be interpreted, or because it is desirable to leave the specification of X to be settled in the circumstances of each case.

Rights and discretion in this situation are compatible, and are a common feature of welfare systems. The needs of individuals and the forms of poverty are infinitely variable; if those needs are to be met and poverty alleviated, it is necessary to allow a degree of discretion in the treatment of particular cases. A well-known debate occurred in Britain in the earlier years of the welfare state as to whether poverty relief ought to be based on clear rules or left to official discretion. R. M. Titmuss, who had great influence on the development of the British system, contended that while certain types and levels of benefit should be protected by precise rules creating entitlements, it was necessary, in addition, to allow considerable discretion so that officials would have the freedom to deal with individual needs as they arose, without the

---

[41] This is a claim right in Hohfeldian terms; see W. N. Hohfeld, *Fundamental Legal Conceptions as Applied in Judicial Reasoning* (Yale UP, 1919). For discussion of Hohfeld in the context of welfare rights, see Wellman, *Welfare Rights*, ch. 1.

restrictions that rules impose.[42] Rules and lawyers, he argued, breed a pathology of legalism, an insistence on strict application of the rules without regard for either the special features of the case in hand, or the 'rapidly changing human needs and circumstances'. Far from being opposed to welfare rights, Titmuss was deeply committed to the notion; but he could see that a strict, rule-based stipulation of rights, although having many virtues, was not the most effective way of relieving poverty. On this view, some rights would on balance be better advanced by official discretion than by strict rules, formal procedures, and adjudication.[43]

In practice, it has proved difficult to implement a discretionary system, and the tendency in recent years has been to simplify matters by providing clearer rules as to the thresholds of entitlement.[44] The important point is, however, that the debate was not between having rights to welfare and having welfare depend entirely on discretionary decisions; the issue was whether rights to welfare were protected more effectively by a rule-based system or one that left some discretion to officials.

The difficulties in settling the most effective strategies of decision-making, of weighing up the advantages and disadvantages, have been considered. The most effective strategy in giving effect to welfare rights depends on some such calculation. Some emphasis may be put on discretion, not in order to allow deliberation as to whether or not there is a right, but rather to work out the meaning and content of a recognized right. That decision may depend upon various factors, such as the particular circumstances, the amount of resources available, and the potential claims of others to a similar right; but these matters affect the content of the right, not its existence. The point of characterizing such situations in terms of rights is to give a particular emphasis and orientation to the reasoning process by making clear the object of any discretionary element, and thereby excluding from consideration matters which are not relevant to it. Understood, in this sense, discretion is not only compatible with the existence of rights, but may be an essential component in working out their meaning and content, and thereby giving them full effect.

---

[42] Titmuss, 'Welfare "Rights", Law and Discretion' and *Essays on the Welfare State* (London, 3rd edn., 1976). See also T. H. Marshall, *The Right to Welfare* (London, 1981), esp. ch. 5.

[43] 'Welfare "Rights", Law and Discretion'.

[44] For discussion, see David Donnison, *The Politics of Poverty* (London, 1982).

There may be, nevertheless, difficulties in making rights dependent upon discretionary assessments. Naturally, the more abstract and indeterminate are the standards which govern its content, the more discretionary the right becomes; one consequence is that the scope for extraneous matters entering into the official's calculations is widened, and the difficulties of independent and objective scrutiny compounded. In that event, the grant of a benefit may in practice become dependent on satisfying conditions which serve extraneous social goals. Another, related consequence is that as the discretionary element widens, the value of the right is reduced; there may even come a point where its content is so dependent on discretionary assessments that the very coinage of rights is debased. Part of the point of a right is, after all, to mark out and protect a specific interest; if the boundaries as to the scope of the protection are so unclear and changeable, then much of that point is lost.

There are a number of factors to consider in determining the most effective way of giving effect to 'discretionary rights'.[45] The desire to decide each case in the way that achieves optimum realization of objects may have to be compromised, in order to reduce the opportunities for considering extraneous matters, and to give a hard and permanent core to specific rights. It is also important to insist that officials be able to justify their decisions, and in doing so to point to recognizable purposes and standards, and to show that the matters relied on are justified within them. Moreover, an important insight in R. M. Dworkin's writing is that rights may derive from a normative basis of principles that are more abstract and indeterminate than rules; this suggests a particular method of reasoning in extrapolating and developing the content of those rights. Constraints of those kinds may, of course, remain rather nebulous and easily satisfied; but the point to be urged is that it is possible to extend and develop those constraints within discretionary contexts, especially when rights are at issue.

So far we have been concerned with the relationship between rights and discretion, and with the general utility of the concept of rights in discretionary contexts. Accepting the importance of rights in such areas, the final issue is whether a discretionary power is to be

---

[45] Tom Campbell has used this expression to refer to positive rights of the kind we are discussing. See his 'Discretionary "Rights"' in N. Timms and D. Watson (eds.), *Philosophy in Social Work* (London, 1978). Campbell distinguishes three senses of discretionary rights according to the extent to which the specific content of rights depends on discretionary assessments.

construed in terms of rights; in other words, how is an official to know whether he is dealing with rights. Here we may suggest two different ways that officials might regard a grant of discretion. One would be that, in the absence of clear directions to the contrary, a grant of discretion involves, unavoidably, considerations of public policy wider than and possibly in conflict with individual interests, and therefore with any notion of rights. To put the point slightly differently, the conscientious official concerned to formulate a legal and political theory which would explain and justify the vesting of discretionary powers in officials, might conclude that his primary duty is to keep a roving eye on the general public interest and to exercise his powers accordingly. The parole authority, for example, might see itself as a surrogate legislator, charged with the task of advancing, through ways that appear opportune from time to time, the public interest in the general reduction of crime. Its decisions might seek both to reflect public opinion, and in other ways to lead it, as ideas about crime and imprisonment change. Accountability lies to the executive and the legislature, and, should the board's views become unacceptable, those authorities have the power to intervene.[46]

On an alternative view, the official concerned to explain and justify his powers might conclude, first, that discretionary powers often are dispensed somewhat impulsively and haphazardly, and that political accountability is an inadequate source of guidance and constraint. He might consider that a justificatory theory needs to be developed along these lines: with respect to any power, he must consider its terms, seek out its purposes, and settle the standards of decision-making. But since the terms of power might be equivocal and the purposes unclear, he may need to refer to wider considerations, in particular the more basic values and principles which the society has adopted, and the nature of the institutions which it has created. By reflective consideration, or what might be called rational reconstruction,[47] of the terms of his powers on the one hand, and these wider considerations on the other hand, he should arrive at a clearer understanding of purposes, and be able to settle with more confidence the general standards to guide his

[46] This is in general the approach taken by the Parole Board; see its annual reports and the Home Office, *Review of Parole in England and Wales* (London, 1981). For recent expressions of judicial attitudes to parole, see *Payne* v. *Harris* [1981] 1 WLR 759, and *In re Findlay* [1984] 3 WLR 1159.

[47] The expression derives from P. Nonet, 'Taking Purpose Seriously' in Gray Dorsey (ed.), *Proceedings of the International Conference of Legal and Social Philosophy* (St. Louis, 1976).

decisions. Some powers might require a continual concern with notions of public interest; others, however, might seem to be concerned primarily with the interests of individuals, and to leave little room for countervailing public policy concerns. Here the notion of rights reappears; our reflective official might conclude that in some cases the object of discretion is to confer rights on individuals; accordingly, the only matters to be taken into account are those directed to working out the scope and content of the rights. He might reach this conclusion by recognizing that important personal interests are at stake, that the legislative purpose demonstrates a sufficient concern that those interests be protected, and that there are, therefore, grounds for duties on the official to provide the protection. In the case of the prisoner seeking parole, for example, the penal authority might conclude that the legislative purpose, interpreted in the context of society's principles about punishment and personal liberty, is that offenders have a right to parole once certain conditions have been met, and that further considerations of public policy should not be allowed to trump that right.[48]

There is no reason in principle why officials should not approach their powers in this way; indeed, it is difficult to see how any other approach could be justified, once it is accepted that all officials must seek out the rational and purposive basis of their powers. As a matter of practicalities, however, such an arrangement provides at best an insecure foundation for rights; if rights are to be taken seriously, they should be given more precise and unequivocal legal protection, rather than be left to the discretion of administrative officials. But if powers continue to be conferred on officials in a somewhat haphazard way, then it is important to have some view as to how officials ought to approach the exercise of those powers, and such a view should include consideration of rights.

The main difficulty, perhaps, is in seeing what is gained by concern with rights in discretionary contexts. In the parole example, any conclusion that rights are at issue follows from the interpretation of purposes; similarly, the justification for taking some matters into

---

[48] An analogy may be drawn with a judge's sentencing discretion; in a recent decision the High Court of Australia in reviewing a sentencing decision held that an estimate of the offender's future dangerousness to the community was not a proper consideration in fixing the sentence *R*. v. *Veen* (1979) 53 ALJR 305. For commentary, see R. Tomasic, 'Preventative Detention and the High Court' (1981) 55 *ALJ* 259. By contrast, the attitudes of British officials and courts to parole is contrary to any suggestion that the prisoner may have rights; see the material referred to in note 46.

account rather than others also depends on construing purposes. So it is considerations of purpose that justify any conclusion by the parole board that the point of parole is to give the prisoner, upon satisfaction of certain conditions, the opportunity of early release, and that it should not be denied for reasons related to the broader public interest, such as the general deterrent effect on others, or the reduction of crime. There is force in this argument, and it may be that the same conclusions will be reached in exercising discretion, whether or not the notion of rights is employed.

The argument for rights is, however, still of importance. The point is that the purposes of discretionary powers are often unclear, dependent on reconstruction rather than deduction. It may be necessary then to reach into background considerations from which it is concluded that the interpretation of a power is for the benefit of particular individuals. In this way, background factors in the relationship between citizen and state may show that rights are at issue; this conclusion will in turn shape the way more specific issues of interpretation are settled. On the Dworkinian view of rights, once the conclusion is reached that rights are at issue in this sense, important consequences follow: a right is an individuated political goal which should not in general be defeated or undermined by other general and competing social goals. The official would be concerned to work out the nature and content of the right according to the considerations of principle upon which it is based, to the exclusion of matters of policy. In our parole example, the object would be to develop the right to early release in terms of its supporting principles, but being careful to exclude considerations of wider social goals, since these have already been taken into account in the decision to create rights. If, on the other hand, the official does not finally accept Dworkin's distinction between rights-based arguments of principle and goal-based arguments of policy, he might nevertheless find that the emphasis upon rights, based in turn on the primacy of certain individual benefits, simply helps him to understand more clearly the considerations that are appropriate in exercising his powers.

4.24 *Discretionary powers and rights to process*

Earlier in this discussion, a distinction was made between rights in the sense of positive claims to benefits, and rights in the sense of interests that are protected against official interference. We must now consider the relationship between discretionary authority and rights in this second sense; this will lead in turn to consideration of procedural rights. It is a common characteristic of discretionary authority that in order to realize the objects of power it may be necessary to infringe, curtail, or defeat interests which hitherto had the status of private rights. In order to build a new road or to site an asylum for the mentally handicapped, it may be necessary to transgress private rights; rights to land may be defeated by an order for requisition, and rights to privacy or quiet enjoyment, which otherwise would be protected by the law of nuisance, may have to be curtailed. An important issue in the early years of increased state regulation was whether a grant of discretionary authority had to be interpreted subject to private rights; when such questions arose, the courts clearly had little choice if the objects of regulation were not to be defeated, but to accept that, subject to certain refinements, private rights must give way. In terms of our two models of authority, the image created is of a system of private rights and duties upon which is superimposed a system of discretionary authority which, to the extent necessary for the achievement of its objectives, predominates. The effects on private rights might be a relevant matter to take into account, but if considerations of public interest so required, private rights must be relinquished.

The question is whether the fact that private rights are in issue in this way has any significance for the manner in which discretionary powers are exercised. There are close similarities between this and the situation, noted in the previous section, where positive claims are made for conferring on individuals benefits, which are dependent upon considerations of public interest. Whether or not a licence to carry on a trade or profession is granted may be subject to considerations of public policy, such as public order or economic efficiency, which are independent of the merits of any particular application. Similarly, sentencing and parole decisions may be concerned, partly at least, in serving certain broad public policies quite apart from the merits of the particular case.

In both cases, whether in seeking to restrain discretionary actions because private rights or interests are affected, or in influencing their outcome in order to enhance private interests, no claim may be laid to any specific outcome since the decision must be made which appears best to serve the public interest, as expressed in the objects of power. The only claim is of a lower order, namely that, because of the importance of the interests at stake, certain methods and procedures ought to be followed in deciding what action to take. The claim, in other words, is not about outcomes but the processes for achieving outcomes. The issue, then, is whether the notion of rights might be employed, not in order to secure substantive benefits against the exercise of discretionary powers, but in order to regulate the way in which advantages are conferred or withdrawn.[49] The publican, the landowner, and the prisoner may not be able to secure substantive entitlements against discretionary intervention, but they might claim rights as to the methods and procedures used in determining whether the licence is to be granted or renewed, the land requisitioned, or early release ordered.

The basis upon which any claim of rights might be founded is that each person, in addition to his interest in securing outcomes advantageous to him, has an interest in ensuring that his claims be considered and taken into account when courses of action are being determined; it might be added that this is best achieved by certain forms of participatory procedures. It might be argued further that this interest is so important in discretionary systems, where decisions are made affecting substantive private interests, that it ought to have the status of a right. The justification for such a claim has to be sought in terms of the relationship between individuals and the state; this requires as a minimum that proper consideration be given to the effects on private interests when a course of action is proposed in the public interest. This leaves open more detailed questions, to be taken up in chapter 7, as to what it means to take a person's interests into account, what level of consideration is required, what procedures are necessary, and the place of notions of representation and participation. The claim of a right to consideration may be supported by appeal to the normative principles underlying the welfare state: while action may justifiably be taken curtailing a person's private interests or denying him benefits in order to advance the interests of society as a whole, or of particular groups within it, each person must still be accorded a minimum level of consideration. Connections can be drawn between this principle and those values which earlier were suggested as guides in the legal regulation of discretion—reasoned decisions, basic stability in legal relations, and procedural fairness. Part of the justification for those values is that, in the relations between the citizen and the state, they constitute the bare minimum of constraints on official action, if

[49] Much of Charles Reich's discussion is concerned with rights in this sense, see 'The New Property'. For further general discussion of the issue, see H. W. Jones, 'The Rule of Law and the Welfare State' (1958) 58 *ColLR* 143.

individuals are to be treated fairly and in recognition of their particular circumstances. The interest that each individual has in maintaining such constraints might well be expressed in terms of rights to process.

Again, however, the point might be raised as to what is gained by expressing notions of process or procedure in terms of rights. The answer is similar to that already given: rights emphasize that important individual interests are at stake, and that they should not be prejudiced without proper consideration. So, although the outcomes of decisions may mean that one's substantive interests are disadvantaged, and although the decision to prefer one set of interests over another may be left to official discretion, the decision must show that all relevant matters have been considered, and that there are reasons, intelligible and reasonable, for the preferences that have been made. The prisoner may not have a right to early release, but he may claim that he has a right that his unquestionable interest in early release be considered.

There are two final points to be noted. It might be objected that such a right is of such little value as to be virtually worthless, since it does not guarantee any outcome, nor necessarily even have any influence on outcomes. Without exaggerating the importance of good processes, the answer to be made is that rights to process may help to engender more carefully considered decisions and to raise the rational basis of discretionary actions. That is of undoubted worth. The second point is that notions of process become unavoidably merged with substantive issues, so that what is claimed as process may often be a claim of a clearly substantive kind. Consider the prisoner seeking parole: once the claim is made that his interests in liberty are to be taken into account, it is only a short step to claiming that those interests are so important to him that they should not be defeated by just any countervailing public interest. Similarly, the publican and the taxi-driver might claim that their interests in continuing to hold their licences can be defeated only by certain kinds of public interests. In order to resolve such claims, it is necessary to develop some system of ranking of interests, and while that is a matter of substance and the very issue that has been entrusted to the official's discretion, process rights may enhance the rational and critical basis upon which it is determined.

It may further be objected that there is no clear division between process and substance, and that process can be extended to include matters of substance. In a sense this is true, but it is worth considering how the relationship between the two might be developed. One of the main issues in discretionary decisions, where different interests and values have to be weighed and set against each other, is in identifying an objective basis for making such assessments. This is primarily a matter for the official exercising discretion, and at first there may be little evidence of a consistent and coherent approach, each case being decided according to what seemed preferable at the time. It is here that process rights have their place; by allowing parties whose interests are affected to put their case, and to require explanation and justification, officials will be under pressure to find objective and empirical support for their decisions. Consistency in attitude and in the weighing of interests may be part of that development. There may be thresholds to be reached before, say, an interest in personal freedom can be outweighed by an increase in the reduction of crime. The sentencing judge may come to recognize that the prisoner should not be given a longer sentence, unless there are gains to society that can be set against and outweigh the extra loss of liberty. In this way process and substance interact; process encourages the formulation of an objective basis for discretionary decisions, but the substantive issues still remain for the official with discretion.

This effect may be buttressed further by the idea that there is a right to process; process is then seen not just as a general duty on officials, but a duty which has as its correlative the goal of ensuring that individual interests are given full consideration in the discretionary process. If the notion of rights to process were to increase even marginally the level of concern amongst officials with that objective, its role would be justified.[50]

4.3 DISCRETIONARY POWERS AND THE ABUSE OF LIBERTY

One constant stream of criticism of discretionary powers is based on the threat that is allegedly posed to personal liberty. The rule of law is regarded as a fundamental protector of liberty, and, according to exponents of this view, discretionary powers are incompatible with the rule of law and thus constitute a threat to liberty. The rule of law is a variable notion, but to constitutional lawyers it is the views of A. V. Dicey that come most immediately to mind when mention is

---

[50] For further discussion generally of rights within the public law model, see J. Mashaw, '"Rights" in the Federal Administrative State' (1983) 92 *YLJ* 1129; R. L. Rabin, 'Legitimacy, Discretion, and the Concept of Rights' (1983) 92 *YLJ* 1174.

made of the doctrine.[51] In his writings in the late nineteenth and early twentieth centuries, Dicey extolled the rule of law as a principle of vital importance to civilized government. Dicey's views, however, are likely to be dismissed on the grounds that he was so wrong in his understanding both of the concept of the rule of law and the constitutional system of his day, that his views merit no further attention. This attitude is not entirely warranted, and in any event, given that Dicey's writings have been influential in shaping constitutional approaches to discretionary powers, a brief consideration of his main arguments is in order.

Dicey's exposition of the rule of law is so well known that it is sufficient to consider merely two of its principal aspects. First and foremost, Dicey saw the ordinary courts as the primary institutions in the constitutional order, and in protecting individual rights and liberties.[52] The real test of the efficacy of individual rights and liberties is whether and to what extent they are enforced by the courts. Thus, he considered, that, without judicial recognition and enforcement, claims to rights and liberties are pointless. His famous criticisms of the French system make sense only in that light; he denounced the development of a *droit administratif* even though he acknowledged it as a sophisticated system of rules and principles, his reasons being that maintenance of the system was not entrusted to the ordinary courts. Dicey could not accept that without judicial controls there could be adequate checks upon arbitrary action by government officials. Thus it was to the ordinary courts that the task should fall of developing legal principles, to prevent the risks of abuse that accompanied the rise of the administrative state.

The second matter of present interest is Dicey's insistence that no one is to be punished, or otherwise to suffer in person or goods, except for a breach of law established in the ordinary legal manner before the ordinary courts of law. Here the contrast is between a system of authority where the powers of officials are stipulated in general legal rules, and where powers are 'wide, arbitrary or discretionary'. As we have noted, Dicey was not asserting that discretion is a synonym for arbitrariness, but that where there is wide discretion there is a risk of

---

[51] See Dicey, *The Law of the Constitution*; also '*Droit Administratif* in Modern French Law' (1901) 17 *LQR* 302; and 'The Development of Administrative Law in England' (1915) 31 *LQR* 148. For discussion of Dicey's views, see H. W. Arndt, 'The Origins of Dicey's Concept of the Rule of Law' (1957) 31 *ALJ* 117; Ivor Jennings, *The Law and the Constitution* (London, 1958).

[52] Dicey, *The Law of the Constituton*, pp. 188–99.

arbitrariness. Dicey's emphasis lay upon those areas of traditional personal liberties concerning arrest, search, seizure, forfeiture, and detention. In the areas of importance in a liberal state—security of person and property—Dicey considered that the English courts had developed a system of clear and comprehensive principles. He concluded from his comparative studies, however, that in various continental systems officials enjoyed in respect of those matters wide discretionary powers and exercised them in an arbitrary way. Dicey concentrated upon these areas of traditional civil rights, but when he came to consider the more general powers of government, his analysis was guided by the same two principles: the need for legal rules, whether made by courts or parliament, defining and limiting the powers of officials, and the authority of courts finally to adjudicate upon the legality of any action taken pursuant to the rules.

However, when it came to extrapolating these principles to the wider spheres of state legislation which he saw growing around him, Dicey's response portrays puzzlement and confusion. He appears to have recognized that the principles which could be stated with vigorous confidence with respect to traditional personal liberties were not so clearly applicable to powers vested in officials for welfare ends. He recognized that wide powers might be necessary to effect reforms in matters of education, pensions, and insurance, and that such powers had to be exercised according to 'business principles' rather than legal principles.[53] The notion of business principles remains unclear, but seems to connote concern with the efficient pursuit of policy goals and acceptance that a certain amount of discretion in pursuing those goals is inevitable. At the same time, he saw judicial controls being weakened: judicial procedures gave way to looser rules of fairness and convenience; judicial intervention became background and residuary, concerned with the limits of power rather than the substantive considerations governing its exercise. The judges would still have a role but it would be only a shadow of what Dicey considered essential to the rule of law. He had strong reservations in general about the rising welfare state: at the political level he did not welcome the collectivist movements which expanded the activities of the state; at the constitutional level his concern was that powers, whose purposes were beneficient and paternalist, might easily become the engines of arbitrariness and oppression, since they lacked those controls that he

---

[53] See 'The Development of Administrative Law in England'.

associated with the rule of law. So, while Dicey is an important figure
in calling attention to the risks inherent in discretionary powers, his
writings remain ultimately ambivalent, and of little guidance in
refashioning old principles to serve new purposes. By closing his mind
to the possible virtues of a *droit administratif* (which means, after all,
principles of legal control of administrative action), Dicey rejected the
opportunity of initiating a vigorous and effective system of administrative
law.

It is later, in the work of F. A. Hayek, that some of Dicey's concerns
are developed into a full attack upon discretionary powers. In a stream
of writings spread over half a century,[54] Hayek has tried to revive and
develop a particular view of liberal theory from which he draws a set of
principles governing the organization of the state. One theme in this
enterprise is a strong criticism of discretionary powers. Hayek accepts
that discretion in certain of its senses is necessary for the functioning
of government;[55] but discretion is anathema to the liberal state when it
means that officials have powers which affect the private domain of the
individual, and that the criteria for their exercise is left to the officials
themselves. The danger of discretion in this sense is that its exercise
depends upon the preferences of officials, which may in turn be
determined by variable values and purposes. This means, according to
Hayek, that the individual is subject to coercion by state officials, in
that they have control over his affairs in such a way as to prevent him
from planning his life, secure in the knowledge of the nature and limits
of official powers.[56]

Coercion of this kind is a deprivation of liberty in a special and
negative sense; that is, the liberty that results from having a sphere of
activity protected by rules, and with which officials may not interfere
except in accordance with the rules.[57] Now, any state control involves
coercion or the threat of coercion, but not all coercion, on Hayek's

---

[54] The main works for the present discussion are: F. A. Hayek, *The Road to Serfdom*
(London, 1946); *The Constitution of Liberty* (London, 1960); *Law, Legislation and Liberty*
(London, 1973–9); and *New Studies in Philosophy, Political Economy and the History of
Ideas* (London, 1978). For critical discussion of Hayek's views on the rule of law and
discretionary powers, the following are of interest: A. de Crespigny, 'Freedom for
Progress' in A. de Crespigny and K. Minogue (eds.), *Contemporary Political Philosophers*
(London, 1976); R. Haromwy, 'Law and the Liberal Society' (1978) 2 *JLibStud* 11; Raz,
The Authority of Law, ch. 11.

[55] *The Constitution of Liberty*, pp. 211 ff.

[56] *The Constitution of Liberty*, chs 10, 11, and 14, and *New Studies in Philosophy,
Political Economy and the History of Ideas*, p. 134.

[57] *The Constitution of Liberty*, chs. 10, 11, and 14.

view, constitutes a deprivation of liberty. Where power is exercised according to known general rules, the individual is able to live within those rules, and will be coerced only if by his own choice he puts himself in violation. In such a situation he is free in so far as there are parameters within which he must live, and within those parameters he may make his choices, and he is free from official interference in doing so. Conversely, where officials are given powers which may be exercised in ways which interfere with the individual and his private interests, and where it is left to officials to decide in their discretion under what circumstances and in what ways interference may occur, then the individual is threatened with a form of coercion that infringes his liberty.

This argument forms part of a wider theory of constitutional government. According to Hayek there is a particular conception of law to be found in the classical, liberal tradition which has been lost in modern democracies.[58] Within that tradition, law is the principal guardian of freedom, but not every act or decree of government constitutes law in its special sense. Government by law requires the formulation of general rules, and the even-handed application of those rules to all who fall within their terms in an unknown number of future instances. But not merely any rules will do; Hayek argues for a conception of justice according to which rules are just only if they are both general in nature and would receive universal consent.[59] Thus, legal rules properly so-called are those general rules of just conduct which are agreed to by all, and which may be applied impartially without regard to particular results, or to their effects upon specific individuals or groups. Closely associated with this view of law is the separation of powers: Hayek argues for a strict separation of institutions and functions, according to which all laws would be made by a legislative authority, or evolve over time in the way of common law rules; all such laws would be justiciable in the courts, and the functions of the executive arm of government would be limited, since in general the delegation of powers for specific purposes of social improvement would be prohibited.

From this brief sketch of Hayek's version of liberal theory, it can be seen how he is provided with a basis for attacking the structure of the modern state: the widespread delegation of discretionary powers undermines the requirement that authority be exercised according to

[58] *New Studies in Philosophy, Political Economy and the History of Ideas*, ch. 7.
[59] *The Constitution of Liberty*, pp. 107 ff.

general rules; it also muddies the distinction between the legislative and executive branches, and it removes the courts from adjudication upon substantive issues by confining questions of legality to the extent of powers, rather than their content. Closely connected to these matters is the alleged corrupting effect engendered by the pursuit of programmes of social welfare and planning; such pursuits are said to undermine the generality of law, and are incompatible with the limited concerns of commutative justice.[60] Hayek sees the development of the modern state in these directions as the result of various factors, amongst the more important of which are the rise of the doctrine of legislative sovereignty, and democratization of the political process. In the hands of popular majorities, the legislative process can be put to any policy ends, quite apart from whether they serve the ends of justice, or whether they lend themselves to being implemented through general rules.[61] Thus, Hayek urges, it is only by reviving the classical principles of liberalism and constitutional government, and by eschewing notions of social justice in favour of market forces, that modern democracies may be rescued from the perils towards which they have drifted.

In assessing these arguments, I shall concentrate on the way that they bear on discretionary powers. The point in Hayek's argument that appears most perplexing and most difficult to sustain is the association made between questions about the substantive ends to which state power may be put, and the condemnation of discretionary powers.[62] The argument seems to be that any pursuit of social justice, or any attempt to regulate the economy, cannot be done in accordance with the rule of law, bearing in mind the special meaning given to the rule of law. In other words, the argument is that because social engineering may require some vesting of discretionary powers in officials, and because this means a loss of liberty in individuals thereby affected, then the state should avoid attempts at social engineering.

The first point that might be made by way of objection is that, while we have seen that the growth of discretionary powers is associated with the activities of the modern state, the links are more contingent and variable than Hayek allows, and indeed many of the state's activities are pursued through clear and general rules, which are justiciable in

[60] *The Constitution of Liberty*, chs. 15 and 19; *Law, Legislation and Liberty*, pp. 139–46.
[61] *Law, Legislation and Liberty*, chs. 7 and 8.
[62] For further discussion, see Raz, *The Authority of Law* and Haromwy, 'Law and the Liberal Society'.

the courts. The reasons for condemning social justice and economic regulation can be based only partly on the alleged evils of discretion. The more substantive reasons are that such laws are unlikely to comply with Hayek's notion of the rule of law, that is a law which is not only general in its terms, but which is accepted by all, or at least by a majority of both those who are affected by the law and those who are not.[63] It is clear then that these restrictions on state activities are matters of substantive political principles, which must be justified on some basis other than the indirect argument from the loss of liberty.

The second question that arises is whether, anyhow, discretionary powers do inevitably involve a loss of liberty. There is a loss of liberty in its negative sense when an official has power to interfere in an individual's private affairs, and when that interference is not regulated by clear and general rules. It is unnecessary here to repeat the arguments urging against the assumption that one must settle for either rules or discretion, and that discretion is necessarily exercised in an unpredictable and variable manner. Rules can be seen as one specific method of decision-making within a normative framework which has available other ways of constraining the exercise of powers: the use of standards of varying degrees of specificity and normativity, the requirements of rationality and purposiveness, and the consequential concern with consistency and fairness. An undue emphasis on rules may lead one to overlook the efficacy of these other constraints in making the exercise of powers predictable, certain, and without arbitrariness. Hayek is right in calling attention to the potential abuse of power that widespread discretionary powers may allow; his error lies in thinking that the only method of prevention lies in prohibiting discretionary powers, rather than by considering the techniques by which those powers may be brought within an acceptable framework of constraints.

This brings us to a third consideration, the relationship between negative liberty, and other ends and values. While discretionary powers may be limited and constrained in various ways, it is unavoidable that on occasions, for the reasons we have considered, there may be a degree of uncertainty as to the standards to be applied and the likely outcomes. The cost of granting officials relative autonomy in approaching their tasks may be a corresponding lack of certainty and stability in the way they are to be performed. It is this, on Hayek's

---

[63] *The Constitution of Liberty*, chs. 10, 11, 14, and 17.

account, that constitutes coercive powers in officials, and a consequential interference with the liberties of individuals. Without denying either the importance of liberty in this negative sense, or the value of rules in making clear the occasions upon which officials may interfere in private affairs, it should not be assumed either that this is the only important sense of liberty, or that liberty in any of its senses is the only goal worth pursuing through the intermediary of the state. Liberty may be taken in its more positive sense of liberty *to* do things, not just liberty *from* things being done to one.[64] In its positive sense liberty may require an active role on the part of the state, to ensure that individuals have the opportunities positively to achieve their ends. The availability of such opportunities may depend upon the state providing the necessary resources and institutions, and it is precisely this point that forms the basis of many aspects of the welfare state, whether the context be education, urban planning, or social security. Alternatively, such purposes might not be associated directly with liberty at all, but may be justified as ends worth pursuing for a variety of other reasons. In either case, the institutional arrangements most suitable for their achievement might not match Hayek's ideal of the rule of law, and may require powers of a discretionary nature. But, in view of the importance of those other aims, it is not clear why this ideal of the rule of law should be the overriding political principle. The sense of liberty which the rule of law protects will always be important, but not necessarily more important than other ends and values. The relationship between the two must be resolved in the context of specific powers, and the aims which they seek to achieve. This is particularly the case once it is realized that it is not a matter of choosing between the rule of law on the one hand and discretionary powers on the other. The task rather is to find ways in which the pursuit of specific social goals can be both effective, and in compliance with those virtues that give importance to the rule of law. This task is facilitated if questions about the proper activities of the state are kept separate from questions about how to ensure that powers are exercised in accordance with acceptable principles of process.

---

[64] For discussion of the distinctions between positive and negative liberty, see Isaiah Berlin, *Four Essays on Liberty* (Oxford UP, 1969).

5

The Basis of Legal Regulation and Judicial Review

THE analysis so far has been concerned with a number of issues: the nature of discretionary power, its relationship to descriptive and normative theories of law, its place within different models of authority, and the various practical and normative constraints on its exercise. Now the direction changes, and from here on our main interest will be in analysing the nature and scope of legal regulation. This is not in the nature of a complete treatise on the law relating to discretionary powers; rather the point is to identify some of the central issues with a view to seeing how they have been handled by legislatures and courts. In this chapter, the legal framework within which discretionary powers occur is considered, and then the basis of judicial review is analysed in terms of constitutional doctrines and values. In the next chapter, various themes in legal regulation are dealt with; questions about the normative framework within which discretion is exercised, the issue of reasons and purposes, and the evidential basis on which decisions are made. In the final chapter, issues of fair procedures are considered, and this includes an analysis of notions of representation and participation.

5.1 THE BASIS OF LEGAL REGULATION

In an earlier chapter, different senses of discretion were identified and it was shown that discretion might stem from a variety of sources. Now, however, I am concerned with discretionary power in its central sense, and then only when it occurs by express or implied delegation. The legal framework around discretionary powers in this sense may briefly be considered in terms of their sources, the basis of delegation, and the constraining legal principles.

5.11 *The general legal framework*

With regard to the first, the primary source of discretionary powers is

208 *Discretionary Powers*

the legislature. In the simplest case the legislature by statute delegates powers to a subordinate authority, whether it be the executive collectively, a particular minister, a named official, or one or other of a variety of administrative authorities. Whether there is a delegation of discretionary powers, and, if so, its scope, depends on the words of the statute. Typically such expressions as 'the minister in his discretion may do X', or 'the minister may do X' or 'the minister shall do X on such conditions as he thinks fit' indicate a grant of discretionary powers, but whether or not there is may in many cases be a difficult matter of interpretation. In chapter 1, we considered some of the problems that occur in identifying discretion, and how it depends on both the terms of delegation and official attitudes. Legislative delegation is not, however, the only direct source of discretionary powers. A subordinate authority, such as a minister of state, may have power to delegate authority to other officials, and this may take a discretionary form. Whether or not one official may delegate to another in this way depends on the laws of the system, and on the terms of the delegator's own authority. Discretionary powers may originate also in sources other than the express or implied delegation by one authority to another. In the judicial sphere, the common law is itself a source of discretion; the judge's discretion to exclude evidence, for example, derives from such a source. The common law may also be a source of discretion in officials other than judges; the prerogative powers, for example, owe their place to constitutional custom and common law recognition. In some systems, discretionary powers inhere in a particular office by customary practice as, for example, in the French legal system where various local offices like that of mayor and prefect carry with them discretionary authority.

Secondly, there is no general difficulty in Parliament delegating discretionary authority to subordinate bodies. This may take the form of a delegation of discretion to make subordinate legislation, or it may be a delegation of administrative discretion. Arguments are sometimes made on the basis of the separation of powers that, since it is for Parliament to legislate and the administration to implement, delegation is invalid unless there are reasonably clear legislative standards to guide the exercise of discretion.[1] Such arguments, in general, have not been successful, and it is accepted that Parliament may delegate

---

[1] The non-delegation doctrine has had some place in American law. For discussion , see L. L. Jaffe, *Judicial Control of the Administrative Process*, (New York, 1965), ch. 2: K. C. Davis, *Administrative Law Text* (St. Paul, 1972) ch. 2.

powers in extremely wide discretionary terms.[2] Once discretion has been delegated to an authority, the latter has a duty to exercise its powers itself, and is not normaly permitted to further delegate. However, provision for subdelegation may, of course, be included in the terms of the original delegation.

5.12 *The sources, institutions, and methods of legal regulation*

In considering the third matter mentioned—the legal regulation of discretion—it is necessary to begin by adding to my earlier introduction. In section 1.53 a schematic account was given of the way that discretionary decisions may be subject to various types of constraints; in section 2.32 a distinction was drawn between the final merits or substance of a decision, and the framework of constraints within which a decision must be taken. The distinction cannot be precise because matters of merits and substance cannot be separated too sharply from processes, nor conclusionary standards from non-conclusionary. The distinction is none the less important in providing different emphases or orientations. Legal regulation may be taken as a working guide to refer primarily to a network of constraints; that is the various methods, techniques, procedures, practices, and principles which shape, influence or control the discretionary process, but without directly or primarily determining the outcome. The principles and procedures of legal regulation are based on and justified by those political values which are considered to be sufficiently important within a community to extend to all varieties of government actions. Compliance with such values is, as we noted earlier, an important element in showing that a decision is authoritative and justifiable. The four groups of values that can be identified in legal regulation have been stated: rational achievement of purposes, legal stability, fair procedures, and a residue of moral and political values. These are inevitably broad and loosely defined categories, open to extension or modification; in general they constitute not only the rationales of legal regulation as it has emerged, but also are a dynamic, normative basis for developing new principles and extending their scope to new areas of discretion. These categories need not be definitive, as other values may come to be recognized as sufficiently important to constitute general constraints on discretion.

The sources from which the principles and procedures of legal

---

[2] For discussion of the breadth that parliamentary delegation may take, see Griffith and Street, *Principles of Administrative Law*, pp. 110–17; Craig, *Administrative Law*, pp. 372 ff.

regulation derive are various. Naturally, the first place to look for legal constraints is the constitution; where there is a written constitution, there may be general principles which place restrictions on all official actions, and therefore on discretionary decisions. In the United States, the provisions of the Bill of Rights protecting such matters as free speech, due process, and equal protection apply to all decisions by officials. Constitutional principles of this kind normally form part of a belt of constraining standards which must be complied with, but which do not themselves point to a specific result; as standards, they tend to be reason-guiding but non-conclusionary. Where, as in the British system, there is no written constitution, it is necessary to look to statutes as the primary source of legal principles. Two different kinds of provisions commonly are encountered. One kind, by enacting general principles of law, implicitly places constraints on all official actions; for example, statutes prohibiting various forms of discrimination or unequal treatment.[3] There is a close analogy between legal principles of this kind and the provisions of a constitutional bill of rights.

The other type of statute is directed specifically towards regulating discretion by such means as stipulating the procedures to be followed, ensuring the representation of pertinent groups and interests, requiring the formulation and announcement of the policies to be applied, and requiring reasons to be supplied for decisions made.[4] Such provisions often are contained in the parent statute under which the discretion occurs; alternatively, attempts might be made to formulate in general terms a set of principles governing the exercise of discretion. This is one of the objects of the American Administrative Procedure Act which provides a legal framework for the regulation of administrative powers in federal matters.[5] Extensive provisions with respect to rule-making and adjudication cover such matters as the procedures to be followed by agencies and officials, the parties who may be represented, the publication of proposed rules, and the rules of evidence that apply. Provision also is made for judicial review of decisions or actions which are arbitrary, capricious, an abuse of discretion, or otherwise not in accordance with law; or which are in breach of procedures, or unsupported by substantial evidence.[6] This

---

[3] See *Race Relations Act* 1976 and *Sex Discrimination Act* 1975.

[4] See, for example, *Tribunals and Inquiries Act* 1971, s. 12.

[5] *Administrative Procedure Act* 1946.

[6] Note especially, ss. 4, 5, 7, and 10. For discussion, see B. Schwartz and

approach has been followed by a number of states, while others have enacted their own more elaborate statutes, or simply left the formultion of constraints to the courts. The Administrative Procedure Act and equivalent state legislation constitute only the bare bones of a legal framework, which have been given substance by the varying practices of administrative agencies and by a large body of judicial doctrine.

Similarly, in some Australian jurisdictions attempts have been made to advance the legal framework within which discretionary decisions are made, sometimes by creating special tribunals with extensive powers to review administrative decisions, at other times by stating in broad outline the grounds on which actions might be challenged by judicial review. The leading example of the first is the system of federal Administrative Appeals Tribunals, which are empowered, with respect to specified but extensive areas of decision-making, to review the merits of the decision.[7] Sometimes this means that the Tribunal substitutes its view of the merits and substance in particular cases, but it also has the opportunity to develop principles and practices of a more generalized kind. An example of a legislative attempt to stipulate general principles is the Administrative Decisions (Judicial Review) Act which states the grounds for judicial review; those include breach of fair procedures, improper exercise of power, fraud, and lack of evidence. There is then further specification of what constitutes an improper exercise of power; this is defined to include various aspects of rationality and purposiveness, and various matters of a more procedural kind, such as the fettering of powers, or the abdication of powers to another.[8] As with the American legislation, the Australian statute is directed to judicial review, but also provides some guidance to the administrative authorities. Another common feature is that both statutes provide only limited guidance, with questions as to the more detailed and precise legal constraints being left to development by the administrative authorities, the special tribunals, and the courts.

In Britain, the record of statutory innovation has been more limited, so that although the statutory enactment of general principles has often been urged, it has never been achieved. Of the two major reviews of administration and administrative law, the Committee on Ministers'

H. W. R. Wade, *Legal Control of Government: Administrative Law in Britain and the United States* (Oxford UP, 1972).

[7] See *Administrative Appeals Tribunal Act* (Cth) 1975, esp. s.43.
[8] See *Administrative Decisions (Judicial Review) Act* (Cth) 1977, esp. s. 5.

Powers in 1932, and the Committee on Tribunals and Inquiries of 1957, only the latter resulted directly in legislation; and although important, that applies only to certain decisions of tribunals and to the decisions of ministers following a public inquiry.[9] Apart from the Tribunals and Inquiries Act, the legislative contribution to legal regulation has been either by way of special provisions for specific areas of discretion, as mentioned above, or by creating special authorities with powers to scrutinize and influence aspects of discretionary decisions; examples are the Council on Tribunals,[10] the Parliamentary Commissioner for Administration,[11] and the Commission for Local Administration.[12] Similar institutions are to be found in other jurisdictions, and I shall return shortly to comment on their general role.

However, first I should mention the final major source of legal regulation, that is the common law as developed by the courts. The judicial role is twofold: one is interpreting and applying statutory provisions, such as those noted above, which seek to regulate discretion; the other is developing their own principles of judicial review. It is often said to be undesirable that the courts should be responsible for creating principles of review, since this inevitably requires a certain amount of discretion on their own part, and raises important issues of a constitutional kind. Some of these issues are considered later in the chapter; for the moment, we may note that the courts have this power partly because legislatures have been inclined either not to provide statutory guidance, or to provide guidance which requires substantial interpretation.

As for institutions, there are a number involved in creating and developing the principles and practices of legal regulation. Parliament is the primary authority; it has the opportunity through general

[9] The two major efforts at reform are contained in the proceedings of the *Committee on Ministers' Powers* (1932) Cmnd. 4060, and *Committee on Administrative Tribunals and Inquiries* (1957) Cmnd. 218. The resulting legislation is the *Tribunals and Inquiries Act* 1971.

[10] For the background, see the report of the *Committee on Administrative Tribunals and Inquiries* (1957) Cmnd. 218 and the special report on the workings of the Council, *The Functions of the Council on Tribunals* (1980) Cmnd. 7805.

[11] For the background, see the Justice report, *The Citizen and the Administration* (London 1961). For the statutory basis, see *Parliamentary Commissioner for Administration Act* 1967.

[12] For the statutory basis, see *Commission for Local Administration in England, Wales and Scotland Act* 1974. For appraisal of its operation, seen the Justice report, *The Local Ombudsman: a Review of the First Five Years* (1980).

statutory enactment or by provision in specific areas of discretion to stipulate regulatory principles. It also has scope through its various procedures—questions, debates, and committees— to scrutinize aspects of administration and to promote good practices. A detailed study of Parliament's role in influencing different areas of discretion and in stimulating general principles and practices is beyond my present purposes, although such a study would be interesting and illuminating. But apart from any direct influence it may have, another important aspect of the parliamentary role is the creation of special authorities which are then responsible for scrutinizing the decisions of discretionary bodies, and in some areas for devising general guidelines. The main authorities specially created in this way are those mentioned: the Council on Tribunals, the Parliamentary Commissioner for Administration, and the Commission for Local Administration. In addition to bodies similar to these, some Australian jurisdictions have created special Administrative Appeals Tribunals with extensive, general powers of review.

The principal task of the Council on Tribunals is, in its own words, to keep 'under review the constitution, working and procedures of a large number of tribunals, and the procedures of certain inquiries'.[13] This task is carried out in a number of ways: it must be consulted about proposed changes in the procedures of tribunals; it may receive complaints from parties aggrieved by particular decisions; and it has come to have, although not statutorily required, an advisory role in respect of legislative proposals aimed at restructuring existing tribunals and inquiries, or in establishing new ones.[14] So, in the course of what is probably a typical year, the Council on Tribunals, amongst many other activities, received a large number of personal complaints and investigated the eight that fell within its jurisdiction; it made extensive recommendations about questions of fair procedures in relation to the Criminal Injuries Compensation Scheme; it set out objections to proposals that reasons need not always be given for certain decisions of tribunals; it examined twenty-five pieces of draft subordinate legislation with provisions affecting the procedures of tribunals and inquiries; and it was consulted about the rules relating to immigration.[15] It can be seen that the Council has considerable scope in influencing procedural

---

[13] *Annual Report.* 1983–4, p. 1.
[14] For discussion, see C. Harlow and R. Rawlings, *Law and Administration* (London, 1984), ch. 6.
[15] *Annual Report*, 1983–4.

aspects of discretionary decisions, and has developed reasonably clear
and firm guide-lines as to what is required for decisions to be fair in a
procedural sense.

There are two kinds of Ombudsman in Britain, one concerned with
actions taken by central departments, the other with the decisions of
local authorities. In both cases the primary task is to investigate the
grievances of individuals concerning particular actions or decisions.

The Parliamentary Commissioner for Administration has described
his position as standing between the legislature and the executive,
discharging an almost judicial function in the citizens' disputes with
government, and yet forming no part of the judiciary.[16] Whereas the
Council on Tribunals is geared mainly to issues of a general kind, the
PCA is essentially concerned with investigating individual complaints
where there is evidence of maladministration. This involves a wide
range of administrative affairs, but those most common and recurrent
appear to be penal matters, social security, taxation, and citizenship.
However, despite the emphasis on individual complaints, there is
scope for making recommendations of a more general kind in matters
both of policy and procedure. The annual reports to Parliament
demonstrate understandable pride in the PCA when his recommendations have led to general changes of policy and procedure. However,
the need for there to be maladministration before the PCA may
intervene, and the absence of a power to investigate administrative
actions without an individual complaint, are severe restrictions on the
role of the office.[17] But, in so far as there is scope for more generalized
scrutiny, the concerns of the PCA are in the main to reduce
arbitrariness in decision-making; to enhance stability in the relationship between administrative bodies and their clients, for example, by
providing clearer standards and guide-lines about how decisions are
made; and to raise the general level of procedural fairness.

The functions of the Commission for Local Administration are in
many respects parallel at the level of local government to the PCA's at
the level of central government. In its own words, the main object of
the CLA is to investigate the actions of local government in order to
secure both satisfactory redress of individual grievances and better
administration.[18] There is perhaps less scope for developing more

---

[16] *Annual Report*, 1983, p. 1.

[17] For further discussion, see P. Stacey, *The British Ombudsman* (Oxford UP, 1971);
Justice Report, *Our Fettered Ombudsman* (London, 1977); Harlow and Rawlings, *Law and
Administration*, ch. 7, Craig, *Administrative Law*, pp. 239 ff.

[18] *Annual Report*, 1982–3, p. 1.

generalized principles and practices, but there has been particular emphasis on encouraging local authorities to at least develop and publicize their own procedures for the settlement of complaints.[19]

In addition to those various types of authorities, there is the Australian Administrative Appeals Tribunal. Because of its novelty and its potential importance in the regulation of discretionary powers, the background to its creation and its operation is considered in some detail later in this chapter. Apart from the role of such special bodies, it would be misleading to overlook the contribution of the various officials and authorities in the course of their own practice of administration. Amongst the numerous, powerful influences on officials must be counted general ideas of good administration, of not only being effective and efficient, but also of being fair and equitable, maintaining moral ideals, upholding procedural correctness, and generally showing interest in and respect for those affected by official decisions. We saw in earlier chapters the stress that officials place on matters like these; and while there are cases of gross deviation and pockets of incalcitrance, it would be unfortunate to accept an image of administrative officials trying at all costs to remain beyond the pale of general principles of law and propriety. Much of the impetus for good administration comes from within the authorities themselves: the concern to act rationally and purposively, to eliminate arbitrariness, to formulate and publicize guide-lines and policy, to respect procedural fairness, to provide reasons, to treat individuals equally and fairly, are all matters likely to be considered by the administrators as important. Moreover, in addition to the commitments of particular officials to principles of good administration, there are often mechanisms within government organizations for one set of officials to provide guidance to others, and for one set of officials to review the decisions of others. The general and important point is simply that, quite apart from clear directions from the legislature, the courts, or other special bodies, administrative officials may have of their own initiative highly developed principles of good administration.

Finally, in the formulation of legal principles there are the courts. Their opportunities to contribute to principles of good administration arise in exercising common law powers of review, or in interpreting and applying statutory principles couched in general and abstract terms. From a practical, legal point of view, the judicial role has been

---

[19] See Harlow and Rawlings, *Laws and Administration*, ch. 7.

regarded as the centrepiece of administrative law. No doubt some of
the more traditional approaches to administrative law, written primarily as guides for practitioners, have exaggerated the role of judicial
review. That tendency has been corrected in some more recent works,
although they are inclined to err at the other extreme. But it is hard to
assess with precision how important the courts are in the overall
development of legal regulation of discretion; it is also difficult to
calculate the effect of judicial principles on the actions of administrative officials. Those are complex, empirical questions, which await
investigation in different contexts. They are certainly not answered by
a simple counting of the number of times issues actually get before the
courts, but depend on the extent to which general norms are
extrapolated from specific decisions, and on the attitudes to those
norms of administrative officials.

What is clear is that the courts have created through precedent a
body of doctrine concerned directly with the regulation of discretion.
That in itself is one good reason for close analysis of judicial review.
This does not imply the unimportance of other sources of legal
principles, nor does it even imply that judicial review is the most
important. There is, however, an additional reason for paying special
attention to judicial review: this lies in the peculiar position of the
courts in constitutional terms. The fact that they are outside the lines
of direct accountability to the political process makes the position of
the courts problematical in imposing constraints on discretionary
authorities, which are themselves politically accountable. The potential
conflict between the political process and the role of the courts has
made judicial review contentious, not because of the doctrines that
have emerged, but because they are created by courts or depend on the
courts for interpretation. For those reasons, a substantial part of this
chapter is devoted to an analysis of the constitutional basis of judicial
review. Before proceeding, however, there are a number of more
general observations to be made about legal regulation of discretionary
authority.

So far I have given an outline of the sources of legal regulation and
the institutions involved in developing regulatory principles and
practices. Two brief comments should be made finally about the
methods of legal regulation. In the first place, while I have emphasized
the general principles that can be found in the practices of the various
regulatory institutions, it should be made clear that these principles are
created and developed according to different techniques. We have

noted the scarcity of general principles pronounced in statutory form, so that most principles have to be extracted from the diverse practices of the various institutions. Judicial principles, for example, are created and refined in deciding specific cases of review where the general issue is legality; this may be contrasted with the advisory functions of the Council on Tribunals, the investigative role of the Ombudsman, and the scrutiny of the merits by an Administrative Appeals Tribunal. The general point is only that despite these different techniques and opportunities, each institution has demonstrated a concern to develop something in the nature of general principles, and that there is substantial common ground amongst them. Secondly, it is not suggested that the various institutions are equally concerned with formulating general principles; authorities like the courts, the Ombudsman, and the Administrative Appeals Tribunals usually are concerned with resolving specific issues, and have to deal with the substantive merits of those issues to greater or lesser degrees. The concern with more generalized standards and practices is usually a secondary consideration, and it is often a matter of extrapolating the more general ideas from a pattern of particular decisions.

5.13   General issues in legal regulation

The next point to be made clear is the relationship between legal regulation and the objects of discretionary powers. The justification for government activity in general, and the delegation of discretionary powers in particular, is the attainment of whatever social goals are considered to warrant such actions. Those goals must in turn find justifiction in a wider political theory. If the use of discretion facilitates and enhances the realization of such goals, then there is a strong case for discretion. Principles of legal regulation or good administration are in the nature of side-constraints on that process, either directed to enhancing the achievement of desired goals, or concerned to uphold values which are important in any context of government activity, quite apart from the substantive goals sought. This suggests a limited role for legal principles, a role concerned to ensure respect for certain enduring values rather than to dictate the ends of government; however, it is a role based on the assumption that importance is attached not only to what is done in terms of results, but also how it is done in terms of processes. If this is the most justifiable approach to legal regulation, then it implies severe limitations on its scope; it is only one element in a much wider concern to make the actions of officials justifiable and legitimate. This is not to say that there is a precise and settled line defining the scope of legal regulation; any such line is clearly variable and particular doctrines may be more or less exacting. In particular, there is no 'legal' solution to the 'problem' of discretion, as if discretion were somehow a temporary and somewhat illegitimate device, awaiting replacement by law. On the contrary, discretion is a legitimate and central part of modern government, and legal regulation is concerned in its main emphasis to enhance that legitimacy.

This prompts mention of a second point which relates to the supposed incompatibility of 'legal values' and 'governmental values', with the implication that the choice has to be for one or the other. Legal values, it is said, are things espoused by old-fashioned lawyers, and are based on the rule of law, rights, and judicial review. For those more up to date, the important concepts are administrative effectiveness, the political process, and political accountability; and in that world there is little room for legal regulation, adjudication, or courts.[20] However, it is difficult to see what is gained by putting the debate in such terms, since the important task is to develop around the exercise of discretion, in the manner I have indicated, a framework of legal constraints based on the articulation of important values. The question is not whether to go either for some uncertain conception of the rule of law, or for governmental effectiveness; it is rather to consider how legal principles and institutions can be put to service in both enhancing effectiveness and ensuring maintenance of other important values. Legal regulation is part of the wider issue of accountability. Sometimes the controversy is more clearly between judicial review and governmental values, the argument being that judicial review is to a large degree illegitimate. But, again, the haze of rhetoric sometimes obscures the more precise criticisms that are being made; whether it is the very idea of scrutiny or review of discretionary actions by anything resembling a court, or whether it is just the present court system, or indeed the particular group of persons who hold judicial office.[21] I

---

[20] For an account which divides those concerned with administrative law into these two camps, see Harlow and Rawlings, *Law and Administration*, esp. chs. 1 and 2. It must be asked, however, whether the camps have ever been so clearly distinguishable, for although statements can be found expressing rather extreme positions, most writers have been aware of the need to find some middle way between 'legal values' and 'governmental values'.

[21] J. A. G. Griffith's, *The Politics of the Judiciary* (London, 1977) has been a milestone in analysis and discussion of the place of the judiciary. Some qualifications are, however, necessary: firstly, many of the assertions about the judiciary are unsupported by

cannot now go into these various issues, but two brief points are worth making. First, there are strong reasons for having some system of scrutiny of discretionary decisions by an authority which is itself reasonably independent of the administration, even if its powers to intervene are severely limited, to perhaps little beyond ensuring procedural propriety. Some such basic division of powers is an important feature of acceptable government. Secondly, it is somewhat parochial to make the issue of judicial review turn on the experience of the English High Court without reference to imaginative innovations in both the British Commonwealth and Continental Europe.

The third and final point is to suggest that there is a certain unity and coherence amongst different institutions and authorities as to what constitutes good administration, and as to the objects of legal regulation. The basic assumptions as to which values are important appear to be shared in the main by the various authorities concerned, whether Parliament or the courts, the Australian Administrative Appeals Tribunal, the French Couseil d'Etat, or the Ombudsman. There may, of course, be differences in emphasis and disagreements about specific issues; but there does appear to be a substantial degree of common ground with respect to the basic principles. This is an obvious but important point, since it would be mistaken to think of the courts as locked in battle with Parliament and the administration. The disputes are not usually about the underlying principles of regulation, but rather the extent to which one authority should scrutinize the decisions of another.

5.2   THE BASIS OF JUDICIAL REVIEW

There are two issues in the legal regulation of discretion which are likely to become confused and which are extremely difficult to keep apart: one is the question of what legal constraints there ought to be on discretion; the other is the question of the responsibilities of different

empirical investigation (compare Paterson, *The Law Lords*); secondly, if the general implication is that judicial review or any other form of scrutiny by a court, tribunal, or other institution which stands outside the lines of political accountability, is unjustifiable, then the thesis is highly contentious. The general position being argued in this book is that external scrutiny, whether or not called judicial review, and whether or not done by courts, is a desirable aspect of the constitutional arrangements; that any such body unavoidably has some discretion in its actions; but that judicial discretion, like the discretion of any public body, should be and is capable of being used according to justifiable political and constitutional principles.

institutions in devising and applying such constraints. The tensions arising around those two issues are nowhere more apparent than in judicial review. No matter how compelling the reasons are for a particular principle, the courts may decline responsibility for its application on the grounds that that task should be performed more appropriately by some other institution. Conversely, courts are on occasions criticized for particular decisions on similar grounds. Efforts should be made to keep apart the two issues, and in the following analysis the emphasis is on the constitutional position of the courts rather than the substantive principles of review. The object is to examine the values and understandings that have been influential in the development of judicial review, on the grounds that this improves our understanding of recurring issues, and that changes and improvements are likely to be incremental rather than radical, building on past experience rather than beginning afresh.

5.21 *The early judicial approach*

The historical development of judicial review of administrative actions is a fine example of incrementalism, of the piecemeal evolution of a body of doctrine in response to changing political and social factors. To comprehend the modern practice, one ought to trace its development through the intricacies of medieval, revolutionary, and modern British history, to see how the superior courts, from their early position as advisers to the Crown, were able gradually to distance themselves both from it, and from the dominance of the emerging Parliament. It is not possible, however, in the present context to undertake the task, so we must be content to concentrate on a number of points of importance to the modern practice.[22]

In the first place, it is significant that judicial review and the principles on which it is based have been left in the main to be moulded by the courts, rather than stipulated by a constitutional settlement where attention might have been directed to formulating the proper scope of legal regulation. Judicial practice itself has evolved in the course of dealing with individual complaints against one or other of the arms of government, rather than by deliberate and comprehensive stipulation of principles. Flexibility and pragmatism have been necessary to deal with the diversity of administrative bodies and types

---

[22] Some historical background is given in de Smith, *Judicial Review of Administrative Action*; also 11 *CLF* p. 40 and 15 *MLR* 189. See also L. Jaffe and E. Henderson, 'Judicial Review and the Rule of Law' (1956) 72 *LQR* 345.

of decisions; as a result, whatever principles have developed have remained open and general in their terms. This has enabled the principles themselves to be more or less constant, thus creating a sense of continuity over long periods of change. But, within that framework of principles, there is room for substantial change and development which can be understood only by close examination of actual practice and the variables on which it is based. Secondly, judicial review is exercised by the ordinary courts, rather than by a set of special administrative courts. That judicial review consists in applying the ordinary law to the decisions of administrative authorities has been extolled as a notable virtue.[23] The very idea of a special review authority applying special principles to the actions of government bodies has been, until recently, repugnant to the common law tradition. Review has proceeded, therefore, on the basis that all government authorities, whether ministers of state, special tribunals, or local authorities, are subject like ordinary citizens to the ordinary law. But, with the growth of modern governments, the idea, owing much of its force to Dicey, that administrative authorities are subject to the ordinary principles of law is misleading, since the real question is what does the ordinary law mean in these situations. A third factor is that principles of review have not been developed by direct application of whatever constraints on discretion are appropriate, but, at least in modern law, indirectly through the concept of *ultra vires*, that is through defining the limits of authority. The guiding principle has been that the primary task for the courts is to ensure that a subordinate authority does not exceed or misuse its powers; to the extent that there are distinct legal principles governing the exercise of discretion, it has been necessary to characterize them as requirements of *ultra vires*. Of course, *ultra vires* may be given an expansive meaning to accommodate a great range of constraints, but the very fact that this indirect approach has been necessary has hindered a more comprehensive and perhaps more satisfactory evolution of principles. Finally, substantive issues of judicial review often revolve around highly technical legal questions, such as whether a remedy is available or whether a complainant has standing; again, this has hindered a more even and open growth of principles.

Against this background, we may now turn to the general principles on which review is based. This is done by contrasting the attitudes of

[23] See Wade, *Administrative Law*, p. 17.

judges at two different points: on the one hand in the early years of this century when judicial attitudes to extensive government regulation were being formed; contrasted with this are the approaches to be found in more recent decisions, as judges have begun to pay more attention to the issues raised by discretion. Judicial attitudes have not progressed evenly or consistently; decisions from any period can be found which are expansive or restrictive, and the practice of judicial review has been erratic and sometimes confused. But, even so, it is possible to discern a reasonably coherent set of attitudes portrayed in important decisions in the first half of the century, and a reasonably distinct change of attitude in later years. And since my primary aim is, by contrasting two sets of attitudes, to explicate the underlying premises of judicial review, the risk of over-simplification need not undermine the general discussion.

With the expansion of government regulation in the early years of this century, the courts naturally were looked to in the expectation that they might provide some protection to private rights and interests. Their position, however, was complicated: they recognized that traditional ideas of legality, the rule of law, and the primacy of individual rights and liberties were truncated by discretionary powers; and since the source of authority for those powers was nothing less than the sovereign Parliament itself, it was hardly appropriate to meddle with a concept of such political and legal importance. It is in the face of this dilemma—signified by the shift from the private law to the public law model—which became clearer and more immediate in the first half of this century than ever before, that courts have had to approach issues of review. The only resources available, however, were limited ideas of legality and procedural fairness.

This dilemma arose clearly and centrally in 1915 in *Local Government Board* v. *Arlidge*.[24] The facts are simple enough: a local authority was empowered by statute to make an order requiring the closure of any dwelling house if it appeared to the authority to be unfit for human habitation. These powers were used to condemn a private dwelling house. The owner appealed to the Local Government Board which appointed an inspector to hold a public inquiry; the owner and his solicitor attended the inquiry and submitted evidence. At its conclusion, the inspector made his report to the Local Government Board which, after considering the report and the evidence, dismissed

---

[24] [1915] AC 120.

the appeal. The owner sought redress by an order of *certiorari*; his claims were that the appeal had been unlawfully dismissed since the order did not identify the official of the Board who decided the appeal, that he was entitled to an oral hearing by the Board, and was entitled to see the inspector's report. The main issue, then, was to what extent and according to what principles the courts, under the heading of natural justice, would examine the decision of the board, where it clearly exercised a considerable degree of discretion in determining the fitness of the house for human habitation. The specific issue was one of natural justice rather than a direct challenge to the exercise of discretion, but the attitudes of the judges towards discretionary decisions are made clear.

The case reached the House of Lords, and it is the opinions expressed there that are of particular interest. Since specific procedures were not stipulated in the statutes dealing with slum clearance, the question for the courts was whether to require certain procedures to be followed. With possibly one exception,[25] the judges agreed that even though private property rights were at stake, it was not for the courts to enforce their own views of fair procedure. The Lord Chancellor noted that the Local Government Board was not a judicial authority, but was required to exercise executive functions, and that even when, on a more functional analysis, it was acting judicially, it was responsible for setting its own procedures. The basis for this conclusion apears to be that Parliament had entrusted a body with judicial powers, without at the same time specifying the procedures to be followed. Now, parliamentary sovereignty is a powerful principle to invoke, but it is not clear that it requires this conclusion. Other inferences might be drawn with equal justification; silence as to procedures might be regarded as an implicit acceptance that normal judicial procedures, including the hearing requirements, were to be followed.

However, the Lord Chancellor found two more reasons for judicial restraint. One was ministerial responsibility to Parliament; the Local Government Board was headed by the minister, and he was directly responsible to Parliament for his own actions and those of his departmental officials. So, the argument went, since the minister was responsible to Parliament in this way, any procedural inadequacies would be corrected by that process. So again the inference was drawn

---

[25] Lord Parmoor thought that principles of substantial justice did apply here; he also thought substantial justice had been done: [1915] AC, pp. 140–2.

that in the absence of parliamentary revision the procedures followed must be taken to have met with Parliament's approval.[26] Lord Shaw, whose speech has been cited with approval in later cases, described as 'grotesque' any attempt to discover the identity of the official who made the decision in the minister's name, or to subject the decision to judicial scrutiny. He also thought that any disclosure of the inspector's report would be inconsistent with the true theory of complete parliamentary responsibility for departmental action.[27] But, again, the argument for ministerial responsibility does not lead inexorably to the conclusion of extreme judicial restraint. Ministerial responsibility is a broad concept which might be taken in various ways, and, had the court considered two further points, a more satisfactory analysis might have been achieved. Firstly, there are limitations on parliamentary scrutiny of ministerial and departmental actions; so that it might have been concluded that in respect of many sorts of questions of precisely the kind in issue, namely fair procedures, Parliament has little time and, often, even less interest. Secondly, there is no reason to assume that some level of judicial scrutiny is incompatible with ministerial responsibility. The former might be seen to complement and supplement the latter on the ground that there are some matters, including questions of procedure, in which the courts have both experience and expertise.

A second argument used to support judicial restraint was that of administrative efficiency. The Lord Chancellor considered that efficiency would be impaired if the minister were required to have greater personal involvement in the decisions made by his department.[28] Lord Shaw argued even more strongly that the imposition of a duty to disclose the inspector's report would constitute a serious impediment upon the frankness with which staff ought to be able to communicate with each other, and that this in turn would impair departmental efficiency.[29] These arguments seem quaint in the light of modern judicial and legislative attitudes to the disclosure of information; but in 1915 the House of Lords appeared hardly aware of the idea that efficiency might well be in conflict with considerations of justice and fairness. By giving supremacy to efficiency, the courts erected a barrier around the substance of discretionary powers which prevented judicial scrutiny, and which curtailed examination of whether other values might have some place.

[26] [1915] AC, pp. 132–4.
[27] Ibid., pp. 136–7.　　　　　[28] Ibid., p. 133.　　　　　[29] Ibid., p. 137.

The approach in *Arlidge* concluded in extreme restraint in reviewing discretionary powers; its basis lay in a particular view of the requirements of the separation of powers and democratic government. One part of this view concerns the relationship between Parliament and the courts; since Parliament is the sovereign lawmaker it is not for the courts to interfere with parliamentary intentions. Thus judicial review certainly should not enter into the merits of statutory enactments, and in this sense there is a strict separation of powers between the courts and Parliament. But sovereignty extends also to govern the relationship between the courts, and ministers and their departments: since Parliament is the source of delegated powers, and since the minister is in turn answerable to Parliament, then, in a sense, Parliament authorizes and controls any exercise of delegated authority. There is also a strict separation between the courts and the authorities exercising delegated powers, particularly where the authority is not only authorized by Parliament, but is also responsible to it. But why should the doctrine of sovereignty of Parliament have such an impregnable place in the constitution? The answer lies in the link between sovereignty and the democratic process; whatever the original basis of the former (and its origins precede any widespread commitment to democracy), it is now justified on the ground that Parliament is the primary institution of democratic government. Administrative authorities exercising discretion are therefore linked directly to the democratic process. On this account, greater intervention on the part of the courts might appear to be an interference with democratic principles.

There is a second aspect to the separation of powers view portrayed in *Arlidge*; in making efficiency so important in decision-making and in departmental organization, the court seemed to be accepting a functional division between the judicial process and administrative decision-making. Efficiency is the yardstick of good administration, and there is little room for judicial methods and procedures. *Arlidge* rests, therefore, on a particular conception of the separation of powers; a conception which is itself dependent upon a particular idea about the democratic process, and the functional division between courts and adjudication on the one hand, and administrative authorities and discretionary powers on the other. Why the courts should have settled on those particular interpretations of constitutional doctrines is a matter of conjecture. Perhaps their response was not unreasonable, considering the social and political environment at the time; government was expanding in a climate of intense political activity and threatening social instability, ideas of social justice were advancing in efficacy and persuasiveness, and the long struggle for universal franchise was on the point of success. It is not surprising that in this environment judges had no desire to be seen to be obstructing the clearance of city slums.

The decision in *Arlidge* provided something of a touchstone for judicial attitudes to review until several years after the Second World War.[30] Judicial review of discretionary powers did not, in general, extend beyond the minimal procedural requirement that the decision-maker must fairly listen to both sides, a duty which, it has been said, falls on anyone who decides anything.[31] In terms of the substantive basis for exercising discretion the constraints were equally minimal, requiring only that decisions be made honestly and in good faith, with the intention of promoting the objects of power.[32] *Liversidge* v. *Anderson*,[33] one of the most vilified cases in legal history, may seem a disreputable example to cite, but the majority views there expressed, in so far as they characterized the matter as a case of reviewing a minister's discretion, were solidly in the mainstream of judicial attitudes prevalent at the time. The basis of the majority view, which to a considerable extent was also the view of Lord Atkin in his famous dissent, was that discretionary powers conferred on a minister are not to be inquired into by the courts, with a view to scrutinizing the reasons for coming to one conclusion rather than another. The controversial issue in *Liversidge* was whether words conferring powers were to be interpreted as stipulating an objective condition to be satisfied before the discretion came into effect, or whether the meaning of the words was itself to be settled by the minister in the exercise of discretion. The majority may be criticized for construing the words 'reasonable cause to believe' as conferring a subjective discretion, but their attitudes to judicial review, once a matter was recognized as discretionary, were clear reflections of the approach laid down in cases like *Arlidge*.[34]

This approach both to fairness in procedure and to scrutiny of the reasoning process by which a discretionary decision was made was repeated with approval on many occasions. One notable case is *Johnson*

---

[30] There are celebrated exceptions where the courts took a rather more activist role, but these are relatively few and out of step with prevailing attitudes. An outstanding case is *Roberts* v. *Hopwood* [1925] AC 578.

[31] Lord Loreburn in *Board of Education* v. *Rice* [1911] AC 182.

[32] For example, see *Weinberger* v. *Inglis* [1919] AC 606.   [33] [1942] AC 206.

[34] See [1942] AC, pp. 221, 233, 248, 267–70, 279.

v. *Minister of Health*,[35] where Lord Greene MR urged caution in review, and invoked by way of support both parliamentary sovereignty and ministerial responsibility, and the unsuitability of policy-based administrative decisions for resolution by adjudicative processes. The position was little different when discretionary powers were conferred, not on a minister, but on an authority less clearly accountable to Parliament. Lord Greene attempted to state the governing principles in *Associated Provincial Picture Houses* v. *Wednesbury Corporation*.[36] Firstly, a reviewing court must not substitute its own view of the way the discretion should have been exercised for that of the original authority. Secondly, the task for the court was to ensure that certain principles were upheld in the exercise of discretion. Those principles are centred around the idea that an authority must exercise its discretion according to the terms of its powers; it must not base its decision upon extraneous considerations, nor come to a decision which is overwhelmingly unreasonable. Provided that the authority stays within these principles, its decisions of policy and its assessment of the merits of particular cases are beyond judicial regulation. The absence of direct or effective accountability to Parliament was not itself considered a good reason for increased judicial scrutiny.[37]

These principles governing the judicial review of discretionary powers vested in executive and administrative officials were neither novel nor innovatory; they were in the main an application in the administrative sphere of the same principles that traditionally governed the approach of higher courts to discretionary decisions made by lower judicial authorities.[38] There is, however, a certain ambiguity about the approach to judicial review which culminated in the statement of principle in *Wednesbury*. It might be taken to justify the restrained approach of the early years, or it might equally support a more vigorous judicial review as has occurred in recent years. It purports to erect a distinction between the merits of decisions and a notion of legality; in fact, this can never be precise either logically or practically, so that the scope of review at any time depends on whether Lord Greene's

[35] [1947] 2 AER 395.
[36] [1948] 1 KB 223. Note that the position now may be rather different in cases where the discretionary authority is not accountable to Parliament; see, for example, Lord Diplock in *Bromley LBC* v. *Greater London Council* [1983] AC 768.
[37] [1948] 1 KB at pp. 228–30.
[38] See *de Smith*, pp. 279–81, where a range of decisions are listed showing the attitudes of higher courts to the discretionary decisions of lower courts and other judicial type authorities.

statement of principle is interpreted restrictively or expansively. But, before considering how that principle has been developed in recent years, we must turn to the implications for judicial review of the constitutional doctrines that have been identified.

5.22 *The separation of powers*

The idea that government powers should be divided amongst separate and distinct authorities has a long history in western constitutionalism. Some version of it was important in the early development of judicial attitudes towards discretionary powers, and it is linked closely to notions of legality and the rule of law. There is no one fixed separation of powers doctrine, but rather a number of versions which have changed and developed over the course of political history; in any event, it is not the doctrine itself that is important, but its underlying values. Our present purposes are served by taking a pure and ahistorical version of the doctrine, and then considering the values on which it is based, and the modifications to be made if it is to be of importance in the legal approach to discretionary powers.

A pure form of the separation doctrine has the following features: (*a*) the functions of government are to be divided into the legislative, the executive, and the adjudicative; (*b*) different functions are to be vested in separate and appropriate institutions; (*c*) the members of one institution should not be members of any other institution; (*d*) the functions of one institution should not encroach on the functions of another.[39] The image that this pure version creates is of power divided amongst three types of institutions according to function, where each is independent of the other in terms of function and personnel. By this division of powers, each arm of government is able, in a negative way, to prevent the others from dominating the conduct of government. In practice, the four tenets of the pure theory are likely to be modified in various ways; indeed, the separation doctrine is more likely to be successful in achieving its objects if each set of institutions, instead of being confined strictly to distinct and separate tasks, has some power to scrutinize and regulate the functions of others. In judicial regulation of discretionary powers, this is precisely the point in issue: in what

---

[39] The most complete modern account of the separation of powers doctrine is J. M. C. Vile, *Constitutionalism and the Separation of Powers* (Oxford UP, 1967). Other discussions of use are: W. B. Gwyn, *The Meaning of the Separation of Powers* (Tulane UP, 1965); Marshall, *Constitutional Theory*, pp. 97–124; Hans Kelsen, *General Theory of Law and State* (New York, 1961), pp. 269–82.

circumstances, and according to what principles, may courts impose, with justification, constraints upon the powers exercised by other authorities? Thus the separation doctrine is often combined with and to some extent modified by the related idea of checks and balances.[40] The doctrine of checks and balances is itself the modern expression of an ancient theme in British constitutional history, to the effect that the institutions of government should be not only reasonably separate and distinct from each other, but also that the functions of government should be shared amongst institutions.

It is in the writings of Montesquieu that the two themes of mixed government and separation of powers are brought together, and given a modern foundation.[41] Montesquieu saw the importance of each institution—the legislature, the executive, and the judiciary—having distinct functions, but being able at the same time to check and balance each other. He also ascribed to the judicial function a status of greater equality with the other branches and a clearer separation from them than had been the case in earlier writings. But since it was for the judiciary simply to apply the law, Montesquieu did not consider either that it had any major role in checking the other branches, or that it in turn needed to be checked.[42] The development of judicial review of the other branches of government is a later development, and owes much to American constitutional history.[43]

Whether in its pure form or modified by the idea of checks and balances, the doctrine of separation is important because of its role in protecting values. W. B. Gwyn has concluded that, historically, these have been; (*a*) to create greater governmental efficiency; (*b*) to assure that statutory law is made in the common interest; (*c*) to assure that the law is impartially administered and that all administrators are under the law; (*d*) to allow the people's representatives to call executive officials to account for the abuse of their power; and (*e*) to establish a balance of governmental powers.[44] While it is mistaken to ignore the various claims that have been made for the separation doctrine, one

[40] For discussion of checks and balances, see Vile *Constitutionalism*, pp. 18, 93–6, 160, 212–17.
[41] Montesquieu, *The Spirit of the Laws* (New York, 1949 edn.). For discussion, see Vile, *Constitutionalism*, ch. iv; J. Plamenatz, *Man and Society* (London, 1963), vol. 1, ch. 7.
[42] Vile, *Constitutionalism*, pp. 88–90, 96–7.
[43] See E. S. Corwin, 'The "Higher Law" Background of American Constitutional Law' (1928–9) 42 *HarvLR* 149 and 365; James Madison and John Jay, *The Federalist* (London, 1970), essay no. lxxviii.
[44] Gwyn, *The Meaning of the Separation of Powers*, pp. 127–8.

theme that has been especially important, and which is represented in
(*c*) and (*d*), is the relationship between a separation of powers and the
rule of law. The division of powers amongst separate institutions
reduces the powers of any one of them, and the separation of functions
means that power is filtered through various processes in which each
institution has some part to play. Although the degrees of separation
and of checks and balances are enormously variable, there is a close
affinity between a strict version of the separation doctrine and a narrow
version of the rule of law: both envisage that the law will be made by
legislative bodies, in the form of general rules to be interpreted and
adjudicated by courts, and finally implemented by administrative
officials. We have seen how important this union of ideas is in the
private law model. But while that version of the separation doctrine
does not directly limit the scope of government, it is most compatible
with a form of government that is concerned to preserve minimum
conditions of social regulation, and so appears to have little scope
within the public law model, where the reliance is on discretionary
authority. From this, it might be concluded that, within that model, the
separation doctrine cannot have any precise connotations, but may be
regarded as the expression of the good practical sense in not
concentrating too much power in any one authority, and in ensuring
some scope for the decisions of one body to be open to scrutiny by
another. This view is likely to be sceptical of functional differentiation
except in the loosest sense, so that whatever the pattern of division and
mutual checking, it will be the result of diverse pragmatic considerations, rather than a reflection of conceptual distinctions. The courts, in
exercising review, would be one institution among several concerned
with checking and balancing the exercise of discretion, as opportunities
arose and when the policy implications were acceptable.

The question, however, is whether between these two positions
there is scope for a more specific separation doctrine, which provides
guidance for judicial review within the public law model. In
institutional terms, the courts are reasonably distinct and separate
from the other organs of government; the problem, however, is
whether there is sufficient functional differentiation for the allocation
to the courts of distinct adjudicative tasks. This depends on two
factors: the first is whether there are such functional divisions in
modern government; the second is whether any role proposed for the
courts is justifiable in terms of constitutional theory, a matter which

turns in the main on the implications of democratic principles and notions of justiciability.

Initially, it would seem that the classical division of functions into legislative, executive and adjudicative has been subverted within the public law model. These functions never have been easy to define, but it has been suggested by M. J. C. Vile that the traditional categories can be translated respectively into rule-making, rule-application, and rule-adjudication.[45] There are, however, immediate difficulties in applying those categories to discretionary authority. Even if it were conceded that, despite the inevitable overlaps between functions and between institutions, each institution is concerned primarily with one function—legislatures make rules to be applied by the executive/administration and, where necessary, adjudicated by the courts—there is still a greater difficulty to confront. It is characteristic of discretionary authority that all three functions are vested in the same institution or set of officials, so that the functional distinctions may be inappropriate and largely meaningless. It is not so much a matter of formulating rules, but rather deciding questions of policy in pursuing broadly defined goals or applying loose standards. These matters may be resolved incrementally in deciding a particular issue without first stipulating general rules, and the main object may be simply to reach an outcome that is reasonably acceptable, both in terms of broad policy and the interests of the parties. Not only may the one authority have to make decisions of a legislative, adjudicative, and applicative kind, but it need not even perceive or analyse its own task in terms of such divisions.

In the face of this merger of functions in discretionary bodies, it is not easy to see what the role of the courts is to be in reviewing discretionary decisions. If they are to be confined to reviewing those aspects that are clearly adjudicative, then their role would be limited to matters of a preliminary or threshold kind, and therefore largely excluded from the substance of the decision. If, however, they get involved in matters of substance and merits, of policy and strategy, then it is not clear that their role continues to be distinctively adjudicative, and the difficulty of justifying the practice of review then is increased. Judicial attitudes in the earlier part of the century opted in general for the first of these; a grant of discretion signified for them a fusion of powers in the administrative body, and the dissipation of any

---

[45] Vile, *Constitutionalism*, ch. xii generally.

element that was clearly adjudicative. This amounted in a curious way to both an affirmation and disavowal of the separation doctrine; an affirmation in that the courts saw it as no part of their task to tell the discretionary authority how to exercise its powers; but a disavowal in that the courts did not consider whether there were aspects of discretionary decisions, beyond the minimum precepts of legality, which might be suitable for judicial scrutiny.

It is worth considering whether anything can be salvaged from the separation doctrine in defining the role of the courts in reviewing discretion. In the first place, although discretionary authority does constitute a merging of functions, there may be scope for informal, but nevertheless reasonably clear divisions of both functions and personnel. Within an area of discretion, there is often in practice a division of labour, especially between those who make the rules and those who work out their application in specific cases; there is usually some scope for functional differentiation of this kind without undermining the rational effectiveness of decision-making. Connections can be drawn between the separation of tasks within an area of discretion and questions about the best mix of comprehensive planning and incrementalism; advance planning carries with it a tendency towards functional differentiation by laying down standards and procedures in advance; while for incrementalism, the emphasis on the actual case helps to maintain a merger of functions. The courts justifiably might concern themselves with the modes of decision-making employed, both to encourage, where suitable, a separation of functions, at least of an informal kind, and perhaps to oversee to a greater extent the even-handed application in specific cases of general policies and standards.

The separation doctrine may also provide guidance to the courts in a second way. Here, the argument is that there remain important senses in which the legislature, executive/administration, and courts are separate institutions with different constitutional rules. In discretionary contexts, the legislature is concerned not so much to lay down the rules, but to define the scope of regulation, to stipulate the goals to be sought, and the general standards to be applied. Typically, the legislature sets the objectives—alleviation of poverty, reduction of crime, preservation of a balanced environment—and then leaves implementation to administrative bodies. The latter settle the more specific policies and strategies within the defined area, and work out their application in actual cases. The lines of accountability for each are different. The legislature is the creature of the electoral process, and accountable to it; the administration is the creature of the legislature, and while the former is accountable in various ways to the latter, the administration acquires a certain independence and autonomy from the legislature.

It is here that the courts are important. They stand outside the relationship between legislature and administration in two ways: they are not concerned directly with the formulation and implementation of social programmes and objectives, nor are they accountable to the political process, either directly or through the legislature. This suggests that the legitimacy of judicial review depends not so much on accountability to the political process, but rather on advancing fundamental and enduring constitutional values. This gives some guidance to review: judicial review is most justifiable not when it is directed at substantive policy choices that occur in exercising discretion, but rather when it draws on values which form part of the constitutional framework within which discretion occurs. Far from being value free, the justification for review lies in the assertion of certain values as sufficiently important to be constraints on the exercise of discretion. The origins of such values must be found within a general constitutional theory, within which the courts may accept that issues of policy and strategy are in principle for the discretionary body, but still insist that this process should take place against a background of stable, political values whose interpretation and application are suitably left for decision by an authority which stands outside the administrative process.[46] The virtues of this approach are that it enables courts to continue their traditional adjudicative role of developing and applying general standards, that their concerns are still in regulating the relationship between the citizen and the state, and that the separation of powers doctrine is given a fresh basis for development.[47] In making the directions for judicial review more

---

[46] The distinction drawn in the discussion between the substance of decisions and the framework of values within which they are made should not be confused with the 'policy–operational' distinction that has been developed in relation to the liability of public authorities in tort. The latter suggests that the policy aspects of a decision can be separated from the more technical issues as to how those aspects are to be carried out. The distinction drawn in the text is different; it is concerned with the value-constraints on issues of policy and substance, but it makes no claim that those values are not themselves, partly at least, matters of policy, nor does it claim that value-constraints do not influence matters of substance.

[47] For another, modern approach to the separation doctrine which has some

explicit, we need to consider the implications of two further issues, democratic principles and notions of non-justiciability.

5.23 *Democratic principles*

The commitment to democratic ideals has important consequences for both the separation of powers doctrine and the legal regulation of discretionary powers. These ideas are manifested in the legal doctrine of parliamentary sovereignty, and the political principle that Parliament is the principal organ of democratic government. To control Parliament is to control law-making; indeed the expansion of government activity and the consequential burgeoning of discretionary powers are a direct result of democratic majorities using law as an instrument of social and economic regulation.

The combination of political activity and parliamentary supremacy was bound to diminish the significance of the separation of powers doctrine. The apparent incompatibilities between a strict, rule of law version of the separation doctrine and widespread legal regulation, together with the natural association of those two doctrines with non-interventionist government, helped to ensure that reforming governments were inclined not to attach great importance to either. The position, anyhow, of the separation doctrine in British constitutional history has been ambiguous, its incorporation only partial, and then in combination with ideas of checks and balances.[48] Added to this is the difficulty of being sure what the doctrine requires, a task which the Committee on Ministers' Powers faced in 1932 when it attempted to define the functions of government with sufficient clarity to guide the allocating and exercising of powers.[49] But its conclusions were insufficiently convincing to have significant impact on the mode of parliamentary delegation. This does not mean that the separation doctrine has had no place in twentieth-century constitutional history; some developments within the administrative system, such as the use of tribunals, are partly explicable in terms of a concern with the separation of powers.[50] But parliamentary supremacy with its demo-

similarities with the one suggested, see Bert Neuborne, 'Judicial Review and Separation of Powers in France and the United States' (1982) 57 *NYULR* 363.

[48] Vile, *Constitutionalism*, ch. viii.

[49] *Committee on Ministers' Powers* (HMSO Cmnd. 4060, 1932).

[50] See *Committee on Administrative Tribunals and Inquiries* (HMSO, Cmnd. 218. 1957). For discussion of the types of tribunals and their development, see J. A. Farmer, *Tribunals and Government* (London, 1974).

cratic foundations has been the dominant principle; other ideas have had their place, but only in its shadow.

To the courts in cases like *Arlidge*, the extension of the sovereignty doctrine and, hence, democratic principles to discretionary decisions, through the concepts of authorization and accountability, appeared to remove any basis for judicial review beyond threshold, jurisdictional requirements. This fails to take account, however, of the independence and autonomy that discretionary authority tends to encourage. This is the result to a certain extent of the very nature of discretion, but also of the limitations on parliamentary resources and organizational factors within administrative institutions. Parliamentary control may, of course, be improved, but the argument suggested earlier is that it can never be complete, and that a certain autonomy in administrative bodies exercising discretion is inevitable and even desirable. The directions that courts might take in review are, therefore, twofold: one is to try to augment the application of democratic principles within discretionary contexts; the other is to recognize that other values are important objects of judicial attention, even where there is potential conflict between them and democratic principles.

In what sense may judicial review be seen as increasing rather than reducing the democratic nature of discretionary action? The courts are not accountable to Parliament for their actions, nor to the democratic process in any other direct way.[51] They may depend ultimately on Parliament for their powers to exercise review at all, and, like any public institutions, courts are bound to be influenced by the political process. But they are not responsible to Parliament for their everyday decisions, and are left to work out principles of review without detailed direction from Parliament.[52] One way of meeting any charge that judicial review is undemocratic is to see it as enhancing rather than being in conflict with the sovereignty of Parliament. It is common to find judges justifying their actions in reviewing discretion by claiming that they are simply giving effect to Parliament's implicit intentions.[53]

---

[51] For discussion of the idea of accountability, see *Local Government Board* v. *Arlidge* [1915] AC 120. These ideas have been analysed closely in recent years in the Australian Administrative Appeals Tribunal. See Brennan J. in *Re Drake and Minister for Immigration and Ethnic Affairs* (No. 2 (1979) 2 ALD 634; also J. Goldring, 'Responsible Government and the Administrative Appeals Tribunal' (1982) 13 *FLR* 90.

[52] For examples of legislative stipulation of standards of review, see *Administrative Decision (Judicial Review) Procedure Act* 1977 (Cth.).

[53] For judicial dicta, see *Padfield* v. *Minister of Agriculture* (1968] AC 997. For discussion, see Wade, *Administrative Law*, pp. 43 ff. and 256 ff.

The difficulty is that since this approach depends on reconstructing parliamentary intention, or simply ascribing one to it, it can be invoked to justify review at virtually any level. Parliamentary sovereignty is turned into an empty, but extremely capacious doctrine, which can accommodate a range of positions. However, while courts claim that they are giving effect to parliamentary intentions, and hence enhancing the democratic basis of administration, administrative authorities also claim that they are authorized by Parliament to act as they do. Therefore, the conflicts that arise between two competing conceptions of sovereignty can be resolved not in terms of sovereignty itself, but only by reference to other, independent doctrines. Indeed, the doctrine of parliamentary sovereignty is itself of little use in determining the scope of judicial review.

There are other senses in which judicial review of discretion can be linked to the democratic process. These are twofold: one is that democracy, in the representative sense of individuals and groups being able to bring their interests to bear on decision-making, can be extended into the discretionary process, and that the courts might involve themselves in that extension. This is followed up in chapter 7. The other approach is that democracy means more than simply majority rule, that it connotes a relationship between each individual and the majority, within which the individual is guaranteed certain protections, and that these in turn may constitute fetters upon majority rule. The argument is that the values inherent in this fuller sense of democracy might be tapped by the courts in exercising review; the justification for their actions would then be that they are enhancing democratic principles rather than acting against them.

This view of democracy has an important place in American constitutional law. American jurists have long pondered the justification in a democratic society for courts being empowered to determine the compatibility with constitutional precepts of legislative and administrative actions. In protecting values like free speech, due process, and equal protection against legislative and administrative encroachment, the bill of rights is expressed in abstract terms, so that a court's views may conflict with the views of an elected assembly or politically accountable administrator. There is then a clash over the scope of those values between the courts and politically responsible institutions. An alternative approach is to see the values protected by the bill of rights not simply as matters of substantive importance in themselves, but as values which are related to and enhance the democratic nature of the system. Free speech, then, is protected because it advances the democratic process; equal protection is important because it ensures that minority groups are properly represented in the political process, and in the outcomes that result. A proponent of this view is J. H. Ely, who argues that the great constitutional decisions of the Supreme Court in the Warren years should not be interpreted as attempts to place certain values beyond democratic control, but rather as reinforcing the democratic process itself.[54] On Ely's argument the courts are concerned with constitutional process; with the framework, the ground rules, the principles of democracy. Within that framework, substantive policy decisions as to the ends and goals to be sought are for the legislative and administrative authorities; but it is for the courts to determine the meaning and scope of the framework.

The difficulties in extending this approach to judicial review of discretionary actions are several. First, there is uncertainty as to what are the values of democracy, since there is nothing equivalent to the bill of rights of the American constitution, and in practice courts do not tend to think of their role as linked to democratic principles, except in the somewhat fictitious manner mentioned. These objections need not be conclusive, however, since the working-out of a conception of democratic values may be regarded as part of the judicial task. In performing that task, the courts may take guidance from the experience of American constitutional law and political theory generally. The second objection is more fundamental: in order to have a concept of democracy as rich as that suggested by Ely, it is necessary to have a complete political theory about how society should be organized, and there is no clear way of distinguishing between questions about the ground rules on the one hand, and questions of a substantive, political kind on the other. This is the basic flaw in the 'process' approach to American constitutional law: defining the ground rules of democracy is an exercise in substantive political theory; it requires taking a view of the relations between the individual and the majority, which means in turn having a full theory of government. How much of that theory is labelled as 'democratic principles' is a matter of opinion, since process values are also substantive values.[55] It is

---

[54] Ely, *Democracy and Distrust*.

[55] Some of the most important comments on process-based approaches to judicial review are: Paul Brest, 'The Substance of Process' (1981) 42 *OhioStLJ* 131; R. M. Dworkin, 'The Forum of Principle' (1981) 56 *NYULR* 469; J. D. Grano, 'Ely's

common for such accounts to begin with a fundamental value like equal concern and respect for each person, and from this to create a version of democracy. This is Ely's approach.[56] On the other hand, the very same principle is used by Dworkin to generate a complete and substantive theory of the relationship between the individual and the state.[57] Just how the line is to be drawn within such a theory between matters of process and matters of substance remains unclear. The difficulties, in short, are twofold: firstly, questions of process or democratic principles require decisions about substantive political values; secondly, within a political theory there is no objective way of separating the ground rules of democracy from other substantive values.

These arguments cast doubt on approaches to judicial review which depend on a clear distinction between the requirements of democracy as procedure or process and issues of political substance. But even if these difficulties are conceded, it might be argued that, nevertheless, there is a legitimate role for the courts in working-out a theory of democracy and applying it through their decisions. This would involve courts in questions of substantive theory, but it is not clear why they should be barred from such endeavours. The practice of judicial review at any level requires courts to have a view about democracy; *Arlidge* portrays one view, later cases another. Moreover, the politicization within the public law model of the administrative process means that issues about democratic principles become more intricately woven into the issues that arise for review. Questions about fair procedures and the representation of interests—what interests are to be considered, what constitutes consideration—are central to the development of judicial review within the public law model, and can be answered only within some theory of democracy. Should the case from necessity be insufficient justification for courts developing a view of democratic principles, then arguments from principle are also available. Courts, like any other officials, must have a view of their place in the constitutional order; within any preferred viewpoint, it may

Theory of Judicial Review: Preserving the Significance of the Political Process' (1981) 42 *OhioStLJ* 167; M. Tushnet, 'Darkness on the Edge of Town' (1980) 89 *YLJ* 1037; L. Tribe, 'The Puzzling Persistence of Process Based Constitutional Theories' (1980) 89 *YLJ* 1063; D. J. Galligan, 'Judicial Review and Democratic Principles: Two Theories' (1983) 57 *ALJ* 69.

[56] Ely, *Democracy and Distrust*, p. 82.
[57] Dworkin, *Taking Rights Seriously*, ch. iv.

be accepted that Parliament is supreme, but that, nevertheless, there are many issues on which it takes no stand. Since courts often have to step into such gaps, it is preferable that they have some theoretical bearing to guide their actions. Part of that theory should be about the principles of democracy, in terms of which specific decisions may be justified. Provided that proper scope is given to important doctrines like parliamentary sovereignty, it is difficult to see major objections to courts upholding in their decisions a version of democratic theory.

The working-out of a theory of democracy may be an important part of judicial review, but that is not its exclusive concern. Principles of democracy form only part of a complete political theory, and, for reasons similar to those for adopting a view of democratic principles, the courts should be concerned with something more comprehensive. The same arguments from necessity and principle apply, but two further questions arise: what is the basis on which such a theory is to be built, and does the concern with such a theory create a conflict with democratic principles? The substance of any such theory finally depends on each judge's understanding of the values which are considered important within the society, together with his own critical appraisal of them. The theory which each judge settles on or, more accurately, works at must accommodate the positive constitutional values that are to be derived from political and legal practice; those provide the basis of his theory. But his own principles of critical morality are also important, partly because they may be necessary in interpreting constitutional practice, and partly in order to direct such practice towards ends and values which appear more enlightened. Such a theory would include a version of democracy, but it would extend beyond to include a wider view of the relationship between individuals and the state, and between minority and majority groups. It would include development of basic notions of rationality, purposiveness, and moral principles. It would also be concerned with the relationship between the courts and other institutions, especially the legislature and administrative authorities. Such a theory need not be static, but is likely to develop as circumstances and a judge's own ideas become clearer. Its practical importance lies in guiding judicial review and in constituting a framework of principles within which decisions may be justified.

Is such an approach undemocratic? The basis for any such claims might be twofold: firstly, that courts are not politically accountable; secondly, that such an approach brings courts into conflict with

institutions which are politically accountable. The first may be met
with the rejoinder that, while courts are not acountable for their day-
to-day activities, they are part of a political system from which their
position and powers derive, and which may, in the longer term, control
and restrict their activities. It is hard to see in what sense courts are
acting contrary to democratic principles when, within this environment, they concern themselves with substantive values, which of
course they do in all areas of law. As to the second part of the claim, a
judge's theory as to his role in the constitutional order must take
account of parliamentary sovereignty, and the extent to which
administrative authorities are authorized and accountable, either to
Parliament or to a wider sense of democratic process. A theory which
took no account of parliamentary sovereignty would be unthinkable
and unlikely to survive; but exactly what parliamentary sovereignty
means, especially in its application to delegated discretionary powers,
has itself to be worked out in terms of a broader theory. Provided that
judges take proper account within their theories of such concepts, it is
difficult to see in what sense their actions might be considered
undemocratic.

To sum up, the relationship between judicial review and principles
of democracy can be interpreted in various ways; judicial review may in
some senses enhance and in other senses detract from democratic
principles. Any justification for judicial review on the basis that the
courts are upholding the constituent rules of democracy in a neutral
and objective manner is doomed to fail. The argument has been,
however, that judicial review is concerned with substantive values,
which include a view of democratic principles, and that such an
approach can be justified in terms of a general theory as to the position
within the constitution of the courts and other institutions.

5.24 *Adjudication and justiciability*

Quite apart from the restraints imposed by democratic principles, early
judicial attitudes were influenced by the idea that matters of discretion
were in some way unsuited to the adjudicative process and thus to
judicial review. This idea, hinted at in *Arlidge*, became of central
importance in *Liversidge*; there a number of judges distinguished
between matters suitable for resolution by adjudicative processes, and
those which are discretionary.[58] Matters of discretion vested in

---

[58] *Liversidge* v. *Anderson* [1942] AC, pp. 221, 248, 261–7, and 279. Compare Lord
Atkin at p. 243.

government authorities were considered non-justiciable, meaning in this context unsuited for adjudication, because, according to Lord Wright, they were over 'statecraft and national policy,' they did not lend themselves to trial-type proof, and the executive was entitled to act upon secret information, the disclosure of which would be contrary to the national interest.[59] The notion of 'non-justiciability' is used in a number of senses, which can be divided into two general categories. The first is where it is used to indicate that for certain kinds of policy reasons there is to be no review, such as the fact that the decision is of a political nature or is politically sensitive, or it is wartime or an emergency of some other kind, or there is some strong reason for leaving the decision to another authority. Reasons like these, which may grow into clear legal policies, are expressed sometimes in terms of non-justiciability. The reasons for that classification are likely to be mixed, but part at least of the rationale is that the courts do not wish to intervene in the decision because, for constitutional reasons, it is best left to some other body.[60] In a second and stricter sense, however, non-justiciability refers specifically to the fact that a particular issue is analytically unsuited for resolution by adjudicative procedures. Here appeal is made implicitly to effectiveness; certain issues are settled most effectively by adjudicative processes, while others are not, and to force the latter into adjudicative forms is to reduce the rational effectiveness of decision-making. It is in practice difficult to keep apart the two senses of non-justiciability, since the same situations may involve elements of both, and the reasons given by courts for not intervening do not always make clear the distinction. So, for example, issues of national security may be non-justiciable, partly because such matters just are better left to the ministers of the Crown, and partly because the kinds of decisions in issue are analytically unsuited to adjudication.[61] Both senses are important in the analysis of judicial review, but I shall begin with the second sense and then make some

[59] Ibid., pp. 261–7.
[60] For judicial discussion of non-justiciability generally, see: *Attorney-General* v. *Gouriet* [1978] AC 435, esp. pp. 491, 512, 524, *Victoria* v. *Commonwealth and Heydon* [1975] 134 CLR 338; *South Australia* v. *Commonwealth* (1961–2) 108 CLR 130 at p. 154; *Commonwealth Aluminium Corp.* v. *Attorney-General* [1976] QdR 231 at p. 262.
[61] Elements of both senses of justiciability are to be found in the judgments in *Council of Civil Service Unions* v. *Minister for Civil Service* [1984] 3 WLR 1174, but perhaps the dominant concern is with the second and more important sense; see esp. pp. 1183 ff. This seems to be reflected also in the emphasis on justiciability being the important factor, rather than the fact that the powers in issue had their source in prerogative.

brief remarks about the first. The second sense of non-justiciability relies on three premises which will be examined in turn: that there is a distinct adjudicative function; that certain types of issues are resolved effectively by judicial procedures while others are not; and that courts, as traditionally constituted, are suited to adjudicative tasks.

The first of these, the question of what constitutes a specifically adjudicative function, has been the subject of extensive judicial consideration, since it is an issue of importance in constitutional systems which are based on a strict separation of powers; it has also been important in administrative law in deciding whether natural justice applies. Judicial solutions have differed, sometimes being based on whether rights are at stake, or whether decisions are made within existing standards, or yet again according to the procedures to be followed. But the results have been unsatisfactory enough for Geoffrey Marshall to conclude, after a review of the authorities, that 'the common law courts have failed to provide us with a single set of reasonably unambiguous criteria for calling a procedure "judicial" '.[62]

Academic analysis has been more fruitful, with L. L. Fuller's classic formulation the centrepiece. On Fuller's view, the distinguishing feature of adjudication is that it confers on an affected party a special mode of participation in decision-making, which consists in each party being able to present proofs and reasoned arguments for a decision in his favour.[63] The second factor is a special relationship between participants and adjudicator, in that the latter must base his decisions on the proofs and arguments that have been presented by the former.[64] The stronger this relationship, the more significant participation becomes, and the more clearly the process is adjudicative. The third element is that there must be some underlying basis of agreement between the parties. The clearest case occurs where there is a binding rule to be applied; arguments and proof can then be centred around the facts and the meaning and application of the rule, and the adjudicator's decision is based on rational application of the rule to the matter in issue. But, according to Fuller, adjudication may extend

---

[62] G. Marshall, 'Justiciability' in A. G. Guest (ed.), *Oxford Essays in Jurisprudence* (Oxford, 1960), p. 277. For comment, see R. S. Summers, 'Justiciability' (1963) 26 *MLR* 530.

[63] L. L. Fuller, 'The Forms and Limits of Adjudication' (1976–9) 92 *HarvLR* 353 at p. 364. See further P. Weiler, 'Two Models of Judicial Decision-making' (1968) 46 *CanBR*. 406; R. Stevens, 'Justiciability: The Restrictive Practices Court Re-Examined' 1964 *PL* 221.

[64] Fuller, 'The Forms and Limits of Adjudication', p. 338.

beyond the application of rules; it may be appropriate provided that there is some common, agreed standard, or even a community of purpose, within which particular decisions may be worked out.[65] The development of much of the common law, for example, may be seen as a successful case of adjudication, since there has been traditionally an underlying commitment to a system of private property and free exchange.

There is a close correspondence between adjudication in Fuller's sense and the tasks that courts typically undertake. Their concern is, generally, to resolve issues between identifiable parties who present arguments and proofs, usually within the context of commonly accepted doctrinal standards. There may be room for interpretation, but the adjudicator's decision is an application of those standards, and is responsive to the arguments and proofs that the parties propose. Moreover, the usual method is incremental, deciding in the particular case only what is necessary for the resolution of that case, and so allowing standards to develop and become more precise in a case by case manner. There is also a forward-looking aspect since each decision serves as a precedent for the future; but the main concern is to resolve the issue in the present case. With the emphasis so clearly directed to that end, it is difficult, relatively unusual, and in various ways risky for courts to attempt to formulate comprehensive standards for the future. When this does happen, the principle enunciated is likely to be the formulation of a general standard which is amply supported by precedents.[66]

The characteristics of adjudication are made clearer by contrasting the process of legislation at the opposite end of the spectrum. Here the object is to create general standards for the resolution of an indeterminate number of cases in the future. The decision-maker is concerned with assessments of policy to ensure that the standards are in accordance with the public interest, and that in specific cases their application will produce good results. Similarly, the basis of participation is different; adjudication typically allows the participation of only those who are involved in the issue in a direct way, and whose primary concern is to advance their own interests. The public interest, in so far

[65] Ibid., p. 378.
[66] There is a wide-ranging literature on the nature of adjudication. Examples are: D. L. Horowitz, *The Courts and Social Policy* (Washington, 1977), chs. 2 and 7; R. S. Wells and J. B. Grossman, 'The Concept of Judicial Policy-Making' (1966) 15 *JPL* 286; Howard J. Woodford, 'Adjudication Considered as a Process of Conflict Resolution: a Variation on Separation of Powers' (1969) 18 *JPL* 339.

as it connotes interests over and above those of the parties involved, typically is not represented. In legislating, a wider basis of participation is desirable to ensure that the legislator has before him a full view of the public interest. The nature and focus of argument and proof also changes; argument is likely to be directed at the overall social advantage of a proposed standard, and the object of proof is likely to shift from establishing facts relevant to a specific issue, to eliciting evidence and opinion relevant to the proposed standard. The scope of the inquiry may be widened to include an assessment and evaluation of empirical evidence, and to consider expert opinion. These characteristics, taken together, constitute a sense of legislation which may be set against adjudication. Between the two, there are intermediate positions depending on how unsettled the standards are, on how widely the basis of representation and participation is drawn, and on how closely the final decision is based on the arguments and proofs presented.

The reason for identifying a distinct sense of adjudication is the idea that certain types of decisions are made most effectively by judicial procedures while others are not. The implication is that adjudication has a certain instrumental integrity which is undermined if it is employed to deal with unsuitable tasks. This captures the idea of non-justiciability in its clearest sense; tasks which are not suited for adjudicative processes are not justiciable. This issue arises in discretionary contexts in allocating tasks in the first place, in performing those tasks, and in reviewing them. But since the scope of review may turn on the extent to which the initial discretionary decision is justiciable, consideration must first be given to the exercise of discretionary powers. Here we shall follow the earlier division of discretionary decisions into those clearly adjudicative, those clearly legislative, and the remainder which are a mixture of the two in that they are individualized (and so veer towards adjudication), and yet contain elements of policy (and so veer towards legislation).

What is it about such situations which makes them unsuited to adjudication? Fuller's account emphasizes the special mode of participation within adjudication, but the most important variable is the degree to which decision-making is governed by set standards. Where there is a firm, but perhaps informal, division of powers so that individual decisions are made by one set of officials applying general and concrete standards laid down by another set, problems of non-justiciability largely disappear: the formulation of standards may be dealt with in accordance with appropriate legislative procedures, and the individualization part in accordance with adjudicative procedures. However, in practice there remains a great mass of discretionary decisions where there is a continuing tension between the merits and circumstances of the particular case, and considerations of underlying policies. The result is that such decisions do not fit readily into the adjudicative framework. In the first place, the standards governing the decision are likely to be abstract and indeterminate, or in conflict with each other, so that the official is left with a degree of freedom in reaching a decision which, all things considered, seems the best in the circumstances. Even where the standards are laid down fairly precisely, it may be desirable for the official to depart from them in order to advance some sense of the public interest. Secondly, the parties may be able to participate in the proceedings by offering arguments and proofs, but again the symmetry, characteristic of adjudication, between the mode of participation and the logic of the decision is lost; the object of participation in such cases is not to show how settled standards apply to the facts, but to urge that one policy rather than another be selected, or that conflicting policies be resolved in one way rather than another. A wider range of interests may be affected, and so open the way for participation by a greater number of groups. Thirdly, the reasons on which the official finally decides need not be confined to the arguments and proofs put before him by the parties, but may include considerations of wider policy concern. The official is not an impartial judge whose primary role is to settle a dispute between parties according to settled standards; his duty is to realize certain goals and to shape his decisions accordingly, and his concerns may be with the future rather than the past. His sources of information and advice may also be broader than that supplied by the parties, and his decision may depend as much on opinion and speculation as proven facts.

The conclusion that seems most obvious is that the farther discretionary decisions depart from the adjudicative model, the less suitable they are for review by the courts. Immediately, however, a number of qualifications must be made. In the first place, while all discretionary decisions contain a core of evaluation and assessment of a policy kind, this may be a relatively minor aspect of the decision, and it may be more to do with the circumstances of the particular situation than with a general policy of wide-ranging implications. This is likely to be the case where the standards are fairly clear and the situations requiring departure from them well settled. In such cases, the exercise of discretion complies rather closely with the adjudicative mode, so that judicial review could not be objected to on the grounds of non-justiciability. Indeed, there should be no automatic assumption that discretion connotes non-justiciability; the force of any such claim depends on close examination of each area of discretion.

The second qualification is that even where discretionary decisions depart significantly from the adjudicative model, so that the outcome depends on assessments of policy and subjective evaluation, there may be, nevertheless, aspects which are stable and recurring, and objective enough to warrant judicial scrutiny without the integrity or effectiveness of the discretionary part being undermined. There is no warrant for the assumption in *Arlidge* that a discretionary decision is inherently non-justiciable, and so beyond the pale of review. Procedural matters may be proper matters for external scrutiny, and in chapter 7 it is argued that the courts may rightly be involved in extending participatory procedures into the discretionary context. Another aspect suitable for review relates to the constraints that derive from rationality, purpose, and morality. Whether there is a foundation of evidence for a finding of facts, whether there are reasons for decisions which are intelligible in their own right and reasonably related to purposes, whether the decision strategies are rationally supportable, has a reasonable attempt been made to provide settled standards—these are some of the issues arising in relation to rationality and purpose that seem justiciable enough to be the basis of judicial review. Similarly, the enforcement of moral constraints on discretionary decision-makers, whether in allowing a suspect access to his lawyer[67] or prohibiting the use of deportation where it amounts to double punishment,[68] are aspects of decisions which, although highly inconvenient for officials and perhaps forcing substantial reorganization of decision-procedures, are eminently suited to adjudicative pronouncement. In other words, while final determination of policy and assessment of particular situations may be inherently non-justiciable, and therefore unsuited to judicial review, discretionary decisions are made, nevertheless, within a framework of constraints which are suited to external scrutiny and analysis.

However, the suggestion that, by concentrating on aspects of

---

[67] *Mapp* v. *Ohio* (L961) 367 US 643.

[68] This issue has arisen in a number of decisions of the Australian Administrative Appeals Tribunal. For a general survey, see M. D. Kirby, 'Administrative Review: Beyond the Frontier Marked "Policy–Lawyers Keep Out"' (1981) 12 *FLR* 121.

procedure and background constraints, judicial review can avoid violating the non-justiciable elements of discretionary decisions is open to question. In the preceding section, in dealing with the problems of accountability that arise in judicial review, we considered the difficulties in separating background or process principles from the core of discretion. The same problem occurs here; virtually any aspect of a decision, no matter how closely it relates to the merits, can be characterized as one relating to the minimum requirements of rationality or purpose. In *Secretary of State for Education and Science* v. *Tameside MBC*,[69] the discretionary part of the Secretary's decision was made to depend on an issue of fact which could be attacked for lacking evidential support; in *Bromley LBC* v. *Greater London Council*,[70] the wide discretion of the GLC in organizing public transport was made conditional upon satisfying rather simplistic judicial views of what constitutes efficiency and sound business principles. Even matters of procedure can be linked to the substantive merits, in that the procedure adopted may reflect the authority's view as to how to achieve most effectively the objects of power.

Here another side of the non-justiciability issue is brought out. The idea is that some tasks can be achieved effectively only by considering a number of complex matters which are weighed and assessed according to the best judgment of officials. By singling out some one factor or requirement as of irreducible importance, judicial review may have the effect of distorting the overall complexity, of underplaying the importance of other factors, and so reducing the effective realization of objects. This is not itself a conclusive argument against judicial review of discretionary issues, but rather an important qualification in setting the extent of review. Effectiveness in exercising discretion is a complex notion, and the decision as to what constitutes the most effective way of say, running a transport system, or deciding on the parole of prisoners, is a matter requiring assessments and judgments of a subjective kind. But such matters are not always or totally impervious to objective assessment; they are partly dependent on agreed axioms as to what constitutes rational action, and it may be defensible to require that at least reasonable threshold requirements be met. The fact that courts do on occasions exceed those thresholds and penetrate to the core of discretion does not itself mean that efforts to set the thresholds should be abandoned.

[69] [1977] AC 1014.   [70] [1983] 1 AC 768.

From the discussion so far, a number of tentative conclusions can be drawn. In the first place, matters arising for decision are neither simply justiciable or non-justiciable; there are degrees of both depending on how closely the issue comes within the core sense of adjudication. Moreover, while an issue may in a general sense be non-justiciable, there may be aspects which are reasonably suitable for adjudicative procedures and for review by a judicial authority. Secondly, questions about justiciability cannot in practice be divorced from other sources of guidance in setting the bounds of judicial review—the separation of powers, accountability and democratic principles, and in general an overall view of the place and function of courts in the constitutional arrangements. Justiciability can be treated as a discrete, analytical concept, but in judicial review of discretion it tends to become intermixed with those other considerations in deciding exactly where the line is to be drawn between the framework of constraints and the core of discretion. It is also here that the analytical sense of non-justiciability merges with the other sense of the term defined above. Non-justiciability in that other sense is likely to be invoked when the court concludes that the discretionary assessment is best left for some other authority. This conclusion in turn is likely to be reached by invoking some established general policy ground like national security or emergency, or, alternatively, by considering that to be in the particular circumstances the most desirable outcome. So in *Arlidge* any conclusions about non-justiciability cannot fully be separated either from considerations about ministerial reponsibility to Parliament or the separation of powers, since these factors are important in judicial deliberations as to which issues are to be decided by which authorities. But the two senses of justiciability are not necessarily compatible. The upshot may be that matters analytically towards the justiciable end of the spectrum are deemed for those other reasons non-justiciable, and vice versa. How those two senses have been regarded in more recent judicial decisions is considered briefly later in this chapter; the general point of importance, however, is to recognize the role that the different concepts have in fixing the extent of judicial scrutiny of discretion.

It has been accepted in the discussion so far that judicial review is most effective when it is directed at aspects of administrative decisions that are of an adjudicative kind. Often this is supported by the claim that there are institutional limitations on the capacities of the courts to enter into the actions of administrative authorities, and so support is gained for limited rather than extensive review. Courts do not appear to have the special skills and expert knowledge that are required, for example, in assessing the economic basis of a licensing system. Nor can they easily acquire those skills; judges depend for their information, and to an extent their education, on the evidence that is put before them in the course of a case. Moreover, courts do not have the continuing conduct and administration of areas of regulation, but are required to deal only with occasional situations. It is often argued that it is difficult for courts in deciding the particular case to obtain a sufficiently informed view of the general context. We considered earlier the idea of complexity; polycentricity is another way of expressing a similar point: social issues are extremely complex because they are affected by and in turn affect in ways that may be unpredictable a range of matters beyond the immediate issues. Courts may be unaware of or fail to understand the complexities, so that their rulings can have unforeseen consequences; and since courts are not engaged in continuing administration, those consequences may go undetected or unremedied.[71]

A related argument has been put by Martin Shapiro, who casts judges in the role of generalists rather than specialists.[72] In the course of a year's work a judge may be required to deal with a great variety of specialized and complex matters. But these are brief encounters, concerned only with particular aspects and unlikely to be repeated. As generalists, courts are not involved in the overall policy planning necessary for the administration of an area of state activity, nor in the day to day decision-making that administration requires. They lack the skills and training of full-time administrative officials, and, in exercising review, are outsiders looking in on complex, administrative subsystems. Their skill is, typically, a critical ability to assess the cogency of evidence and arguments that others place before them, and to test the conduct of administration against a few relatively simple standards deriving from reason, purpose, and fairness.

Observations like these are important in understanding that the scope of judicial review is not a factor of abstract functional analysis only, but also of the institutional characteristics of courts; the justiciability of issues depends, in other words, partly on practical judicial capacities. The early judicial attitude may have been overly circumspect, whereas in more recent years a touch of caution may have

[71] See J. Jowell, 'The Legal Control of Administrative Discretion' and Horowitz, *The Courts and Social Policy*, ch. 7.

[72] Shapiro, *The Supreme Court and Administrative Agencies*, ch. 1.

led the courts to take fuller account of the complexities involved. In *Bromley*, for example, the courts allowed review to depend upon an evaluation of whether the Greater London Council was conducting its transport policy in accordance with sound business practices.[73] And yet that is the very kind of issue upon which expert opinion differs, and in which the practices actually followed may be evaluated in different ways.

Nevertheless, it may be mistaken to assume that the courts are good at adjudicating only in Fuller's sense. It is perhaps a law of evolution that institutions develop and adjust, and acquire distinctive characteristics, not so much as a matter of deliberate planning, but in response to the tasks set for them. Adjudication in Fuller's sense may have been the traditional occupation of courts, but if they are required to deal with discretionary decisions, they may develop new capabilities without undermining their traditional position of reasonable independence and authority. Abram Chayes has suggested a number of directions that this might take:[74] (*a*) Judges have a certain professional independence of the political process, but are not necessarily naïve about political considerations. (*b*) Judges are not suited ideally to overall policy control, but since many discretionary decisions are incremental, in that the object is to find a satisfactory solution to a problem, judges may be good at appraising that process. (*c*) Courts are in a good position to ensure that there is adequate representation and participation of interests, and in turn the court hearing does provide a public forum for interested parties to put their cases. (*d*) In discretionary decisions involving issues of policy and strategy, the provision and evaluation of information of a wide-ranging kind may be important, and the adversary process may have unexpected strengths in bringing information forward and vigorously testing it. (*e*) The judicial inquiry may be an effective forum for bringing grievances about discretionary decisions in that courts must make a decision, and may bring to bear the critical scrutiny of an outsider. (*f*) The courts are not locked into a complex administrative structure, and so are able to make an independent assessment of problems, and even to seek advice and information from sources independent of the administration. None of these amounts to a radical departure from the traditional judicial

---

[73] *Bromley LBC* v. *Greater London Council* [1983] 1 AC 768.

[74] Abram Chayes, 'The Role of the Judge in Public Law Litigation' (1976) 89 *HarvLR* 1287.

function, and taken together they suggest ways that might be pursued in advancing both the scope and propriety of judicial review.

To conclude, taking non-justiciability in its strict sense to mean unsuited for adjudication, then it is an important idea in assessing the scope for judicial review of discretionary actions. However, there are still three directions that review might take: in ensuring that there is an informal division of powers so that decisions are made pursuant to standards settled in advance, where this may be done without undermining the objects of the power; in developing participatory procedures; and in maintaining a basis of rationality and purposiveness, and conformity with critical moral principles. These are directed at the background framework of decision-making rather than substantive merits in particular cases, but it is recognized that no clear line can be made between the two. It has been stressed also that non-justiciability may refer not only to analytical unsuitability for adjudication, but also to policy reasons for not intervening with a decision made by another authority. The two senses are important in examining judicial review, and although they are often run together, efforts should be made to see the specific role of each. Finally, although there are practical limitations on the capacity of courts when dealing with administrative regulation, there are signs that they may be able to develop expertise which goes beyond the strict task of adjudication.

5.3 CHANGES IN JUDICIAL ATTITUDES

About half-way through the century the signs of change in judicial attitudes to review began to appear. In 1952 the courts revived the doctrine that errors of law on the face of the record were reviewable,[75] thus giving themselves a limited basis for looking into the discretionary process where there is an official record. The concept of jurisdiction has been extended to allow courts to characterize as jurisdictional, errors which otherwise might be regarded as concerned with merits.[76] The rules relating to standing have been eased to allow a wider basis upon which individuals or groups may challenge a discretionary decision, and technical restrictions on the scope of remedies have been modified.[77]

[75] R. v. *Northumberland Compensation Appeal Tribunal, ex parte Shaw* [1952] 1 KB 338.
[76] *Anisminic Ltd* v. *Foreign Compensation Commission* [1968] 2 QB 862; also *Re Racal Communications Ltd* [1981] AC 374.
[77] For a general account, see de Smith, *Judicial Review*, part 3.

Of greatest importance, however, is the attitude of the courts in reviewing discretion itself. The increased review has various aspects. The discretionary control exercised by ministers and other officials over the disclosure of official information has come under judicial scrutiny.[78] In a less systematic way, the courts have begun to show interest in the facts upon which decisions are based, to ensure that there is an evidential basis for them,[79] and that the opinions and evaluations of a policy nature are also supported by rational considerations.[80] A duty of procedural fairness has been held to apply not only to judicial, but also to a wider spectrum of discretionary decisions.[81] Perhaps most importantly, the courts have begun to look into the reasoning process of decision-making in order to test the appropriateness of the reasons against the purposes of the power;[82] this has meant, on occasions, venturing far into the discretionary process. The consequences of these changes of direction are, firstly, an emphasis on fair procedures, and, secondly, a greater concern with the rational, purposive, and moral basis of decision. But before examining some of the main themes, we shall consider the implications of these changes generally and in relation to constitutional doctrines.

In *Padfield* v. *Minister of Agriculture*,[83] the minister had discretionary powers to deal with complaints made to him about the operation of the pricing system within the Milk Marketing Board. The statute empowered the minister, in his discretion, to refer the complaint to a committee of investigation which would consider the matter and then report back to him; he then had a further discretion whether to act on the committee's recommendations. A complaint was made and the minister decided, for a number of reasons which he made known, not to refer it to the committee for investigation. His reasons were based on the general nature of the milk marketing scheme and the desirability, in his opinion, of leaving it to the marketing board, which consisted of representatives of milk producers, to fix the prices. A challenge to the minister's decision, on the ground that he had not exercised his discretion in accordance with the purposes of the statute, was upheld by the House of Lords.

---

[78] Ibid., pp. 35–46.   [79] See section 6.41 below.
[80] See *Sagnata Investments* v. *Norwich Corporation* [1971] 2 QB 614.
[81] See de Smith, *Judicial Review*, ch. 4.
[82] For example *Padfield* v. *Minister of Agriculture* [1968] AC 997. Also, see, Lord Diplock, 'Administrative Law: Judicial Review Reviewed' 1974 *CLJ* 233.
[83] [1968] AC 997.

No new approach was enunciated, but, in applying the standards of *Wednesbury*, judicial opinions were divided. The minority of judges considered it to be inevitable and appropriate that the minister should act according to the policies which, in his opinion, provided the basis for the marketing scheme.[84] Provided that he did not act for reasons which clearly were unrelated to that scheme, it was not for the courts to assess the merits of his reasons. The majority approach was different: beginning with the principle that discretionary powers are conferred to promote the policy and objects of the statute, the majority proceeded to consider whether the minister's reasons for exercising his discretion one way rather than another were consistent with those objects and policies.[85] They concluded that he had misunderstood his powers, and that the reasons he gave for his actions were not within the statutory purposes.

This view has set the pace for later cases. The courts have examined the Home Secretary's discretion to revoke television licences which had been purchased in advance to avoid a future increase in fees,[86] the Secretary of State's powers to give directions to the Civil Aviation Authority, and his prerogative powers to designate suitable trans-Atlantic carriers to the United States government under treaty,[87] directions given by the Secretary of State for Education to a local education authority concerning the changeover to comprehensive state schooling,[88] and the business principles upon which the Greater London Council is to conduct its transport policy.[89] The courts do not always enter into such a close examination of reasons, but, in such cases, that is usually because of some additional reason of public policy which is taken to be more important; for example, the need to avoid grave harm to the national economy by a threatened strike,[90] or the importance of bringing defiant councillors to book, and thus preserving good government.[91]

The minority views in *Padfield* may be seen as generally continuing the approach that is dominant in the earlier cases: primary account-

---

[84] The leading minority judgements are Diplock LJ [1968] AC, pp. 1010–15 and Lord Morris, pp. 1040–4. Note that Lord Diplock now regards his approach in that case as too timid; *O'Reilly* v. *Mackman* [1982] 3 WLR 1096 at p. 1105.

[85] Lord Reid, ibid., pp. 1029–34.

[86] *Congreve* v. *Home Office* [1976] QB 629.

[87] *Laker Airways* v. *Department of Trade* [1977] KB 643.

[88] *Secretary of State for Education and Science* v. *Tameside MBC* [1977] AC 1014.

[89] *Bromley LBC* v. *Greater London Council* [1983] 1 AC 768.

[90] *Secretary of State for Employment* v. *Aslef* (No 2) [1972] 2 QB 455.

[91] *Asher* v. *Secretary of State for the Environment* [1974] 1 Ch 208.

ability for ministerial actions lies to Parliament and the political
process; the separation of powers requires the courts to stand back
from the decisions of executive and administrative authorities, and, in
any event, such matters are unsuited for judicial determination. The
majority view, however, marks subtle but important shifts in judicial
attitudes to those matters. Scrutiny of reasons and purposes is justified
on the basis of the sovereignty doctrine, but with consequential
diminution in the importance of the other side of the sovereignty
doctrine, namely that delegated authorities are primarily responsible to
Parliament. In *Padfield*, the administration of the milk marketing
scheme is the very sort of thing that Parliament might have taken a
close interest in, and yet the minister's responsibility to Parliament was
not seriously considered as a reason against review. The apparently
casual reference by the Master of the Rolls to 'questions in the House'
suggests a scepticism of parliamentary scrutiny, and a recognition that
once discretionary powers are conferred they do, in a way, become
independent of Parliament.[92] A similar premise underlies the speeches
of the majority in the House of Lords: once a statutory scheme has
been created, its daily workings pass out of the hands of Parliament;
Parliament may change the scheme by legislation or put pressure on
the minister to modify his policies, but it exercises little control over
the administrative operation of statutory provisions. In *Congreve*, it was
made clear that, since the minister's policy to revoke licences
purchased in advance was adopted without express parliamentary
direction, it was for the courts to pass judgment on it.[93] There is a
certain realism in recognizing such administrative autonomy and the
limited efficacy of accountability to Parliament. The next step is to
examine specific cases of discretion in order to ascertain the manner
and degree of accountability to Parliament and the political process.
Only after such an examination can a reviewing court begin to
determine with respect to a particular issue whether the avenues of
political accountability are sufficient, or whether they ought to be
supplemented by judicial scrutiny. The existence of some degree of
accountability to the political process does not necessarily exclude
judicial review, since there may be aspects of a discretionary decision
which ought to be subject to legal regulation, quite apart from whether
or not accountability for the final merits lies to the political process.
The degree of judicial scrutiny is justifiably influenced by the

[92] See Lord Denning [1976] 1 QB, p. 1006.
[93] [1976] 1 QB 629.

adequacy of other forms of accountability, both as to merits and outcome, and as to more permanent regulatory values.

There are also implications for democratic principles. The courts continue to stress that the merits of discretionary decisions are for the delegated authorities; judicial practice suggests, however, a failure to understand that once an examination of reasons and purposes is undertaken, there is no logical stopping-point between legality and merits. As judicial review advances in that direction, so that questions of merits become involved, democratic principles become blurred. However, we have seen the complexities and pitfalls in arguments from democracy, and, in particular, in using such arguments to justify any particular approach to judicial review. This does not mean that ideas of democracy play no part, but only that such arguments must be made with great care. Moreover, courts must be prepared to enter into consideration of such matters, simply because any approach to review involves unavoidably some view of democracy and the division of powers amongst different institutions. It is unsatisfactory to proceed on the basis that because judicial review is concerned with defining the limits of parliamentary intentions, any degree of review is justified, and no issue of democratic principles arise. Some conception of democracy inevitably enters into any determination of the right balance between Parliament, the autonomy of discretionary authorities, and the role of the courts. Similarly, as is shown in chapter 7, understandings of democracy are involved directly in settling matters of procedure, representation, and participation. It is to be stressed, however, that democratic principles are not the only sources of guidance in setting the bounds of judicial review. My argument has been that there are basic political values, of which the principle of democracy is but one, and which provide much of the basis for judicial review. Such regulatory values, while clear enough in abstract terms, need to be articulated and developed within the various areas of discretion. There is some evidence, although somewhat tentative and fragmented, that the courts in exercising review are beginning to address themselves to such matters, particularly with respect to the requirements of rational decision-making, and various aspects of fairness.[94]

Finally, the activist approach of the majority of *Padfield* signals a shift in attitude regarding justiciability. Any presumption that may have

[94] For examples, see *Council of Civil Service Unions* v. *Minister for Civil Service* [1984] 3 WLR 1174, esp. Lord Diplock; *In re Preston* [1985] 2 WLR 836; *In re Findlay* [1984] 3 WLR 1159; *Green* v. *Daniels* (1977) 51 ALJR 463.

existed to the effect that discretionary decisions are unsuited for judicial review no longer stands. One of the minister's arguments in *Padfield* was that the policies of the milk marketing scheme were linked to wider economic factors and ideas of equity amongst producers, and that it was appropriate for the minister to apply these in dealing with complaints. Some judges were receptive to arguments of this kind, but the majority did not regard the policy nature of the minister's decision as an obstacle to review. In other cases, appeals to non-justiciability have succeeded. In *Aslef (No 2)*, reference was made to the variety and complexity of the matters which the minister might properly take into account, and to the irreducibly evaluative nature of his final decision.[95] The same attitude has appeared in decisions dealing with the eviction by local authorities of residential tenants;[96] powers of management may be exercised for reasons quite apart from the tenant's record, and, short of bad faith, any assessment of their decisions is beyond judicial scrutiny. Similarly, some efforts have been made to show why issues of national security are not justiciable.[97] There is clear merit in overcoming the idea that discretionary decisions are presumptively and incorrigibly non-justiciable. But to make good use of non-justiciability it is necessary to analyse decisions, and to identify those aspects which are most suited for adjudicative resolution; it is also necessary to have a view about the functional capacities of different authorities, as well as the courts. Little of this is to be found, however, in the modern cases, so that non-justiciability is in danger of becoming another empty doctrine, able to be invoked to achieve whatever outcome is desired for other reasons.

The judicial approach manifested in *Padfield*, and extended in later cases, has been important in clearing away obstacles to judicial review of discretionary actions. However, this is still in a sense the pre-history of judicial review. The time is ripe to reassess the idea that judicial review consists in giving effect to parliamentary intentions. It can be accepted that much of judicial scrutiny is concerned with interpreting statutory terms, and that Parliament has the last word in setting the principles and limits of review. However, it can also be accepted that judicial review extends beyond interpreting statutes, that the doctrine of sovereignty is itself a common law doctrine which forms part of a wider framework of common law ideas, and that courts have a

[95] Buckley LJ [1972] 2 QB, pp. 494 ff.
[96] For example, *Bristol District Council* v. *Clark* [1975] 1 WLR 1443.
[97] See *Council of Civil Service Unions* v. *Minister for Civil Service* [1984] 3 WLR 1174.

legitimate role and a constitutional duty to devise and extend the principles that are suitable constraints on discretionary authority. This means recognizing that the assumptions of the private law model are inadequate in dealing with the exercise of authority within the public law model. Before considering lines for developing judicial review, brief examination should be made of an Australian experiment to extend review to the merits.

5.4 REVIEW OF THE MERITS: AN AUSTRALIAN EXPERIMENT

Discussion of judicial review of discretionary powers generally is conducted on the assumption that the scope of review should not extend directly to the merits of decisions. In recent years in Australia there have been departures from this assumption by creating a system of administrative appeals tribunals dealing with matters within the jurisdiction of the federal government. The tribunals have powers to review in selected areas the decisions of ministers, their departments, and other officials and authorities. The statutory grant of powers to the tribunal is expressed in the widest terms; it may exercise, generally, all the powers and discretions which are conferred on the person who made the decision; it may affirm, vary or set aside the decision, and it may substitute its own decision or return the matter to the original authority for reconsideration in accordance with any directions or recommendations of the tribunal.[98] When the Attorney-General introduced the bill, he referred to the tribunal as 'machinery provided by Parliament for adjudication';[99] but although it has various curial features, is independent of the administration, and is immune from direct political control, its functions are not confined to those traditionally considered judicial. Its jurisdiction does not extend to all administrative actions, but only those that are brought by parliament expressly within its powers. Many of the tribunal's decisions are concerned with aspects of administrative actions that are suited to adjudicative processes: matters of fact and evidence, interpretation of legal provisions, ensuring the fair and consistent application of policies and guide-lines made by the minister or other authorities, and maintaining fair procedures. In those matters, the tribunal is unhindered by

---

[98] *Administrative Appeals Tribunal Act* 1975 (Cth.), s. 43(1).
[99] *House of Representatives Debates*, 1975, vol. 93, p. 1187.

the normal constraints on courts and has been able to establish a firm basis of review.

However, because of the widely drawn statutory powers under which it operates, the tribunal often is required to consider the substantive merits of discretionary decisions. In many matters, it may discharge this duty without straying far from the adjudicative process. In other cases, however, where powers are vested in the discretion of a minister or other senior official, this duty may take the tribunal to the centre of matters of high policy. In the two reports which led to its creation, it was envisaged that the tribunal would be concerned less with the merits of policy than with its application; the tribunal's task would be to ensure that decisions in particular cases were not oppressive, discriminatory, or otherwise unjust.[100] But no such reservations were made in the statute, and when the question came before the Federal Court in *Drake* v. *Minister for Immigration and Ethnic Affairs*,[101] it declined to infer any restrictions on the breadth of the tribunal's powers. Where issues of policy are involved, the tribunal may treat the stance taken by the minister or other official as a relevant factor in its deliberations, but it must not abdicate its duty of deciding whether the decision was 'the correct or preferable one in favour of a function of merely determining whether the decision made conformed with whatever the relevant general government policy might be'.[102]

In later cases, the tribunal has attempted to devise guide-lines as to how it should proceed in the light of the Federal Court's directive. It must not accept ministerial or departmental policy without question, and yet there are reasons of a constitutional kind for making some accommmodation with ministers and their departments. The first president of the tribunal, Mr Justice Brennan, who moulded its early development with insight and imagination, distinguished between adjudicative decisions and discretionary decisions; in the latter, there are inevitably issues of policy to be settled. Issues of policy divide into categories: policies settled at the political level, and policies settled at the departmental level. The tribunal may depart from both, but 'it would be manifestly imprudent for the tribunal to override a ministerial policy and to adopt a general administrative policy of its

---

[100] *Commonwealth Administrative Review Committee*, Report 1971, para. 300; *Committee on Administrative Discretion*, Final Report 1973, para. 172.

[101] (1979) 2 ALD 60.

[102] Ibid., pp. 69–70.

own.'[103] The tribunal might depart from a policy, whether ministerial or departmental, to avoid injustice in a particular case, but in general its approach towards the substance of policy should be one of restraint. Three reasons were given to support this stance: the tribunal is not linked into the chain of responsibility from minister to government to Parliament, its constitution and membership is not appropriate for the formulation of general policy, and it is unsupported by a bureaucracy fitted to advise on policy.[104]

The tribunal is still in its early years and it is too soon to expect its role to be defined with precision. Policy issues have arisen mainly in relation to the deportation of immigrants for drug offences; as a result, there has not been a wide spectrum of matters within which to test the implications of Brennan J.'s guide-lines. However, the deportation cases do reveal some of the difficulties likely to be encountered. In the first place, it is not easy to maintain the distinction between the merits of a general policy and the merits of its application in specific cases.[105] The very judgment that the policy works injustice in a particular situation depends, normally, on a commitment to some other standard or set of standards which would be contravened by the general policy. In any case, some members of the tribunal have been openly critical of the deportation policies themselves.[106] Secondly, the fact that the minister's policies have been stated in a set of guide-lines and tabled in Parliament does not appear to have been a major factor in the deliberations of some members of the tribunal. Even policies with the best political credentials may be based on false or unacceptable premises, or may be morally offensive or insupportable for some other reason. Nevertheless, considerable concern has been expressed by commentators at the implications for constitutional principles of the tribunal censoring government policy. Thirdly, however, there has been little opportunity for testing and developing the two other factors given by Brennan J.—the tribunal's unsuitability for formulating general policy and the absence of an attendant bureaucracy—as reasons for restraint in exercising review. But, again, the deportation cases throw some light on these matters. The tribunal might not be the most appropriate body for devising a deportation code, and anyhow

---

[103] *Re Drake and Minister for Immigration and Ethnic Affairs (No 2)* (1979) 2 ALD 634, p. 644.
[104] Ibid.
[105] Brennan J. develops this distinction in 'New Growth in the Law—The Judicial Contribution' (1979) 6 *MonLR* 1.
[106] For a review of the deportation cases, see Kirby, 'Administrative Review'.

that is not its function; but that does not obviously detract from its capacity as an outside body to expose the weaknesses in existing policies. Moreover, where exposure depends mainly, as in deportation matters, on rational scrutiny and moral evaluation, the absence of a supporting bureaucracy is not likely to be a major consideration. That last factor is of course of greater importance in areas where policies turn on issues of a complex economic and social kind, and require for their effective application a continuing course of decisions. It is clearly necessary to be careful in characterizing the capacities of the tribunal in a general way; its strengths and weaknesses depend so much on the kinds of issues with which it deals.

It is interesting to notice how the very same issues which have shaped attitudes in the context of judicial review are at the centre of the debate as to how the tribunal should approach its tasks: accountability and democratic principles, and to a lesser extent the separation of powers; justiciability and the suitability of different institutions for different tasks. There are significant differences, but both the courts and the Administrative Appeals Tribunal, in defining their respective roles, must take some stand on these matters in developing an understanding of the place of each in the constitution. We may conclude by considering briefly some of the implications of these issues for the tribunal.

The fact that the tribunal stands outside the line of accountability to Parliament, and so to the democratic process, is of course important, although it is unclear as to precisely what inferences are to be drawn. The tribunal is not accountable to Parliament for particular decisions but it is the creation of Parliament, its powers derive from Parliament, and areas of jurisdiction allotted to it depend on a deliberate decision by Parliament. It is still true that the tribunal is not linked to Parliament in the same way as a minister, and this is a factor to be taken into account in defining the tribunal's attitude to ministerial discretions. It is not clear, however, why the fact that a ministerial policy has been scrutinized by Parliament is of great moment; Parliament may legislate and thereby give binding force to, say, its deportation policy. If it chooses not to, but delegates the policy issues to its ministers, then that is to adopt a different strategy; subsequent parliamentary approval (whatever exactly that connotes) of the minister's policies may be of little constitutional effect. It is, at best, one factor which the tribunal might consider relevant to its approach in a particular case. But there are other factors: appeal might be made to a principle or value which has wide support in the community or in other areas of law and practice, or which might be, for moral reasons, a principle which ought to be adopted even if to do so is to move ahead of public opinion. Some of the reasons given in the deportation cases are of these kinds. Why should the tribunal not concern themselves with the moral basis of double punishment or the empirical basis of deterrence? Similarly, the tribunal might appeal to a view of democratic principles which is more sophisticated than mere majority rule, and which recognizes that the tribunal has a role to play in protecting minority interests, thus enhancing rather than being in opposition to democratic ideas. These are the sorts of arguments to which the tribunal might appeal; they must be worked out step by step as new situations arise. But there is no reason for thinking that the tribunal is somehow illegitimate, a cuckoo in the democratic nest.

Similar sorts of considerations apply with respect to questions of justiciability and institutional capacities. Two brief points may be noted. Firstly, it is important to distinguish between the tribunal's task of reviewing actual decisions, and the administative tasks of formulating general policy. The tribunal's decisions are likely to have implications for general policy, but its policy-making role is limited and indirect, and its primary concern is still with individualized decisions. Secondly, and notwithstanding, there may be occasions where the tribunal would be ill-advised, for the reasons Mr Justice Brennan suggested, to take upon itself a rigorous examination of policy matters with far-reaching social and economic consequences, because of its lack of expertise and its limited capacities. But again, these matters can be worked out only as opportunities arise and as experience accumulates.[107]

5·5 DIRECTIONS FOR JUDICIAL REVIEW

Realist approaches to judicial review contend that the courts, like all other state institutions, are concerned with policy results and are influenced by a host of matters which are constantly changing. Martin

[107] For general commentary on the Administrative Appeals Tribunal, the following are useful: G. D. S. Taylor, 'The New Administrative Law' (1977) 51 *ALJ* 804; D. Pearce, 'Courts, Tribunals and Government Policy' (1980) 11 *FLR* 203; J. King, 'The Role of the Judge in Relation to Public Administration' (1980) 39 *AJPA*. 1; J. Goldring, 'The Foundations of the "New Administrative Law" in Australia' (1981) 40 *AJPA* 79 and 'Responsible Government and the Administrative Appeals Tribunal' (1982) 13 *FLR* 90.

Shapiro advances such a view, the corollary being that courts are not doing anything that is different in principle from the activities of other officials.[108] The opposite view might be put in Dworkinian dress: judges do have a distinctive role which is to proceed according to principles rather than policies, and to uphold the rights of individuals against the state.[109] The analysis of this chapter suggests that, in a system which in many respects fits the public law model, the truth lies somewhere between the two. Judges in exercising review of discretionary decisions are concerned with two primary objectives: one is to maintain, in so far as the limited powers of courts are able, an acceptable balance between political institutions, the other is to ensure that decisions are made in accordance with constraints which are based finally on fundamental political values and policies. It may still be maintained, however, that the primary object of external judicial scrutiny, whatever form it takes, is not in 'governing', but in formulating the conditions which are to be satisfied, as necessary rather than sufficient, if governmental decisions are to be acceptable. Within the public law model there is no one, single benchmark against which review can be tested; many of the assumptions which served in the private law model have been subverted, so that the task for review is more complicated and the directions it might take more diverse.

In this uncertain endeavour, there is, however, guidance to be derived from two sources: from one come the constitutional principles we have been considering—the separation of powers, parliamentary sovereignty and democratic principles, justiciability and institutional capacities; from the other come the values considered in 2.32—the rational basis of decision-making, the provision of reasonably stable decision standards, the concern with fair procedures, and principles of basic morality. The latter provide the basis of constraints on the exercise of discretion, while the former provide the constitutional values to guide the courts in deciding the extent of their responsibility for advancing those constraints. These two sources of guidance do not stipulate results but provide the kinds of considerations in terms of which results are to be sought and justified. Even within the confines of such guidance, the emphasis may be put in one way rather than another, and a range of conclusions is possible. Questions of interpretation, of different understandings of the constitution, and policy factors inevitably enter into this process; but this does not mean

---

[108] *The Supreme Court and Administrative Agencies*, ch. 1.
[109] *Taking Rights Seriously*, ch. iv.

that any conclusion is as good as another. The object of argument and reflection is to develop and refine the guiding doctrines, and to show by persuasion that, while there may be no one right answer, some answers are clearly insupportable and, amongst those that remain, some are better than others.

There are signs of realization that the assumptions implicit in the private law model are inadequate in developing a more modern approach. However, the willingness to move away from their earlier stance has tended to produce, so far, little more than unprincipled forays into discretionary decisions. The next step is to reflect more closely on how the constitutional doctrines and the background values can be translated into the public law model. The necessary standpoint or theoretical understanding cannot be achieved by logical deduction from simple principles, for example that judicial review is giving effect to the will of Parliament; rather, it can be achieved only by extrapolating doctrines and values, and by assessing and reassessing their application as understanding advances and circumstances change.

In a recent and striking statement, Lord Diplock has acknowledged that in addition to illegality and procedural impropriety, irrationality in an official action is itself a basis for judicial review.[110] Irrationality was defined in terms of the *Wednesbury* test of unreasonableness, which in turn was said to apply 'to a decision which is so outrageous in its defiance of logic or of accepted moral standards that no sensible person who had applied his mind . . . could have arrived at it'.[111] The association of logic and morality under the concept of rationality raises interesting issues, and in any event the practical consequences of irrationality as a separate head of review remain uncertain. The suggested test erects a threshold so low as to be easily surmounted, and anyhow courts have for some time been employing, implicitly, some such test. The significance of the statement lies perhaps in the fact that once irrationality is recognized as an independent ground of review, closer consideration may be given to developing, under the capacious concept of rationality, more exacting criteria of review. Indeed, the discussion in the next chapter demonstrates that there are already links to be drawn between various specific heads of review, and a concept of rationality. In addition to notions of rationality, there also

[110] In *Council of Civil Service Unions* v. *Minister for the Civil Service* [1984] 3 WLR 1174 at p. 1196.
[111] *Ibid.*

are signs of greater judicial attention to fairness, in a mixture of procedural and substantive senses. It is too early to claim substantial progress in developing wider notions of fairness, but it is in accordance with the general argument of this chapter to suggest that this concept will be advanced increasingly in regulating discretion.

These developments are modest, and it is by no means certain that a sophisticated system of judicial review will emerge. In any case, courts are likely to remain substantially confined in their capacity for expanding review. In the absence of statutory authorization, they are unlikely to be as innovative or exacting as the Australian Administrative Appeals Tribunal, for example. But, even within its confines, judicial review may progress markedly in the construction of a body of doctrine suitable to the exercise of discretionary powers in the public law model.

5.6 CONCLUSION

The object of this chapter has been to consider the general framework of legal regulation of discretion, and to examine in some detail the premises and assumptions on which judicial review is based. The scope for legal regulation of discretion may be thought of in terms of a plane stretching between two points: at one end there is complete review in the sense that the reviewing authority considers the merits and substitutes its own view; at the other end is review in its narrower sense, something akin to judicial review in its earliest years, where the object is to ensure compliance with minimal notions of legality. Between these two points there are various intermediate positions which are illustrated in the practices of the authorities considered; the Administrative Appeals Tribunal for example, provides a more exacting review than the courts, while in turn the practices of the courts have also changed by extending incrementally the scope for review.

Where the practice of any particular authority—whether courts, ombudsmen, or special tribunals—is to be placed along this plane is determined largely by three variables: the constitutional position of the authority, and in particular its relationship to the political process; the procedures and techniques by which the authority operates, for example whether it is investigative or adjudicative, whether it may initiate action itself; and thirdly the principles and standards sought to be applied. Each of these variables requires interpretation and application, and thus involves a considerable degree of judgment and opinion. For these reasons disagreement about the best approach to be adopted by any particular authority, and whether more and different authorities ought to be created, is unavoidable. The scope for different views can be seen in the development of judicial review and in the continuing arguments about its rightful place. A similar analysis might be made of each of the other authorities that are involved in regulating the exercise of discretion. Perhaps we may end with the simple point that any particular view must be argued for in terms of these variables, and there is no fixed yardstick at which judicial review, or any other form of review is to be aimed. Nevertheless, I have suggested the general directions which judicial review might profitably take, based around the variables mentioned; recent judicial practice has taken some steps towards this approach, but obviously there is still much to be done in working out a coherent and justifiable approach. Some aspects of the contemporary approach are considered in greater detail in the following chapters, and at various points suggestions are made as to how that approach might be developed further.

6

Themes in Legal Regulation and Judicial Review

Now that the general basis of legal regulation and judicial review has been considered, a number of specific themes may be examined. The underlying object is to consider the extent to which the general themes of rationality, purposiveness, and background principles are manifested in judicial review; where there are obstacles to the further development of legal principles, those obstacles are examined and appraised. The analysis begins with the disclosure of reasons; the disclosure of general reasons before decisions and specific reasons after decisions are basic requirements of good decision-making. But since those requirements are not insisted upon in any general way, the case for disclosure is examined and the arguments against considered. The second theme is the normative framework within which decisions are made, with particular attention being paid not only to the no-fettering doctrine, but also to the positive case for standards being laid down. The final themes concern more clearly the substance of reasons: the problems that occur in ascertaining purposes, the relevance and irrelevance of reasons, and questions about reasonableness and the evidential basis of facts and policies.

6.1 REASONS FOR DECISIONS

The general principles that discretionary decisions should be made according to rational reasons means: (*a*) that there be findings of primary facts based on good evidence, and (*b*) that decisions about the facts be made for reasons which serve the purposes of the statute in an intelligible and reasonable manner. Actions which do not meet these threshold requirements are arbitrary, and may be considered a misuse of powers. Since questions arising under (*a*), and questions about the content of reasons under (*b*), touch on the substance of discretion, they are considered in section 6.3. In this section we are concerned with the more formal issue concerning the disclosure of reasons.

The duty to act rationally is a basic political principle, as we have seen, and it is implicit in a range of legal doctrines. But while there is a duty on officials to act rationally, it is a separate question whether there is a legal duty to make their reasons known, either generally or to the parties affected. The disclosure question has two aspects: one consists of making known in advance the reasons in the sense of the standards and considerations that will govern the decision; the other consists of supplying the reasons for having made a decision in a particular way.[1] The case for disclosure in those two senses depends partly on arguments from rationality and partly on fairness. An official may act rationally without disclosing his reasons, but disclosure is likely to enhance rationality; it may tend to make an official reflect more carefully on his task, to be more diligent in identifying and specifying objects and purposes, and to take greater care in applying them to the circumstances. Disclosure in advance of the standards to be applied has the added advantage of allowing parties to direct their arguments and proofs more directly and economically to the matters in issue; it also provides a source of information which might be highly relevant to the decision. The argument from fairness is that when the state takes action which is directed against an individual or affects him in important ways, there is a duty to follow procedures which show respect for that person. This would require, normally, that a person be told in advance the basis on which action is to be taken, and given reasons after the event for the decision. These issues are treated more fully in chapter 7, where it is shown that arguments from fairness are not without their difficulties. However, it may be accepted that on the basis of rationality and fairness there is a good case for disclosure of reasons. The joint grounds of fairness and rationality are not always strictly compatible, since the former may impose constraints which detract from the latter; but, generally, fair procedures also contribute to rationality.

Disclosure of general reasons in advance of decisions and disclosure of particular ones afterwards have qualities in common which derive from rationality and fairness. The main difference is that while disclosure in advance assists parties in preparing their evidence and

---

[1] This distinction is generally overlooked. See M. Akehurst, 'Statement of Reasons for Judicial and Administrative Decisions' (1970) 33 *MLR* 154; G. A. Flick, 'Administrative Adjudications and the Duty to Give Reasons—A Search for Criteria' 1978 *PL* 16.

marshalling their arguments for the decision itself, disclosure after the event enables parties to decide whether the decision is sound, and whether a challenge might be made to it. Disclosure is particularly important in the discretionary context in removing ambiguity and uncertainty as to why a decision was made. There is a good case for disclosure at both points. The Franks Committee in Britain and similar committees in Australia and America have recognized the importance of reasons after the event,[2] and their respective recommendations have led to the imposition in some contexts of statutory duties of disclosure.[3] Less attention has been paid to the disclosure of reasons before the event, although this sometimes is dealt with in specific statutes by stipulating the standards to be applied or the matters to be taken into account. In both cases, the statutory requirements tend to be piecemeal and unsystematic, with the courts being left to settle reasons requirements. Since it is accepted generally that there is no general common law duty to give reasons, failure to do so does not itself invalidate the decision. However, we shall see that there are various ways in which the failure to give reasons may be the basis for establishing invalidity on other grounds.

6.11   *Disclosure of reasons and factors before decisions*

It would be unusual for an authority to make decisions in the exercise of its powers without first formulating, even if tentatively, some general policies, standards, or guide-lines; in some cases it might also gather together a body of knowledge and opinion about how to settle the issues likely to arise, and, on the basis of evidence and facts, form impressions and views which are likely to be relied on in decision-making. Individual decisions, in other words, are bound to be made within a context of policies and attitudes, and against a background of factual assumptions. The extent of an authority's duties to formulate guiding standards is one issue which is considered in section 6.2; my present concern is not with the extent of that duty, but with the extent to which such policies, standards, opinions, and facts to be relied on, must be disclosed to interested parties. The extent and significance of

[2] *Committee on Administrative Tribunals and Inquiries* (HMSO Cmnd. 218, 1957) (Franks Report); *Committee on Administrative Discretion* (Cth Parl. Paper No. 316, 1973) (Bland Report), para. 172(a)(ii); *Administrative Procedure in Government Agencies* (Senate Doc. No. 8, 77th Congress, 1st Sess. 1941), pp. 29–30. See also, the Justice–All Souls Report, *Reviews of Administrative Law in the United Kingdom* (Discussion Paper, 1981).
[3] For example: *Tribunals and Inquiries Act* (UK) 1971, s. 12 and Schedule 1.

any such duty naturally varies as decisions range across the spectrum of types earlier identified; in cases close to the adjudicative mode, reasonably precise standards would be expected, and it is those to which duties of disclosure would apply; in cases of, say, specific policy decisions, there might be little more than very abstract and indeterminate policies to be disclosed. Bearing in mind variations of those kinds, a few remarks need to be made about the extent of any general duty of disclosure.

It is often the case in practice that what may be called the decisional factors acted on in the exercise of discretion are not disclosed in advance. The extent of any duties to disclosure, and the actual practice of different authorities in making disclosure, is highly variable. Parliament has not attempted to provide by statutory enactment any general duty of disclosure; what statutory duties there are tend to be found in specific statutes, but even there the requirements as to the existence and extent of any duties to disclose vary greatly. If any generalization may be ventured, it would be that there exists no consistent and universally applied statutory policy. Authorities are often left to decide for themselves the extent to which disclosure of decisional factors ought to be made; and again both the ways of disclosing and the degree of disclosure are greatly variable. Indeed, in a number of areas like social security, immigration, and compensation for criminal injuries, it is usual to find that while there is extensive disclosure of some guide-lines, there are others which are kept secret. In other contexts, such as planning, there is considerable controversy as to the extent to which disclosure should be made of background reports and expert opinion. Where disclosure is denied, it is usually for what are called rather loosely reasons of efficiency, but just what this connotes, and how the balance is to be struck with the strong and obvious case for disclosure, has not been the subject of systematic analysis. The strength of that case finds support in the practice of special bodies like the Parliamentary Commissioner for Administration and the Council on Tribunals. But this support is in the main implicit, with more attention being paid to the importance of explaining a decision after it has been made.

The issue has come to a head in a number of judicial decisions which provide some support for a general duty of disclosure, and which have provided a forum for consideration of the issues involved. So the Criminal Injuries Compensation Board has been held to a duty to inform an applicant for compensation of any principles that it intended to use in its decisions;[4] in deciding on the suitability of applicants for a gaming licence, the Gaming Board should give 'sufficient indication of the objections raised against him such as to enable him to answer them';[5] and where the Board of Trade had laid down firm guide-lines for allocating subsidies to manufacturers, it was required to give applicants the opportunity of addressing arguments to show why the guide-lines ought to be modified or made exceptions to in that case.[6] However, there are decisions explicitly denying the existence of any legal duty of advance disclosure where the authority has discretion: a local authority in exercising its powers of management, regulation, and control of housing is under no duty to disclose the standards and factors that are acted on in evicting tenants;[7] the Boxing Board of Control may deny an application for a boxing manager's licence without disclosing even the gist of the standards that it is applying.[8]

The issue of prior disclosure generally arises either in the context of the no-fettering doctrine or as an aspect of natural justice. As to the first, an authority may adopt general standards provided that the circumstances of each case are considered to determine how the standards are to apply or whether they perhaps ought to be modified. So in *British Oxygen* v. *Board of Trade*,[9] the House of Lords held the formulation of guide-lines to be in order provided that each applicant was given the chance to address arguments as to how its case should be dealt with; something which could be done only if the existence and content of the guide-lines were disclosed.[10] Such cases might appear to support by implication the prior disclosure of proposed standards. However, the position is not quite so clear, since the no-fettering doctrine usually requires only that the authority should direct its attention to the particular case, not that it must give a party whose interests are in question the opportunity of being heard. The no-fettering doctrine and natural justice have developed along independent lines and do not always coincide.[11]

---

[4] *R.* v. *Criminal Justice Injuries Compensation Board, ex parte Ince.* [1973] 1 WLR 1334 at p. 1345.
[5] *R.* v. *Gaming Board, ex parte Benaim and Khaida* [1970] 2 QB 417, at p. 431.
[6] *British Oxygen* v. *Board of Trade* [1971] AC 610.
[7] *Cannock Chase DC* v. *Kelly* [1978] 1 WLR 1.
[8] *McInnes* v. *Onslow-Fane* [1978] 1 WLR 1520.   [9] [1971] AC 610.
[10] For a similar approach in other cases see: *Cumings* v. *Birkenhead Corporation* [1972] 1 Ch 12; *Schmidt* v. *Secretary of State for Home Affairs* [1969] 2 Ch 149.
[11] For discussion of this divergence, see D. J. Galligan, 'Nature and Function of Policies within Discretionary Powers' (1976) *PL*, pp. 355-7.

As an aspect of natural justice, prior disclosure comes within the principle that a party likely to be affected by official action should know the case against him, and be given an opportunity of meeting it. This formulation may seem more suited to decisions of an adjudicative kind rather than decisions of, say, a specific or general policy kind; but, leaving aside for the moment the object of natural justice with respect to more policy-based decisions (which determines the significance and extent of disclosure), it is not always accepted that there is in discretionary contexts any general duty of disclosure of decisional factors.[12] In *McInnes* v. *Onslow-Fane*, the Boxing Board of Control was not required to inform the applicant of the standards to be applied or the considerations to be taken into account.[13] The Board's powers are discretionary in a clear sense; the empowering statute gave only the barest guidance and, while each applicant had an interest in obtaining a licence, there was no question of rights being affected or legitimate expectations being thwarted. In deciding against any duty to disclose reasons, either in advance or after the event, a number of justifications were offered. An examination of those shows the principal arguments that the courts have advanced against disclosure.

One reason against prior disclosure is connected to the scope of judicial review; wider disclosure would create greater demand on courts to review the suitability of the standards, and to test their application to the facts. The more information there is about how a decision was made, then the greater scope there is for finding something to challenge. But to use this as an argument against disclosure is to linger in the shadow of *Arlidge* rather than to follow the lights of *Padfield*; the point is that disclosure of the standards, or any other information, does not itself commit courts to anything in terms of review. The two matters are best kept separate; the courts have their own means for regulating review, and it is a strange argument that uses the possibility of greater review as a reason against enhancing rationality and fairness.

A second and more generally applicable objection to disclosure, which appears under many guises, relates to administrative efficiency. If the Boxing Board were required to make prior disclosure, it would be necessary to have a provisional procedure at which the standards could be disclosed, and an indication given of how they would apply in that

---

[12] Natural justice usually is defined in terms which include prior disclosure of standards and considerations; see de Smith *Judicial Review*, p. 156.
[13] [1978] 1 WLR 1520.

case.[14] A related argument is that administrative bodies have difficult tasks to perform; authorities like the Boxing Board or the Parole Board have to assess complex matters, and acquire with experience a sense of what is appropriate.[15] The imposition of procedural hurdles might obstruct the efficient execution of those tasks.[16] To these familiar arguments there are two replies. Firstly, we must recall the distinction between efficiency and effectiveness. Greater disclosure of decisional factors, although administratively inconvenient, may enhance, nevertheless, the rational basis of decisions; that is, it may help to produce decisions which achieve a closer congruence between general objects and results in actual cases and so be highly effective. If interested parties know the proposed basis for making decisions, they may be able by their arguments and evidence to show how to deal best with the present case, or even provide reasons for modifying the decisional factors. Talk of efficiency, however, usually connotes a thin sense of expedition and economy which tends to be impeded by procedural constraints like the requirement of disclosure. Speed and economy are of course components of good decision-making, but such factors, together with the more general problems that arise from limited resources, are constraints on the extent of any duty of disclosure rather than decisive reasons against its existence. In other words, arguments from efficiency do not meet the strong case for disclosure, they rather affect the extent of disclosure in different situations. Moreover, arguments based on the costs of additional administrative burdens like disclosure must be treated with caution, since there is the familiar phenomenon whereby administrative practice tends to be able to adjust to and absorb new constraints without loss of effectiveness or overall efficiency, even though such constraints might initially have appeared onerous. This might well occur, should disclosure of decisional factors become an integral aspect of everyday practice.

The second reply to the argument from efficiency is based on procedural fairness. Fair procedures impose on decision-making constraints which are always in a sense inconvenient. But fair procedures are based partly on their contribution to rational outcomes, and partly on their links with other values. A more complete examination of the requirements of fair procedures is made in the next chapter, where it is argued that notions of fairness have a significant

---

[14] Ibid., pp. 1532–3.
[15] With respect to the Parole Board, see *Payne* v. *Lord Harris* [1981] 1 WLR 754.
[16] [1978] 1 WLR at p. 1535.

place in discretionary contexts, a place often buttressed by the claim that there are individual rights to good and fair procedures. If that kind of argument is accepted, and if prior disclosure of decisional factors is an important facet of fair procedures (a matter not accepted in the boxing decision),[17] then that case is not defeated by just any argument from efficiency or cost. Again, as suggested above, matters of costs are relevant to the scope of disclosure, but do not override the duty itself. On the basis of these considerations, there is a good case for a presumption in favour of prior disclosure, the extent of which is variable depending on the type of decision in issue, the circumstances of particular discretions, and the capacities of different authorities; that presumption may not normally be overriden, however, merely on the grounds of administrative costs or convenience. It might perhaps be overriden, or at least qualified, by conflicting matters such as the confidentiality of information; it might even in a rare case be overriden by circumstances of emergency. It is hard to see in the boxing case that there were adequate grounds on any count to defeat that presumption.

A third argument against prior disclosure might be based on non-justiciability. In the boxing manager's case it was said that there may be many reasons for refusing a licence: the personal characteristics and background of the applicant, or reasons of general policy concerning the regulation of boxing. There may be 'no case against him at all',[18] the implication being that there is nothing to disclose and, in turn, that there is nothing to which arguments can be directed. But we saw in the previous chapter that issues are not simply justiciable or non-justiciable; that is a matter of degree to be assessed only by careful analysis of decisions. It may turn out that the Boxing Board had been applying fixed and detailed standards; by that very fact, the issue would become to a degree justiciable, and a strong case for disclosure would be made out in terms of both rationality and fairness. Even where the standards are left relatively abstract to be individualized incrementally in the circumstances of each case, the support for disclosure of those standards remains. Disclosure should not be dependent on the decisions being adjudicative; disclosure may be equally important in consultative procedures where the object is to ensure that, in settling issues of policy, the views and interests of the parties are considered.

This leads to a final comment about the extent of the duty to

[17] Ibid., at p. 1532.
[18] Ibid., at pp. 1533–4. A similar point is often made in decisions relating to the penal process; see *Payne* v. *Harris* [1981] 1 WLR 754.

disclose decisional factors. If the general duty is made out on grounds of effectiveness and fairness, then the practical question is what exactly that duty requires. In the first place, it would be mistaken to think that disclosure makes sense only in decisions of an adjudicative kind; the modes of participation appropriate to more discretionary decisions, the dominant of which is perhaps consultation, still depend on interested parties being able to address arguments and evidence to matters of policy, opinion, and fact. So, although the decisional factors in more discretionary contexts may be less specific and less settled than in adjudication, that factor affects the manner and degree of disclosure not the general duty. The extent of that duty may be affected also by the resources and capacities of the authority, the subject matter in issue, and the nature and importance of the interests affected. But, as I try to show in the final chapter, these are matters which always affect the design and requirements of good and fair procedures.

To conclude, there is a persuasive case based on rationality and fairness for the prior disclosure of standards and considerations. It seems of sufficient weight to create a presumption in favour of disclosure, unless there are clear and strong policy reasons to the contrary. The arguments that courts tend to rely on are generally unconvincing, and rarely amount to serious consideration of the basis of disclosure, or of the relationship between fairness and administrative convenience. A presumption in favour of disclosure may encourage courts and officials to consider more carefully this relationship, and to be more explicit in formulating and weighting reasons that outweigh it. Administrative convenience is rarely a good reason; on the other hand, there may be genuinely countervailing factors like confidentiality in relation to national security or other important aspects of the public interest.[19] It might also be legitimate to withhold disclosure where the discretionary power relates to matters of high constitutional significance, such as gubernatorial powers with respect to parliament and the executive.

---

[19] For a striking decision in a different context but relevant by analogy, where national security prevailed over procedural fairness, see *Council of Civil Service Unions* v. *Minister for Civil Service* [1984] 3 WLR 1174. With regard to confidentiality, it is often possible to disclose the general purport of confidential information while keeping secret the details and sources. An approach along these lines would help to remove the sense of unfairness that persists in cases like *R.* v. *Gaming Board, ex parte Benaim and Khaida* [1970] 2 QB 417.

6.12   *Disclosure of particular reasons for decisions*

The case for explaining why a decision has been made also turns on arguments from rationality and fairness. An adequate explanation should include findings of fact as well as the reasons for acting on those facts in a particular way. On the assumption that post-explanations do marginally enhance the rational basis of decisions, and that there is at stake an important aspect of fairness, again there is a strong case for disclosure. There is also the additional factor that disclosure after the decision may facilitate judicial scrutiny of discretionary powers. These considerations again would seem to create a presumptive case for disclosure, to be overridden only for clear and powerful policy reasons.[20] The legal requirements, however, are fragmented, partly dependent on statute and partly on common law. Where there are statutory provisions, they typically require a general statement of reasons, and then leave it for the courts to decide on their adequacy;[21] where there are no statutory provisions, the issue is left entirely to the common law.

Statutory requirements regarding reasons are to be found either in statutes of general application to classes of authorities or types of decisions, or in the specific statutes under which discretion occurs. One example of the first is the Tribunals and Inquiries Act in Britain, dealing with the decisions of most tribunals and inquiries; another example is the Australian Administrative Appeals Tribunal Act which enables a person whose interests are affected by certain types of discretionary decisions to require a statement setting out (*a*) the findings on material matters of fact, and (*b*) the evidence or other material on which the findings are based, and (*c*) giving reasons for the decision. Apart from these statutes of more general application, there are in the various jurisdictions various specific statutes imposing more or less exacting duties as to the giving of reasons. There remain, however, many areas of discretion which are relatively immune from statutory requirements, the penal process being a notable example. Despite the continued existence of such areas, there is, as noted earlier, an increasingly strong and widespread commitment to the

[20] For further discussion, see R. L. Rabin, 'Job Security and Due Process: Monitoring Administrative Discretion Through a Reasons Requirement' (1976–7) 44 *UChicLR* 60. (The argument for disclosure based on autonomy must be considered in the light of chapter 7).

[21] On the adequacy of reasons where there is a duty to disclose, see *Re Poyser and Mills' Arbitration* [1984] 2 QB 467, *Mountview Court Properties* v. *Devlin* (1970) 21 P&CR 689 and *Elliott* v. *Southwark LBC* [1976] 1 WLR 499.

provision of reasons as an integral part of good administration. The annual reports of the Council on Tribunals, for example, portray a deep concern that the giving of reasons be extended across a wide range of discretionary matters. The Council has urged that, save where a case is made out for an exception in particular circumstances, reasons should be given in writing by all tribunals for all their decisions.[22] This, it may be suggested, is likely in time to become an axiom applied to all discretionary decisions, unless there are clear and established policies in specific contexts against revelation as, for example, in matters of national security.

Turning now to the approach of the courts in judicial review, it has been true generally that there is no duty to give reasons for discretionary decisions in the sense that failure to do so would be a ground of invalidity. The position is not now so clear because of developments in three directions. In the first place, failure to give reasons may be held to constitute an improper exercise of power. An industrial tribunal charged with assessing compensation for unfair dismissal has been held to have a duty to state the reasons for its award, and to show how the figure was reached.[23] The guiding standard was to award whatever sum was 'just and equitable', and so, although it was not discretionary in the strongest sense, the tribunal did have a reasonably broad assessment to make. Again, a lands tribunal in exercising discretion as to costs has been held to be under a duty to act judicially, with the consequence that any departure from the practice that a successful party be awarded costs must be explained and justified.[24] In both of those cases the discretion in question was considered to be of a judicial kind; where the power is more clearly policy-based, the existence of a duty to explain is likely to be less certain.[25]

Secondly, in the absence of a specific duty to give reasons, failure to do so may be instrumental in establishing impropriety on some other ground. In *Padfield*, the minister gave reasons for not referring the milk producer's complaint to the committee of inquiry, but it was made clear that had he not, the court would have inferred that there were no good reasons, and thus concluded that his powers had been misused. This idea is often quoted but rarely acted upon, since it is first

[22] *Annual Report*, 1982–3, p. 4.   [23] *Norton Tool* v. *Tewson* [1973] 1 WLR 45.
[24] *Pepys* v. *London Transport Executive* [1975] 1 WLR 234.
[25] For example, *McInnes* v. *Onslow-Fane* [1978] 1 WLR 1520; *Cannock Chase DC* v. *Kelly* [1978] 1 WLR 1.

necessary to show that there is some evidence of abuse. The question is likely to arise when a challenge is being made to the propriety of purposes, or in considering whether matters taken into account are extraneous. Obviously, it is difficult to make that inquiry without a statement of the official's reasons. It has been said in the context of deportation that the minister would be ordered to disclose his findings and reasons only if the applicant for review could show a prima-facie case of impropriety or provide some basis for suspecting the minister's good faith.[26] In *Padfield*, there appeared to be a prima-facie case of impropriety, so that had the minister not given reasons to explain and rebut that appearance, it would have been inferred that no good reasons existed.[27] However, judicial eagerness to find sufficient signs of impropriety in some cases, and hence to require reasons, may be offset by a corresponding reluctance in others; for example, a minister's action in intervening in a strike planned by train drivers,[28] or the decision of a minister to require an extraordinary audit of the records of a local housing authority acting in breach of rent regulations.[29] There is unavoidable circularity in the very idea that a prima-facie case of impropriety has to be established before reasons will be required, when it is the reasons themselves that are likely to be the best evidence of impropriety.

A general difficulty is that the judicial approach to reasons tends to depend on whether the discretion in issue is one which the courts are prepared to review: if it is, reasons are likely to be required; if it is not, then courts will avoid drawing any conclusions from the absence of reasons. The decisions as to disclosure of reasons is dependent, therefore, on a prior assessment as to the suitability of the issue for judicial review. In the latter case, talk about failure to show a prima-facie case of impropriety is camouflage for the fact that the decision has been made not to engage in serious scrutiny. Now while there would be little point in requiring reasons if the decision has been made on other grounds that an action is largely non-justiciable, there would be considerable merit in separating the two issues. One undoubted gain would be that criteria might be developed about non-justiciability,

---

[26] *R. v. Governor of Brixton Prison ex parte Soblen* [1963] 2 QB 243.
[27] [1968] AC 997.
[28] *Secretary of State for Employment* v. *Aslef (No. 2)* [1972] 2 QB 455.
[29] *Asher* v. *Secretary of State for the Environment* [1974] 1 Ch 208. For a recent example of the courts' attitudes to the provision of reasons and their reluctance to make such provisions a ground of review, see *British Airways Board* v. *Laker Airways Ltd* [1984] 3 WLR 413.

while leaving the question of the provision of reasons to be settled according to its relevant merits. Should the decision be made in a particular case for exacting review, the absence or inadequacy of reasons is likely to be highly revealing. As Woolf J. has noted recently, the absence of reasons will often show that the issue has not properly been considered, or the proper thought processes gone through; inadequate reasons will often show that there has been failure to consider something of importance, or that the wrong matters have been considered.[30]

A third approach to the giving of reasons is through natural justice. Whether natural justice includes giving reasons depends on the complexities of the modern law; but, in general, the demands of natural justice are greatest when the decision is of a judicial nature, and the party's interests are matters of rights or settled expectations. Where the power is more clearly discretionary and the party's interests less settled, the requirements of natural justice are less stringent, and do not always include an explanation of reasons. There are, however, some indications to the contrary; the High Court of Australia has held that, in deciding how to use an extremely broad discretion relating to taxation on trust income, the Commissioner of Taxation should make known the factual basis upon which he acts,[31] although it does not seem to have been argued that he ought also to disclose the standards he applied. There are suggestions in English cases that officials should disclose the standards they used, and the way they are applied to the facts; Lord Denning has insisted that a district council of a trade union give its reasons for refusing to confirm the election of a shop steward, since once elected by his fellow workers he had an expectation of being confirmed.[32] The majority, however, considered that in those circumstances, fairness did not extend to giving reasons.

The same approach suggested in respect of prior disclosure might also be adopted for disclosure of reasons after the decision. On this approach, there would be a presumption in favour of disclosure, subject to the possibility of important, countervailing policy considerations. As with prior disclosure, the reasons given against post-disclosure have been unconvincing, usually either invoking notions of administrative

[30] *Crake* v. *Supplementary Benefits Commission* [1982] 1 AER 498.
[31] *Giris* v. *Commonwealth Commissioner of Taxation* (1969) 119 CLR 365, esp. Barwick CJ. But against that may be set the decision of the High Court in *Salemi* v. *Minister for Immigration and Ethnic Affairs (No 2)* 14 ALR 1.
[32] *Breen* v. *Amalgamated Engineering Workers Union* [1971] 2 QB 175.

efficiency, or failing to accept that procedural fairness provides a good reason for explaining decisions. On other occasions, the absence of a duty to give reasons has been an expedient way of limiting judicial review.

Where there is a duty to give reasons, the further question arises as to what constitutes adequate reasons. This tends to be left, even where the duty is of statutory origin, for final determination by the courts. It has been said that the reasons must be reasons which are not only intelligible, but which deal with the substantial points that have been raised.[33] If this seems to be still a rather vague requirement, a more specific and useful working rule might be adopted along the lines of the Australian Administrative Appeals Tribunal Act, set out above; it covers the three vital elements of fact, evidence, and reasons, the last being taken to include any policies and standards, and an outline of the reasoning process by which they are applied to the particular case.

There are, however, two familiar points to be considered; this can be brief since the issues are similar to those raised in section 6.11. The first concerns the variability as to what constitutes adequacy of reasons; within the terms of the working rule suggested there is scope for substantial divergence from one situation to another, and, it might be argued, there are often good reasons for not being able to meet even that threshold. Again, questions of adequacy of reasons and the extent of the duty to provide reasons depend on several factors: the mode of decision-making, the resources of the authority, and the nature of the interest of particular individuals and groups. So adequacy might require in the case of adjudication or modified adjudication a fairly detailed statement of facts, evidence, and reasons; however, adequacy in respect of decisions which are more policy-based might be met by a statement of broad policy, a general outline of the background of facts, estimates, and opinions, and a rather impressionistic account of how different factors have been weighed and evaluated in producing the outcome. But although adequacy is dependent on factors like these, it is important to ensure that, within these constraints, the threshold requirements are met. The second point concerns efficiency, or, more broadly, the costs that result to administration from an onerous requirement of reasons. The approach to this is along the lines previously suggested; such constraints affect the extent of the duty, but must not be seen as reasons for not imposing the duty.

[33] *Re Poyser and Mills' Arbitration* [1964] 2 QB 467.

6.2 THE NORMATIVE FRAMEWORK

The next step is to consider the normative framework within which discretionary decisions are made. The question here is in what ways and to what extent do the courts in judicial review concern themselves with that framework. The discussion in chapter 3 and 4 suggested that rational decision-making occurs within a context of standards, although the standards may vary in their degrees of precision, specificity, and bindingness. A number of more specific points were suggested. Firstly, that the ideas of comprehensive planning and incrementalism are useful ways of representing the range that is open, the former suggesting an attempt to formulate precise and comprehensive standards, the latter suggesting a substantial degree of flexibility in dealing with situations within loosely defined standards. Some of the practical and normative factors that may influence an authority in settling the decision structure were considered; we also saw that the normative framework may shift and change, so that what begins as highly incremental may, over a course of decisions, come to be governed by clear and fixed standards, while what begins as an attempt at formulating comprehensive standards may assume incremental attributes in response to the problems that arise. Secondly, there is a complex relationship between general standards and the very idea of rational and purposive decision-making. In order to act rationally and purposively, it is necessary to proceed in accordance with some general standards, and, in turn, each decision entails a commitment in some sense to general standards. Considerations of consistency from one decision to another may also add to the case for general standards, and an official normally would be expected to follow his own previous decisions, or give reasons for not doing so. Standards might also be related to fairness in that it may be unfair to have action taken against one's interest without stipulating in advance the criteria; they might also help to remove a sense of unfairness that results from inconsistency. At another level questions about standards are connected to political values: in guiding the official in making decisions, and thus enhancing accountability; in providing some stability in legal relations, and thus enabling those who are likely to be affected by discretionary decisions to plan their actions. Just what configuration of standards and openness, planning and incrementalism, is adopted in different areas of decision-making is a matter of complexity and variability depending on a variety of overlapping and conflicting factors. The question is whether the courts might have an active role in supervising the development of a suitable normative structure.

6.21 *The no-fettering doctrine*

There are broadly two directions that judicial review might take: the more positive one of influencing the form that the framework of decision-making takes, and in particular of ensuring that standards are formulated; and the more negative one of preventing the making of decisions according to inflexible rules.

In so far as the courts have entered into this question at all, they have concentrated on the latter and have developed the no-fettering doctrine, which may be summarized in this way: (*a*) an authority in the exercise of a discretionary power may, but is under no duty to, adopt or create a set of standards upon which its decisions may be based; (*b*) those standards must not be treated as rules to be applied automatically to situations that come within them, but must allow consideration of the merits of each case; (*c*) consideration of the merits of each case means that the authority must direct itself to the case, and then decide whether the standards should apply, whether they should be modified, or whether, in the circumstances, an exception should be made to them.[34] The courts are not always consistent in their attitudes to the relationship between general standards and the particular case, and may take a more or less restrictive view.[35] There is some support for adding two more limbs: one (*d*) would create a link with natural justice, namely that an authority has a duty to allow an interested party to direct arguments against general standards with a view to showing how they should be applied in the present case, or why they should be modified or not relied on at all. However, as we have noticed, the link between no-fettering and natural justice is not established firmly,[36] so that discretionary standards may be applied without notice and hearing, either because there is no duty to disclose the standards, or

[34] For detailed discussion, see Galligan, 'The Nature and Function of Policies within Discretionary Powers'. For a recent example of the doctrine in the context of parole, see *In re Findlay* [1984] 3 WLR 1159.
[35] Compare *British Oxygen* v. *Board of Trade* [1971] AC 610 with *Sagnata Investments* v. *Norwich Corporation* [1971] 2 QB 614. In the recent Australian case, *R.* v. *Clarkson, ex parte Australian Telephone and Phonogram Officers' Association* (1980) 39 ALR 1, it was held that the Conciliation and Arbitration Commission may formulate a general principle and follow it in particular cases. See also *Attorney-General* v. *Ng Yuen Shin* [1983] 2 WLR 735.
[36] For further discussion, see: Galligan, 'The Nature and Function of Policies within Discretionary Powers', pp. 355–7.

because no hearing is required where the standards have been disclosed. Furthermore (*e*) where an authority does set itself standards and discloses them, it may be under a duty to apply them, and to depart from them only after giving parties an opportunity to be heard, although again this may depend on the subject matter of the discretion and on the extent to which disclosure may be regarded as an implied undertaking to those affected.[37]

When it comes to explaining the no-fettering doctrine, two partially satisfactory accounts can be found. Firstly, there is the constitutional principle that an authority must not legislate unless it is clearly authorized. Where general standards are so concrete and binding that the only question is whether the facts of a case come within them, they amount to legislation. Standards which are adopted in the exercise of discretion, and which operate as something less than binding rules and more in the nature of guide-lines, are acceptable because they retain a degree of flexibility in dealing with specific cases. To ask why this element of flexibility should be important is to raise the second part of the rationale of the no-fettering doctrine; here the idea is that discretionary powers are conferred in order to achieve in individual cases the best results, all things considered, something which tightly drawn rules may prevent.

These explanations for the no-fettering doctrine are not entirely satisfactory. In the first place, the distinction between 'legislating' in the sense of stipulating binding rules, and doing something less than legislating in the sense of formulating standards or guide-lines of lesser normative force, is not compelling. The former constitutes legislating in a very clear case, but the latter might also be legislating in a real enough sense, so that differences between the two are matters of subtle emphasis. Secondly, the emphasis put on treating each case on its merits can be exaggerated. In many areas of discretion, the object is simply to regulate an area of activity, and precise standards might be the best way of doing it. It should not be assumed that, because there is discretion, there is necessarily something in the very nature of the matter in issue which prevents rational and effective decision-making according to rules. Indeed, examples were given in chapter 1 where courts have themselves rapidly converted a discretionary matter into one governed by strict rules. So while there often will be an element of

---

[37] For an example, see *Pepys* v. *London Transport Executive* [1975] 1 WLR 234, but contrast the two different attitudes demonstrated in *R.* v. *Secretary of State, ex parte Asif Khan* [1984] 1 WLR 1337 and *In re Findlay* [1984] 3 WLR 1159.

individualization in deciding on the admissibility of an item of evidence, the allocation of costs, or an assessment of damages, in other areas the 'rational and proper operation' of an area of regulation may require that there be firm general principles to be followed in particular decisions. In so saying, Mr Justice Stephen was amongst the majority of the justices of the Australian High Court in accepting that the guide-lines on the fixation of wages laid down by the Full Bench of the Conciliation and Arbitration Commssion might be applied by a single Commissioner, even without considering (according to some justices) whether or not he should depart from them.[38]

This is not to suggest that the no-fettering doctrine generally is misconceived in its application to the discretions of officials. There is often little virtue in making decisions according to precise and inflexible rules, and there is rarely a good case for preventing oneself from taking account of the special circumstances of a case. The no-fettering doctrine serves both rationality and fairness in bringing home to authorities the importance of these two matters, and of maintaining some concern for the special characteristics of specific cases. The real criticism is that, by confining their attention to the no-fettering doctrine, the courts have neglected to consider whether they might play a more active part in shaping positively other aspects of the normative framework.

The no-fettering doctrine is a negative constraint on the exercise of discretion; its object is to prevent the translation of discretion into binding rules, thus leaving no room for variation in particular cases. Implicit in the doctrine and part of its rationale is that consistency in decisions, while clearly important, is not to be regarded as the overriding concern. There is, however, also a positive side to the doctrine, which recognizes the importance of general consistency in decisions, and that stated policies and standards should not be departed from without good reasons. There are signs to be found in recent cases that this positive side of the no-fettering doctrine is coming to be recognized. Accordingly, an authority may be required to apply consistently its established standards and guide-lines unless it gives good reasons for departure.[39] The scope and application of this doctrine is so far unsettled in two respects. Firstly, while it has been

---

[38] *R. v. Clarkson, ex parte Australian Telephone and Phonogram Officers' Association* (1980) 39 ALR 1 at p. 12; see also similar suggestions in *British Oxygen v. Board of Trade* [1971] AC 610.

[39] *R. v. Secretary of State, ex parte Asif Khan* [1984] 1 WLR 1337.

applied to various types of discretionary decisions, including decisions by the Home Secretary regarding immigration, its appeal has been found less compelling in the penal system.[40] Secondly, there is uncertainty as to whether the authority may depart from existing standards for any reasons which it considers appropriate (within the scope of its discretion), subject to allowing interested parties an opportunity to be heard; the alternative suggestion is that the reasons must be good reasons, a matter for final determination by the courts. These matters are likely to be left reasonably open, to be settled in particular cases, depending on how exacting the courts wish to make their review.

Subject to those matters, the development of the positive doctrine can be justified as another way of raising the rational basis of discretionary decisions, and of demonstrating the general importance of legal stability. We have earlier noted the complexities of the notion of consistency, and I have shown that consistency is not the only matter of importance in discretionary decisions. Nevertheless, there is not only a general case for consistency, but by requiring rational explanation by an authority for departure from or modification of its own standards, the overall rational basis is likely to be enhanced. There can also be seen running through this doctrine, and the doctrine relating to disclosure of decisional factors before and after decisions, a certain unity and coherence.

6.22 *The formulation of standards*

The present legal position is that an authority is at liberty to formulate general standards, subject to the no-fettering doctrine, but whether or not it does so is, in the absence of statutory requirements, a matter for it to decide. The question is not exactly whether or not to have general standards since purposive, rational decision-making entails reliance on standards at some level of generality; the issue is whether there ought to be legal duties to articulate the standards that are implicit in decisions, and to formulate standards more explicitly in advance of decisions.

The present legal position is governed partly by statute and partly by principles of common law. Power may be delegated for the express or implied purpose of making delegated legislation, and in that event there are legal rules for guiding and testing the validity of outcomes. Where the delegation is not legislative, but more clearly one of

---

[40] *In re Findlay* [1984] 3 WLR 1159.

administrtive discretion (a distinction not always easy to make), the position is different. The delegation may include a specific duty to formulate standards of decision-making, a process which may carry with it additional duties to consult groups with interests in the matter. For example, the British Housing Corporation is required by statute to set criteria for the registration of housing associations, and to consult housing associations in doing so.[41] An analogy can be drawn in those circumstances with delegated legislative powers, which are usually subject to duties both to formulate general standards, and to consult interested groups. It may even be argued that the formulation of general standards should be reserved for legislative bodies and processes, rather than vested in a variety of administrative bodies. This, of course, is to raise again the arguments about why there should be discretionary powers at all; it is sufficient to accept that there are good reasons, and, in addition, that there are advantages in an administrative body being able to formulate, change, and abandon standards without the formalities that attach to delegated legislation. The principal disadvantage is that statutory delegations of discretion do not normally include a duty in the authority to formulate and publish its standards, although again there is general support by bodies like the Council on Tribunals and the Parliamentary Commissioner for Administration for the formulation by discretionary authorities of reasonably clear and settled policies, standards, and guide-lines.

Where there are no statutory duties, the burden shifts to the courts, which in this matter have been mainly silent, perhaps partly because of the idea that each case of discretion depends on its merits, and partly because the determination of decision strategies is an integral part of discretion. However, there does seem to be more scope for judicial scrutiny than the courts have allowed themselves. One approach would be to link the question of setting standards to natural justice. The extension of fair procedures might be taken to include a firm duty to have standards and to disclose them. But since there is no clear duty even to disclose standards (section 6.11), the further step of requiring standards has naturally not been taken. A comparison may be made with the concept of procedural due process in American law.

There the question of discretionary standards is approached in two ways; one involves the formal, rule-making procedures which must be followed by federal agencies under the Administrative Procedure Act

---

[41] *Housing Act* 1979, s, 13(4).

and by various state authorities under similar state law.[42] Formal rule-making broadly resembles delegated legislation in the British context. The second, more informal side, recognizes that the setting of standards is always important in the exercise of discretionary powers. Standards may derive from the terms of delegation, as in Britain, and indeed there is the federal constitutional doctrine, often reproduced at the state level, that a delegation of power must be accompanied by standards guiding its exercise. This doctrine, however, has not been enforced in recent years with any rigour, and despite occasional outbreaks of interest in its revival, delegations of discretion subject to only the loosest standards are likely to be upheld.[43] An alternative approach, which has had the support of K. C. Davis,[44] is for administrative authorities to be under a duty to create their own standards. This can be achieved by general statutory enactment, such as the Revised Model State Administration Procedure Act issued in 1981 which provides that each agency shall adopt rules embodying appropriate standards, principles, and procedural safeguards, which the agency is to apply in exercising its power.[45] In the absence of statutory duties, there are signs that some American courts consider it a common law duty for the agency to create standards, on the grounds that 'due process means that administrators must do what they can to structure and confine their discretionary powers through safeguards, standards, principles, and rules'.[46]

Another approach to the formulation of standards by discretionary authorities combines the separation of powers and the delegation doctrines. The argument is that a delegation of discretionary authority constitutes, partially, a delegation of legislative powers and that there is a constitutional duty on a legislative authority to formulate standards. So, if Parliament in delegating authority does not set standards, that duty passes to the discretionary body. This is to take an extended view of the legislative process, but it is compatible with the view of discretionary authority as a merging of the legislative and adjudicative

---

[42] For an account of the American position, see B. Schwartz, *Administrative Law* (New York, 1976) ch. 4.

[43] Ibid., ch. 2.

[44] For an account of these views, see Davis, *Discretionary Justice* or *Administrative Law Text*. (See also section 4.1 above.)

[45] The terms of the Revised Model State Administrative Procedures Act, 1981 are set out in K. C. Davis, *1982 Supplement to Administrative Law Treatise* (St. Paul, 1982), ch. 8.

[46] *Historic Green Springs* v. *Beugland* 497 F. Supp. 839. (ED Va. 1980). For comment, see Davis, *1982 Supplement*, pp. 188–9.

functions. The separation of powers doctrine may also be called in aid: the separation doctrine, although modified in modern constitutions, still provides a sound basis for attempting to distinguish, even if informally, between the legislative and adjudicative aspects of discretionary authority. The formulation of general standards by the authority itself before applying them in specific cases is one way of achieving the main idea behind the separation doctrine. And, on the basis of the view of judicial review taken in chapter 5, it is appropriate that the courts should concern themselves with the separation doctrine in discretionary contexts, and in particular with the formulation of standards. These are matters of process and method rather than substance, and are based on the kinds of values that are properly the domain of the courts.

These two lines of approach, one based on due process, the other on the separation doctrine, provide a doctrinal basis upon which judicial principles governing the formulation of standards might be developed. The question remains, however, as to the objects sought to be achieved. Considering the diversity of factors that bear on the shaping of the normative framework of decision-making, it would be inappropriate for the courts simply to insist that all discretionary powers tbe rendered into a system of clear and binding rules. This might sometimes be suitable, but in many cases it would be to gloss over the reasons for having discretion and for sometimes retaining a highly incremental approach. A blanket requirement of rules would also have the effect of divorcing the policy-making part from the decision in particular cases, and might reduce the capacity of those directly affected to make any impact on policy. In many cases, decisions as to the most appropriate strategies of decision-making, in terms of effectiveness and other factors, is so tied to the substance of discretion that they are resolved most suitably by the discretionary body rather than the courts.

For these reasons, the choice of decision strategies should remain primarily in the hands of the administrative authority, subject of course to statutory guidance. Nevertheless, the courts might have a legitimate role in hedging around this process a number of principles and constraints. These would be based on the idea that administrative authorities have a general duty to direct their attentions to the decision strategy to be followed, and to make public their conclusions and their reasons for them. This duty could be made more specific in a number of ways. (*a*) The authority should direct itself to the issue of standards, and formulate at some level of particularity the basis upon which it will proceed in making decisions. Standards may be given a wide meaning ranging from very abstract criteria to fairly precise rules; they include the specification of factors which may or must be taken into consideration, and some attempt might be made to rank them in importance. (*b*) Where standards are left at a highly abstract level so that substantial discretionary assessments have to be made in individual cases, reasons should be given for adopting that approach. A complete absence of standards would never be justified, and in practice the question would be whether the standards set are sufficiently specific. An authority might have good reasons for taking an incremental approach, with an emphasis on resolving problems as they occur, and on extrapolating more general standards from actual cases rather than by advance stipulation. (*c*) Once standards have been set, an authority would be expected to follow them unless it considered either that they should be modified in order to avoid an unacceptable result in a particular case, or that they were simply no longer appropriate. But, any change of standards in general or departure from them in particular cases ought to be explained and justified. (*d*) Where decisions are made on an incremental basis, efforts should be made to articulate the standards that implicitly are relied on, and in this way to create general standards. Consistency from one case to another is not an overriding concern, but it has a place of importance, and there are generally good reasons for linking precedents and in that way creating standards. They need not be binding precedents, but they should be persuasive and followed unless there are reasons for acting otherwise.

The point of imposing duties along these lines would be to enhance the rational basis of decisions and to reduce arbitrariness, to provide guidance upon which expectations might be built and hence to satisfy a sense of fairness, but without forcing adminstrative bodies into a rigid, rule-governed framework. The courts as independent generalists are in a good position to oversee compliance with these constraints, while final responsibility for settling particular strategies remains with the discretionary body. Nevertheless, there are objections that might be raised to this approach. The suggested duties to be imposed on officials might be satisfied in a formal and perfunctory manner. If judicial review is to have any real impact, it may be necessary for courts to go farther, and enforce specific views about the most appropriate strategy to be adopted in a particular area of discretion. There are arguments for and against extending the judicial role; nevertheless, it is worth sketching the outlines that a more demanding approach might take.

In section 3.3, a case for clear and certain standards was considered in circumstances where specially important interests are at stake. This might be put in terms of a presumption in favour of standards where there is a strong public interest, and it is at risk of being harmed seriously and perhaps irremediably by a discretionary decision; it would also apply where there are personal interests relating to bodily liberty and integrity, and to welfare. The presumption would apply also where there is a strong likelihood of abuse. The presumption in favour of clear and precise standards where any of these conditions apply would not be inflexible, and could be modified on occasions in order to place decisions on a more incremental basis. The possible reasons for doing so are numerous: they might relate to the nature of the task to be peformed, or lack of experience in dealing with a matter, or because the interest in question may be better protected by procedures other than a prior formulation of standards. Some examples may be given. Where the authority can show that the complexity of a problem makes it difficult and unwise to stipulate standards in advance, then it may be acceptable to proceed incrementally, but only on the condition that parties whose interests are directly in issue be given an indication of the lines that will be followed, and an opportunity to put their cases. Again, it might be in the very nature of the discretionary task to work out a solution which constitutes an acceptable compromise amongst interests; then the personal interests at stake might be guaranteed better recognition through procedures which guarantee full participation in the decision. Another way of putting the point would be that where special interests are at stake or where the risk of abuse is high, the protections that are normally provided by settled standards may be secured through alternative procedures.

Just how far courts should follow this line of approach need not be determined in the abstract. To take steps in that direction requires the formulation or evolution of a theory of interests; it also takes the courts into the administrator's territory to an extent that recommends a cautious and incremental approach by the courts themselves. Moreover, such an approach is only one of several ways of raising the rational and moral basis of discretionary decisions, and should be understood and developed in its relationship with those others. The object has been to demonstrate that there are numerous steps that might be taken by courts in increasing review of the normative framework, each drawing the reins of review a little tighter.

6.3   THE SUBSTANCE OF REASONS

Important as it is that discretionary authorities should meet the procedural demands discussed in the preceding section, discretionary decisions are also and primarily about substantive outcomes, about settling on a decision of one kind rather than another, or selecting one course of action rather than another. Our concern in this section is to consider the extent to which matters of substance are subject to legal regulation. Where a decision is invalid because it simply falls outside the terms of delegated authority, it is unnecessary to examine the reasons for making it; but where the decision is of the kind that is within power, it may, nevertheless, be invalid because it has been made for bad reasons. It is often the case that an appeal lies from the discretionary decisions of one authority to another, whether the latter be a tribunal, court, or other administrative body. The existence of appeals depends generally on the governing statute, and may range in scope from a full reconsideration of the merits to rather restricted points of law. Whatever the type of appeal may be, there is likely to be, to greater or lesser degrees, some scrutiny of reasons and substance. Such matters might also on occasions be subject to examination by the Parliamentary Commissioner for Administration or the Commission for Local Administration. Questions of reasons and substance might also arise in judicial review, not directly because courts are confined to issues of legality, but nevertheless in a real enough way since a judgement of legality may depend on an assessment of the reasons by way of explanation and justification.

The discussion may begin with a reminder of two points which link the present issue to the argument in chapter 5. The first concerns the criteria against which the reasons for decisions are to be assessed. The governing criterion is the intention of the delegating authority as expressed in the terms of delegation; at its simplest, an exercise of discretion must comply with their terms of the statute or other instrument of delegation. If the statute (and statutory delegation is taken as the central example) stipulates with clarity and precision the matters to be considered in decision-making, then an assessment of validity will be a relatively simple inquiry; judicial review is likely to be confined to being satisfied that each factor has been considered, and that the decision as a whole has not been unreasonable. However, it is both a sign of discretionary powers and one of its characteristics that the matters to be taken into account are left open to be settled under the broad guidance of purpose; and what is taken into account then depends on the policies and goals being sought. So, whether the reasons for decisions are valid or not turns on whether those policies and goals are within statutory purposes. For example, the validity of decisions made by a local authority in fixing the fares on public transport depends on whether the policies sought to be realized are within the purposes of its powers.[47] Purposes may be stated at a level of high abstraction, or even left largely unstated. The power to release prisoners on parole, for example, is in the main unguided by clear statutory purposes, or by more specific statutory policies. In order to assess whether the reasons for decisions are good reasons, it may be necessary first to determine the objects or purposes of the discretionary power, and then to assess whether the reasons properly come within them. Once this inquiry is undertaken, the line between matters of interpretation and the merits of discretion becomes difficult to maintain.

The second point concerns the role of the courts. The governing criteria for judicial review is said to be the intention of the legislature, as interpreted by the courts. Statutory interpretation is rarely an easy matter, and in the context of discretionary powers the normal difficulties are compounded. It is necessary not only to construe words and ascertain their meaning, but also to reconstruct background circumstances and underlying objects and values. This process may be divided broadly into different parts: (*a*) ascertaining purposes in general; (*b*) identifying the constraints and background considerations which derive from the statute and from sources outside it, whether from the constitution, the common law, or judicial policy; (*c*) deciding whether specific reasons, and the policies on which they are based, come within and constitute an acceptable working-out of those general purposes. These parts are naturally interwoven and in practice are not always distinguished from each other; instrumental policies might not be separated from general purposes, and background constraints may have their effect in the definition of purposes. It is convenient, however, to retain this division between the three parts in considering the problems that occur in judicial review of reasons and purposes.

---

[47] See *Prescott* v. *Birmingham Corporation* [1955] Ch 210.

6.31   *Ascertaining purposes: the issue of interpretation*

Judicial review is based around the general doctrine that discretionary decisions must be in accordance with the purposes authorized by the terms of the delegation, and must not advance or depend on purposes that are not authorized.[48] Judicial determination of the purposes of discretionary powers is an aspect of the general task of statutory interpretation, which is itself a matter of considerable interest and complexity. Naturally, one begins with the words used; where they have a clear, ordinary meaning, or perhaps an artificial but settled meaning, it may be unnecessary to go any farther. Alternatively, the decision may be so clearly outside the authorized purposes that a detailed analysis of possible alternatives is unnecessary. So when a vegetable seeds committee, which was charged with maintaining during wartime an adequate supply of seed, sought to control seed merchants in order to advance its own trading and financial interests, its regulations were held to be outside the permitted purposes.[49] It is more likely, however, that things will not be so simple; rather than being derived from the meaning of words, purposes may have to be ascertained by a process of reconstruction from the words and whatever other materials are available.

The first question in understanding the process of reconstruction is to consider its objectives. Stated simply, the aim is to give meaning to those words of a statute which are relevant in ascertaining the purposes of a grant of discretionary power. Thus the primary object of interpretation and the main constraint—whether in relation to a statute, a past decision, a novel, or a poem—is to give meaning to the words of the text as they appear. The next question is what means are to be employed in achieving that aim? Is it to ascertain what actually was intended by those who enacted the statute, and, in that event, which intentions count when the statute is the product of collective efforts? Alternatively, the object might be to arrive at a notional intention: what would those who enacted the statute have intended had they thought about it at the time, or were able to think about it in its present setting? Each of these approaches is subject to well-known objections.[50] A third possibility is to ignore questions of real or notional

---

[48]   For statements and analysis of the general principle, see de Smith, *Judicial Review*, pp. 325–33; Craig, *Administrative Law*, ch. 10.

[49]   *Yates* v. *Vegetable Seeds Committee* (1945) 72 CLR 37.

[50]   For general discussion of the problems of interpretation and various approaches to it, see: Rupert Cross, *Statutory Interpretation* (London, 1976); G. R. MacCallum,

intentions and simply derive the meaning of the words themselves. This has its own problems: it is naïve to think that words have meaning in an objective and defined sense; they have meaning only in so far as it is ascribed to them in a given context. Their meaning depends on that context—on its values, understandings, and history—and on the interpreter and his specific and individual values and concerns within that context. Finally, it is not simply a case of ascribing any meaning to the text, to 'deconstruct the text' as it is sometimes called, since that is to ignore the objective constraints that there are upon the interpretative process.

None of these possibilities or any other of a like kind expresses adequately the method for arriving at meaning. Rather interpretation involves each of them in this sense: the aim is to arrive at the meaning of a text and that is achieved by considering the words in their context; for this purpose context means both the general environment of history and values in which the text occurs, and more specific factors such as the intentions of the legislator and the nature of the problem at the time, compared with the problem as it is now perceived. Factors like these assist in settling the meaning of a text, but none of them can be regarded as a substitute for the text itself. It is equally mistaken to regard any one of these factors, such as the views expressed at a constitutional convention, as irrelevant.

Interpretation does not consist in ascribing just any meaning that anyone may choose, since there are two important constraints on the process: interpretation occurs within a specific community of interests, and is conducted according to by-and-large agreed standards.[51] The idea of the first is that in any context interpretation occurs as part of a recognizable enterprise which has its objects and its modes of operation: literary criticism and philosophical analysis, as well as statutory interpretation, occur within a community in this sense. There may be room for diversity within an enterprise, but there must be enough common ground for the activity to be recognized as 'judging'

'Legislative Intent' in Summers, *Essays in Legal Philosophy*; MacCormick, *Legal Reasoning and Legal Theory*, pp. 203–13.

[51] For interesting discussions of interpretation and, in particular, ideas of reconstruction: Stanley Fish, 'Working on the Chain Gang: Interpretation in Law and Literature' (1982) 60 *Texas LR* 551. See also K. Abraham, 'Three Fallacies of Interpretation: a Comment on Precedent and Judicial Decision' (1981) 23 *ArizLR.* 771 and 'Statutory Interpretation and Literary Theory' (1979) 32 *RutLR* 676; R. M. Dworkin, 'Law as Interpretation' (1982) 60 *TexasLR* 527 and 'The Forum of Principle' (1981) 56 *NYULR*, pp. 471 ff; O. M. Fiss, 'Objectivity and Interpretation' (1982) 34 *StanLR* 739.

or 'literary criticism'. The idea of community of enterprise is not novel, but it is of special importance in adjudication, and nicely expresses the institutional environment within which courts operate, or the 'integrity and coherence of law as an institution'.[52]

The second constraint consists in those standards which, within an interpretative community, govern interpretation. There are rules for interpreting poems and novels; there are also rules about how to regard past cases, and there are rules and maxims of statutory interpretation. Compliance with the rules does not guarantee a right or best or even sound interpretation, but failure to comply means that the enterprise itself has failed, and the substantive interpretation loses whatever authority it might have had. Naturally, the rules may be more or less settled and precise; in this regard, law may differ from other interpretative enterprises in that there typically exists in the former an easier basis than would normally be the case for establishing the authority of rules.

The three crucial elements in interpretation are, then, the text and its environment, the interpretative community, and the rules of interpretation. Within the confines of those elements, interpretation is neither entirely subjective—the context, the community, and the rules impose a certain objectivity—nor is it completely objective since there is still room for personal judgment and assessment. The nature of the interpretative community may change, as may the rules of interpretation, and in the context of judicial reconstruction of statutory purposes these possibilities are especially important.

In the first place, there are really two interpretative communities: judges and administrative officials. Questions about the existence and extent of discretion may be answered differently by each; the same applies to questions about statutory purposes. Each has different concerns and is subject to different constraints, and so is prone to construing purposes differently: the administrator in terms of problems and projects, subject to the political and institutional constraints of the kind considered in chapter 3; the court in terms of rather uncertain and unspecific values and standards. Secondly, the rules of interpretation within the emerging public law model are in a state of flux and disarray: the governing standard—that parliamentary intention is supreme—provides only the most general guidance and can accommodate a range of possibilities; beyond that there are few

---

[52] Fiss, 'Objectivity and Interpretation'.

specific standards so that judges have little to rely on other than abstract constitutional principles. Judicial interpretation is likely, therefore, to be variable and to appear unprincipled, since there is substantial necessity for each judge to develop his own working standards. Moreover, each judge must resolve not only the normal problems of statutory interpretation, but implicit in his task is the duty to define the division of labour between the courts and the administrative officials whose discretions are in question. Virtually any issue can be turned into a question about purpose, and yet one of the basic judicial principles is that a distinction must be made between defining purposes and the merits of decisions within those purposes. When it comes to locating an intermediate position between the two, the lack of guidance from the disciplining rules is acute.

This is the context in which the interpretation of statutory purposes occurs.[53] It is clear that within the limits of the text, the interpretative community, and the disciplining rules, judges have to reach into a substratum of political undertstandings in order to ascertain statutory purposes. In considering the legality of actions based on implementation of the Greater London Council's plan substantially to reduce fares on public transport, a matter the council was committed to in its election manifesto, the House of Lords had to consider the meaning of a statutory duty on the council to promote the 'provision of integrated, efficient and economic transport services for Greater London'. It also had to consider the duty on the London Transport Authority to have 'due regard to efficiency, economy and safety of operation', and then further to decide what background constraints there were on exercising a broad discretion for social welfare purposes.[54] Implicit in the opinions of the judges are views about the relationship between Parliament, local authorities, and the courts, about the respective responsibilities of a local authority to rate-payers and the users of public transport, and about the relationship between the social objectives of a transport system in relation to other social goals that a local authority might undertake. The fact that these matters were not discussed explicitly in no way diminishes their importance in the decision. Similarly, when Lord Denning explained his reluctance to

[53] Specifically on the interpretation of purposes, see A. M. Bickel and H. H. Wellington, 'Legislative Purpose and the Judicial Process: The Lincoln Mills Case' (1957) 71 *HarvLR* 1.

[54] See *Bromley LBC* v. *Greater London Council* [1983] 1 AC 768. For comment, see H. S. E. Gravelle, 'Judicial Review and Public Firms' (1983) 3 *IntRevLaw&Econ* 187.

investigate the minister's reasons and purposes in preventing a strike by train drivers partly in terms of the 'emergency' of the situation and the 'grave threat to the national economy', and partly because no threats to 'life, liberty, or property' were in issue, he was relying on a specific but unstated view of the political system, and the values that constitute its foundation.[55] These are but two examples of numerous cases, where in the quest for purposes the courts have had to make decisions about the political values and understandings in terms of which the administrative process is to be viewed.[56]

Questions about purposes may arise in different ways.[57] The issue may be whether or not to investigate purposes, a matter which is settled in accordance with the constitutional doctrines we have considered, or, once an affirmative decision has been taken, the criteria to be followed in making the investigation; alternatively, questions about purposes may occur in assessing whether the reasons acted on are relevant and proper. These issues, however, are less distinct than they seem, and in each case, directly or indirectly, the courts have to enter into questions of purposes and interpretation. The question is whether that process can be made more objective both in arriving at an understanding of purposes, and in settling the background constraints on their achievement. An element of subjectivity is inherent in interpretation, so that the important issue may be simply which authority, the courts or the administrative officials, is to have the final say. However, there does seem to be some scope for raising the objectivity of interpretation of purposes, firstly by adopting a general approach which recognizes more explicitly the problem in issue, and secondly by developing specific 'disciplining rules' which provide guidance in particular situations.

In taking the first step, the courts may come to accept that interpretation requires them to consider the values and political implications inherent in a grant of power, and in being prepared to offer reasoned opinions about the stance they take. This is one of the

---

[55] *Secretary of State for Employment* v. *Aslef (No 2)* [1972] 2 QB 455.

[56] For other examples, see *Roberts* v. *Hopwood* [1925] AC 578; *Chertsey UDC* v. *Mixnam's Properties Ltd* [1965] AC 735; *R.* v. *Hillingdon LBC, ex parte Royco Homes* [1974] 1 QB 720; *R.* v. *Governor of Brixton Prison, ex parte Soblen* [1963] 2 QB 243; *Asher* v. *Secretary of State for the Environment* [1974] 1 Ch 208.

[57] There are signs of increased judicial willingness to investigate issues of purpose: in addition to *Padfield*, see *Television Corporation* v. *Commonwealth* (1963) 109 CLR 59; *Congreve* v. *Home Office* [1976] QB 629; *Newbury DC* v. *Secretary of State for the Environment* [1981] AC 578; *Re Toohey, ex parte Northern Land Council* (1982) 38 ALR 439.

important points that R. M. Dworkin has argued for; judges are under an obligation to construct a general political theory which best fits the materials to be considered, and which in turn guides them in interpreting new cases. It is not necessary to accept Dworkin's own preferred theory based on rights in order to join in his claim that judges are required, when reconstructing the purposes of planning powers, or parole, or deciding the obligations of a housing authority in evicting tenants, to make decisions based on some view of the relationship between the individual and the state, and thus of the nature of the constitution and the type of democratic system that supports it.[58] Judges cannot be expected suddenly to have a complete and coherent theory about their role in exercising review, but by reasoned consideration of statutory texts against the backdrop of constitutional doctrines, a set of standards and guide-lines should begin to appear.

Some efforts have been made in this direction. In *Padfield*, where there was no express indication of legislative intention in respect of the minister's discretion to refer a complaint about the milk marketing scheme, Lord Reid examined the history of the scheme as a whole; from this he was able to acquire some idea of the object of the investigatory procedure.[59] He found that the minister not only had a discretion to refer individual complaints, but also a further discretion as to whether any action should be taken after the committee had reported. From this he concluded that the earlier discretion was intended to be much narrower than the later; in the later, the minister was more clearly accountable to Parliament, whereas the former provided an important safeguard, to be initiated by an individual, on the working of the scheme. Assistance could be derived from considering the interests in issue; on the one hand the interests of producers in having their complaints considered, on the other hand a range of public interests over which the minister clearly was intended to have control. A comparison of the wording of the two discretions suggested there were differences between them—one was directed towards general policy, the other towards individual complaints; overall policy control could be retained by the minister under the wider power, while allowing greater status to private interests under the weaker discretion. By analysis of this kind, Lord Reid was able to reach

---

[58] This theme runs through a number of Dworkin's writings; for example, 'Law as Interpretation' (1982) 60 *TexasLR* 527.
[59] [1968] AC 997.

an interpretation of the statutory purposes which in turn provided a basis for assessing the minister's reasons for acting as he did. The analysis might have been taken farther, and other conclusions might have been drawn; but there is a commendable attempt at interpretation which recognizes the relationship between the words of the statute, its context, and the underlying political values.

6.32 *Background constraints*

The second strategy in making interpretation more objective can be seen in the context of background constraints. Discretionary powers do not occupy an otherwise empty terrain, but are superimposed on an intricate network of interests and values, with the consequence that the relationship between the objects of power and the background constraints may be both subtle and complex. The decision to build a new highway, for example, will set in train a host of repercussions: it is likely to affect existing transport arrangements and the economic interests in them, to reduce traffic on existing roads, and thus affect the provision of local services; the route selected may run across someone's land, and interfere with a variety of activities associated with its use; it may increase pollution, and have harmful effects on the neighbouring environment and ecology. Similarly, discretionary powers to sentence offenders, or to parole or deport them, raise issues as to what moral and political values are to be preserved against discretionary preferences; are powers conferred in such discretionary terms unrestrained within their area of authority, or are they subject to reservations deriving from ideas about personal liberty?

Questions like those commonly occur in interpreting discretionary powers. The task for courts is often to determine whether loosely defined purposes are to be read subject to a specific legal or moral principle, or a public or private interest. In one case, for example, the courts had to decide the validity of conditions attached to planning permission, according to which any houses built were to be occupied by people on the council's housing list. The question then was whether the council's planning powers could be used to achieve objects relating to the provision of housing; in turn, that question depended on whether account was to be taken of the consequences of conditions imposing on the developers substantial duties incompatible with the normal rights of land ownership. The court concluded that planning purposes are subject to those reservations.[60]

[60] *R.* v. *Hillingdon LBC, ex parte Royco Homes* [1974] QB 720.

The difficulty is that while there is always a range of interests and considerations in the background, it may not be clear which are protected against discretionary actions. Where there is a broad grant of discretion, interpretation is likely to revolve around the relationship between the general objects on the one hand, and particular interests and factors on the other. The relationship might itself be complex; an interest might have complete legal protection against discretionary interference, or there might be presumptive protection capable of being rebutted, or it might be simply that an interest must be taken into account in the reasoning process. Within each of those categories there may be scope for even more subtle variations. In order to raise the objectivity of interpretation, it is necessary to develop settled standards and guide-lines for handling the relationship between general powers and those background factors.

Where there are express legal provisions protecting values or interests, a grant of discretionary power normally would be construed subject to them. The sources and types of constraints were noted in section 5.1: they may derive from constitutional sources or be the creation of statute or common law. They can be diverse in character, ranging from the provisions of the Bill of Rights 1688 to statutes prohibiting forms of discrimination. Such legal provisions do not have a clearly superior status to statutes conferring discretion, but the presumption is that, subject to clear words to the contrary, the latter will be regarded as subject to the former. The provisions of the Bill of Rights, prohibiting the levying of money for government purposes without parliamentary authorization, have been invoked in support of a general principle that discretionary powers may not be used to impose levies or taxes without express or implied authorization.[61] Of greater contemporary signficance, as a source of constitutional constraints on discretionary powers, is the European Convention on Human Rights and Fundamental Freedoms.[62] The Convention has not been adopted in English municipal law, but the doctrine is emerging that legislation is to be interpreted in accordance with its provisions,[63] subject only to clear evidence of parliamentary intention to the contrary.

[61] *Congreve* v. *Home Office* [1976] QB 629.
[62] The provisions of the Convention are contained in S. H. Bailey, D. J. Harris and B. L. Jones, *Civil Liberties* (London, 1980), p. 18.
[63] For discussion and judicial statements, ibid., pp. 5 ff. The reading of discretionary powers subject to the principles of the Convention has become especially important in the penal system; see for example *Raymond* v. *Honey* [1983] 1 AC 1 and *R.* v. *Secretary of State for the Home Department, ex parte Anderson* [1984] 2 WLR 725.

In the early days of modern state regulation it was not uncommon for the argument to be advanced that discretionary powers were to be exercised subject to the private rights of individuals; such arguments were naturally given short shrift, for to do otherwise would have been a vain attempt to maintain in the face of political change what has been described as a Victorian bill of rights.[64] Where there is some choice as to both the objects to be pursued and the specific courses of action required, the position is more complex. The highway might equally well go across a tract of vacant land as through the middle of someone's farm; although that vacant tract might harbour wildlife whose habitat and survival would then be threatened. Discretion will normally require some policy choices and the trading of one value or interest against another, and it is generally in the nature of discretion that these are matters for the administrative authority rather than the courts.

However, certain private interests may acquire a position of special importance in the face of discretionary power, the clearest cases being private legal rights.[65] Where it is possible reasonably to achieve the objects of power without affecting or compromising private rights, there is a presumption that discretion will be restricted accordingly. Discretionary powers are taken to override private rights without compensation only where there is clear and unambiguous authorization as an irresistible inference from the statute read as a whole.[66] Where the conditions imposed by a planning authority in its discretion on the use of a site as a caravan park were so onerous as substantially to reduce existing rights to use the site in that way without compensation, it was held that the exercise of powers was improper. The empowering statute could not be construed as authorizing that consequence, and so the discretion had to be exercised subject to that restraint.[67]

Most cases have been concerned with rights of a proprietary or pecuniary kind, but the same principles apply in respect of civil rights.

---

[64] Lord Patrick Devlin, 'Judges as Lawmakers' (1976) 39 *MLR* 1.

[65] Whether there are rights in issue may itself be a difficult matter: see for example *Bradley* v. *Commonwealth* (1972) 128 CLR 557.

[66] *Minister for Housing and Local Government* v. *Hartwell* [1965] AC 1134; *Colonial Sugar Refining Co. Ltd* v. *Melbourne Harbour Trust Commissioners* [1927] AC 343; and *Chertsey UDC* v. *Mixnam's Properties Ltd* [1965] AC 735.

[67] There may be connections between the presumption against interference with private rights and the presumption that appears to prevent discretion being used for objects of economic redistribution in the absence of express authority. See *Roberts* v. *Hopwood* [1925] AC 578 and *Prescott* v. *Birmingham Corporation* [1955] Ch 210.

In an early Australian decision, *City of Melbourne* v. *Barry*,[68] the issue was whether the municipality's discretionary power to make by-laws for a variety of purposes, including suppressing nuisances and regulating processions, was sufficiently wide to include a by-law severely restricting the use of streets for public processions. The by-law had the effect of prohibiting processions, unless the written permission of the municipal council were obtained, a permission which might be granted or refused entirely according to the council's discretion. The High Court held the by-law not to have been authorized by the terms of the parent statute, and in order to reach this conclusion it was necessary to decide upon the purposes for which the power had been granted. A vital factor in the decision was a presumption that the common law rights to use the streets for public gatherings and processions should not be removed or restricted in the absence of clear authorization.

The presumption against a curtailment of rights may extend beyond clear cases of interference with rights to include the incidents that accompany rights. We have seen how, in *R.* v. *Hillingdon LBC ex parte Royco Homes*,[69] restrictive conditions attached to the grant of planning permission for the construction of homes were held to be improper. The basis for the conclusion was the effect of the conditions on the incidents that normally pertain to the ownership of property; it comes close, however, to extending the presumption against interference beyond proprietary rights to include the loss of a pecuniary advantage or the imposition of a financial disadvantage. Links can be drawn between this and the other doctrine that a tax, or levy, or other financial imposition may not be imposed without express statutory authorization. The fusion of these two ideas occurred in *Congreve* v. *Home Office*,[70] where the only apparent basis for declaring improper the Home Secretary's revocation of television licences, purchased in advance in order to beat an increase in fees, was that those who had done so would lose the financial advantage gained by early purchase. In its anxiety to come to the rescue of aggrieved licensees who faced the prospect of paying the same amount for their television licences as everybody else, the Court of Appeal hardly considered whether the power to deprive private citizens of a financial advantage might be a rational and reasonable aspect of the minister's discretion to revoke

[68] (1922) 31 CLR 174.
[69] [1974] 1 QB 720.
[70] [1976] QB 629.

licences. The fact that the discretion had that consequence without clear statutory authorization seemed to the court conclusive.

The same background assumptions can be seen in cases where an authority with a clear discretion has been held to be under a duty to exercise it in a particular way. *Sheffield* v. *Morrell* is an example, where the courts, after confirming that 'may' always means 'may', nevertheless construed it as meaning 'must', for the sole reason, it seems, that a landlord's rights to possession were in issue.[71] A similar idea appears in an interesting and more subtle way in *Padfield*: the minister there had discretion to refer to a committee of inquiry the complaints of dairy farmers about the operation of a statutory milk marketing scheme. The judgements holding invalid the minister's reasons for not making a reference can be read in a number of ways, but a recurring theme is that the minister had special responsibility towards those producers who had made the complaint, such that once it had been made he had a prima-facie duty to have it investigated by the special committee.[72] Non-referral required special justification, and since the minister's reasons were thought to be inappropriate or insubstantial, his duty had not been discharged. The minister's presumptive duty to investigate is based on the private economic interests of the producers. This did not remove completely the minister's discretion, but it shaped the way the matter was to be approached by placing the onus on him to show good reasons for not acting in furtherance of those interests. Once the onus is put in this way, it is clear that the kinds of reasons open to the minister for refusing to refer are very limited; if he thought the complaint frivolous or vexatious, for example, or if a similar complaint had already recently been rejected by the committee.

It is not always easy to predict which interests short of rights will have a favoured position in interpreting discretionary powers. In *Bristol DC* v. *Clark*,[73] the local authority served notice to quit on a council tenant whose rent was in arrears, and who in other ways was an unreliable tenant. The authority sought possession of the premises under its general statutory powers to manage, regulate, and control council houses. The question was whether these general powers were to be read subject to wider purposive considerations based on the 'social service responsibilities' of the local authority, in particular a responsibility not to create homelessness, and thus to consider alternatives to eviction. The tenants argued that the authority did not need the

---

[71] [1929] 2 QB 180.   [72] See especially Lord Reid, [1968] AC pp. 1030–3.
[73] [1975] 1 WLR 1443.

premises for the provision of housing to others, and that, considering the consequences of eviction for the present tenants, the council had misused their powers. The issue might be put in terms of whether the general discretion is to be read against the interest of the tenants in not being made homeless. The novel claim caused the judges to pause, but only briefly, before holding that there was no evidence to show that those wider factors had not been taken into account by the authority, and that all things considered the result was reasonable. There could be no suggestion of an initial presumption against eviction; the authority was free to see the issue as one of efficient management so that the tenants' interests were at their highest a relevant consideration to be traded off against other policy matters.

Judicial practice has been similarly uneven in respect of civil rights and liberties. Despite Lord Denning's avowed support for liberty as well as property, claims relating to speech, movement, association, and security of persons have not attracted the same status in construing discretion as those pertaining to property. The principle of *Barry* was clear, and might have been extrapolated to cover a range of civil rights; but it has proved to be difficult to construe discretionary powers subject to any such constraints. One difficulty is that rights in these areas are generally of a residual kind, Hohfeldian liberties rather than claim rights, and so without the firm status of property rights. This is even more clearly the case where the interests at stake are simply those general but fundamental interests that each person has in not being physically constrained, and in being able to move, speak, and associate freely. Evidence of the judicial approach to civil interests can be seen in various ways within the penal system, particularly the parole decision, and in areas of immigration and deportation. Here the breadth of discretionary powers is typically considerable and the importance of the personal interests indisputable; but there is no sign that their existence creates any presumption in interpreting purposes, nor even in settling subtle but often crucial questions as to the onus of proof. In *R. v. Governor of Brixton, ex parte Soblen*,[74] where the issue was whether the Home Secretary had used his deportation powers to achieve extradition, the alien's interest in not being returned to a country where he faced criminal charges added no weight to his unsuccessful argument that the minister ought to be required to disclose his reasons, and that the court ought to examine them closely

---

[74] [1963] 2 QB 243; also *Utter* v. *Cameron* [1974] 2 NSWR 50.

in the light of the purposes of deportation. Similarly, in the penal system, the courts are reluctant even to review discretionary decisions regarding prison discipline and the refusal of parole, let alone allow the civil interests involved to affect the way those decisions are to be made.[75]

6.33   *Explicit moral factors*

There is little to be gained by attempting a precise classification of the different types of background constraints on the exercise of discretion; indeed any attempt to identify specifically moral considerations is likely to founder, since most background constraints are traceable to or can be characterized in terms of moral principles. However, because specific moral principles are often directly and explicitly relevant to discretionary decision-making, brief consideration of some of the more important issues is pertinent.

Moral principles and values can be relevant to discretion in two main ways. In the first place, there is the question to what extent a discretionary authority may take into account or even explicitly base its decision on a point of morals; secondly, there is the question to what extent a reviewing court will positively require consideration of moral principles by the administrative body. With regard to the first of those, it is clear that discretionary decisions often encounter moral issues, and that it is not only right but desirable to give to them full and proper consideration. It is in precisely such contexts, as suggested in my earlier discussion, that conflicts between pragmatism and expediency on the one hand and moral values on the other are most directly and sharply focused. We have also noticed the concern so often apparent in the attitude of officials for congruence between their moral attitudes, including to some extent their interpretation of community morality, and their actions. The most cursory examination of areas such as the decisions of police, prosecutors, sentencing judges, and parole boards, will reveal how important are ideas of fairness, responsibility, guilt and deserts. In other contexts, consideration of issues like the responsibilities of mining companies towards conservation, the duties of housing

---

[75] See *R.* v. *Board of Visitors of Hull Prison, ex parte St. Germain* [1979] 1 QB 425. However this case does represent an important step in judicial review which may be the beginning of wider review; see also *R.* v. *Secretary of State for the Home Department, ex parte Anderson* [1984] 2 WLR 725; *O'Reilly* v. *Mackman* [1983] 2 AC 237; and *In re Findlay* [1984] 3 WLR 1159.

authorities to the homeless, or the attitudes of a rugby club to apartheid, may only thinly veil important moral questions.

Indeed the latter of these examples can be used to illustrate the general attitude of reviewing courts to reliance by discretionary bodies on moral principle. In that case, *Wheeler* v. *Leicester CC*,[76] the council had resolved in its discretion to terminate the use of its recreational facilities by a local rugby football club on the ground that the members of the club were not prepared unanimously and unequivocally to condemn apartheid and the visit by some of the club's members to participate in sporting events in South Africa. After differences of opinion in the Court of Appeal, the House of Lords held that, while the council was entitled, indeed required under the Race Relations Act to take into account and give substantial weight to the club's attitude to apartheid, the council was not entitled to make fulsome condemnation a necessary condition of a favourable decision. This approach is typical: provided that a particular moral point satisfies the test of relevance to the objects of the discretion, and provided that the weight put on the moral point is not excessive, then the decision is properly made. While the test is easy enough to state, it is to be noted that each of the provisos imports a test of reasonableness.

The second question concerns the role of the courts in positively requiring compliance with or at the least consideration of moral principles. It is useful here to distinguish between what might loosely be called substantive principles and procedural principles. Whether the courts regard a substantive principle to be so important that failure by the original authority to take it into account and to accord adequate weight to it would result in the decision being invalid, must be determined according to the normal criteria of purposes, relevance, and reasonableness. Failure by a sentencing judge to consider factors of retribution and deserts, or a parole board to consider the moral culpability of an offender, might well be deemed a sufficiently grave error to undermine the legality of the decision. The fact that the matter in issue is of a clearly moral kind does not change the general judicial approach; but it is likely to be more difficult to persuade a court that failure to take a moral principle into account is a sufficient omission to warrant review, than to persuade the same court that some factor has been improperly taken into account or given excessive importance. However, this observation is not unique to moral principles but is likely to be true with respect to judicial review generally.

[76] [1985] 3 WLR 335.

Procedural principles also may be connected to moral values, and the question then is to what extent courts will review a discretionary decision for violation of some such principle. Lord Diplock, it will be recalled, stipulated procedural impropriety as a separate and sound ground for judicial review, and the general importance of fair procedures as a basis for legal regulation of discretion has already been discussed. Typically such issues arise under what has come to be known as natural justice, but there is no reason to regard the categories of procedural fairness as closed. Two brief points may be noted. Firstly, there is a noticeable tendency to argue for senses of procedural fairness which clearly are linked to but extend beyond a more traditional view of natural justice. The extension of ideas of natural justice to discretionary contexts is examined in the next chapter, where it is shown that the term 'natural justice' has to a large extent been replaced simply by 'fairness'. The very use of the broader, less precise concept invites new and wider conceptions of fairness. This has opened the way for closer judicial scrutiny of the relationship between officials and those affected by their decisions, a scrutiny which considers whether there has been anything in the nature of a holding out by the official as to how decisions will be made. Considering that a holding out has been held to extend not only to express and direct assurances but also to the indirect inferences that may be drawn from self-imposed guidelines, the potential for extending procedural fairness is considerable.[77]

Secondly, there may be other aspects of procedural fairness which will come to have a place in judicial review of discretionary decisions. One example is fairness in the sense of like treatment, often expressed in terms of consistency. The discussion in section 4 would suggest that great caution is needed in interpreting and applying the principle of consistency, but nevertheless it is an aspect of procedural fairness that often is invoked. It has been said by Mr Justice Mason of the Australian High Court that 'consistency in punishment—a reflection of the notion of equal justice—is a fundamental element in any rational and fair system of criminal justice';[78] it is doubtful whether that view is accepted widely, but arguments based on the idea commonly are

---

[77] *R. v. Secretary of State for the Home Department, ex parte Asif Khan* [1984] 1 WLR 1337. For more general discussion, see *Attorney General* v. *Ng Yuen Shin* [1983] AC 629, and *Council of Civil Service Unions* v. *Minister for Civil Service* [1984] 3 WLR 1174.

[78] *R. v. Lowe* (1984) 58 ALJR 414 at p. 415.

encountered in sentencing review.[79] In the wider context of discretionary decisions, attitudes have been rather more cautious, and are
perhaps best summed up by another Australian judge Mr Justice
Deane: consistency in decision-making may be an aspect of fairness,
but there is more to fairness than consistency.[80]

To sum up then the argument in the preceding sections concerning
purposes and background constraints, when courts embark on an
investigation of the purposes of discretionary powers their aim is not to
arrive at a comprehensive definition, but rather to determine the
relationship between broadly specified objects and specific, personal,
background interests. In so far as there is a consistent judicial
approach, it is one which favours private rights relating to property,
and pecuniary and economic interests incidental or closely connected
to property. Rights and interests of this kind are favoured by
presumptions of varying strength against interference by officials in
exercising discretionary powers. Civil rights may attract the same kind
of presumption, but those and other non-proprietary rights and
interests are more likely to be regarded only as factors to be
considered. The favoured status conferred on property rights and
related interests might be questioned on two grounds. Firstly, it rests
on obsolete distinctions between property rights and interests which
happen historically to have been surrounded with firm legal protection,
and other non-proprietary interests which are nevertheless of equal, if
not greater importance, and which are affected often seriously and
directly by discretionary powers. Secondly, there is little evidence to
show that the courts are concerned to develop a framework within
which the relationship between general discretion and personal or
group interests is to be understood. Outside the limited areas of
proprietary interests, it appears either to have been accepted that there
are no constraints on discretion generated by the interests at stake, or
that there is to be a balancing of considerations which is somewhat
crude and, in the absence of a more settled yardstick, somewhat
haphazard.

This is not to suggest, however, that interpretation of the purposes
behind discretionary powers, and the background constraints on its

---

[79] See the other judgments in *R. v. Lowe* (1984) 58 ALJR 414 and *R. v. Griffiths*
(1977) 137 CLR 293.
[80] *Nevistic v. Minister for Immigration and Ethnic Affairs* (1981) 34 ALR 639; see also
the analysis by Mr Justice Brennan in *Re Drake and Minister for Immigration and Ethnic
Affairs (No 2)* (1979) 2 ALD 634.

exercise, can be made an easy and entirely objective matter. The situations in which discretion occurs are enormously variable, and similar situations may be dealt with differently in the terms of the governing statutes; there is also the problem of divergences amongst judges, and the fragmentation of law into pockets which bear little relation to each other. It may be argued, nevertheless, that as the public law model of authority becomes more firmly established, the legal issues of interpretation are likely to recur according to identifiable patterns, and in that situation there is scope for strengthening the rules of interpretation by closer analysis of the relationship within discretionary contexts between the citizen and the state.

6.34   *The relevance and irrelevance of reasons*

Questions about purposes often arise in testing whether the reasons for a decision are sufficiently related to general purposes. Usually this is referred to as an inquiry into the relevance or irrelevance of the matters taken into account. In settling questions of relevance and irrelevance it is not always necessary to reflect on purposes at all; if the relevant factors have been stipulated by statute and are meant to be comprehensive, a decision is invalid if any one of them is neglected. Similarly, if all listed factors are taken into account, the decision normally is valid, subject only to the possibility of gross unreasonableness in assessing the importance of each. More typically, however there is neither mandatory stipulation of the matters to be taken into account, nor an assumption that those stated are to be treated as exhaustive. In that case, the validity of a discretionary decision is assessed by first defining purposes, even if only in outline, and then deciding whether the reasons for a decision relate to them in a sufficiently clear and reasonable manner.

Relevance is used in two different senses; one is whether a particular factor is so rationally or logically related or unrelated to the objects of the discretion that it ought to be taken into account, or not, as the case may be. For example, the question has arisen whether a local authority, using its slum clearance powers to requisition a group of buildings for demolition, was entitled to consider what had transpired at an earlier inquiry; conversely, there was a dispute about whether it had failed to take into account changes in the law and policy relating to housing, which were said to be highly relevant.[81] The court

---

[81] *Elliott v. Southwark LBC* [1976] 1 WLR 499.

found for the council on the grounds that the first was a matter that might properly be taken into account, and that the second, which ought to have been taken into account, had properly been considered. The question in cases of this kind is almost an evidential one of deciding what range of matters are related sufficiently closely to the issue as a matter of logic and reason.

Indeed, in understanding relevance in this sense (which may be referred to somewhat loosely as logical relevance) an analogy may be drawn with the law of evidence: a piece of evidence *a* is relevant to issue *b*, if *a* tends to show that *b* is the case; if *a* is not probative in this way, it is excluded as irrelevant. In discretionary decisions, reasons which fail to satisfy this test are irrelevant, and should not be acted on; conversely, reasons which do satisfy the test are logically relevant, and are normally proper elements to consider in making a decision, subject to exclusion for other reasons.

There is, however, a second type of situation where the issue of relevance is more clearly concerned with an assessment of the policies that may be advanced within the scope of discretion. If a matter is taken into account because it serves a policy *p*, then the question is whether *p* may legitimately be pursued; this is resolved by inquiring whether *p* represents an improper purpose, or, alternatively, whether *p* as an instrumental policy is incompatible with purposes. The courts do not tend to distinguish between the two, and the way the matter is approached is unlikely to make a difference to the outcome. In *Padfield*, the minister's reasons for not making a reference to the committee of inquiry were held to be irrelevant, because they were based on policies falling outside the range of those that might properly be considered. Whether this is seen as a case of improper purposes, or as an inappropriate policy for giving effect to agreed purposes, depends finally on the level of abstraction at which purposes are expressed. The minister and the judges did not disagree in *Padfield* about the general objects of the milk marketing scheme, but rather about the policies that might be deployed in the realization of those objects. Relevance and irrelevance in this sense depend on an inquiry into purposes and objects, rather than an inquiry into the rational links between an issue and the pieces of evidence that might help in its resolution. So when the Australian High Court, in *Murphyores* v. *Commonwealth*,[82] held that the environmental effects of mining were

[82] (1976) 136 CLR 1.

proper factors to consider in deciding whether to allow the exportation of minerals, it was not deciding a question of logical relevance, but whether protection of the environment was a proper object to take into account in exercising a discretion of this kind.

Once it is established that a policy is a proper one to follow, logical relevance may again be helpful in deciding which factors are relevant or irrelevant to that policy. Moreover, with respect to any issue that arises in the exercise of discretion—whether a person is in extreme need, or fit to run a public house, or whether a house is fit for human habitation—there are certain matters which must be taken into account if the inquiry is to be rational and reasonable. But such matters of logical relevance readily merge into matters of policy; so in deciding whether a reason must positively be taken into account, it is often necessary to fall back on an analysis of general purposes, and on the relationship between them and particular values and interests. Further, there may be subtle but important differences between whether a factor may be taken into account or whether it must be. In *Murphyores*, the environmental consequences of mining were proper matters to take into account, but whether it would have been wrong for the minister not to take them into account is a different matter. The difference between may and must sometimes is to be resolved by considering whether the factor in issue is one required to be taken into account as a matter of logical relevance; more often, however, the difference depends not on logical relevance, but on an assessment of objects and purposes.[83] In this way, questions of relevance and irrelevance become part of the inquiry into objects and purposes, and so encounter the familiar issues of interpretation.

Within the general issue as to whether factors are relevant or irrelevant, whether they may or must be taken into account, the question may be whether certain interests are to be considered and, if so, what it really means to be considered. If the discretionary process is seen not so much as applying stated objects according to logical reasoning and technical experience, but at least partly as a means for finding a compromise between competing interests, then outcomes are likely to depend to some degree on which interests are considered. An important question then for both administrative officials and the courts

[83] *Roberts* v. *Hopwood* [1925] AC 578; *Prescott* v. *Birmingham Corporation* [1954] 3 AER 698; *Taylor* v. *Munrow* [1960] 1 WLR 151; *Bromley LBC* v. *Greater London Council* [1983] 1 AC 768; *R.* v. *Secretary of State for the Environment, ex parte Norwich City Council* [1982] QB 808.

is to decide which interests must be counted in exercising discretion. This occurs not only in deciding which interests the discretionary body must consider, but also in relation to participatory procedures, since, if there is a duty to consider certain interests, then there is a presumptive case for allowing those interests to participate in decision-making.

There are close links between the inquiry into which interests are to be considered, and the earlier discussion of background constraints. The spectrum of positions can be put in this way: (*a*) matters which are unrelated logically to a given issue, or are related to an issue which pertains to an improper purpose; (*b*) matters which are relevant and may, but need not, be taken into account; (*c*) matters which must be taken into account; (*d*) matters which carry a rebuttable presumption that they will not be affected by discretionary decisions; (*e*) matters which have an immunity from discretionary actions. Underlying this spectrum, which runs from interests of tenuous connection to rights with legal or constitutional protection, is the common issue of how much interests and values are to count in discretionary decisions: do they count at all; if so, what weight do they carry when compared with other interests and values?

In the first place, the courts clearly have taken various positions which are reflected in their attitudes to background constraints and in the method of giving presumptive protection to certain interests. The suggestion already made is that this approach is inadequate in dealing with the range of discretionary powers. The second question, then, is what approach should the courts adopt, or, perhaps more accurately, what direction might they take in developing a theory about the relevance and status of interests. Perhaps the simplest approach is a version of interest representation which requires simply that all those whose interests, taking a broad sense of the term, are affected by a discretionary decision ought to be considered. Provided all interests are considered, no complaint may be made against the outcome, even if it is unfavourable. This approach might be supported by the Poundian idea that since there is no objective basis for giving priority to one set of interests over another, the function of legal institutions is to satisfy as many interests as possible.[84] Subscription to some such principle would have the salutary effect of requiring the courts to ensure that any interests affected by discretionary actions have the opportunity of bringing its claims to bear on the administrative

---

[84] Roscoe Pound, *Contemporary Juristic Theory* (California, 1940), pp, 77–80.

authority. This approach has the added advantage of defining the role of courts with reasonable objectivity, since their task would not go beyond ensuring that interests have the chance of being represented, and that the officials in fact consider their claims. Provided it could be seen from the official's reasons that each claim had been considered, questions of weighting and outcomes would be a matter for the authority.

There are some attractions to such an approach, but there are also difficulties which are taken up in the next chapter. The general objection is that such a view is acceptable only if it forms part of a more sophisticated theory which includes some sense both of justice and democratic principles. In sketching such a theory, a number of premises may be relied on. Firstly, there is the idea of reflexive rationality, that in the relative absence of clear, objectively defined goals, an administrators perceptions of purposes and the relationship with other aspects of society are influenced by the claims that are put before him. If outcomes are shaped by inputs, then the rules governing inputs are extremely important. Secondly, it is necessary to have some theory of interests in deciding which are to qualify for representation and consideration, and in allotting to them some weighting, even if of a threshold kind, within the discretionary process. In this regard, two ideas might be invoked; one is that there is more to democracy than either majority rule or domination by the most powerful groups; there is the idea of the rights of individuals and minorities against majorities. This may help courts in ensuring the representation of minority interests, and in erecting around them procedural barriers to be surmounted before action may be taken to their detriment. The other idea, which is not unrelated, is to recognize that some substantive theory of the relative importance of different interests is necessary in settling questions of purpose and relevance. A theory such as that already suggested might be taken as an example. Individual interests are divided into two main categories, one relating to personal liberty, the other to personal welfare, and, within each, specific interests may be ordered according to their relative importance. The image created is of a society comprising individuals, around each of whom are clustered a range of interests of varying importance in constituting and preserving persons as distinct, relatively autonomous, and worthy of protection. Some interests are fundamental to that end, and warrant firm protection against conflicting considerations; others are less central, and are more open to being balanced against other factors. So, for example, the interest one has against bodily constraint is of such central importance that it may be curtailed only for strong and clear reasons; freedom of speech, however, is less central and, therefore, is more readily balanced against other interests.

The development of some such approach towards interests would be a significant part of a theory of interpretation which could be applied to discretionary authority. An analysis of the interests in issue would help in establishing an approach to purposes; the more important the interest, the stronger the basis for construing discretionary authority in a way favourable to it. Something of this can be seen in Lord Reid's approach in *Padfield*: the interests at stake were sufficiently important to require good reasons, if a decision were to be taken contrary to them. This did not remove the minister's discretion, but it certainly channelled it so that the onus was on him to show why a reference was not made. Had he stated more clearly and fully his interpretation of the objects of the overall scheme and the policies he would pursue, he might have scotched the judicial doubts; in fact, his explanation was patchy, and some of the reasons he offered were unsatisfactory. How far courts might go in developing such an approach to interests can be answered in different ways, but there is a case for the exertion of some control in the form of presumptions, procedural hurdles, or simply by requiring evidence that important interests have rationally and reasonably been considered.

Enough has been said to demonstrate the lines along which judicial review of purposes and reasons might develop, and some of the difficulties to be encountered. Central to this issue is interpretation, connoting constant tension and interaction between the words of the statute and the background environment, between objectivity and subjectivity, between the roles of administrative officials and the courts. These tensions and interactions are inherent in both interpretation and judicial review, and are best understood and channelled rather than ignored or sought to be removed. The important task for the courts in reviewing these aspects of discretionary decisions is to recognize that they have a legitimate role in developing constitutional doctrines and canons of interpretation, that this is not in any sense a neutral business, but that positions taken must be defended and justified, and that this in itself requires the adoption and specification of a theoretical standpoint.

6.4   EVIDENCE AND REASONABLENESS

An authority exercising discretion may have satisfied the different legal constraints so far considered; it has followed the correct procedures, its decision is based on reasons which are within purposes, and it has considered the right matters. There are, however, two final grounds on which judicial review might proceed: one concerns the evidential basis for findings of fact, the other is the residual notion of reasonableness.

6.41   *The evidential basis of facts and policies*

A basic aspect of rational action is that the facts on which decisions are founded should be supported by good evidence. This means that for any finding of fact f which counts in the reasons for decision, there ought to be evidence from which, as a matter of logic and experience, f may be inferred. In drawing inferences from the evidence, there is inevitably an element of personal and subjective judgment which may connote discretion; but the question whether there is a reasonable basis of evidence for f may be assessed in more objective terms. So, in the discretionary context, it can be accepted that the drawing of factual inferences is for the authority, subject to the condition that there be a basis of evidence, a matter which might well be left to judicial supervision.

In describing the supervisory functions of the courts over issues of evidence, English courts tend to talk in terms of 'no evidence' and American courts in terms of 'substantive evidence', and although there are differences between them, the tests in fact applied under either heading are variable, and often connote a notion of reasonableness: is there a reasonable basis of evidence for f, or, alternatively, is f a reasonable finding in the light of the evidence. Whether the test is expressed in terms of reasonableness or in some other way, it is necessarily dependent upon a substantial element of judgment and opinion as to whether it is satisfied, and so may be made more or less exacting.

In recent years, the British courts have taken steps to enforce a duty on administrative officials to have a foundation of evidence for the factual basis of their decisions. It has been held that a minister in exercising his slum clearance powers must have good evidence for being satisfied that a pair of houses are unfit for human habititation.[85]

[85] *Ashbridge Investments Ltd* v. *Minister of Housing and Local Government* [1965] 1 WLR 1320.

A similar principle applied in a more discretionary situation where the minister, again in exercising his clearance powers, declared a building to be 'reasonably necessary' for the satisfactory development of the cleared area. His decision was quashed on the ground that he had acted on no evidence, or that he had come to a conclusion to which, on the evidence, he could not reasonably come.[86] These are typical examples of numerous cases which in recent years have taken this approach. There have always been ways in which judicial scrutiny could extend to consideration of the factual basis of decisions, either through the jurisdictional fact doctrine, or by characterizing questions of fact as issues involving the interpretation of statutory provisions, and so as matters of law. The more recent approach is significant in allowing findings of fact to be the direct objects of review. The efficacy of the doctrine is partly dependent, however, on administrative officials being under a duty to state their reasons and findings.

While judicial review based on the no-evidence or reasonable-evidence rule does not create great difficulties where a finding of fact is central to the administrative decision, the position becomes more troublesome when the decision is more clearly discretionary. One problem is that the distinction between fact and discretion is neither neat nor precise. Questions characterized as factual entail the recording of perceptions and their classification into shared, familiar categories. When the categories are familiar, the process of classification goes unnoticed; but when they are unfamiliar or artificial, the classification may involve elements of discretion, either in interpreting the meaning of the concept, or in deciding whether the evidence establishes its existence in the present case. Whether someone is 'undesirable as an inhabitant of Britain' entails facts and discretion, since the category in question depends on variable criteria which are not stipulated. It is then a question of how far the courts should go in assuming control over the definition of concepts which include elements of assessment and judgment. Problems of a related kind arise when it is necessary to decide whether a set of facts comes within a category which is abstract, imprecise, or complex. It may be possible in both situations to distinguish between the primary facts and the evaluation, characterization, or appreciation of them, but in practice there is no clear line between the two.

---

[86] *Coleen Properties Ltd* v. *Minister of Housing and Local Government* [1971] 1 AER 1049. See also *Sutherland Shire Council* v. *Finch* [1969] 123 CLR 657; *Secretary of State for Education and Science* v. *Tameside MBC* [1977] AC 1014.

These problems are accentuated when judicial review is extended to scrutiny of the policies which are employed in the exercise of discretionary powers. In *Sagnata Investments* v. *Norwich Corporation*,[87] the local authority, pursuant to a previously adopted policy, refused a permit for an amusement centre in Norwich on the ground that, because of the effects they might have on children, such places were socially undesirable. It was held by a majority of the Court of Appeal that the council acted improperly, one of the grounds being that it had no evidence to support its policy. One judge spoke of the failure to bring evidence either of harm to the young caused by fun parlours in neighbouring towns, or evidence of particular harm being likely to result in Norwich. Lord Denning dissented, and considered that matters of policy of this kind were essentially matters of opinion which were entrusted by Parliament to the local authority, and in respect of which it was responsible to its electors.

These opposing views nicely capture the two central problems: the tension between raising the rational basis of discretionary decisions by requiring that the reasons for action be based on good evidence, and on the other hand the fact that questions of policy and judgment—of what is the best course of action to take—are also dependent on opinion, and a view of social aims and values. The arguments for the former are that matters of policy are always dependent to some extent on empirical knowledge; in *Norwich*, it might have been possible to bring evidence not only of the social effects of fun parlours in other places, but also evidence of a psychological and sociological kind about the general effects of such institutions on the behaviour of children. These arguments apply generally; unless there is a substratum of objective evidence for the reasons and policies acted on, discretionary decisions are liable to the charge of arbitrariness. Powerful examples of arbitrariness in that sense are to be found in the penal system where decisions are made about offenders on the basis of unproven assumptions about human behaviour, and unsupported predictions concerning future conduct. It is clear that rigorous judicial scrutiny of the empirical basis on which sentencing and parole decisions are made would greatly reduce the arbitrariness ingrained in such areas.

Judicial review of the evidential and empirical basis of discretionary decisions can be made more or less exacting, depending on where the

---

[87] [1971] 2 QB 614. For fuller discussion of *Sagnata*, see Galligan, 'The Nature and Function of Policies within Discretionary Powers' pp. 339 ff. See also *R.* v. *Flintshire CC Licensing Committee, ex parte Barrett* [1957] 1 QB 350.

line is drawn between a minimum threshold of evidence, and a
sufficient level of evidence to show that the course of action is in the
circumstances the most rational. The higher the level of evidence
demanded, the more difficult it is for an administrative body to act on
unsupportable assumptions and opinions, and to that extent the
rationality of decisions is enhanced. The difficulties are, first, that
questions of evidence are prone to embrace matters of policy and
opinion, and thus bestow on them a sense of objectivity that is not
always warranted; secondly, according to the division of powers,
matters of policy and substance are for the administrative authorities
rather than the courts. How far the courts go in demanding evidential
support must be determined, therefore, according to constitutional
doctrines and the nature of the decision, the capacities of the
administrative body, and the nature of the interests that are affected.

The difficulties in determining the most suitable course for judicial
review of the evidential basis has become a central issue in American
administrative law. Judicial review within the federal jurisdiction is
centred around two general standards which apply in different
contexts; one is the substantive evidence rule which applies to
administrative adjudication, the other is the arbitrary or capricious test
which applies when an administrative agency is formulating general
rules. It is unnecessary to go into the procedural details, or into the
debate as to whether these amount substantially to the same test.[88]
Taken together, these standards are similar to those used in British
law, and in each jurisdiction the tests are subject to interpretation, and
may be made more or less stringent in their demands. In recent years
in America, a mood of judicial activism has been noticeable which has
taken the form of more exacting review of the rational basis of
discretionary decisions. It has been described as a distinct move from
an incremental approach to one of comprehensive, rational planning,
to a synoptic rather than a piecemeal approach, and the threshold
requirement of rational reasonableness has given way to the 'hard look
doctrine'.[89] This lethal-sounding device has been described as a
reluctance by the courts to be content with the 'intuitive plausibility of

[88] For a useful discussion, see J. Skelly Wright, 'The Courts and the Rulemaking
Process: the Limits of Judicial Review' (1974) 59 *CornLR* 375 and P. R. Verkuil,
'Judicial Review of Informal Rulemaking' (1974) 60 *VaLR* 185.

[89] For an excellent discussion of the background to the hard look doctrine as part of a
trend by American courts away from incrementalism towards comprehensive planning,
see C. S. Diver, 'Policymaking Paradigms in Administrative Law' (1981) 95 *HarvLR*
393. See also Verkuil, 'Judicial Review of Informal Rulemaking'.

the link between the policy announced and the statutory standard';[90] the agency must be prepared to demonstrate to the court that the course of action chosen not only advances its goal, but is superior to any alternative 'advanced by outside participants or conceived by the agency itself'.[91] Under the hard look doctrine, the courts have demanded that the agency specify its goals, identify the alternatives, analyse the consequences of each, and optimize their choices.

The hard look doctrine plunges the courts directly into a searching examination of the evidential and empirical basis of decisions. It does of course have its difficulties and its detractors, as can be seen from an interesting decision of the Supreme Court in *Vermont Yankee Nuclear Power Corp. v. Natural Resources Defence Council.*[92] The issue was the validity of two decisions by the Nuclear Regulatory Commission (NRC) granting nuclear power plant licences. At a technical level the legal issues were whether the NRC could be required to follow procedures beyond those specified in the Administrative Procedure Act or other statutes; but, at a substantive level, the issue was whether the NRC was required to disclose the factual basis of proposed rules for measuring the environmental effects of radioactive waste, and to reply in detail to the criticisms and evidence submitted by interested parties against them. It was argued that the NRC failed to explore adequately the environmental consequences of its policies, which had been attacked by the Natural Resources Defence Council. The argument was upheld by the Court of Appeal, and the licences granted to operate power plants were declared invalid; in the Supreme Court that position was reversed on rather technical, procedural grounds, but the decision, while not amounting to outright rejection of the hard look doctrine, has been taken as a significant damper on it, and has provoked extensive comment.

The Supreme Court decision has been condemned by Richard Stewart who commends the hard look doctrine as an important progression in judicial review in enhancing the rational basis of discretionary decisions.[93] He argues that the courts have a legitimate

---

[90] Diver, 'Policymaking Paradigms in Administrative Law', p. 411.

[91] Ibid., p. 412. For a good example of the exacting levels of review that result from this synoptic approach, see *Citizens to Preserve Overton Park* v. *Volpe* (1971) 401 US 402.

[92] (1978) 435 US 519. For discussion, see S. Breyer, '*Vermont Yankee* and the Court's Role in the Nuclear Energy Controversy' (1978) 91 *HarvLR* 1833.

[93] '*Vermont Yankee* and the Evolution of Administrative Procedure' (1978) 91 *HarvLR* 1805. For a perceptive account of *Vermont Yankee* in the British context, see Jack Beatson, 'A British View of *Vermont Yankee*' (1981) 55 *Tulane Law Review* 435.

role in extending the scope of review even without congressional authorization, and that the hard look doctrine forces administrators to create a record showing the basis on which they have proceeded, thus giving participating parties the opportunity to examine, criticize, and offer alternatives. The final decision of policy is left to the agency, but that may become a somewhat hollow form since it would be hard to justify a course of action other than that most supportable on the evidence. Other critics have welcomed *Vermont Yankee* as a 'needed corrective to an unwholesome trend'.[94] Clark Byse has argued that the hard look doctrine, when pushed too far, constitutes an unjustifiable intrusion by the courts into roles that are suitably performed by administrative agencies. On this view, Congress has delegated to the agency the authority to settle such issues of policy, and to determine how its resources are best deployed. However, such arguments to some extent beg the question since virtually any judicial role, active or passive, can be justified in terms of legislative intention. Moreover, it is difficult to see why, in areas such as nuclear energy, the standards of rational decision-making should not be high, and the onus put on discretionary authorities to justify their policies. The upshot seems to be that, despite the restraints of *Vermont Yankee*, American courts continue rigorously to review in many important areas of discretion the factual and empirical basis of policies adopted, and courses of action proposed.[95]

The British courts have not yet adopted the hard look approach, nor has there been a major trend towards ensuring the optimal or comprehensive rationality of discretionary decisions. Lord Diplock's view that irrationality is a separate ground of review has rapidly been assimilated into judicial orthodoxy.[96] But, as we have seen at various points, while rationality is of fundamental importance to judicial review of discretion, it is a movable feast; like Keynes's ball of wool, it has no sharp edges, and as with all such complex concepts, rationality has to be interpreted, and it may be pitched at different levels, and so be more or less exacting. However, tentative steps have been taken as the courts extend their examination of purposes, relevancy and the evidential basis. One point to notice is that the developments in those

---

[94] Clark Byse, '*Vermont Yankee* and the Evolution of Administrative Procedure: A Somewhat Different View' (1978) 91 *HarvLR* 1828.

[95] See *Industrial Union Department* v. *American Petroleum Institute (Benzene)* (1980) 448 US 607; *American Textile* v. *Donovan (Cotton Dust)* (1981) 101 SCt 2478.

[96] See *Council of Civil Service Unions* v. *Minister for Civil Service* [1984] 3 WLR 1174.

various areas are to be seen as linked, and as parts of a unified approach. There are also links between questions of evidence and disclosure of reasons with relevancy, and what it means to take into account an interest or circumstance. There are also connections with participation by interested parties, since one of the main arguments for participation is to enhance the rationality of decisions. So, while questions of evidential support might be resolved at a number of positions between a low threshold of no evidence and an extremely 'hard look', the position taken may vary from one context to another, and is to be determined in line with those other, related doctrines. The second point is that beyond reiterating the general approach suggested to judicial review, it is doubtful that any more specific guidance can be given as to the most satisfactory degree of judicial scrutiny of evidential matters.

6.42   *Reasonableness and unreasonableness*

The reasonableness or unreasonableness of a discretionary action is said not to be a matter of direct concern in judicial review. Courts do not determine reasonableness, but only legality. Nevertheless, the notions of reasonableness and unreasonableness are implicit in much of the practice of judicial review; indeed, it has been suggested by Bernard Schwartz that reasonableness is the one unifying concept that runs through judicial review:[97] in settling purposes, deciding relevance and irrelevance, and in assessing the adequacy of evidence, the concept of reasonableness often unavoidably serves as the common touchstone. But since reasonableness is one of those concepts more potent in appeal than illuminating in analysis, there are arguments against putting it more clearly at the centre of judicial review. It seems preferable to require both administrators and courts to argue directly for a particular interpretation of purposes or relevancy, or for a certain level of empirical support, rather than invoke reasonableness as if it provides conclusive support for whatever position is preferred. Reasonableness rightly and inevitably constitutes the basis for any practical judgement, whether the administrator's or the court's, so that the issue typically for judicial review is which of a number of possible reasonable positions is to be supported; that judgment depends on more than incantation of reasonableness, the very concept in issue.

[97] *Administrative Law*, p. 663.

Nevertheless, it does seem that despite occasional disclaimers,[98] reasonableness is coming to have a more prominent and explicit place in judicial review; for that reason it is worth considering briefly the ways in which it may be employed. Firstly, we may distinguish between an express statutory requirement of reasonableness, and the role of reasonableness in common law doctrines. Discretionary powers conferred subject to a standard of reasonableness have had a chequered history in the hands of the courts, but, subject to notable exceptions, such standards are regarded generally as providing a firmer basis for judicial review than might otherwise exist.[99]

As a part of common law doctrines of judicial review, reasonableness appears in a number of ways. Firstly, following Lord Greene's famous statement,[100] unreasonableness might refer simply to the fact that a decision is for some other reason *ultra vires* because of an improper purpose, irrelevant matters, or inadequate empirical support. Secondly, reasonableness may constitute a condition of last resort, so that a discretionary decision could be considered invalid if it were so unreasonable that no reasonable authority could have made it.[101] The idea is that attention is focused not directly on the reasonableness of the decision, but on whether it is the kind of decision that a reasonable authority would make. There are difficulties with this test. Firstly, what a reasonable authority would do depends ultimately on some idea of what constitutes a reasonable decision. To emphasize the reasonableness of the authority rather than the decision is not to propose a different test; its real effect is to stress that the decision must be highly or grossly unreasonable before it is to be considered invalid. Secondly, it has been pointed out that this residual test is redundant since situations which would qualify could always be recharacterized as questions about purposes or relevancy.[102] While this is in general true, it is just possible to imagine decisions which are totally unreasonable in result, even though no fault can be found in the premises. The judge who gives the rapist a suspended sentence may have considered all the

[98] *Chief Constable of North Wales Police* v. *Evans* [1982] 1 WLR 1155, per Lord Hailsham at pp. 1160–1. Compare *Liversidge* v. *Anderson* [1942] AC 206 and *Secretary of State for Education and Science* v. *Tameside MBC* [1977] AC 1014.

[99] For discussion, see Craig, *Administrative Law*, pp. 360 ff.

[100] *Associated Provincial Picture Houses* v. *Wednesbury Corporation* [1948]1 KB 223.

[101] Ibid. For application of the test, see *Luby* v. *Newcastle-Under-Lyme Corporation* [1964] 2 QB 64; *British Airways Board* v. *Laker Airways Ltd* [1984] 3 WLR 413.

[102] Craig, *Administrative Law*, pp. 358–09.

right matters, but have come to a totally unreasonable conclusion.[103]

There is a third sense in which reasonableness may operate, and it is this that is most important. Here reasonableness appears in providing guidance as to whether an action is within purposes, whether a background factor is to be overridden, whether a matter is relevant and whether it has been adequately considered, and whether there is evidential support for a finding or policy. In such matters the ultimate object is to decide whether, say, a condition imposed on planning permission is within purposes, but, in order to arrive at that decision, a notion of reasonableness is likely to be invoked. So conditions imposed on planning permission, which in effect required the applicant to build and dedicate to the public a new road without compensation, were considered to be beyond the legitimate objects of planning;[104] but, to reach that conclusion, an assessment of the reasonableness of the conditions had to be made. Similarly, the decision mentioned earlier that a local authority, in deciding whether to allow use of its facilities by a local rugby club, had put too much emphasis on requiring the club's total commitment to anti-apartheid, depended implicitly on a criterion of reasonableness. The authority was entitled to take such matters into account, but to make them conditions precedent to a favourable decision was held to be unlawful. Despite the disclaimers that the courts are to assess the reasonableness of discretionary decisions, it is clear that in practice reasonableness has a central role in judicial review. This seems to be inevitable, the only question being that raised previously, whether reasonableness and unreasonableness are really useful terms in justifying the stance taken in judicial review, or whether there is a high risk of them becoming empty terms of self-justification.

Finally, there is a fourth sense of reasonableness worth noting. Here reasonableness means fairness. To act unfairly is not necessarily to act unreasonably, but where there is unfairness in a sense that courts will act upon, it might on occasions be referred to in terms of unreasonableness. The usual sense of unfairness relevant to judicial review is procedural fairness, a matter touched on earlier in this chapter and considered more fully in the next. In such contexts, it is

---

[103] For examples which come close to this, see *R.* v. *St Albans Crown Court, ex parte Cinnamond* [1981] QB 480 and *R.* v. *Boundary Commission for England, ex parte Foot* [1983] 1 AER 1099.

[104] *Hall* v. *Shoreham-by-Sea UDC* [1984] 1 WLR 240. See also *R.* v. *Hillingdon LBC, ex parte Royco Homes Ltd* [1974] QB 720; *Esmonds Motors* v. *Commonwealth* (1969) 120 CLR 463.

not normally necessary to introduce the notion of unreasonableness, since unfairness is itself a sufficient ground for review. However, issues of procedural fairness may, by a subtle shift of emphasis, be seen as matters of substantive fairness. So, where the Home Secretary published criteria which he had formulated in the exercise of his discretion governing the entry of foreign children for adoption, he was held, in effect, to be bound to apply those criteria in deciding a particular application for entry.[105] It was held to be unfair and unreasonable for the Home Secretary to create expectations by the publication of criteria, and then to apply different criteria. Unless prior notice of changes to the criteria were given, or unless some overriding matter of public policy could be cited in the particular case, the Home Secretary was held to be bound to comply; to depart would have been to introduce irrelevant factors. In this way procedural requirements may place constraints on the substance of decisions. Such an approach would also have important implications for the no-fettering doctrine, but it must be noted that judicial behaviour in this issue is variable, and usually it is sufficient if the discretionary body gives to interested parties an opportunity of being heard before departing from stated criteria.[106]

The question might still be posed whether the requirement of rational reasonableness in all official decisions ought to be itself a head of judicial review. This is of course to ask in another way how far courts should get involved in the merits of decisions. Accepting that there is no clear line between the merits of discretion and questions of legality, the positions that might be taken in judicial review can be calibrated as follows: (*a*) a rational basis test of a threshold kind such that decisions which failed to comply would be so lacking in reason as to be arbitrary; (*b*) a higher standard of rationality which is encapsulated in the idea of reasonableness; and (*c*) the more demanding standard which is well expressed in the hard look doctrine of American law. These are only rough categories along a spectrum of great subtlety and variety, but they highlight the broadly different directions that might be taken. The English approach seems to waver between the rational basis and reasonableness categories, while

---

[105] *R.* v. *Secretary of State for the Home Department, ex parte Asif Khan* [1984] 1 WLR 1337.
[106] See, for example, *O'Reilly* v. *Mackman* [1983] 2 AC 237 and *Attorney-General of Hong Kong* v. *Ng Yuen Shin* [1983] AC 629. Note also the related case of *In re Findlay* [1984] 3 WLR 1159.

American law vascillates between the reasonableness and hard look tests.

When it comes to considering the most acceptable level of judicial review, we must be content to note two points. Firstly, the courts in practice shift between the different levels in accordance with the kinds of factors that are by now familiar: the constitutional doctrines, the nature of the institution and its powers, the interests in issue. It seems also that judicial review is bound to fluctuate in this way for those kinds of reasons, and that few benefits are to be gained from a uniform, rigid approach. Subject to that qualification, there is a general case for the court being involved more directly in examining the rational basis of discretionary decisions. To require a parole board, nuclear licensing authority, or noise protection body to provide reasons, that those reasons show how relevant matters and interests have been taken into account, that interested parties have been heard and their arguments considered, that there is empirical evidence supporting proposed courses of action, and that reasoned explanation can be given for choosing one course rather than any other—is certainly to provide exacting standards for administrative decision-making; it also takes the courts well into the discretionary process. Secondly, to return to our original enquiry it is not clear that an explicit head of judicial review based on the concept of reasonableness would be an innovation of substantial merit.

6.5 CONCLUSION

The general object of this chapter has been to examine those themes in legal regulation, and in particular in judicial review, which are of greatest significance in relation to discretion. It has been necessary to be selective, but the issues considered are of interest because they are undergoing rapid development, or because they demonstrate important themes and problems. A number of themes can be seen running through the analysis. Firstly, there is the recurring issue of how the rational basis of decision-making can be increased. This is a major concern in matters like the disclosure in advance of standards of decision-making, and the disclosure of reasons after the decision has been made; it is also an important factor in the no-fettering doctrine, in the question of how far standards should be laid down in advance, and in considering how far the courts should go in examining the substance of reasons. Notions of stability and fairness also have a place in a number of these areas. A second theme concerns the relationship between the authority exercising external scrutiny, in this case the courts, on the one side, and Parliament and the administrative authority on the other side. Each area of review demonstrates the general point made in chapter 5, that questions about principles of review become closely intermixed with questions about the relationship between the different institutions. The third theme has been to examine some of the problems that are concealed under the traditional heads of review, and in doing this it has been necessary to identify and examine some of the assumptions underlying such matters as the judicial scrutiny of purpose, the question of relevance and irrelevance, and finally matters of reasonableness. The general point is that judicial review is always concerned about the extent to which legal values are to be imposed on discretionary decision-making, and on the relationship between the courts and the other institutions of government in making and applying decisions about basic underlying values.

7

Fair Procedures in Discretionary Decisions

THE question of fair procedures in discretionary contexts has been in recent years of increasing concern to the legislature, court, and administrative authorities. This chapter deals with that issue and considers the ways in which traditional procedural doctrines, based around the ancient principles of natural justice, have been developed and extended to take account of discretionary powers. The analysis goes beyond that, however; it begins by considering the basis of procedural fairness, for without some theoretical stance it is difficult to assess the course of legal doctrines and to suggest lines for further development. It is also necessary to consider the place that the concepts of representation and participation have in the design of procedures. The reader will recall the suggestion in chapter 2 that there are limits on the capacity to regulate discretionary powers by general legal norms, and that, accordingly, participatory procedures are important in influencing outcomes and in securing their legitimacy. An attempt is made in this chapter to show how these ideas can be translated into specific procedural requirements. The concept of consultation is considered and shown to be especially helpful in linking discretionary powers to the broader political system, and in devising appropriate modes of participation. Finally, within this general framework, procedural doctrines developed by the courts are considered.

7.1 RATIONALITY AND FAIRNESS IN PROCEDURES

Questions about fair procedures arise at many points in political and legal systems. At the political level, the guiding standard in answering such questions is often some version of democracy with its emphasis on procedures securing participation in the political process; at the legal level, it is the judicial trial that commonly provides the yardstick for setting and measuring procedural practices. Fuller's model of adjudication, with its emphasis on reasonably settled standards, the delineation of a specific set of contested issues, the opportunity for each party to participate through proof and argument, and the reasoned decision of an impartial adjudicator, contains a notion of procedural fairness which is often taken within the law to be the very quintessence of fairness. However, since discretionary powers do not always fit easily into that model, it is necessary to look beyond the special case of adjudication and to identify a wider and more general basis for fair procedures.

The primary consideration in designing procedures is to provide a practical and rational means for arriving at whatever outcome is sought. In a criminal trial the main object is to make an accurate finding of guilt or innocence, and so the most suitable procedures are those most conducive to that end. There is not necessarily one best procedure, and different procedures may be more or less effective; it is not clear, for example, that the adversarial procedures of the common law trial are more effective than an inquisitorial approach in distinguishing the guilty from the innocent. The selection of procedures is a matter of trial and error, of finding the most rational means for achieving a given outcome. Provided the procedures do serve the desired outcome as rationally as possible, they are good procedures; and provided that the outcome is itself just, then the procedures are just.

The difficulty is that not even the most carefully selected procedures always produce the correct outcome; in a criminal trial, the innocent may on occasions be found guilty and the guilty innocent. In matters of this kind, procedures no matter how good can never be perfect, so that it is possible to achieve only what John Rawls has called imperfect procedural justice.[1] This is the case in criminal and civil trials and in most types of administrative decisions. Not only are procedures unavoidably imperfect, but the costs of procedures in achieving even tolerable levels of accuracy can be high. So it may be necessary to make comparisons between the costs of procedures in raising the rationality of outcomes, and the costs of settling for outcomes where the margins of error and the reductions in rationality are increased. If two in every ten of those acquitted of a criminal offence are guilty, it might be

[1] Rawls; *A Theory of Justice*, pp. 85–7. For further discussion of procedures, see Barry, *Political Argument*, pp. 102–6. Also a number of useful essays are contained in J. R. Pennock and J. W. Chapman (eds.), *Due Process* (Nomos XVIII) (New York UP, 1977).

possible to improve the trial procedures so that only one in ten acquittals is wrong; but the costs of the procedures might be greater than the gains in outcome. The costs might involve extra judges, lawyers and policemen, and longer trials; the gains, however, of having one less guilty person go free might be small.[2]

So the first point is that the selection of procedures is not just a matter of finding the most rational means for achieving outcomes; it also involves assessing the costs and benefits of procedures in order to achieve marginal gains in outcomes. The second point is that any comparative assessment requires a prior decision as to what factors are to count; in order to carry out a cost benefit analysis, it is necessary to know what to cost and what value to put on it. There are obvious gains in reducing the acquittal rate of the guilty, but those same procedures may raise the conviction rate of the innocent; similarly, gains in economy and expedition in deciding claims for social security benefits might not only reduce the accuracy of outcomes, but also leave disappointed claimants with a sense of grievance and moral opprobrium. Matters like these are important and complex even where the object is to arrive at a dispassionate calculation of costs and benefits, since some price has to be put not only on clear gains or losses as to outcome, but also on the way people perceive procedures and what they consider to be fair. Such calculations are especially important and difficult in designing procedures in discretionary contexts.[3]

The relationship between procedures and outcomes can be seen in criminal and civil trials; in both, the main object of the procedures adopted is to put before the court an account of the circumstances which is as complete as possible to enable an accurate adjudication to be made. A similar congruence between procedures and outcomes is at the basis of the doctrine of natural justice; here the principal requirement is that a party whose rights are affected by an official action is to be informed of the case against him and given an opportunity of answering it. That person is likely to be in a particularly good position to produce evidence and arguments which cast light on the matter in issue. Had the vicar in *Bagg's* case[4] given the insolent

---

[2] For a detailed analysis of the costs and benefits of procedures, see R. A. Posner, 'An Economic Approach to Legal Procedure and Judicial Administration' (1972–3) 2 *JLegStud* 399.

[3] Some of the factors that might be built into a calculus of this kind are considered in J. L. Mashaw, 'The Supreme Court's Due Process Calculus for Administrative Adjudication in *Mathews* v. *Eldridge*: Three Factors in Search of a Theory of Value' (1976) 44 *UChicLR* 28.   [4] (1615) 11 CoRep 936.

verger the opportunity of explaining his behaviour, extenuating circumstances might have been revealed of a kind which were pertinent to whether or not he should be dismissed; similarly, the Wandsworth Board of Works might have found, had they given Mr Cooper an opportunity to explain himself, that there were good reasons for not pulling down his house.[5] But, although there clearly are grounds for listening to the case that might be put by the person whose interests are directly in issue, there also clearly are limits to the time and resources that could sensibly be invested in the inquiry; beyond a certain point the costs of inquiry may exceed the marginal gains in the rationality of the outcomes.

On the account so far, questions of procedure are seen in terms of instrumental rationality, in settling upon means which achieve desired ends. In so far as notions of fairness or unfairness are relevant, they depend on substantive outcomes. It may seem, however, that there is more to fairness in procedure than that. Indeed, there are two further factors to be considered. Fairness is sometimes taken to include side constraints that may be imposed upon the procedures adopted in realizing given ends. In a criminal trial, there are rules against self-incrimination and the admission of certain kinds of confessional evidence. These constraints cannot be explained adequately in terms of instrumental rationality, but depend more directly on protecting certain values which are sufficiently important to warrant some diminution in instrumental rationality.

Now, while such side constraints may form part of any assessment of the fairness of procedures, there seems to be a second, more elusive quality which is a positive requirement of procedures being fair. The importance placed on procedural fairness can hardly be accounted for if it consists solely in an analysis of costs and benefits; that analysis has to be made, but the claim from fairness is that the calculation is subject to certain restrictions. Such restrictions may take either of two directions: they may claim that a certain level of accuracy in achieving outcomes is required if procedures are to be fair; alternatively, values may be invoked which are independent of outcomes, but which impose constraints on the methods for achieving outcomes.[6]

---

[5] *Cooper* v. *Wandsworth Board of Works* (1863) 14CB (NS) 180.
[6] For discussion of procedural fairness, see T. M. Scanlon, 'Due Process' and David Resnick, 'Due Process and Procedural Justice' both in Pennock and Chapman, *Due Process*, and William Nelson, 'The Very Idea of Procedural Justice' (1980) 90 *Ethics* 502.

7.11   *The proportionality principle*

The first of these challenges the idea that the level of accuracy of procedures is entirely dependent on a policy decision as to how much society is prepared to pay. If this is just a matter of policy, it would be permissible to decide in respect of a certain area, say deportation decisions, that a very low level of accuracy is acceptable and so procedures adopted of the most rudimentary kind. The argument from fairness claims, on the contrary, that some minimum levels of accuracy must be reached. This claim has most force when personal rights are in issue; for example, each person has a right not to be convicted of a crime that he did not commit. Since procedures for determining guilt are unavoidably imperfect, mistakes sometimes are made. However, if that right is to be taken seriously, there is a duty on the community to provide procedures which guarantee a high level of accuracy. This does not mean that the highest level of accuracy must be attained at any cost; some sense of proportion has to be maintained between the importance of the right and the resources that society can be expected to make available in maintaining it. R. M. Dworkin, who argues along these lines, suggests that there are two rights in issue: one is the right to have the moral harm in a wrongful conviction given a value in criminal procedures, which reflects its value in the general morality of the society; the other is the right to have that value and weighting applied consistently to all cases.[7] The practical outcome is that those rights guarantee procedures, which in turn guarantee a certain level of accuracy of outcome. The fixing of precise procedures may be a difficult task, but whatever position is taken must be justifiable in those terms. And the guiding principle is that 'once the content of the right is determined, then the community must furnish . . . at least the minimum level of protection against the risk of injustice required by that content, even though the general welfare . . . suffers in consequence'.[8]

This argument has particular force in relation to criminal procedures, but it applies equally to civil cases; the question is whether it applies to discretionary decisions. An initial difficulty is that Dworkin's argument for guaranteed procedures is made to depend on there being rights at stake—such as the right not to be wrongly convicted in criminal law or held negligent in civil law; it is said not to apply when it

[7] R. M. Dworkin, 'Principle, Policy, Procedure' in Tapper, *Crime, Proof and Punishment.*
[8] Ibid., p. 211.

is only personal interests rather than rights that are affected. In discretionary contexts rights are sometimes in issue; it is arguable, for example, that in the famous American case, *Matthew* v. *Eldridge*,[9] where the question was whether social security benefits could be terminated without a hearing, the beneficiary had rights to welfare. If so, the administration was not free simply to decide questions of procedure according to an assessment of relative costs, but had to give a weighting to the claimant's right, and then fashion procedures accordingly. The Supreme Court did not take this view and upheld procedures which were settled on a more clearly utilitarian basis, and which did not require a hearing.

Rights in this sense may be in issue; we saw in section 4.23 that the object of discretion, properly construed, may be the creation and maintenance of rights. In that case, the level of procedural accuracy must be proportionate to the importance of the right. However, in most cases of discretionary powers, rights in that sense are not in issue; it is only interests or rights otherwise existing that are affected, and so the case for guaranteed procedures would not apply. But this seems unduly restrictive; why should it be only rights in this special sense that attract procedural protection, especially when, within the public law model, rights have in important ways been displaced from the centre of the stage? There are two ways of possibly overcoming this difficulty: the first is to argue for an extended view of rights; the second is to argue that, in any event, there are duties to be accurate even in respect of interests. With regard to the first, although there might not be rights in the special sense, there may be procedural rights not to have one's otherwise-existing rights and interests prejudiced by official decisions which are based on inaccurate assumptions or inadequate evidence. This could be supported by pointing out the nature of modern authority where, within the public law model, discretionary powers have such a pervasive role, and where an individual's interests may be left largely unprotected.[10] There may be good reasons for discretionary powers and for accepting that they are to be exercised on policy grounds; there are also good reasons for ensuring that proper consideration be given to the personal interests that are affected, and

---

[9] (1976) 424 US 319. For discussion, see Mashaw, The Supreme Courts Due Process Calculus' and Dworkin, 'Principle, Policy and Procedure'.

[10] Support for this argument might be found in the line of approach taken by C. A. Reich in 'Individual Rights and Social Welfare: the Emerging Legal Issues' 74 *YLJ* 1245 and 'The New Property' in Macpherson, *Property*.

so for a notion of procedural rights. This would include a right to levels of accuracy in decisions that are commensurable with the nature and importance of the interests. In short, a theory of regulation within the public law model might consider accurate procedures as a sufficiently important and individualized goal to constitute rights.[11]

If one hesitates at ascribing rights in this way, an alternative case can be made for minimum procedures in discretionary decisions. The argument, then, is that important interests may be affected seriously by discretionary decisions, and that this is itself a strong reason for minimum levels of accuracy. Decision-makers have a duty to act rationally, and a duty, based on the principle of concern and respect, to consider the interests that are affected by their decisions; from this, threshold conditions as to what constitutes 'taking into account' may be derived. One such condition would be the maintenance of some sense of proportion between the relative importance of the interest and the levels of accuracy of decisions affecting them. Just as rights may be allotted a relative weighting in the political values of the society, so the relative importance of interests could be calculated. That, of course, would require the difficult task of commensurability between the relative importance of interests and the minimum procedures required; but that difficulty pertains whether it is rights or interests in issue. The minimum procedures required in respect of interests might not be as exacting as those for rights, but that is not an argument against giving some weighting to interests. Nor does this prevent officials from making choices amongst interests, or of acting to the detriment of one or other; it means only that in doing so, minimum procedures must be satisfied. These arguments seem to me persuasive and useful in guiding the design of procedures. The upshot is that there must be some sense of proportion between the relative importance of the rights or interests at stake, and the levels of accuracy to be aimed at in setting procedures. We shall see the development of this idea in the course of this chapter.

7.12 *The importance of participation*

The second basis for fairness takes a different course: it is aimed not at ensuring minimum levels of accuracy of outcome, but at the form

---

[11] Dworkin's approach to rights as individualized goals is useful here. See *Taking Rights Seriously*, ch. 4. It must be said, however, that the use of the rights approach in the way suggested in the text is unlikely to have Dworkin's support; see 'Principle, Policy and Procedure'.

procedures are to take. The general argument is that, in order to be fair, procedures must satisfy certain conditions which usually centre around the ideas of unbiased decision-making and a particular mode of participation—knowing the issue, having a chance to put one's case, and being given reasons. The first of those may be put aside since bias normally would be ruled out on grounds of rationality. It is the second, the idea that there must be a certain mode of participation, that is of most interest, and which may be seen as a vital element in the proper consideration of a person's interests. Some form of participation usually would be an important aspect of instrumental rationality, since the parties most affected by an action may be able to offer information and argument which would enable a better decision to be made. Participation is also efficacious in preventing elements of arbitrariness and in exposing what J. S. Mill called 'sinister interests'. Now while this provides a firm base for participatory procedures, it is to some degree contingent, and circumstances can be imagined in which those whose interests are affected might be excluded on the grounds that they have nothing to contribute to the rationality of the decision. It is then important to know whether there are constraints from sources independent of instrumental rationality which must be met if procedures are to be fair.

The difficulty lies in establishing the foundation for any such claim. Lawrence Tribe has suggested that 'the right to be heard from, and the right to be told why, are analytically distinct from the right to secure a different outcome; these rights to interchange express the elementary idea that to be a *person*, rather than a thing, is at least to be consulted about what is to be done with one'.[12] So a right is claimed which, independently of outcomes, secures a specific mode of procedure. At the base of this claim there seems to be a principle of respect for persons: this is a fundamental political value, and in order to satisfy its demands in making political choices, the interests of each person, in so far as they are relevant, ought to be considered. However, it is difficult to make the step from a general duty of respect to any specific mode of procedure. Once various interests have been considered, choices have to be made amongst them, and, more specifically, a person's interests can be considered without necessarily allowing that person to engage in some form of participatory process. The notion of 'taking into account' a person's interests can be considered at different levels, but

[12] Lawrence Tribe, *Constitutional Law* (New York, 1978), p. 503; also quoted by Dworkin, 'Principle, Policy and Procedure', p. 223.

it is only in an exacting sense that it would require personal participation. Decisions affecting one's interests are taken regularly at different levels of the political process, subject only to the most attenuated forms of personal participation; decisions are also made in an acceptable way about categories of people, such as children or mental defectives, without participation. The search for a link between respect for persons and personal participation finally falls back on the weaker, but by no means unimportant, instrumental claim that the most effective champion of one's interests is normally oneself.

These difficulties might to some extent be overcome by presenting the case for participation directly. Participation in decision-making is regarded widely as an important political value: it is the cornerstone of democratic political systems; it is also of such centrality to the judicial trial that denial would draw an immediate charge of unfairness. Participation has similar importance in other contexts—in industrial organizations, corporations, and indeed virtually any social body that makes decisions. It is one of the universally acclaimed values against which it is hard to find a voice of dissent.[13]

Why, then, does the idea of participation induce such approbation? One explanation is in terms of the good effects that participation has on the individual himself; by participating, the individual fulfils some part of his character and adds to his sense of worth as a person. However, this is surely a contingency that might follow from participation, rather than an incontrovertible truth about the nature of participation. Alternatively, participation might be justified in terms of self-government; it is only by participating that one is able to have some control over the outcomes of decisions, and to have such control is an essential aspect of one's dignity and self-respect. But neither parts of the argument appear to be self-evident. Participation does not guarantee any level of control; I may participate, and yet find the outcomes totally contrary to my wishes. Similarly, I may find ways of fulfilling my sense of personal integrity quite independently of self-government.

[13] The best account of all is W. N. Nelson, *On Justifying Democracy* (London, 1980), chs. iii and vi. For other accounts of participation: J. R. Pennock and J. W. Chapman (eds), *Participation in Politics* (Nomos XVI) (New York UP, 1975); G. Duncan and S. Lukes, 'Democracy Restated' in H. S. Kariel (ed.), *Frontiers of Democratic Theory* (New York, 1970); J. Lively, *Democracy* (Oxford, 1975); J. R. Pennock, *Democratic Political Theory* (Princeton UP, 1975); C. Pateman, *Participation and Democratic Theory* (Cambridge UP, 1970); D. F. Thompson, *The Democratic Citizen* (Cambridge UP, 1970).

An alternative and more persuasive approach can be based on a rather subtle combination of these ideas. According to classic theories of participation deriving from Rousseau and especially J. S. Mill,[14] the dual foundations are improvement of both the community and oneself. The community is improved in the sense that the outcomes of decisions have to be justified to those participating; this tends to produce, not necessarily outcomes that are in my interests, but at least outcomes for which I can see the justification. Part of the justification consists not only in outcomes, but in showing that the outcomes have been reached by justifiable methods and rules. W. N. Nelson suggests that the central concept is open government;[15] participation contributes to open government, open government contributes to the need to justify official actions in terms of morally acceptable principles, and the need to justify contributes to better decisions. The other part of the argument is that those participating in government are required also to develop their sense of moral principles in order to evaluate and criticize decisions. In this way, the justification of participation in public decision-making is based on the interwoven ideas of community and personal improvement. It is not possible here to consider possible objections and refinements to this approach; it fits closely with the underlying theme of this book that officials must justify and account for their decisions, and although the links between participation and this sense of communal and personal improvement are ultimately empirical, they are sufficiently intuitively compelling to be accepted as a working basis for the importance of participation in discretionary decisions.

It may be concluded that the case for participatory procedures rests on their importance in contributing to rational and effective outcomes, and on their links to social and individual improvement, which we may refer to simply as good government. The question then arises as to how the significance of these two factors is to be calculated in the design of procedures. As instrumental to substantive outcomes, participatory procedures would have to be considered of substantial importance in assessing the costs and benefits of possible procedures. However, the significance of participation to good government suggests that it is to have a weighting which, in the cost-benefit

[14] Mill's discussion is contained in *Considerations on Representative Government* (London, 1964 edn).
[15] *On Justifying Democracy*, p. 118. My own account has benefited substantially from Nelson's.

calculus, gives it some protection against other considerations. Here an appeal has to be made to political practice and political values; both provide support for a general theory in which participatory procedures have a special importance, such that they should not be outweighed by just any argument of policy. It might even be said that within the political theory of democratic societies, participation is considered of such importance that each person has a right of an abstract political kind to participate in decisions which directly and seriously affect his interests. But even without the support of such a claim of right, there are good grounds for accepting that in the ranking of political values participation has a position of importance. Its twofold basis warrants a presumption that procedures are to include the opportunity for those affected to participate. The form and extent of participation may vary, ranging from minimal participation in the political process to the form of participation familiar in a judicial trial; but the presumption of participation in principle should be rebutted only by other factors which are of at least equal importance. It is within this framework that more specific issues of procedure are to be settled.

This rather lengthy discussion may be summed up as follows. (*a*) Ideas of good and fair procedures, or due process, are concerned primarily with achieving given outcomes rationally and effectively; they are concerned not only with positively achieving outcomes, but also in ensuring against arbitrariness in doing so. In this sense procedures are instrumental to outcomes, and are fair in so far as the outcomes are fair. (*b*) Rational outcomes are not the only concern; there may be other values which put constraints on the procedures followed, and may even have the effect of reducing their rational basis. (*c*) Since procedures are usually imperfect in achieving desired outcomes, the question arises as to what levels of accuracy are to be considered acceptable. This might be determined on a purely cost-benefit analysis, but there is a case for requiring a weighting to be put on the personal rights and interests that are at stake, and for maintaining commensurability between that weighting and the appropriate procedures. This 'proportionality principle' requires a difficult calculation; it does not eliminate the need for weighing costs and benefits, but it provides the procedure to be followed in making and justifying such calculations. (*d*) A central issue in questions of procedure is whether individuals or groups are able to participate and, if so, the form participation is to take. The case for participation is dependent partly on its instrumental role in achieving rational outcomes; it also depends on the value put on participation as related to good government. In fixing procedures, participation is of significant weight in the cost-benefit calculus; it also warrants a special weighting as an important political value. This can be expressed in terms of a presumption in favour of participatory procedures in discretionary decision-making, subject only to strong and clear reasons to the contrary.

The application of these factors to discretionary decisions can now be considered. The first question is what sort of procedures contribute most effectively to rational outcomes. It might be thought that there are only two types of procedure, one associated with the political process, the other with adjudication. But we have seen that within discretionary authority, reasonably distinct types of decisions can in practice be identified; in section 7.31 this classification is matched to appropriate modes of participation. In particular, consultation is advanced as a mode of participation that generally is appropriate in relation to the policy aspects of discretionary decisions. In order to develop the notion of consultation it is necessary, because of the merging within the public law model of political and legal spheres, to analyse the relationship between areas of discretion and the general political system. The second issue concerns the role of participatory procedures; in discretionary contexts, because of the relative autonomy of administrative officials, participatory procedures are important in contributing to principles of good decision-making and accountability. But before considering these matters in more detail, we must give an outline of the institutional setting within which procedural principles are developed.

7.2 INSTITUTIONAL RESPONSIBILITY FOR PROCEDURES

Procedural matters are not the exclusive prerogative of courts, but the courts have developed a distinctive notion of fair procedures, and have been influential in extending that notion or aspects of it to other areas of decision-making. In principle, the legislature and the administration are primarily responsible for settling the procedures to be followed by the many and diverse institutions and officials. And there has been in recent years a concern to develop procedures which are both fair and effective. As G. Ganz has written in her study of administrative procedures, 'the most important development has been the recognition that an administrative decision is not a narrow contest between two parties but a determination of what ought to be done in the public interest in a particular case.'[16] The point is that the traditional approach to procedures, which derives from the judicial trial where the issue is well defined and adversarial procedures are reasonably suitable, is not entirely appropriate in many areas of discretionary decisions where there is a continuing issue. Thus legislative and administrative authorities have experimented with a range of new procedures: in some areas these are directed towards conciliation, to achieving consensus between conflicting interests;[17] in other areas the adversarial approach has been replaced by investigatory procedures,[18] or by inquiries based on wide public participation;[19] and in still other areas of administration the emphasis has been on informality.[20] But the commitment of Parliament and the administration to procedural innovation has been less than complete, and the success of experiments variable.

Procedural issues are also central to the work of bodies like the Council on Tribunals and the Ombudsman. But since my main concern in this chapter is to examine some of the problems that arise with respect to procedures, the following analysis concentrates on the judicial doctrine of natural justice. The courts continue to have an important role in settling questions about fair procedures, and, indeed, this has become one of the most litigated areas of administrative law. An analysis of the difficulties encountered by the courts in extending the adjudicative models of fair procedures into discretionary contexts provides a useful point at which to begin.

But first a note on the relationship between legislative and judicial responsibilities; the primary responsibility for setting the procedures to be followed in discretionary areas lies with the legislature or other authority conferring discretion, and to a lesser degree with the discretionary body itself. The legislature often specifies procedures either in the terms of a grant of power or in a general statute of interpretation. Legislative requirements vary considerably, but there is

---

[16] G. Ganz, *Administrative Procedures* (London, 1974), p. 1.

[17] For example: *Rent Acts* 1968, *Race Relations Act* 1968, and *Industrial Relations Act* 1971. See Ganz, *Administrative Procedures*, ch. 2.

[18] For example: Restrictive Practices Court, and Monopolies and Mergers Commission. See Ganz, *Administrative Procedures*, ch. 3.

[19] For example: inquiries into local government reorganization, and the building and siting of major roads. See Ganz, *Administrative Procedures*, ch. 4.

[20] For example: various areas of decision-making relating to social welfare. See Ganz, *Administrative Procedures*, chs. 2 and 3.

evidence of a growing concern to stipulate the procedures to be followed; yet it is still not unusual to find discretionary powers being conferred without mention of such matters. In such cases, it is for the delegated authority to devise its own procedures, either by setting down a code or by adopting something much less formal.

Where Parliament does specify procedures, it is not for the courts to substitute their own views; but they have considerable scope where either the statute is silent or the procedures laid down are insufficient. The courts naturally have some discretion in deciding what is adequate, and they appear to be more inclined now than previously to supplement statutory procedures, and positively to impose procedures where statutes are silent.[21] They are assisted in this endeavour by the guiding principle that Parliament is to be presumed not to authorize decision-making according to unfair procedures. The occasions on which courts may intervene, and the procedural conditions they require when they intervene, depend on the meaning of the judicial principles of procedural fairness. Where statutory procedures are comprehensive, they are to be followed even if they do not meet judicial standards; but where it is possible to regard the statutory procedures as an outline rather than a comprehensive scheme, or where there are none at all, the courts are likely to require compliance with procedures which meet their own understanding of fairness. It is in this way that judicial notions of fair procedures bear on the exercise of delegated powers; it is also clear that in settling matters of procedure judges are not simply extending what they take to be legislative intention, but are forced to develop their own views about what is required.

The judicial approach to fair procedures is expressed in terms of the two principles of natural justice: that one should be heard before action is taken against one's interests, and that the decision-maker should not be biased. These two principles have grown out of adjudicative proceedings, and are most at home where the emphasis is on the existence of settled standards, the delineation of a specific issue, the opportunity to participate through argument and proof, and the reasoned decision of an impartial adjudicator. But while natural justice is suited to adjudication in terms of rational outcomes and fairness, participatory procedures in discretionary contexts are more varied.

---

[21] For general discussion of the development of the law relating to fair procedures, see de Smith, *Judicial Review*, pp. 156–75.

7·3 PARTICIPATORY PROCEDURES IN
DISCRETIONARY CONTEXTS

In considering those variations, we may begin by identifying the modes
of participation that are suited to the different types of decisions that
occur.

7.31 *Types of decisions and modes of participation*

As decision-making moves away from the adjudicative model of private
law and becomes more clearly discretionary and centred in the public
law model, the specific mode of participation inherent in adjudication
is less suitable; the question then is what are appropriate alternatives.
In section 3.1, four types of decision-making were identified:
adjudication, modified adjudication, specific policy decisions, and
general policy decisions. These depict the four broadly distinct
positions between a central sense of adjudication through to the
general policy concerns that are characteristic of legislation. That
progression is a function of a number of factors: the extent to which
the decision-standards range from being clear, settled, and precise to
being abstract notions of public policy; the range of groups and
interests whose concerns ought to be considered in the decision; the
extent to which the decision-maker is an impartial judge or has to
decide according to his own policy preferences; and, of most concern
for our present concerns, the mode of participatory procedures that are
appropriate.

Again, we may begin with Fuller's idea that there are discrete types
of decision procedures which have the following characteristics: each
has a certain completeness and inner logic, which includes a specific
mode of participation by parties, and is suitable for the effective
realization of specific tasks. Apart from adjudication, Fuller identified
various types of procedure ranging from voting in elections to
managerial direction.[22] Within the private law model, *adjudication* is the
dominant type of procedure, the appropriate mode of participation
being the presentation of arguments and proof to meet a specific case,
which is to be settled in accordance with settled standards, by an
adjudicator who bases his decision on interpreting and applying given

---

[22] For references to adjudication, see note 63 chapter 5. For an account of these other
forms, see L. L. Fuller and M. Eisenberg, *Basic Contract Law* (United States, 3rd edn.,
1972), pp. 89 ff. For extended discussion, see R. A. Macdonald, 'Judicial Review and
Procedural Fairness in Administrative Law' (1979) 25 *McGillLJ* and (1980) 26 *McGillLJ*
1.

standards, in accordance with the proofs and arguments put before him by the parties. But, while individualized discretionary decisions retain strong elements of adjudication, adjudicative procedures are less suitable as decisions move from adjudication to modified adjudication to specific and general policy decisions, in accordance with the factors above.

As that progression occurs, the adjudicative mode of participation also becomes less appropriate and gives way to the notion of consultation. *Consultation* connotes the presentation of arguments and proofs in order to influence the way issues are to be settled, where the decision-maker has a duty to hear and consider, but may decide for reasons which go beyond the submissions of the parties, and may act according to standards which are defined only broadly or settled only in the course of the decision.[23] Before developing the notion of consultation, two other decision procedures which may have some scope in discretionary contexts are worth noting. One is *mediation* which applies where the object is to reach agreement between the parties, and where the task of the mediator is to oversee and facilitate the negotiating process.[24] The other is decision by direction or *fiat* where there is no provision for participation; this may be especially useful in order to deal with an emergency, or to gain an economic or business advantage.

Why then are adjudication and consultation, with some limited scope for mediation and fiat, the modes of participation most relevant in discretionary contexts? The answer is partly logical, and partly a matter of the values on which the public law model is based. It is logical in the sense that adjudicative and consultative procedures are effective in certain contexts in achieving rationally the objects of decisions. Some aspects of discretionary decisions, especially decisions about how an individual is to be treated, are concerned with the application of reasonably settled standards to the facts, and so are suited to adjudication. Other aspects, however, are concerned with working out the best policy result in the circumstances, and, in that case, consideration ranges beyond the particular circumstances to wider aspects of public interest; consultation is then a suitable

[23] On consultation, see M. Eisenberg, 'Participation, Responsiveness and the Consultative Process' (1978) 92 *HarvLR* 410.
[24] On mediation, see L. L. Fuller, 'Mediation: its Forms and Functions' (1971) 44 *SCLR* 305; M. Eisenberg, 'Private Ordering Through Negotiation, Dispute Settlement and Rule-Making' (1976) 89 *HarvLR* 637; Macdonald, 'Judicial Review and Procedural Fairness', pp. 20 ff.

procedure since it ensures that account is taken of the parties' interests, but also recognizes that preference may have to be given to one rather than another, and even that all may be subject to a wider sense of public interest.

The case for these modes of participation is based also partly on the political values which form the backdrop to discretionary decisions. There are two aspects to consider. One is the recognition that what counts as effective realization of the objects of a discretionary decision may be partly dependent on a background theory about how decisions are to be made. For example, the route for a new road might be selected on the basis of economy and the satisfaction of traffic needs; alternatively, it might be selected not just on those factors, but also on the importance of minimizing the interference with other interests which are bound to be affected. Which course is selected depends on which background theory is adopted: one emphasizes a simple view of effectiveness which might best be achieved according to business principles without participation by interests affected; the other emphasizes a more pluralist understanding of society, and accepts that effectiveness may have to take account of and be influenced by a diversity of interests. The other way in which background values are important is in directly influencing the form procedures take; participation is one such value and the presumption in favour of participation guides the design of procedures.

The question may be raised as to why officials in deliberating on policy matters should be required to take account of the individual interests that might be effected? Why not proceed by fiat and decide according to a simple view of objects and effectiveness? The first part of the answer is related to my earlier suggestion that the making of value choices and the preferring of one interest over another are unavoidable in the exercise of discretion. Secondly, the 'effective realization of objects' is often not an objective notion but depends partly in complex areas of decision-making on reflexive rationality, that is on curbing conflicting interests and subsystems in order to find some acceptable balance amongst them. In other words, discretionary decisions are concerned, within their confined areas, with the same kinds of tasks and choices that are characteristic of decision-making within the general political process. The importance attached to the representation of interest and the capacity to participate in the political system carries over to administrative areas.[25]

[25] For discussion of ideas of representation, see J. R. Pennock and J. W. Chapman (eds.), *Representation* (New York, 1968).

Connections with democratic ideas are also important. By extending representative and participatory ideas into discretionary decisions, the democratic basis of the total system may be revitalized. On the more idealistic accounts, of which responsive law is a good example, that extension is a way of achieving social harmony and consensus. More sceptical accounts, however, make no claims for any close connection between representative and participatory ideals and social consensus, but support the former as the only procedures that are acceptable in making decisions, where there is no objective notion of the public good, and where the groups and interests within society are inevitably in conflict to greater or lesser degrees. On this approach, the decisions of government are likely to favour some interests over others, but some legitimacy may be gained by the fairness of procedures in ensuring the representation and participation of individuals and groups. This is part of the idea of reflexive rationality; since there are limits on the capacity to regulate society by objective, general norms, the emphasis shifts to the procedures by which outcomes are achieved.

Whichever view is taken, the representation of interests in some form and according to some theory is important at both the general political level and in discretionary decisions.[26] It might be argued, nevertheless, that direct representation and participation in the policy aspects of discretionary decisions are unnecessary. On this view, effective representation is to be achieved through participatory procedures at the general political level; discretionary decisions then will naturally reflect the same spectrum of views and interests. But, no matter how fair and effective representation is at the general political level, there is no guarantee that discretionary decisions will be its mirror image. Because of the relative autonomy inherent in discretionary powers, there is no necessary symmetry between influences operating at the political level and the outcomes of discretionary decisions. The only basis for any such assumption is the untenable view which sees administration as a matter of implementing, in an

---

[26] For further analysis, see D. F. Thompson, 'Bureaucracy and Democracy' in G. Duncan (ed.), *Democratic Theory and Practice* (Cambridge UP, 1983). For discussion of the problems in making administrative authorities representative and accountable: R. C. Martin (ed.), *Public Administration and Democracy* (Syracuse UP, 1965), especially the essays by Thompson, Egger and Appleby; Herman Finer, 'Administrative Responsibility in Democratic Government' in F. E. Rourke (ed.), *Bureaucratic Power in National Politics* (Boston, 1965); E. S. Redford, *Democracy in the Administrative State* (Oxford UP, 1969); F. Marini, *Toward a New Public Administration* (New Jersey, 1971), ch. 6; J. P. Witherspoon, 'The Bureaucracy as Representatives' in Pennock and Chapman, *Representation*.

objective and neutral manner, policies settled at the political level. But whatever guidance the political system does provide, the need for representation of interests in administrative decisions is not removed.

Another approach is to regard the officials themselves as representing various interests and groups. Officials are not normally the representatives of distinct groups and interests, in the sense of being elected or appointed or made accountable to them in any direct manner. However, they may be representative in the sense that the same diversity that constitutes the total society will be reflected in the views of officials. Sam Krislov has suggested that there exists an isomorphism, or parallel, between the larger system and the smaller, so that the diversity of views at the macro political level is reflected in actions at the micro administrative level.[27] But there are difficulties. One is that even though there might be an isomorphic relationship between the total society and administrative authorities, there is no guarantee that the relationship will hold within specific areas of decision-making. There are many variables that affect the selection of officials for particular tasks, and the way they perform once appointed. Another difficulty is that within an administrative bureaucracy there are various forces and influences which affect decision-making, and which are likely to interrupt and distort any close parallels between the composition of the bureaucracy and the general society. The issue, however, is not one of perfect representativeness, but whether administrative authorities, tested by their actions, are more or less representative than other institutions. There is some evidence to suggest that, on that test, administrative bureaucracies closely parallel other political institutions. This is an important aspect of representation, but it is not a satisfactory substitute for more direct methods of representation in the administrative process.

The case for the mode of participation characteristic of consultation may be summed up as follows: (*a*) that mode contributes to the instrumental rationality of discretionary decisions; (*b*) it flows from commitment to the general principle of participation as an important aspect of open government; and (*c*) it follows from the commitment to representative and democratic government, since discretionary powers merge into and in a sense form part of the general political system. And, while representation does not entail participation, the former usually is best achieved by the latter.

[27] Samuel Krislov, *Representative Bureaucracy* (New Jersey, 1974).

7.32 *Two levels of authority and the principle of selective representation*

On the basis that consultative procedures have a clear place in discretionary contexts, the question remains as to their objects and the restrictions on them. Are areas of discretionary authority to be seen as small-scale political arenas which replicate so far as possible the general political process? In answer to this, we must consider further the relationship between the general political system and administration.

It has been useful to depict discretionary powers as subsystems of authority within which officials may act in relative independence of other systems and of legal control. It is now necessary to recognize the many and varied connections between discretionary powers, and other sub systems and sources of external influence, in particular the general political system. We may adopt the distinction which E. S. Redford has made between the macro political system and the micro systems constituted by discretionary powers.[28] An important feature of the complex and variable relationship between them is that micro systems are products of the macro system: the latter determines what micro systems are to be created, and the powers they are to have; in doing so, the macro system provides some indication of the factors that have brought the micro system into existence, and the purposes it is to serve, even if only in broad outline. The macro system may intervene to change the terms of authority of the micro system, or to impose specific constraints, or to overcome the effects of past decisions.

It is within this relationship that micro systems may be characterized as part of the political process. In democratic systems the principles of representation operate at both levels: at the macro level individuals and groups are able to be represented to greater or lesser degrees, and to participate in the political process in various ways. This does not mean that decisions made at the macro level are necessarily the results of consensus, but it does indicate that the delegation of powers to an administrative authority for specific purposes is the result of a process based on democratic principles. This has a number of implications for decision-making at the micro level. First, the macro system provides what Redford describes as direction and adjustment: no matter how open the discretionary process may be, there is always some direction from the macro level in terms of tasks, purposes, and roles.[29] But not

---

[28] Redford, *Democracy in the Administrative State*, esp. chs iv and v.
[29] Ibid., pp. 188–204.

all conflicts and choices are settled at the macro level, so that adjustments between competing interests must be made at the micro level. Directions from the macro level help to define the public interests in issue, and from this some guidance can be derived as to how issues are to be resolved in making adjustments and compromises between interests. The administrator's task is not to grant victory to the interests that are most powerful or vociferous, nor to strike just any compromise between conflicting interests; rather a continuing balance must be maintained between the conceptions of the public interest that derive from the macro system, and the resolution of conflicts at the micro level.

Directions flowing from the macro level also provide guidance in identifying and limiting the interests that are relevant at the micro level. A range of interests may be affected by the decisions of administrative authorities, but some are affected more clearly and directly than others; in deciding different levels of representation, lines have to be drawn. This may be facilitated by recognizing that representation can occur in different ways and degrees at different levels of political activity; while all interests may join in the political process at the macro level, greater selectivity is necessary at the micro level. Representation at the macro level need not mean exclusion at the micro level, but the degree and effectiveness of representation at the former, may be an important factor in settling that issue at the latter. Conversely, clear failure or ineffectiveness of representation at the macro level may be a good reason for increased representation at the micro level.

The relationship between the two levels of authority can be made clearer by an example. Take welfare: the general question of welfare is considered at the general political level; groups and interests have the opportunity to make their views known, and to influence the minds of officials and legislators. The government may have its own ideological commitments, but its general approach to relieving poverty is bound to be influenced by public discussion and the activities of pressure groups. Out of this, some general policies are likely to emerge and finally to be expressed in legislation. The general objects of poverty relief will be settled and resources allocated. The next level of political activity then comes into operation. This means the formulation of more specific policies as to how the resources are to be used, and the setting of priorities amongst different objects; for example, how much is to be devoted to housing standards, how much is to be put aside for children. At this level a more restricted range of interests might be considered; those which are specifically concerned with particular aspects of poverty relief, such as associations devoted to the protection of children or the homeless. Many groups and interests are excluded from consideration at this point, because they have had the chance to participate at the more general level, and their interests are not sufficient to warrant further participation. Once policies have been settled and, as usually would be the case, translated into rules and guide-lines, we move to the third level, the application of the guide-lines to specific cases; how much relief does X get? Here the primary concern is with X's personal circumstances and, accordingly, there is little room for interest groups to be involved. This part of the decision approaches the adjudicative end of the scale, and naturally X has a strong case for being able to present his case and establish his circumstances.

This is a simplified description of the way decisions are made; it may not be possible in practice to distinguish so clearly between the different levels of representation, and in some cases the policy aspects arise only in the course of an individualized decision. Its point, however, is to illustrate, through the different levels of representation, the relationship between the macro political system and discretionary powers. Within an area of discretionary authority, issues of representation occur at different levels, but in each they are to be resolved by considering the relationship between the macro and micro systems, and the guidance that the former provides for the latter. This process may be referred to as 'selective representation'.

To sum up, a suggested approach to representation and participation in discretionary decisions is as follows. Firstly, where the interests of a person or group are entitled to be represented, it is to be assumed that normally representation is achieved best by personal participation. The second question is whether the interests affected and the possible consequences to them are of sufficient importance to warrant procedural protection. This is to be determined according to a theory of interests within which some ranking can be made according to relative importance. Without now suggesting any particular theory of interests, although my own preference is along the lines set out in chapter 4, it is intended that interests be construed widely to include not only those related to welfare and liberty, but also less tangible interests such as those relating to the quality of the environment. Questions may also arise as to who is entitled to represent particular interests. Leaving that aside, once it is accepted that certain interests warrant procedural protection, the third question is the form such procedures are to take. It is suggested that consultation normally will be the appropriate mode; it is rationally instrumental in achieving outcomes, it satisfies the presumption of participation, and it ensures representation.

The common features of consultation are (*a*) the participating parties are able to ascertain the matters that are to be decided, the general policy choices that have been made or are in the balance, the empirical evidence, and the expert advice upon which the official is acting or proposing to act; (*b*) the participating parties are able to put before the decision-maker arguments and evidence directed towards any of these matters; (*c*) the official considers the arguments and evidence, and finally gives a reasoned explanation for the policy choice he makes. Consultation is connected closely to the notion of open government and, to be successful, depends vitally on the availability of information, the breaking-down of government secrecy, and the containment of claims of confidentiality. Consultation may, therefore, serve well the values on which participatory procedures were earlier justified, especially the relationship between participation and open government. Each of the common features of consultation can be made more or less exacting and thorough, so the final question is how are the precise requirements of consultation with respect to a particular matter to be determined. There are two guiding factors. The first is the proportionality principle: the relative importance of the interests must be assessed, and procedural resources allotted which, within the range of resources available, fairly reflect that importance. The second is the principle of selective representation: account must be taken of the opportunities that have existed at other points for representation and participation by those interests; that assessment will depend partly on comparing the potential consequences of the decision for other interests, and the opportunities they have had to participate.

7.33 *A note on mediation*

To concentrate on adjudicative and consultative procedures is not meant to imply that other modes of decision-making have no place in the public law model. Consultation is a particularly apt mode of procedure with respect to the policy aspects of discretionary actions; however, it may be desirable in some contexts to go beyond consultation and seek agreement between the parties and the administrative authority. In those circumstances, mediatory procedures are especially suitable: firstly, they emphasize the importance of reaching agreement, where negotiations are conducted in an environment which is guided at best by very broad standards, where there is some equality of bargaining power, and where agreement is in the interests of the parties. Secondly, an agreement reached in this manner is likely to be regarded with greater trust, and accorded greater bindingness, than a decision made in the exercise by an official of his powers. Thirdly, mediation matches various aspects of the public law model where there may be no clear notion of public interest beyond the peaceful settlement of a dispute. These undoubted advantages have led to suggestions that mediatory procedures should be regarded as the paradigm of fair procedures in the modern state.[30]

Without rejecting mediation as having some scope, there are, however, important limitations. Firstly, on Fuller's exposition, mediatory procedures, like adjudication and consultation, have their own integrity as procedures, and are suited to fairly specific circumstances; primarily disputes between two parties, such as the partners to a marriage, or a trade union and an employer.[31] As the number of parties increase, mediation is less appropriate. Secondly, mediation is most efficacious when the parties consider their interests to be served best by agreement. Thridly, it is necessary to ensure that, whatever scope there is for different solutions to a problem, any particular solution, and thus any agreement, is within the public interest. For these reasons, the scope for mediation is real but limited, and unlikely to serve as the dominant paradigm of fair procedures.

7.34 *Problems of pluralism*

Approaches to discretionary decision-making which advocate increased representation through participation have in the background a pluralist view of political systems. The central tenets of pluralism are that society is made up of a number of groups with overlapping interests of an economic, religious, ethnic, and geographical kind, and that political decisions are reached in accordance with set procedures by a process of reciprocal constraints, adjustments, and compromises

---

[30] See Fuller, 'Mediation', R. A. Macdonald, 'Judicial Review and Procedural Fairness in Administrative Law: II' (1980) 26 *McGillLJ* 1.

[31] Fuller, 'Mediation', pp. 330 ff.

amongst the groups.[32] On the simplest view of pluralism, political decisions are made by the resolution of potential conflicts into compromise and consensus. According to this view, which has been called the arena theory,[33] decisions are made in this way at various points in the political system. A more sophisticated version, known as the umpire theory,[34] recognizes that groups may become large and powerful, and that the state may have to take a more active role in setting the procedures for resolving disputes, and in controlling their activities. However, the state is still not a full and active participant, but more in the nature of an umpire. On either version, it is essential that all individuals and groups be able to participate and have their interests represented in the political market-place.

The shortcomings of pluralism are well known, and need be mentioned only briefly.[35] In the first place, while pluralism may be descriptively correct in depicting society in terms of overlapping and conflicting groups and interests, it is questionable whether it provides a sound normative basis for political decision-making. The claim appears to be that conflict followed by adjustment amongst groups is itself a legitimate and possibly the most democratic way of making decisions. This conclusion is often a reaction to the failure to find any more positive basis for decision-making, but it is nevertheless based on a normative claim which has to be justified. Even if all groups are able to participate on a reasonably equal footing, the normative claim that decisions are to be made by compromise and consensus may still be challenged. Alternative principles might be argued for, based on a view of distributive justice, or on a ranking of individual and public interests, or on some other set of moral principles.

A second and more serious difficulty is that pluralism does not appear to provide any criteria for decision-making. This difficulty

---

[32] Connolly, *The Bias of Pluralism*, p. 3. The literature on interest group pluralism is extensive; the following are a selection from among the most important: R. Dahl, *A Preface to Democratic Theory* (Chicago UP, 1956), and *Pluralist Democracy in the United States: Conflict and Consensus* (Boston 1967); Lindblom, *The Intelligence of Democracy*; D. Truman, *The Governmental Process* (United States, 1957); R. J. Harrison, *Pluralism and Corporatism* (London, 1980).

[33] This is Connolly's expression: 'The Challenge to Pluralist Theory', p. 8.

[34] Ibid.

[35] Connolly provides a useful summary of the main criticisms: 'The Challenge to Pluralist Theory'. For further selections of the critical literature: Peter Bachrach, *The Theory of Democratic Elitism: A Critique* (Boston UP, 1967); John Dewey, *The Public and Its Problems* (New York, 1967); C. W. Anderson, 'Political Design and the Representation of Interests' (1977) 10 *CompPolStud* 127.

becomes apparent in deciding which interests are to be considered, and how choices are to be made between them. Roscoe Pound advanced a jurisprudential version of pluralism according to which the first problem is answered by considering only those interests that actually make demands on the system.[36] But this is unsatisfactory; there may be various real interests which, because of their subordinate position in the society, are incapable of pressing their claims, and that in itself is hardly a justifiable basis for ignoring them in public decision-making. Similarly, it is difficult to see any criteria for choosing between interests, or for taking measures to protect weaker groups, unless principles extraneous to pluralism are invoked. This leads to the problem of bias; in the absence of external standards both for deciding whether all relevant interests are represented, and for choosing amongst competing interests, the more powerful and better-organized groups are likely to exert a dominating influence, and thus create bias in their favour.

These difficulties, characteristic of pluralism generally, are likely to occur in discretionary contexts. At its simplest, the pluralist approach to administrative discretion envisages a number of groups with competing interests urging upon the administrative body a number of solutions that it might adopt. In finding a decision, the official does not begin with a firm conception of the public interest, but allows one to emerge through interaction and adjustment amongst the groups. In terms of our earlier analysis, the pluralist image matches the idea of radical incrementalism where decisions are made according to the circumstances as they occur, modulated by whatever combinations of interests are in play. The public interest thus consists in whatever result emerges from the process, and the administrative system may be seen as a series of small-scale political arenas where groups may participate, and where the officials' tasks are to settle on courses of action reached by adjustment and compromise. But what interests are to be allowed to compete, what is to be done about interests which, although affected, are unable to compete, what decision criteria are to be applied in weighing and choosing between interests when there is no consensus, and how is bias to be eliminated?[37]

---

[36] Pound, *Contemporary Juristic Theory*, pp. 60–7, 79–80 and *Jurisprudence* (volume 3). For discussion, see J. Stone, *Social Dimensions of Law and Justice* (Sydney, 1966), pp. 175–6.

[37] For discussion of the problems of pluralism in the administrative law context, see R. Stewart, 'The Reformation of Administrative Law' (1978) 88 *HarvLR* 1669. See also S. Lazarus and J. Onek, 'The Regulators and the People' (1971) 57 *VaLR* 1069.

There may be no complete solution to these problems in the discretionary context, just as there is no complete solution in the political context. But the approach to be taken towards alleviating these difficulties depends on what view of pluralism is held, and what is expected to be gained by increased representation and participation in discretionary decisions.[38] Since there are grave difficulties with both the arena and the umpire theories, a third version of pluralism may be suggested: guided pluralism. Guided pluralism accepts that society is divided into a complex of groups and interests, but it maintains that decisions are made within some framework of values and standards which guide the extent of interest representation, and help to provide criteria for weighting and assessing interests. This is especially important in discretionary contexts where there is guidance flowing from the macro political system. The macro system, through the terms of the statute, provides goals and objects, and gives some indication of the political values sought to be achieved; there may also be a background of more fundamental political principles and ideas, based on ideals of justice and long-range views of the public interest. Within this framework some (but not complete) guidance can be found as to the objects and extent of increased representation and participation at different levels. Participation is not just to ensure that one's interests are considered, but is also concerned with improving the rules of decision-making through the notion of open government. Similarly, the very idea of consultation suggests that the object is not to identify the most powerful interests, but to put before the decision-maker a wide view of the public interest, which includes but is not defined in terms of the interests affected.

The notion of guided pluralism does not remove all the practical difficulties, the inevitable conflicts that occur, or the necessity to make hard choices between conflicting interests; similarly, it does not remove, but may reduce, the tendency for certain interests to dominate the decision-process. But the fact that there is no perfect resolution of those difficulties is not a reason for abandoning attempts to create theoretical and practical systems, which regulate the clash of interests and guide officials towards acceptable ends. To fall back on cruder versions of pluralism just because there can be no perfect solution to the exercise of discretionary powers is to misconstrue the relationship between the macro and the micro systems, and to accept an approach

[38] For further discussion, see C. W. Anderson, 'Political Design and the Representation of Interests'.

to decisions which even if coherent has little to commend it. The general approach here is that, as modern societies move towards the public law model, the task is to develop general standards within which discretionary powers are to be exercised and controlled. Increased representation and participation is part of that enterprise, not a replacement for it.

7.35   *Problems of corporatism*

An alternative to interest group pluralism in understanding issues of representation and participation in decision-making is known as corporatism.[39] Corporatism has been defined as a system of interest representation in which the constituent units are organized into a limited number of singular, compulsory, non-competitive, hierarchically ordered and functionally differentiated categories, created, recognized, or licensed by the state and granted a monopoly in representing interests within their respective categories, in exchange for observing certain controls on their selection of leaders and their articulation of demands.[40] Corporatism differs from group pluralism in that while the latter tends to be loosely organized and voluntary, corporate institutions tend to be formalized and to have specific legal status. Typical examples are trade unions, employers' organizations, consumer councils, and financial institutions. It is often suggested that the growth of corporate bodies of this kind is a characteristic of modern societies, and that this has had significant impact on both public decision-making and the democratic structure, and must be taken into account in understanding the administrative process.[41] Corporatism has two specially important aspects: firstly, a large part of political activity is displaced from the political arena and occurs within corporate structures. Problems are likely to be resolved by negotiation between corporate bodies rather than in accordance with a wider view of the public interest. Secondly, corporatism has important con-

[39] For a selection of the writings on corporatism: Otto Newman, *The Challenge of Corporatism* (London, 1981), p. 9; S. Brittan, 'Towards a Corporate State' (1975) xliv *Encounter*; L. Panitch, 'The Development of Corporatism in Liberal Democracies' (1977) 10 *CompPolStud* and 'Recent Theorizations of Corporatism: Reflections on a Growth Industry' (1980) 31 *BJSoc*; A. Cawson, 'Pluralism, Corporatism and the Role of the State' (1978) 13 *Govt&Opp*.

[40] This is the definition suggested by P. C. Schmitter, 'Still the Century of Corporatism' in F. B. Pike and T. Stritch (eds.), *The New Corporatism* (Notre Dame UP, 1975).

[41] On the legal implications of corporatism, see: Unger, *Law in Modern Society*, ch. 3; Poggi, *The Development of the Modern State*, esp. ch. vi.

sequences for the democratic structure; if political activity is concentrated within corporate structures, then it is important that they should be organized on democratic lines.

In the context of administrative discretion, corporatism has the effect of moving the focus of political power from the macro political system to the internal workings of corporate bodies, and to the agreements reached between them; the macro system is weakened, and may not be able to give administrative authorities the necessary direction and guidance. It may be able to do little beyond specify the problems that need to be solved, while the only effective influence on administrative officials may come from the corporate bodies which have an interest in the matter. Without the security of a clearly defined public interest, administrative authorties may come to accept that they have little authority beyond endorsing outcomes effectively settled within and between corporate bodies.

The consequences of corporatism create in turn a number of problems for administrative discretion.[42] Firstly, there may be an imbalance between those interests which are protected within corporate structures and those which are not. And, since it is unlikely that all interests relevant to a particular area of discretion will be protected in this way, there is the problem of ensuring that they are considered in decision-making. The requirement that other, non-corporatist interests also be consulted may become a hollow form. Secondly, what may be in the interests of corporate bodies and their numbers is not necessarily in the public interest. Unless the public interest consists in whatever solutions are acceptable to corporate bodies, there may be disjunction between the two. Thirdly, if the effective point of decision-making is concentrated within corporate structures, it may be, given their semi-public, semi-private nature, that they are more difficult to control than the more public processes of administrative authorities. Moreover, the legitimacy of outcomes achieved by corporate bodies depends on the democratic nature of their internal processes; indeed, the problems of ensuring representation and participation of interests are moved partly from the administrative sphere to the corporate.

It is possible that society may become so dependent on corporate structures that there will be neither scope nor need for a wider political and legal system. However, it does not seem that that stage has yet been reached. There are undoubtedly deeply entrenched corporate

---

[42] For valuable discussion, see: Anderson 'Political Design' and Harrison, *Pluralism and Corporatism*, ch. 10.

structures which have a major effect on public policy, but there is still room for political and legal activity outside them; there also seems to be some capacity to modify the impact they have. Again, we must have recourse to the importance of the macro political system in directing the exercise of discretionary powers, and to the creation and extension of principles based on ideals of rationality, respect for persons, and democratic principles, which will in turn lead to fuller conceptions of the public interest, of representative and participatory government, and of other mediating principles directed against arbitrariness and unfairness. Fulfilment of the first set of principles depends on the macro political system being prepared to specify with greater certainty the objects to be achieved in discretionary contexts, the values that are important in doing so, and the interests to be considered. The second set of constraints depend for their efficacy and acceptability on the increased awareness of administrative officials and reviewing courts of the problems of corporatism. It is likely that their responses will be slow and piecemeal; this is inevitable and perhaps desirable considering the complexity and importance of the issues at stake, and considering the difficulty of devising satisfactory methods of regulation.

7.4 JUDICIAL PRINCIPLES OF PARTICIPATORY PROCEDURES

Against this background to matters of procedure, we may turn to the development of more specific judicial principles. That has occurred not by direct application of general precepts of fair procedure, but by incremental extension to discretionary decisions of the specific doctrines of natural justice which have their origins and most exact application in adjudication. This has had the effect of excluding certain kinds of decisions from the scope of fair procedures; it has also meant that even in the more expansive approach of recent years, the adjudicative model has remained the paradigm.

7.41 *The common law background*

The modern law begins with *Ridge* v. *Baldwin*[43] in 1964. Prior to that, the application of natural justice was confined in general to decisions of administrative officials which were of an adjudicative nature. The

---

[43] [1964] AC 40.

criteria for characterizing a decision as adjudicative could be flexible, and in pre-twentieth-century cases that characterization was likely to be inferred whenever private rights were affected. The courts in fact appear to have been less concerned with the conceptual classification of decisions as judicial, than with ensuring that where rights were at stake natural justice should apply. Thus discretionary decisions were likely to be made subject to natural justice when rights were affected; it might also be insisted in such cases that there was a duty to act judicially, but that would be satisfied by virtue of the affect on rights, rather than according to an additional functional analysis. So, in *Cooper* v. *Wandsworth Board of Works*,[44] the board was held to be subject to natural justice in deciding whether to demolish Cooper's house, even though its powers were clearly discretionary. The court's insistence that the board's functions were nevertheless judicial makes sense, therefore, only if the judicial quality is inferred from the fact that rights were affected.

In the early years of this century, the characterization of decisions as judicial became more important to the application of natural justice. The cautious approach of the courts in the face of burgeoning discretionary powers led them to emphasize the connection between the judicial nature of decisions and natural justice. It was not sufficient that rights were affected, since the broadest discretionary powers might have direct and serious effects on rights. Natural justice, with its fairly specific connotations, came to be confined to those decisions which could be characterized as judicial or quasi-judicial. Even allowing for a certain judicial discretion in deciding when natural justice applied, this had the consequence that discretionary decisions which were not regarded as sufficiently adjudicative, escaped procedural restrictions beyond a rather empty requirement that they be fair.

It was not until *Ridge* v. *Baldwin* that the courts began to reconsider the application of fair procedures in discretionary contexts. The facts are well known: a chief constable was dismissed by the watch committee under powers which provided that the committee 'may . . . dismiss, any borough constable whom they think negligent in the discharge of his duty, or otherwise unfit for the same'.[45] The basis of the dismissal was negligence, but no specific charge was formulated. The question was whether natural justice applied, and, if so, whether it had been breached. The House of Lords, by a majority, gave an

---

[44] (1863) 14 CB (NS) 180.   [45] [1964] AC at p. 41.

affirmative answer to both questions. The main speech is that of Lord Reid. He held that the present situation fell squarely within a long line of authorities 'to the effect that an officer cannot lawfully be dismissed without first telling him what is alleged against him and hearing his defence or explanation'.[46] The chief constable had a strong personal and financial interest in retaining his office; he also had a strong interest in being required to resign (an option open to the watch committee) rather than being dismissed, since in the former case but not the latter his pension entitlements would have been saved. Moreover, it made no difference that the power to dismiss from office, or to deprive him of other rights or privileges, was discretionary. Here there were two elements of discretion: whether there was negligence was left to the assessment of the watch committee; if it found negligence, there was a further discretion as to what action should be taken. Finally, Lord Reid reasserted the principle that, where rights are affected by an administrative decision, the hearing principle applies, and it is not necessary to find some further requirement that the authority is required to act judicially. Or, to put it another way, if the hearing principle only applies when there is a duty to act judicially, that duty will be inferred from the fact that rights are affected.

The primary significance of *Ridge* v. *Baldwin* is its reaffirmation of the principle that natural justice applies to decisions which affect rights, and so to a wide range of discretionary decisions. But once natural justice is extended in this way, a number of questions arise. One is whether natural justice applies to interests wider than rights. There are suggestions in Lord Reid's judgment that it may; at one point property rights and privileges are grouped together to suggest that they have the same significance.[47] Similarly, the implicit criticism of the decision in *Nakkuda Ali* v. *Jayaratne*,[48] where the controller of textiles was held entitled to cancel a dealer's licence without complying with the hearing principle, gives some hint that it might indeed apply to such cases. Just how far it extends has become a major issue in later cases. Secondly, uncertainties remain as to the implication of *Ridge* v. *Baldwin* for discretionary decisions. Lord Reid drew a distinction between two kinds of discretion; one is the type in issue in the present case, where there may be an element of policy, evaluation, and assessment, but where nevertheless the question is how a particular person ought to be treated, and where the choice occurs within a fairly

[46] Ibid., p. 66. [47] Ibid., pp. 68 ff. [48] [1951] AC 66.

limited scope. In such cases, an analogy may be drawn between the official's discretion, and the elements of judicial discretion that regularly occur in adjudication. The watch committee's decision is not exactly one of adjudication, but there are similarities; for this reason, modified adjudication seems an apt description. On the other hand, there are discretionary powers which involve a much wider range of choices and require a wider consideration of the public interest. These differ from modified adjudication in two ways: they affect directly a wide range of individuals, and the decision-maker's main concern may be to give effect to a general policy or to find the best policy outcome in the circumstances. These are the types we have referred to as specific and general policy decisions. It would be unreasonable, according to Lord Reid, to require in these circumstances application of the principles of natural justice to every individual whose interests are affected.[49]

It was unneccessary in *Ridge* v. *Baldwin* to pursue these matters, but in the development of fair procedures in discretionary contexts they are of great importance. Natural justice is said to apply to discretionary decisions only when rights are affected and the decision is one of modified adjudication; what is required where rights or other interests are affected by specific or general policy decisions is left open. Moreover, many decisions fit uncomfortably between these two categories; the issue may be about how an individual is to be treated, and yet have policy implications of a wider kind which affect both the public interest in general and the particular interests of others. *Ridge* v. *Baldwin* offers little guidance in these matters, and subsequent judicial attitudes have been varied; some have maintained Lord Reid's distinction between the two categories, natural justice applying in one, lesser notions of fairness in the other; other judges have merged the distinction in order to develop a more broadly based notion of procedural fairness. It is convenient in considering the lines of judicial development to follow the distinction between decisions about how to treat an individual or situation, adjudication or modified adjudication, and decisions of a specific or general policy kind.

7.42 *Fair procedures in modified adjudication*

In considering fair procedures in individualized decisions, some guidance may be drawn from the earlier discussion. Decisions about

---

[49] [1964] AC at p. 72.

how to treat a person or situation—fixing the sentence, granting parole, issuing a licence, deciding need, determining habitability—involve both adjudicative and consultative elements. They are close to the adjudicative model when the standards are clear and settled, when participation is confined to the person whose interests are directly in issue, and when the primary question is how the standards apply in that case. The adjudicative mode of participation, which is the basis of the principles of natural justice, is most rationally suitable in such cases. What exactly is required within the hearing principle depends on the levels of accuracy sought, and this in turn is determined by the proportionality principle.

Decisions about how to treat a person or situation may also involve issues of general policy. This occurs when the policies are settled in advance, but the question arises in the course of a specific decision whether they ought to be changed or modified; alternatively, policy issues can arise where the particular case is decided according to what seems best in terms of general considerations of public policy. The first might occur in sentencing where the offender wishes to challenge a settled standard on the ground that its policy implications are wrong; the second is prevalent in matters such as licensing where the grant or refusal depends on an assessment of what is best, all things considered, within broadly defined standards. In both situations, there is a mixing of the adjudicative and the consultative. There is adjudication in the sense that the decision is still about how to treat a particular person or situation within these standards, and there is consultation in the sense that the outcome depends to some degree on issues of policy which may extend beyond the present case.

The mixing of the adjudicative and the consultative in this way adds to the complexity of procedures: it means that different modes of participation may have to be combined in the one decision; it also means that consideration should be given to whether parties other than the person directly affected should be allowed to participate, since their interests may also be affected by the decision taken on matters of policy. These issues are to be approached with suggestions earlier in this chapter, but two points should be noted. Firstly, it is usually the case that the person who is the direct object of the decision—the offender being sentenced, the prisoner seeking parole—has a special and direct interest in the outcome; so, even though adjudication may merge into consultation, procedures should allow a reasonable opportunity to that person to address not only the facts relating to his circumstances, but also the policy issues, at least in so far as they bear directly on his situation. Secondly, it is not necessarily the case that a wider range of interests should be represented and consulted whenever individualized decisions involve an element of policy. That depends on an assessment of the nature of the policy issue, and particularly on the relationship between it and wider interests; it also depends on the opportunities that exist at other points in the system for representation and participation by those interests. In applying this principle of selective representation, it may be necessary to compare those opportunities with others available to the person whose interests are directly in issue. For example, the prisoner who wishes to argue that, in considering parole, his behaviour in prison should count more than his past record of convictions, is making claims of policy, but it is the kind of policy matter that he should be allowed to address, and which need not be opened up to wider consultation of interests. On the other hand, Mr Laker's application for a licence to operate trans-Atlantic flights directly raises policy issues which should not be resolved without consultation of interests wider than the applicant's.

A general approach to participatory procedures in respect of modified adjudication can now be formulated. (*a*) The adjudicative mode is appropriate in so far as the standards are settled, the decision is concerned primarily with applying those standards to the specific circumstances, and the parties affected are few in number. (*b*) Persons whose interests are directly in issue should be allowed to participate in accordance with the principle of proportionality. (*c*) As the standards become less settled, so that a greater concern with policy issues enters into individualized decisions, and a wider range of interests is affected, consultation becomes the appropriate mode. (*d*) The parties whose interests are most directly affected may still have a claim to special participation, but other parties may also seek to participate in accordance with the principle of selective representation.

7.43 *Judicial extension of fair procedures*

Since *Ridge* v. *Baldwin* the development of the law has been variable; it is not clear that it has unfolded according to any clear pattern, let alone that suggested above. However, it is useful to examine the three main issues that have arisen: firstly, what interests are adequate to attract the participatory requirements of natural justice; secondly, whether the mode of natural justice is dependent on the classification of powers as judicial; thirdly, how the policy elements in discretionary decisions are to be handled.

After the decision in *Ridge* v. Baldwin, questions have arisen as to whether private interests of a status less than legal rights attract the hearing principle. The issue may arise with respect to interests of an economic or commercial kind, such as continuing to hold a licence to trade or practise a profession,[50] or even perhaps in obtaining a licence in the first place,[51] or continuing to hold an office or position;[52] there may be interests of a more personal and civic kind, such as retaining one's place at a tertiary educational institution,[53] or in not suffering penalties within penal institutions,[54] or in not being denied continued residence within a country.[55] The types of interests that might be subject to discretionary powers are numerous and varied; many are considered sufficient to attract the participatory procedures of natural justice, but some are not.

An assessment of the importance of interests is significant in two ways: firstly, the more substantial the interests that are affected by discretionary decisions, the stronger the claim for procedural accuracy and so for exacting procedures; secondly, the importance of the interests at stake is relevant to the claims that may be made for participation in those procedures. But some interests are considered to be of insufficient importance to require any procedural constraints, beyond honesty and the absence of caprice. Examples are a resident alien's interest in continuing to live in Britain,[56] a boxing referee's interest in obtaining a manager's licence,[57] and minicab drivers' interests in entering airports to obtain passengers.[58]

It is not always clear how the line is drawn between those interests which qualify for participatory procedures and those that do not. One possibility is to distinguish between rights and non-rights. The major drawback to this distinction is that many important interests then

---

[50] For example, *R.* v. *Barnsley MBC, ex parte Hook* [1976] 1 WLR 1052.

[51] For example, *McInnes* v. *Onslow-Fane* [1978] 1 WLR 1520.

[52] For example, *Ridge* v. *Baldwin* [1964] AC 40; *Breen* v. *Amalgamated Engineering Workers Union* [1971] 2 QB 175.

[53] For example, *Glynn* v. *Keele University* [1971] 1 WLR 487.

[54] For example, *R.* v. *Board of Visitors of Hull Prison, ex parte St Germain* [1979] 1 QB 425.

[55] *Schmidt* v. *Secretary of State for Home Affairs* [1969] 2 Ch 149.   [56] Ibid.

[57] *McInnes* v. *Onslow-Fane* [1978] 1 WLR 1520.

[58] *Cinnamond* v. *British Airports Authority* [1980] 1 WLR 582. Although in this case the previous course of illegal conduct by the cab drivers was a vital factor in deciding the point of natural justice.

would be denied procedural protection, and anyhow, within the public law model, the arguments for participatory procedures depend on the relative importance of different interests, not on the distinction between rights and interests. An alternative basis of division is the idea of a legitimate expectation. This was invented by Lord Denning in the course of deciding that no duty of natural justice was owed to a resident alien, since he had no legitimate expectation that he would be allowed to continue his residence.[59] A similar approach has been taken in the licensing field to distinguish between forfeiture or non-renewal of an existing licence, and refusal to grant a licence in the first place. So natural justice was denied to an applicant for a boxing manager's licence since he had no initial basis for expecting that his undoubted interest in gaining a licence would be realized.[60] On the other hand, the expectation that a person will be extended the customary freedom to enter a race meeting on payment of the entrance fee was held to be legitimate.[61]

If there is a legitimate expectation about the course or outcome of a discretionary decision, then that provides the basis for participatory procedures; the underlying point being that it would be unfair to thwart such expectations unless, as Lord Diplock has put it, rational grounds are given and there is a chance to comment. The difficulty, however, lies in identifying the criteria for legitimate expectations. There appear to be three situations. In the first place, legitimate expectations are inferred from the nature of the interest at stake. If that interest is a right, the expectation is that it will not be affected

---

[59] *Schmidt* v. *Secretary of State for Home Affairs* [1969] 2 Ch 149. See also *R.* v. *Gaming Board, ex parte Benaim and Khaida* [1970] 2 QB 417 and *Cinnamond* v. *British Airports Authority* [1980] 1 WLR 582. It is interesting to notice the links between the idea of legitimate expectations in the context of natural justice, and the general importance of legal stability. We have also seen how the disappointment of expectations may be taken to constitute a sense of unfairness. See. A. M. Honoré, 'Social Justice' and the discussion in section 3.44. For recent judicial discussion, see *F. A. I. Insurance Ltd* v. *Winneke* (1981–2) 151 *CLR* 342, *O'Reilly* v. *Mackman* [1983] 2 AC 237, *Attorney General* v. *Ng Yuen Shin* [1983] AC 629, *In re Findlay* [1984] 3 WLR 1159, *R.* v. *Secretary of State, ex parte Asif Khan* [1984] 1 WLR 1337, *Council of Civil Service Unions* v. *Minister for Civil Service* (1984) 3 WLR 1174, *R.* v. *Secretary of State, ex parte Brent LBC* [1982] 2 WLR 693.

[60] *McInnes* v. *Onslow-Fane* [1978] 1 WLR 1520.

[61] *Heatley* v. *Tasmanian Racing and Gaming Commission* (1977) 137 CLR 487. For comment, see P. F. Cane, 'Natural Justice and Legitimate Expectation' (1980) 54 *ALJ* 546. It is not always clear whether the expectation refers to the likely course or outcome of the decision, or to being given the opportunity of making one's case. It seems that while the latter is sufficient it is not necessary, since expectations as to the former are a sufficient basis for some sort of hearing.

detrimentally without following procedures that include something in the nature of a hearing. Some really important interests, often of an economic kind, will also give rise to the necessary expectations. Indeed where rights or certain interests are in issue, procedural requirements may be inferred without explicit reference to expectations, the procedural duties being taken to follow from the very nature of the right or interest; but whether fuller explanation of such cases would reveal implicit reliance on a notion of expectations, remains unclear. In the second situation, legitimate expectations are created by undertakings or assurances given by the authority to the persons affected. This idea, which is sometimes expressed in terms of a holding-out, is understandable enough when an express undertaking of consultation has been made. However, the position becomes more complex and the scope of the doctrine more uncertain when the holding out is inferred indirectly from the actions of the authority, actions such as the formulation of policies or guidelines. There may even be a third category in that from the mere fact that one has enjoyed in the proximate past a benefit or advantage, such as a licence or concession perhaps, legitimate expectations are created that one will not be deprived of it in the future without the appropriate participatory procedures.

Reliance on the notion of legitimate expectations has increased, but it is not without its critics and its difficulties. One problem lies in the relationship between the first category and the other two; in the first, participatory procedures follow from the nature of the interest in issue, while in the others, participatory procedures depend on a relationship, whether express or implied, between the discretionary authority and the person affected. These really are different sources of procedural fairness, but the relationship between the two remains unclear and it is difficult to know when and in what circumstances an interest will be sufficient itself to attract participatory procedures. Moreover, while it is important to recognize that relationships may give rise to ideas of fairness and in turn procedural constraints, this should not obscure the fact that ideas of procedural fairness may have their origins in the very nature of a particular interest, quite independently of any relationship. Secondly, where procedures do derive from a relationship, the interest in issue would seem, logically, to be irrelevant. And yet even in those cases, there appears to be an implicit reference back to the nature of the interest, suggesting perhaps that no matter what the relationship or the expectations created within it, some interests, such as the prisoner's interest in parole, just do not qualify for procedural protections. Thirdly, in so far as expectations are based on implicit undertakings or past practices, there has to be a factual enquiry into the way different discretions are in fact exercised. This seems bound to lead to haphazard results, varying with the practices of officials rather than the nature of the interests in issue. Moreover, there is a danger of circularity in that expectations may come to depend on whether participatory procedures are in fact employed; if they are, the expectations are legitimate, if not, they are illegitimate. This can hardly be a satisfactory basis for deciding how to deal with a novel situation.

Once it is established that the interests in issue warrant procedural protection, it is necessary to consider what the requirements are. In cases of modified adjudication, the dominant mode is likely to be adjudicative, with resulting emphasis on the mode of participation suitable to adjudication, supplemented by elements of consultation. It is necessary, however, to be careful in characterizing the type of procedure. It may be that, in cases which appear superficially to be adjudicative, the interests are not in issue in a way which creates that special relationship between official and individual which is characteristic of adjudication; the only issue may be one of general policy thus making the mode of participation consultative. The principle of selective representation then comes into effect, and it must be asked whether the individual's interest is different from or is affected in a different manner from the interests of others.

This may be clarified with an example. In *Nashua* v. *Shannon*,[62] a special carbonless paper imported into Australia was classified as category A for assessment of excise duties. This was a concessional rate which applied when a suitable equivalent was not produced in Australia. It later came to the official's notice that there were suitable equivalents being manufactured locally, and the special classification was revoked. The revocation was challenged, one issue being the denial of natural justice. The court held that, although there was no legitimate expectation that the concession would continue throughout the period, the kind of interest at stake was one that normally would attract natural justice. However, that initial presumption was overridden by the fact that the official's decision was 'unrelated to factors personal to the applicant and will depend upon matters appertaining to the goods themselves in relation to tariff policies and considerations

---

[62] (1981) 58 FLR 325.

applied by the department'.[63] So the reasons are: firstly, that questions of tariffs are clearly matters of policy, and these are constantly changing; secondly, there is nothing about the circumstances of the company that is relevant to the decision; thirdly, the company has no greater interest in the content of policies than any other importer, so that it would be inappropriate to engage, in the course of deciding one case, in consultative procedures about how the goods were to be classified. This decision illustrates nicely the present approach to participatory procedures.

Another stumbling block in the judicial development of participatory procedures is the continuing uncertainty over the extent to which the hearing principle is dependent upon the classification of powers as judicial. The distinction between judicial and non-judicial functions is not always made, and there is high judicial authority for disregarding it, and applying the hearing principle to discretionary decisions which affect rights and interests.[64] There is, however, a persistent view that the hearing principle applies to judicial decisions while non-judicial decisions import a different notion of fairness. The reasons for making the distinction differ. It may be a matter of semantic convenience; natural justice or the hearing principle refers to the mode of participation applicable to judicial decisions, while fairness refers to the mode suitable for more distinctly discretionary decisions. It may, however, have substantive connotations; natural justice refers to distinct procedural requirements based around notice and hearing, and is appropriate in judicial decisions, while fairness refers to lesser requirements which are largely undeveloped and unpredictable. There is then a strong incentive to force decisions into the judicial mould, and since the criteria for characterizing decisions as judicial are fairly flexible, such attempts have a good chance of success. The consequence may be that in respect of decisions that cannot be characterized as judicial the procedural constraints are minimal.

In view of these consequences, it might appear preferable to abandon any attempt at functional classifications in determining procedural matters. However, a case has been made by Mr Justice

---

[63] Ibid., p. 338. Note also *Bread Manufacturers of NSW* v. *Evans* (1981) 56 ALJR 89, where Gibbs CJ expressed a similar idea. Here the Commission, in deciding whether to allow an increase in the price of bread, had to make a general decision of a discretionary character which affected all consumers and sellers of bread. See section 7.44.

[64] Lord Reid in *Ridge* v. *Baldwin* [1964] AC at p. 74 ff.; Aickin J. in *Heatley* v. *Tasmanian Racing and Gaming Association* (1977) 137 CLR 487 at p. 498; *R.* v. *Barnsley MBC, ex parte Hook* [1976] 1 WLR 1052.

Wooten in *Dunlop* v. *Woollahra* for retaining the classification in order
'to preserve the concept of natural justice, with its traditional content
(in particular the right to a hearing), as a concept applicable to a certain
class of function—the traditional class containing virtually all judicial
functions and many administrative functions to which it is appropriate'.[65] So the dependence of natural justice upon powers being
classified as judicial is justified as the best way of ensuring the
application to a wide range of administrative decisions of precise
participatory procedures.

   The next step in the argument in *Dunlop* was to define what counts
as judicial. The category clearly is meant to be expansive, but what is
the criterion of appropriateness? Here reference was made to the
criteria suggested in *Durayappah* v. *Fernando*[66] for setting the application of natural justice: (*a*) the nature of the rights or interests in issue;
(*b*) the circumstances and occasions on which the authority is entitled
to act; (*c*) the consequences that may result to the rights and interests.
We have dealt with (*a*) and (*c*) which are closely linked; the crucial
factor now is (*b*). Here a distinction was drawn between decisions that
are in a real sense individualized, and decisions which are concerned
with general categories, with 'imposing a common rule over a large
number of properties'.[67] This latter case is, in a loose sense, legislative:
it requires consideration of public welfare and the amenity of the
locality; it affects a wide class of persons who have a similar interest to
that of the present suitor; and, finally, the action is taken by an elective
body which is thus answerable to the local community. A genuinely
individualized decision, however, depends on there being some issue
between the council and the landowner to be resolved; it entails
consideration of the merits and consequences for particular individuals
and their properties. If the decision is individualized in this sense, it is
sufficiently judicial for the hearing requirements of natural justice to
apply. If it is a decision of general policy, and thus of a legislative
nature, more variable and normally lesser procedural standards apply.
The *Dunlop* case was held to fall into the second category, since the
issue concerned a local council passing resolutions of a general kind
imposing limitations on the height of buildings in a certain residential

---

[65] [1974] 1 NSWR 446 at p. 470.   [66] [1967] 2 AC 337.
[67] [1974] 1 NSWR 446 at p. 476. For further discussion of the distinction between
individualized decisions which attract the adjudicative mode of participation, and
decisions of a more policy kind, see the useful comments of Gibbs CJ in *Bread
Manufacturers of NSW* v *Evans* (1981) 56 ALJR 89 at p. 94.

area. The council had to consider specific applications by a development company, but the resolutions went beyond those applications, and applied to any proposals that might be made in the future. Fairness to the specific applicant was satisfied in these circumstances, it was thought, by allowing it to address the council's planning committee.

This interesting decision warrants a number of comments. The first point is that judicial is defined by way of contrast with legislative; notice also that this is more subtle than simply asking whether or not there are issues of policy to be settled. A decision can be individualized and therefore judicial even though policy elements are involved, provided that they are connected to the individual's specific circumstances; the contrast is rather with policy issues which depend for their resolution on wider and more general factors. In that case, the resolution of policy issues is suited to consultative procedures not adjudicative. Wooten J. does not specifically employ the idea of consultation, but his analysis fits neatly into that concept. Secondly, however, the objection might be raised that many cases of discretionary decisions fall somewhere between the two; they involve issues of policy which are linked to the immediate circumstances, and which also involve wider considerations of public policy. Such decisions are both individualized and of general policy interest, and that is the point of calling them modified adjudication. But this mixture can be accomodated if Wooten J.'s analysis is seen not as an attempt to define 'judicial' for the purpose of deciding whether natural justice applies, but as an approach to determining what is required by procedural fairness with respect to different elements of a discretionary decision; some are suited to adjudicative procedures, some to consultative, and which side of the line any aspect falls has to be determined by considering the factors we have discussed.

Thirdly, if there is criticism to be made of Wooten's approach, it is in over emphasizing the participatory procedures applicable in adjudicative decisions, while leaving policy or legislative decisions to the vague notion of fairness. Since fairness can mean virtually anything, this is unsatisfactory; the procedures and mode of participation suited to general policy issues have to be governed by more precise concepts with specific connotations. I have argued on the basis of instrumental rationality and political principles for the notion of consultation as a means for approaching issues of procedure; whether or not this particular concept is the best may be open to discussion, but little progress can be made if the only concept available is fairness.

Perhaps we may sum up in this way. Because terms like judicial and natural justice carry with them the scars of battles fought in the past, there is much to be said for expunging them from discussions of procedure. The difficulties that they have created in the history of participatory procedures adds support to that suggestion. The main rejoinder, however, is that functional classifications, including adjudication, inescapably reappear in settling procedural matters. All that can finally be urged is that it is not the concepts that are confused, but the way in which they are employed; the way forward is to recognize the presumptive case for participatory procedures in discretionary contexts based on instrumental rationality and the value of participation. Once that is accepted, the proper role for conceptual classifications, like judicial and legislative, can be understood; they serve not in providing the conditions to be met before participatory procedures are justified, but as useful concepts in determining precisely what these procedures are to be.

Once it is shown that the interests are important enough to warrant procedural protections, whether within the adjudicative or consultative modes, the next task is to determine more precisely what is required. The guiding factors within each mode are the presumption of participation, the proportionality principle, and the principle of selective representation. Where the rights or interests in issue are of great importance, like the right not to be wrongly convicted, the levels of accuracy required are high; where the interests are of a lesser kind, lower levels of accuracy are acceptable. These calculations require a view as to the relative weighting of interests on the one hand, and, on the other hand, devising a scale of procedures ranging from the least demanding to the most. The two scales can then be put side by side, with the most important rights and interests corresponding to the most exacting procedures. The claim is not that there is some natural affinity between the two, nor that the scale is finely tuned, but only that it is a satisfactory way of representing and acknowledging the relative importance of different interests within a general legal theory.

The courts are not often explicit in evaluating interests in this way, but the process can be detected at work below the surface. The criminal trial with its exacting procedures is an obvious example, so also are administrative decisions affecting personal and property rights. The general presumption that notice and hearing are required in such cases is based on a similar evaluation. However, with the extension of fairness to interests broader than rights, it is not always recognized in judicial decisions that a similar evaluation has to be made in settling procedural matters; nor is it always recognized, when an evalution is made, that it requires more than an *ad hoc* balancing of considerations.

A good example is *Payne* v. *Lord Harris*,[68] which concerned the scope of procedural fairness in parole decisions. The prisoner claimed to be entitled to make representations to the local review committee and the parole board, and to be told the reasons for refusing to recommend his early release. He also argued that in the event of the Home Secretary not acting on the parole board's recommendation, reasons should be given. The members of the Court of Appeal set about defining the procedural requirements by looking at the reasons in favour of the prisoner's arguments, then by listing the reasons against. The former were based jointly on the importance of reasons and representation in ensuring reasonable accuracy, and on a more moral notion of individual respect. The reasons against were practical and expedient: the difficulties of giving the reasons of a body of five members, the danger that they would become short and stereotyped, the greater likelihood of challenges being made, and the general increase in the costs of administering a parole system. When the costs and benefits are tallied in this way without clear criteria of assessment, it is not surprising that the arguments from expedience should prevail. An alternative approach, however is to evaluate the importance of the personal interests at issue, and the consequences for them; the value placed on personal liberty is extremely high, and although there are differences between the prisoner seeking release and the accused being tried, some links can be made between the two in assessing the relative importance of the former. An attempt should then be made to fix a corresponding level of procedures. Assessments of commensurability cannot be exact, but unless some attempt is made to determine such matters, there is no way of comparing public against private interests. If the presumption of participation is added, the prisoner seeking parole has a clear case for procedures which ensure reasonable levels of accuracy and which include personal participation.

One of the main difficulties in fixing the scope of participatory procedures with respect to modified adjudication is in dealing with the consultative aspects. Here selective representation is important. In some cases the adjudicative and the consultative are separable and,

[68] [1981] 1 WLR 754. See also *R.* v. *Secretary of State for the Home Department, ex parte Gunnell, The Times* 3.10.83.

because of opportunities to participate at other points in the system with respect to policy, parties subject to the decision may have no special claim within the confines of that decision to consultation. *Nashua* v. *Shannon* is to be viewed in this way; the fixing of tariff rates is clearly of wide-ranging concern, and a matter which is suitable for determination at a high administrative level, rather than in the course of a specific decision where the only body represented is the one company whose interests happen to be in issue. The conclusion follows, however, not simply from the existence of policy factors of a general kind, but by analysing the position of the particular party in accordance with the criteria suggested. In applying that criteria, it is necessary to dissent from the view that matters of policy are to be settled once and for all in the political process, and that it is inappropriate that they should become issues in individualized decisions. That view can be detected in some of the cases where participatory procedures are denied in respect of aspects of policy.[69] K. C. Davis has argued on such lines in distinguishing between 'legislative' and 'adjudicative' facts.[70] The latter are facts which relate to the parties and their circumstances and can be established by evidence; the former, 'the general facts which help the tribunal decide questions of law and policy and discretion'. The point of Davis's distinction is that while a party should have a hearing on adjudicative facts, he need not be heard in respect of legislative facts, since they involve matters of policy to be settled according to wider considerations.

The case against this is, firstly, that individualized elements and matters of wider policy may be so intertwined that the former have an important influence on the way the latter are perceived and resolved. The decision once made may have policy implications of a general kind, but the immediate concern is to deal with the case in hand. Secondly, the very fact that the policy issue arises in dealing with some peson's particular circumstances is often enough to confer on him an interest over and above that of others affected by the policy implications. This is recognized in the law relating to fettering, where part of the rationale for not allowing the adoption of fixed rules is to leave open the opportunity of reconsidering in the particular case general policy decisions that have already been taken. Finally, there may be individuals and groups who have not in fact had reasonable or equal opportunities to influence policy at the other levels; it is then

[69] For example *McInnes* v. *Onslow-Fane* [1978] 1 WLR 1520.
[70] Davis, *Administrative Law Text*, pp. 160–1.

hardly unfair that they be allowed to address arguments towards the policy issues when their interests are directly subject to discretionary powers.

In practice, the extent to which general policy matters are to be open to consideration in the course of a decision depends on a number of factors: the number of cases that must be decided, the importance of the interest at stake, the resources and capacities of the deciding body, the degree to which policy choices have been translated into firm standards, and the likelihood that particular cases may raise novel or unforseen issues. In some situations, procedural fairness may be satisfied by making available the criteria of decision-making, and giving the person affected an opportunity to put his case in its best light; in other situations, where there is a different combination of factors—the interests at stake, the small number of parties likely to be involved, the relatively unsettled policies—the case for fuller consideration of policy may be stronger. In other words, a significant variable is whether individualized decisions are made pursuant to a comprehensive plan or left to be worked out incrementally. In the former case, there is likely to be a division between the guide-lines, and their implementation in particular cases. Interest group consultation is then most appropriate at the first level, while individualized adjudication characterizes the second. Where the mode is incremental, policy-making and policy-application become merged and so, accordingly, do the modes of participation.

Indeed, the synoptic-incremental distinction is also useful in drawing attention to one of the unfortunate side-effects of a too sharp division in individualized decisions between policy-making and policy-application. It may be that, although the decision is policy-based, in fact precise guide-lines have been laid down for deciding individual cases. In the boxing manager's case,[71] where participatory procedures were denied because the decision was policy-based, it would have been highly relevant to know whether the licensing authority had fixed standards; if it had, then, while it may not have been necessary to allow elaborate arguments as to their relative merits in general, it certainly would have been important that they be made known to him, and the opportunity be provided for arguments and evidence as to their application in his case. In *Heatley* v. *Tasmanian Racing and Gaming Commission*,[72] where natural justice was held to apply to the discretion-

---

[71] *McInnes* v. *Onslow-Fane* [1978] 1 WLR 1520.
[72] (1977) 137 CLR 487.

ary decisions of the Commission barring Heatley from entering a
racecourse, it was not clear whether the Commission acted upon
settled standards or whether it decided each case on its merits within a
broad policy framework. But the implication is clear that, in the first
situation, any self-imposed guide-lines ought to be made known.
Without disclosure, the point of allowing representations by the person
affected is undermined. We noted earlier *R.* v. *Criminal Injuries
Compensation Board, ex parte Ince*,[73] where the Criminal Injuries
Compensation Board was required to inform an applicant for
compensation of the standards adopted to guide its discretion, and to
give her an opportunity to address arguments in respect of them. This
is surely preferable to an approach which makes no attempt to
ascertain the standards of decision-making, or to make them known to
affected parties.

To sum up the general argument is that participatory procedures are
not to be settled by *ad hoc* and variable balancing of policy factors. A
justificatory theory is required for whatever approach is taken, and
while there are various possible theories, one is suggested here which
is based around: (*a*) assessment of the relative importance of interests,
and the proportionality principle; (*b*) the distinction between the
adjudicative and consultative modes, and the recognition that within
each, procedures can be more or less exacting; (*c*) the principle of
selective representation.

7.44   *Participatory procedures in specific and general policy decisions*

While it was unnecessary for Lord Reid in *Ridge* v. *Baldwin* to be
specific about the application of fair procedures to policy decisions,
whether specific or general, that issue has since arisen with increasing
frequency. Some indication has been given in the earlier discussion of
how these issues are handled in relation to the *Dunlop* and *Nashua*
cases. The point of this section is to extend that discussion by
considering more fully some of the points arising in creating
participatory procedures.

Although the lines between different types of decisions cannot be
drawn too sharply, it is useful to follow the earlier distinction between
modified adjudication on the one hand, and discretion in deciding on a
specific policy matter (for example, whether to construct a new town or
a motorway) or in formulating a general policy (for example, whether

---

[73] [1973] 1 WLR 1334.

to grant subsidies to a certain type of industry, or to abolish fixed fees charged by solicitors). The difference between these last two types depends on whether the policy issues arise in respect of a particular situation, or whether it is more in the nature of a general policy for application in a number of situations. It is characteristic of both types of decisions that they have fairly direct effects on a number of individuals and groups. A general approach to the application of participatory procedures in decisions of these kinds has been outlined. There may be elements of adjudication to be settled, but the dominant mode of procedure is consultative, and this becomes more clearly the case as decisions are closer to the policy end of the spectrum. The two guiding principles in participatory procedures are again proportionality and selective representation. These are normative principles which should guide Parliament, administrative bodies, and the courts in the design and development of participatory procedures. It is these principles that give substance and meaning to the concept of procedural fairness. Without claiming that any of these authorities are committed unequivocally to such principles, or that procedures have developed in accordance with them, it is important, nevertheless, to uncover the connections and divergences between actual practice and underlying principles.

Parliament generally is assumed to have the main responsibility for setting consultative procedures, and it is a common characteristic of statutory schemes to provide for consultation with respect to matters of policy. For example, there are extensive statutory schemes of consultation with individuals and groups in areas of planning, welfare, and economic regulation. Statutory provisions often are incomplete, however, so that it is left to officials as part of their discretion to determine the extent of consultation. Such matters may then come before the court in the course of their general concern with fair procedures, and in recent years it has been made clear that review may extend into the development of consultative procedures. One of the stumbling blocks hindering that development is that the context in which questions of consultation arise are usually highly discretionary and policy-laden; the courts have, accordingly, been naturally hesitant in imposing procedural constraints where Parliament has been silent. Such an approach might be justified on either or a combination of two grounds, one stemming from a substantive theory of procedural fairness, the other from the background principles governing the relations between the courts and Parliament. With regard to the first, it is difficult to see how any cogent and comprehensive theory as to the basis of participatory procedures could make a sharp distinction between discretionary decisions of a modified adjudicative kind and those of a more clearly policy kind. The approach suggested in this chapter recognizes that differences between the two are differences in degree, and that both have a clear place within a general theory of procedures. And since the courts have made substantial progress in developing an approach to individualized, adjudicative decisions, they are committed to a general theory which must either apply to decisions involving general policy, or show some principled basis for excluding them. Secondly, the relationship between the courts and Parliament is open to being construed in varying ways according to the particular interpretation given to background principles. We have considered those principles and shown how judicial involvement in procedural matters might be justified. There may be no correct judicial approach, but, whatever stance is taken must be justified by the elaboration of principles and policies. There are signs that the courts are beginning to do just that, and to claim a legitimate role in advancing procedural fairness even in highly discretionary contexts.

A striking example of judicial insistence on consultative procedures with respect to a general policy decision is *R.* v. *Liverpool Corporation, ex parte Liverpool Taxi Fleet Operators' Association*[74] (referred to as *Liverpool Taxi*). Here the city council had power to license such number of hackney carriages as it thought fit. The council gave an assurance to the associations representing existing licence holders that it would not increase the numbers without consulting them. At a public meeting of the council, the chairman of the licensing sub-committee gave an undertaking that the number of licences would not be increased until certain future events had occurred. Some months later, however, the council resolved to increase the numbers. Litigation followed, the central issue being whether the council had a duty to consult the existing licence holders before adopting this resolution. The economic interests of the existing licensees in restricting the number of licences and the detrimental effects of the council's resolution were undisputed. For that reason, and because of the assurance that had been given, it was held to be a matter of fairness that the licence holders be allowed to make representations which the council should consider in settling policies about the optimum number of taxis.

[74] [1972] 2 QB 299.

The assurance given by the council to the existing licensees was clearly a factor of importance in the court's decision, although Lord Denning for one was of the view that in these circumstances consultation was a requirement of the general duty of fairness. The assurance amounted to a holding out which, to use the modern parlance, created legitimate expectations; and to have disappointed those expectations would have been unfair. The requirement of legitimate expectations has come to dominate decisions about procedural fairness here in a way similar to that in modified adjudication. Whether there is to be consultation with particular individuals or groups often is made to depend on whether there has been in respect of that group a holding out of the kind considered earlier. But again the ambiguities and inadequacies of that concept apply equally here; and the general point is that while the special relationship between officials and citizens which stems from a holding out may be a sound basis for fair procedures, it would be unfortunate if this were to conceal the fact that the broader basis for procedural fairness is the nature of the interests in issue and the likely consequences to them. There is wide recognition of this at the general political level, in the design of statutory schemes, and in recent judicial decisions.[75]

Once the threshold requirements relating to the adequacy of interests are met, the question as to the scope of consultative procedures arises. That question is best answered, it is suggested, under the guidance of the two principles of selective representation and proportionality. Indeed, it is interesting to notice that the enquiry into the adequacy of interests is likely to be subsumed into those two principles; for in applying those principles it is necessary to identify the interests, the way they are affected by comparison with other interests, and the opportunities for influencing policy that have existed at other points in the system. It might be argued with some plausibility that, provided there is a real and identifiable interest, it is unnecessary to try to draw a line between those that warrant procedural protections and those that do not; any such interest attracts fair procedures, so that the important question is what precisely those procedures are to be. In answering that question, the relative importance of different interests will be accommodated.

This can be illustrated through the judgment of Chief Justice Gibbs

---

[75] For recent judicial discussion, see *Council for Civil Service Unions* v. *Minister for Civil Service* [1984] 3 WLR 1174 and *Bread Manufacturers of NSW* v. *Evans* (1981) 56 ALJR 89. But note also *Bates* v. *Lord Hailsham* [1972] 1 WLR 1373.

of the Australian High Court in *Bread Manufacturers of NSW* v. *Evans*.[76]
One of the issues there was whether an association representing the
manufacturers of bread was entitled to be consulted prior to an order
being made by the Prices Commission regulating, and in effect
reducing, the price of hamburger buns. The association argued that,
although under no statutory duty to hold an enquiry, the Commission
was bound to disclose to the association its intention of making such an
order, and that the association should have been given an opportunity
to argue against it. A number of points of interest are to be found in the
judgment of the Chief Justice.[77] First, it was made clear that fair
procedures apply to a wide range of interests, a range that certainly
goes beyond rights. The financial interests here were unquestionably
sufficient. Secondly, the application of fair procedures does not
depend on the classification of a power as judicial, administrative, or
legislative. Thirdly, the decision here was of a highly discretionary
kind, since the object was to make a general decision of a discretionary
character which affected all consumers and sellers of bread. It was as
such a decision of general policy and might be contrasted with 'an act
which directly affects a person individually'. Notice it is not just the
fact that it was a policy decision; the important point is that it was a
matter of policy *and* did not affect any person individually. The
manufacturers of bread have a financial interest, but then so does a
range of others, all in fact who consume bread products. If we ask why
this is signficant—a question that the Chief Justice does not answer
explicitly—the reason would seem to be that the manufacturers have
no greater interest than many others, and that there is no reason to
conclude that the general political process fails to provide representation of all such interests commensurate with their relative importance;
and so the requirements of procedural fairness are met elsewhere.[78]
Fourthly, the Chief Justice went on, even if that is not the case so that
there is a duty to consult the association before making the order, it is
not clear that the Commission failed in its duty. It had received and

---

[76] (1981) 56 ALJR 89.   [77] Ibid. at p. 94.

[78] For other cases where the same point is implicit, see *Creednz Inc.* v. *Governor-
General of New Zealand* [1981] 1 NZLR 172, where Richardson J. says: 'Public
participation is provided for in the form of consultation with the elected representatives
of these persons who are most directly affected. And practicalities must be taken into
account. To give all persons likely to be affected an opportunity to be heard and have
their views conveyed to Cabinet directly or through the Minister would be a major and
potentially time-consuming exercise.' See also *Dunlop* v. *Woolhara* [1975] 2 NSWR
446 and *Nashua* v. *Shannon* (1981) 58 FLR 325.

considered the submissions of the association in favour of a price increase, and presumably the submissions of other interested parties. As in so many situations like this, there cannot be a precise stipulation of the demands of procedural fairness; the guiding principles may be clear enough, but what is required in actual situations depends finally on assessment and judgment. It is not surprising, then, that judicial opinions are often couched in the alternative for that very reason.

There may be occasions when the case for consultation in respect of particular interests clearly is established, and yet precisely what is required may be unclear. I have provided the outline of a central sense of consultation, with the qualification that the actual requirements can be more or less exacting.[79] It is here that the proportionality principle becomes especially significant. And again its application may be demonstrated by reference to the recent case *Bushell* v. *Secretary of State for the Environment*.[80] Here a public local inquiry was held into two draft schemes published by the Secretary of State for the construction of motorways. The first issue arose when the objectors were allowed to call evidence as to the need for the motorway; in the course of that inquiry, it was admitted by the Department of the Environment that its estimates of future traffic needs were based on a departmental publication known as the Red Book. Objectors then brought evidence to show that the methods used in the Red Book were insupportable, and sought to cross-examine witnesses for the department as to the accuracy of these methods, and the resulting predictions as to levels of traffic. The second issue arose when after the close of the inquiry and before the inspector made his report, the department issued new information which showed that the existing roads could carry more traffic, and that revised estimates showed reduced levels of traffic for the future. The objectors sought to have the inquiry re-opened in order to make representations regarding this new information. The minister refused; the inspector recommended that the schemes should go ahead, and the minister accepted the recommendation.

The objectors sought to have the minister's decision quashed by the

[79] For discussion, A. D. Jergesen, 'The Legal Requirements of Consultation' 1978 *PL* 290. For examples, *Lee* v. *Department of Education and Science* (1967) 66 LGR 211; *Agricultural, Horticultural and Forestry Industry Training Board* v. *Aylesbury Mushrooms Ltd* [1972] 1WLR 190.

[80] [1981] AC 75. For perspicuous comments on this case (although taking a rather different approach), see R. M. Dworkin, 'Principle, Policy and Procedure' in Tapper, *Crime, Proof and Punishment*.

courts for failing to allow cross-examination of the department's witnesses, and for refusing to re-open the inquiry. In the House of Lords it was accepted that there was a duty to follow fair procedures; this meant allowing interested parties to address arguments and evidence in a consultative manner. The specific issue, however, was how exacting the consultative process had to be in order to satisfy procedural fairness. This depended on two considerations. One was the extent to which issues, such as whether there is need for a motorway and, if so, what route it should take, are to be turned into questions of fact which can be proved or disproved. This matter is discussed in section 6.4, where we saw the difficulties in transforming broad policy questions into justiciable inquiries. The second matter depends on assessing the levels of accuracy that can be demanded in discretionary decisions; a matter to be determined, it is suggested, in accordance with the proportionality principle. The objectors in the present case were allowed to submit their own evidence as to the need for a motorway, but they were barred from cross-examining the department's witnesses; had this been allowed, it would have provided an opening for investigating the basis of the department's case. This would have led in turn to a more rational decision, and thus enhanced the worth of the participatory procedures. However, that is not the only factor; the costs to society of the inquiry also had to be considered. It had already gone on for a hundred days; it was expensive and might have gone on indefinitely.

The judges recognized the need to draw some such line, and had resort to the familiar idea of balancing—the public interest in an expeditious and economical decision on the one hand, the importance of procedural fairness on the other. The minister's decision, it was concluded, represented a reasonable balance. All things considered, that conclusion appears reasonable, taking into account the interests involved and the consequences to them. The courts did not derive explicit guidance from the proportionality principle, but when there is talk of balancing some such principle may well be in the background.

To conclude, the judicial development of participatory procedures in relation to decisions that are based on assessments of general policy is in its early stages. The opportunities for review do not occur as frequently as in modified adjudication, but there are signs of change; the courts are beginning to consider whether general policy issues may be circumscribed by procedural constraints, and whether to extend the notion of consultation. The general argument here is that there is considerable room for developing that concept in discretionary decisions, and that it has a firm basis in underlying constitutional and legal theory.

7.5 A NOTE ON STANDING

The discussion of participatory procedures so far has been concerned with participation in the discretionary decision itself. A related issue is who may bring or intervene in an action in the courts, challenging the validity of the discretionary action. Although the courts have taken only the most tentative steps towards a more cogent theory, in recent years this question has been well and widely discussed.[81] For that reason my remarks shall be brief, and shall be concerned to relate standing to the approach taken to discretionary powers.

There are two recurring issues: one concerns a person's capacity to seek judicial review of discretion where his private interests in some sense are affected by the decision; the other is where a person seeks to challenge simply on the basis of the public interest in not allowing official powers to be used improperly. In the first, the interests at stake might range greatly, for example from private property rights to one's interest in a clean environment; some such interests may be private only in an attenuated sense, and there may come a point at which they are better characterized as interests which are or should be of general public concern. The point is to distinguish interests in that sense from the special sense of public interest that consists simply in an administrative body acting in accordance with its legal powers.

The issue of standing in the second case is whether a person should be allowed to seek review simply as a concerned citizen. The traditional device of entrusting the public interest to a public official, such as the Attorney-General, may be inadequate, and there is a strong case for individuals being able to seek review in some cases. The difficulty is in fixing criteria, but one possibility would be to require that if no private interest could be shown, then at least a real concern with the decision or its consequences must be demonstrated. The concern might be based, for example, on moral, religious, or aesthetic grounds. Where real concern can be shown, there is a good

---

[81] See Peter Cane, 'The Function of Standing Rules in Administrative Law' (1980) *PL* 303; Craig, *Administrative Law*, pp. 444–57; Joseph Vining, *Legal Identity: The Coming of Age of Public Law* (Yale UP, 1978).

claim for standing, subject to a degree of discretion in the court to consider any clear reason of public policy to the contrary.

To return to the first situation mentioned above, the usual issue of standing to review discretionary decisions is what private interests are sufficient. The prevailing judicial approach can be seen in terms of the private law model: the object of judicial review is to uphold private rights against actions by officials which contravene the law; standing to sue is confined, therefore, to those whose rights or associated interests are affected. There is, however, a serious flaw in the apparent symmetry between the object of review and the standing rules; the object of review is to ensure that officials act within their powers, while the point of standing is to determine who may bring an action. These are two different issues, and determination of the legality question is not linked in any logical way to the decision about who brings the action; the same issues arise on the former whether the action is brought by a person whose rights are transgressed, or by a complete outsider. It is understandable that the only one who would wish to sue, normally, is the person whose rights are affected, especially since, within the private law model, administrative powers are likely to be restricted in scope, affecting rights rather than a wide range of interests.

With the rise of discretionary powers and the emergence of the public law model, two main changes occur. First, the interests affected by discretionary actions are more extensive in range and variable in importance, so that there is greater demand for the power to initiate judicial review. In those circumstances, it is difficult to see why the capacity to sue should be confined to those whose rights are affected, rather than extended to a wider range of interests. The point of making such a distinction might be simply a way of controlling the demand for review; but even if that is a justifiable objective, the method is arbitrary. The second change in the public law model is that, while the object of judicial review is still to determine the legality of administrative actions, what counts as legality may, for the reasons we have seen, require some degree of judicial entry into the discretionary process. Judicial determinations of the legality of discretionary decisions rest partly on how the objects and purposes are interpreted, and what factors are to be taken into account. This in turn depends partly on the arguments and evidence that might be brought by parties whose interests are affected. So, although the judicial inquiry is concerned with the narrow question of legality, it in some respects mirrors the original discretionary decision and may require consideration of some of the same issues. On the assumption that the person whose interests are in issue is usually the best one to advance those interests, there is an additional argument for extending standing to a wide range of interests.

On the basis of these characteristics of the public law model, the general question in issues of standing is which interests are sufficiently important to justify the initiation or intervention in judicial review. The answer is provided by an analysis similar to that made in deciding whether an interest is sufficiently important to warrant participation in discretionary decisions; that is, some ranking of interests according to importance must be made, and some threshold set, which is to be satisfied in order to warrant standing. These tasks must be performed in accordance with some theory of interests, but, for the kinds of reasons that have been given earlier, liberal and extended rules of standing are justifiable since judicial review forms an important element in the development of principles of official accountability in the public law model of authority. The courts have gone some way in that direction by extending standing to 'aggrieved' persons, and more recently, by statutory innovation, the governing criterion is 'sufficient interest';[82] such concepts have to be given meaning and content against some general theory, and the judicial approach is still being developed.[83]

While there are similarities between questions of participation in discretionary decisions and standing to challenge those decisions, there are also differences. In the former, the procedural requirements are more or less exacting depending on the importance of the interests, whereas in the latter, once standing is granted, the usual judicial process ensues, although it is not improbable that the rigour and extent of review may be influenced by the nature of the interests at stake. Moreover, the interests that participate in the original decision need not coincide with those seeking review; indeed, it might only be after the decision that a person realizes his interests have been harmed, and that the only recourse then is to seek review. In short, while there is close similarity between the interests necessary for participation and those required for review, there may be variations according to the different circumstances.

[82] Rules of the Supreme Court, Ord. 53, r. 3(5).
[83] For discussion, see Craig, *Administrative Law*, ch. 12.

7.6 CONCLUSION

The object of this chapter has been to consider the issue of participatory procedures in the exercise of discretionary powers. This has involved two more specific issues: firstly, it has been necessary to examine the basis of procedures, and to identify the underlying values; secondly, it was then necessary to consider the extension of those values to decision-making within the public law model. Under the first of these tasks, it was suggested that the primary object of good procedures is to produce good outcomes; procedures, in other words, are instrumental on outcomes. However, procedures also serve other values, and of special importance in the present context are notions of representation and participation by interested parties. Under the second of the issues mentioned, consideration was given to the extension of the adjudicative mode to take account of the other modes of decision-making that occur in the public law context. Emphasis was placed on consultation as an appropriate mode in many contexts of discretion, but without excluding other concepts like mediation. It was also shown how there is an intermingling in discretionary contexts of political ideas about representation and participation, and the traditional legal conceptions of natural justice. The general argument is that in settling procedural issues, the main guiding principles are those of proportionality and selective representation: the first suggests that a relationship of comparative proportionality is to be maintained between the mode of procedures and the interests affected; the second maintains that the extent of representation and participation by persons affected by discretionary decisions is to be assessed by considering the overall opportunities that have existed at other points in the political and administrative process. Finally, the application and extension of these ideas in the context of judicial review was examined.

Bibliography

Abraham, K., 'Statutory Interpretation and Literary Theory' (1979) 32 *RutLR* 676.
—— 'Three Fallacies of Interpretation: a Comment on Precedent and Judicial Decision' (1981) 23 *ArizLR* 771.
Judicial Decision' (1981) 23 *ArizLR* 771.
Ackerman, B., *Social Justice in the Liberal State*, Yale UP, 1980.
Ackerman, B. and Hassler, W., *Clean Coal/Dirty Air*, Yale UP, 1981.
Adler, M. and Bradley, A. (eds.), *Justice, Discretion and Poverty*, London, 1975.
Adler, M. and Asquith, S. (eds.), *Discretion and Welfare*, London, 1981.
Administrative Procedure in Government Agencies, Senate Document No. 8, 77th Congress, 1st Session 1941.
Akehurst, M., 'Statement of Reasons for Judicial and Administrative Decisions' (1970) 33 *MLR* 154.
Albrow, M., *Bureaucracy*, London, 1970
Alschuler, A. W., 'The Prosecutor's Role in Plea Bargaining' (1961) 36 *UChiLR* 50.
Aman, A. C., 'Administrative Equity: an Anlysis of Exceptions to Administative Rules' 1982 *DukeLJ* 277.
American Friends' Service Committee, *Struggle for Justice*, New York, 1971.
Anderson, C. W., 'Political Design and the Representation of Interests' (1977) 10 *CompPolStud* 127.
Appleby, P., *Policy and Administration*, Alabama UP, 1949.
Archibald, R., 'Three Views of the Experts' Role in Policy Making' (1950) 1 *PolSci* 73.
Arndt, H. W. 'The Origins of Dicey's Concept of the Rule of Law' (1957) 31 *ALJ* 117.
Atiyah, P. S., *The Rise and Fall of Freedom of Contract*, Oxford UP, 1979.
—— *From Principles of Pragmatism: Changes in the Function of the Judicial Process and the Law*, Oxford UP, 1978.
Auerbach, C., 'Some Thoughts on the Hector Memorandum' 1960 *WiscLR* 183.

Bachrach, Peter, *The Theory of Democratic Elitism: A Critique*, Boston UP, 1967.
Baier, Kurt, *The Moral Point of View*, New York, 1965.
Bailey, S. H., Harris, D. J. and Jones, B. L., *Civil Liberties*, London, 1980.
Balbus, I. D., 'Commodity Form and Legal Form: An Essay on the "Relative Autonomy" of the Law' (1977) 11 *LSR* 571.
Baldwin, R. and Hawkins, K., 'Discretionary Justice: Davis Reconsidered' 1985 *PL* 570.

Bankowski, Z. and Nelken, D., 'Discretion as a Social Problem' in Adler and Asquith, *Discretion and Welfare.*

Barry, Brian, *Political Argument*, London, 1965.

Bean, P., *Rehabilitation and Deviance*, London, 1976.

Beatson, Jack, 'A British View of *Vermont Yankee*' (1981) 55 *TulaneLR* 435.

Bendix, R., *Max Weber: An Intellectual Portrait*, London, 1966.

Berlin, Isiah, *Four Essays on Liberty*, Oxford UP, 1969.

Beverley, F. and Morris, P., *On Licence: a Study of Parole*, London 1975.

Bickel, A. M. and Wellington, H. H., 'Legislative Purpose and the Judicial Process: The Lincoln Mills Case' (1957) 71 *HarvLR* 1.

Blom Cooper, L. and Drewry, G., *Final Appeal: a Study of the House of Lords in Its Judicial Capacity*, Oxford UP, 1972.

Bondach, E. and Ragan, R. A., *Going by the Book: The Problem of Regulatory Unreasonableness*, United States, 1982.

Bottomore, Tom, *Theories of Modern Capitalism*, London, 1985.

Braybrooke, D. and Lindblom, C., *A Strategy of Decision: Policy Evaluation as a Social Process* New York, 1963.

Brennan, F. G., 'New Growth in the Law—The Judicial Contribution' (1979) 6 *MonLr* 1.

Brest, Paul, 'The Substance of Process' (1981) 42 *OhioStLJ* 131.

Breyer, S., '*Vermont Yankee* and the Court's Role in the Nuclear Energy Controversy' (1978) 91 *HarvLR* 1833.

Brittan, S., 'Towards a Corporate State' (1975) xliv *Encounter.*

Brice, M., *Coming of the Welfare State*, London, 4th edn., 1968.

Burin, F. S., 'Bureaucracy and National Socialism: A Reconsideration of Weberian Theory' in Merton, *Reader in Bureaucracy.*

Burrows, J. F., 'Statutes and Judicial Discretion' 1976 *NZLR* 1.

Burrows, P. and Veljanovski, C. G. (eds.), *The Economic Approach to Law*, London, 1981.

Busck, Lars, 'The Family Guidance Centre in Copenhagen' in K. C. Davis, *Discretionary Justice in Europe and America.*

Byse, Clark, '*Vermont Yankee* and the Evolution of Administrative Procedure: A Somewhat Different View' (1978) 91 *HarvLR* 1828.

Cairncross, A., 'No Wonder Bertrand Russell Was Afraid of Him', *Guardian Weekly*, 19 June 1983.

Campbell, Tom, *The Left and Rights*, London, 1983.

—— 'The Socialist Concept of Rights' (1982) *BASLP* 82.

—— 'Discretionary "Rights"' in Timms and Watson, *Philosophy in Social Work.*

Cane, P. F., 'Natural Justice and Legitimate Expectation' (1980) 54 *ALJ* 546.

—— 'The Function of Standing Rules in Administrative Law' 1980 *PL* 303.

Carson, K., 'White Collar Crime and the Enforcement of Factory Legislation' (1970) 10 *BritJCrim* 383.

—— 'Some Sociological Aspects of Strict Liability and the Enforcement of Factory Legislation' (1970) 33 *MLR* 396.

Cavadine, P., *Parole: the Case for Change*, London, 1977.

Cawson, A., 'Pluralism, Corporatism and the Role of the State' (1978) 73 *Govt&Opp*.

Chayes, Abram, 'The Role of the Judge in Public Law litigation' (1976) 89 *HarvLR* 1287.

Chipman, L., 'Formal Justice and Rational Individualism' (1978) 67 *ARSP*.

Cicourel, A. V., *The Social Organization of Juvenile Justice*, New York, 1968.

Commission for Local Administration, Annual Report, 1982/3.

Committee on Administrative Discretion, Cth. of Australia Parliamentary Paper No. 316, 1973.

Committe on Administrative Tribunals and Inquiries, Report, 1957 Cmnd. 218.

Committee on Ministers' Powers, Report, 1932 Cmnd. 4060.

Commonwealth Administrative Reviews Committee, Report, Cth. 1971.

Connolly, W. (ed.), *The Bias of Pluralism*, New York, 1969.

—— 'The Challenge to Pluralist Theory' in Connolly, *The Bias of Pluralism*.

Corwin, E. S., 'The "Higher Law" Background of American Constitutional Law' (1928–9) 42 *HarvLR* 149 and 365.

Council on Tribunals, *Annual Reports*, 1983–4.

—— *The Functions of the Council on Tribunals*, 1980 Cmnd. 7805.

Craig, P. P., *Administrative Law*, London, 1983.

Cramton, R. C., 'Comment on Trial-Type Hearings in Nuclear Power Plant Siting' (1972) 58 *VaLR* 585.

Cranston, Ross, *Legal Foundations of the Welfare State*, London, 1985.

Crespigny, A. de, 'Freedom for Progress' in Crespigny and Minogue, *Contemporary Political Philosophers*.

Crespigny, A. de and Minogue, K. (eds.), *Contemporary Political Philosophers*, London, 1976.

Crommelin, Michael, 'Economic Analysis of Property' in Galligan, *Essays in Legal Theory*.

Cross, Rupert, *Precedent in English Law*, Oxford UP, 1964.

—— *Statutory Interpretation*, London, 1976.

Cross, R. and Tapper, C. *Evidence*, London, 6th edn. 1985.

Cyert, R. and March, J., *A Behavioural Theory of the Firm*, New Jersey, 1963.

Dahl, R., *A Preface to Democratic Theory*, Chicago UP, 1956.

—— *Pluralist Democracy in the United States: Conflict and Consensus*, Boston, 1967.

Daintith, T., 'Public Law and Economic Policy' 1974 *JBL* 9.

—— 'The Functions of Law in the Field of Short-Term Economic Policy' (1976) 92 *LQR* 62.

Davis, K. C., *Administrative Law Text*, St Paul, 1972.

—— *Administrative Law Treatise*, St Paul, 2nd edn., 1979.

—— *Discretionary Justice*, Louisiana, 1969.

—— (ed.), *Discretionary Justice in Europe and America*, U of Illinois, 1976.

—— *Administrative Law of the Seventies*, St Paul, 1976.

—— *1982 Supplement to Administrative Law Treatise*, St. Paul, 1982.

Davis, M., 'Sentencing: Must Justice be Evenhanded?' (1982) 1 *Law&Phil* 77.

de Smith, S. A. and Evans, J. M., *Judicial Review of Administrative Action*, London, 4th edn. 1980.

Devlin, Patrick, *Trial by Jury*, London, 1956.

—— 'Judges as Lawmakers' (1976) 39 *MLR* 1.

Dewey, John, *The Public and its Problems*, New York, 1967.

Dicey, A. V., *The Law of the Constitution*, London, 1961 edn.

—— '*Droit Administratif* in Modern French Law' (1901) 17 *LQR* 302.

—— 'The Development of Administrative Law in England' (1915) 31 *LQR* 148.

Dickinson, J., *Administrative Justice and the Supremacy of Law*, Harvard UP, 1927.

Dickinson, John, 'Legal Rules: Their Function in the Process of Decision' (1931) 79 *UPaLR* 833.

—— 'Legal Rules: Their Application and Elaboration' (1931) 79 *UPaLR* 1052.

Diplock, Lord, 'Administrative Law: Judicial Review Reviewed' 1975 *CLJ* 233.

Diver, C. S., 'Policymaking Paradigms in Administrative Law' (1981) 95 *HarvLR* 393.

Donnison, David, *The Politics of Poverty*, London, 1982.

Dorsey, Gray (ed.), *Proceedings of the International Conference on Legal and Social Philosophy*, St Louis, 1976.

Dow, P. E., *Discretionary Justice: a Critical Inquiry*, Ballinger, 1981.

Dugdale, D. F., 'The Statutory Conferment of Judicial Discretion', 1972 *NZLJ* 556.

Duncan, G. (ed.), *Democratic Theory and Practice*, Cambridge UP, 1983.

—— and Lukes, S., 'Democracy Restated' in Kariel, *Frontiers of Democratic Theory*.

Dunsire, A., *Administration: the Word and the Science*, London, 1973.

Dworkin, R. M., *Taking Rights Seriously*, London, 1977.

—— 'A Reply to Seven Critics' (1977) 11 *GaLR*.

—— 'No Right Answer?' in Hacker and Raz, *Law, Morality and Society*.

—— 'Principle, Policy, Procedure' in Tapper, *Crime, Proof and Punishment*.

—— 'The Forum of Principle' (1981) 56 *NYULR* 469.

—— 'Law as Interpretation' (1982) 60 *TexasLR* 527.

Eckhoff, T., 'Guiding Standards in Legal Reasoning' (1976) 29 *CLP* 205.

Ehrlich, I. and Posner, R. A., 'An Economic Analysis of Legal Rulemaking' (1974) 4 *JLegStud* 257.

Eisenberg, M., 'Private Ordering Through Negotiation, Dispute Settlement and Rule-Making' (1976) 89 *HarvLR* 637.

—— 'Participation, Responsiveness and the Consultative Process' (1978) 92 *HarvLR* 410.

Ely, J. H., *Democracy and Distrust*, Harvard UP, 1981.

Faller, B., 'Does Dworkin's Rights Thesis Succeed in Solving the Problem of Judicial Discretion?' (1984) 22 *UWOLR*.

Farmer, J. A., *Tribunals and Government*, London, 1974.

Fayol, H., *Industrial and General Administration*, London, 1949.

Feinberg, Joel, *Social Philosophy*, New Jersey, 1973.

Ferguson, A. R. (ed.), *Attacking Regulatory Problems*, United States, 1981.

Finer, Herman, 'Administrative Responsibility in Democratic Government' in Rourke, *Bureaucratic Government in National Politics*.

Finnis, J. M., *Natural Laws and Natural Rights*, Oxford UP, 1980.

Fish, Stanley, 'Working on the Chain Gang: Interpretation in Law and Literature' (1982) 60 *TexasLR* 551.

Fiss, O. M., 'Objectivity and Interpretation' (1982) 34 *StanLR* 739.

Flathman, Richard, *The Practice of Rights*, Cambridge UP, 1976.

Flick, G. A., 'Administrative Adjudications and the Duty to Give Reasons—A Search for Criteria' 1978 *PL* 16.

Frankel, M. E., *Criminal Sentences: Law Without Order*, New York, 1972.

Freund, E., *The Growth of American Administrative Law*, New York, 1923.

Frey, R. G. (ed.), *Interests and Rights*, Oxford UP, 1980.

Friedrich, C. J. (ed.), *Rational Decision*, New York, 1964.

—— 'Some Observations on Weber's Analysis of Bureaucracy' in Merton, *Reader in Bureaucracy*.

Friendly, H. J., *The Federal Administration Agencies*, Harvard UP, 1962.

Frug, G. E., 'The Ideology of Bureaucracy in American Law' (1984) 97 *HarvLR* 1276.

Fuller, Lon, *The Morality of Law*, Yale UP, 1964.

—— 'Mediation: Its Forms and Functions' (1971) 44 *SCLR* 305.

—— 'The Forms and Limits of Adjudication' (1976–7) 92 *HarvLR* 353.

Fuller, Lon, and Eisenberg, M., *Basic Contract Law*, 3rd edn., 1972.

Galligan, D. J., 'The Nature and Function of Policies within Discretionary Powers' 1976, *PL* 332.

—— 'Guidelines and Just Deserts: A Critique of Recent Reform Movements in Sentencing' 1981 *CrimLR* 297.

—— 'The Return to Retribution in Penal Theory' in Tapper, *Crime, Proof and Punishment*.

—— 'Judicial Review and the Textbook Writers' (1982) 2 *OJLS* 257.

—— 'Judicial Review and Democratic Principles: Two Theories' (1983) 57 *ALJ* 69.

—— (ed.), *Essays in Legal Theory*, Melbourne UP, 1984.

—— 'Arbitrariness and Formal Justice in Discretionary Decisions' in Galligan, *Essays in Legal Theory*.

Ganz, G., 'The Control of Industry by Administrative Process' 1967 *PL* 93.

—— *Administrative Procedures*, London, 1974.

Garfinkel, H., 'The Rational Properties of Scientific and Common Sense Activities' (1960) 5 *Behavioural Science* 72.

—— 'Studies of the Routine Grounds of Everyday Actions' (1964) 11 *Social Problems* 225.

Gifford, D. J., 'Decisions, Decisional Referents, and Administrative Justice' (1972) 37 *Law&CP* 3.

—— 'Discretionary Decisionmaking in the Regulatory Agencies: a Conceptual Framework' (1983) 57 *SCLR* 101.

Goldstein, J., 'Police discretion not to Invoke Criminal Process' (1960) 69 *YLJ* 543.

Goldring, J., 'The Foundations of the "New Administrative Law" in Australia' (1981) 40 *AJPA* 79.

—— 'Responsible Government and the Administrative Appeals Tribunal' (1982) 13 *FLR* 90.

Gostin, L., *A Human Condition*, London, 1976.

Gough, I., *Political Economy of the Welfare State*, London, 1979.

Grano, J. D., 'Ely's Theory of Judicial Review: Preserving the Significance of the Political Process' (1981) 42 *OhioStLJ* 167.

Gravelle, H. S. E., 'Judicial Review and Public Firms' (1983) 3 *IntRevLaw&Econ* 187.

Greenawalt, Kent, 'Discretion and Judicial Decision: the Elusive Quest for Fetters that Bind Judges' (1975) 75 *CollR* 359.

—— 'Policy, Rights and Judicial Decision' (1977) 11 *GaLR* 991.

Grey, J. H., 'Discretion in Administrative Law' (1979) 17 *OsgoodeHLJ* 107.

Griffith, J. A. G., *The Politics of the Judiciary*, London, 1977.

—— and Street, H., *Principles of Administrative Law*, London 1973.

Guest, A. G. (ed.), *Oxford Essays in Jurisprudence*, Oxford, 1960.

Gulick, L. and Urwick, L. F. (eds.), *Papers on the Science of Administration*, New York, 1937.

Gwyn, W. B., *The Meaning of the Separation of Powers*, Tulane UP, 1965.

Habermas, J., *Legitimation Crisis*, London, 1976.

—— 'Towards a Reconstruction of Historical Materialism' 1975 *Theory and Society* 287.

Hacker, P. and Raz, J. (eds.), *Law, Morality and Society*, Oxford UP, 1978.

Handler, J. F. and Hollingworth, E. J., *The Deserving Poor*, United States, 1971.

Hare, R. M., *The Language of Morals*, Oxford UP, 1971.

Harlow, C. and Rawlings, R., *Law and Administration*, London, 1984.

Haromwy, R., 'Law and the Liberal Society' (1978) 2 *JLibStud* 11.

Harper, M. C., 'The Exercise of Executive Discretion: a Study of a Regional Office of the Department of Labour' 1982 34 *AdmLR* 559.

Harrison, R. J., *Pluralism and Corporatism*, London, 1980.

Hart, H. L. A., *The Concept of Law*, Oxford UP, 1961.

—— *Punishment and Responsibility*, Oxford UP, 1968.

—— *Essays in Philosophy and Jurisprudence*, Oxford UP, 1983.

—— 'Between Utility and Rights' in *Essays in Philosophy and Jurisprudence*.

—— 'Bentham on Rights' in Simpson, *Oxford Essays in Jurisprudence*.

Hayek, F. A., *The Road to Serfdom*, London, 1946.

—— *The Constitution of Liberty*, London, 1960.

—— *Law, Legislation and Liberty*, 3 vols., London, 1973–9.

—— *New Studies in Philosophy, Political Economy and The History of Ideas*, London, 1978.

Hawkins, Keith, *Environment and Enforcement: Regulation and the Social Definition of Pollution*, Oxford UP, 1984.

Hector, L., 'Problems of the C.A.B. and the Indepedent Regulatory Commissions' (1960) 69 *YLJ* 931.

Herrmann, J., 'The German Prosecutor' in Davis, *Discretionary Justice in Europe and America*.

Hewart, Lord, *The New Despotism*, London, 1929.

Hirsch, W., 'Reducing Law's Uncertainty and Complexity' (1974) 21 *UCLALR* 1233.

Hirst, P., *On Law and Ideology*, London, 1979.

Hoffmaster, Barry, 'Understanding Judicial Discretion' (1982) 1 *Law&Phil* 21.

Hogarth, J., *Sentencing as a Human Process*, University of Toronto, 1971.

Hohfeld, W. N., *Fundamental Legal Conceptions as Applied in Judicial Reasoning*, Yale UP, 1919.

Home Office, *Review of Parole in England and Wales*, London 1981.

Honoré, A. M., 'Social Justice' in Summers, *Essays in Legal Philosophy*.

Horowitz, D. L., *The Courts and Social Policy*, Washington, 1977.

Hughes, G., 'Rules, Policy and Decision-Making' (1968) 77 *YLJ* 411.

Hunt, Alan, *The Sociological Movement in Law*, London, 1978.

Jaffe, L. L., *Judicial Control of the Administrative Process*, New York, 1965.

—— 'The Illusion of the Ideal Administrator' (1973) 86 *HarvLR* 1183.

Jaffe, L. L. and Henderson, E., 'Judicial Review and the Rule of Law' (1956) 72 *LQR* 345.

Jansen, J., 'Some Formal Aspects of Dworkin's Right Answer Thesis' (1981) 11 *ManLR* 191.

Jennings, Ivor, *The Law of the Constitution*, London, 1958.

Jergesen, A. D., 'The Legal Requirements of Consultation' 1978 *PL* 290.

Jones, H. W., 'The Rule of Law and the Welfare State' (1958) 58 *ColLR* 143.

Jowell, J. L., 'The Legal Control of Administrative Discretion'1973 *PL* 178.

Justice, *The Citizen and the Administration*, London, 1961.

—— *Our Fettered Ombudsman*, London, 1977.

—— *The Local Ombudsman: a Review of the First Five Years*, London, 1980.

Justice—All Souls, *Review of Administative Law in the United Kingdom*, London, 1981.

Kadish, M. R. and Kadish, S. H., *Discretion to Disobey: a Study of Lawful Departures from Legal Rules*, Stanford UP, 1973.

Kamenka, E. and Neale R. S. (eds.), *Feudalism, Capitalism and Beyond*, London, 1975.

—— and Tay, A. E. S. (eds.), *Justice*, London, 1979.

—— *Law and Social Control*, London, 1980.

Kariel, H. S. (ed.), *Frontiers of Democratic Theory*, New York, 1970.

Keeling, D., *Management in Government*, London, 1972.

Kelsen, Hans, *General Theory of Law and State*, New York, 1961.

Kennedy, Ian, *The Unmasking of Medicine*, London 1978.

King, J., 'The Role of the Judge in Relation to Public Administration' (1980) 39 *AJPA* 1.

Kirby, M. D., 'Administrative Review: Beyond the Frontier Marked "Policy—Lawyers Keep Out"' (1981) 12 *FLR* 121.

Korah, V., 'Counter-Inflation Legislation: Whither Parliamentary Sovereignty?' (1976) 92 *LQR* 42.

Krislov, Samuel, *Representative Bureaucracy*, New Jersey, 1974.

Kronman, A., *Max Weber*, London, 1983.

Ladd, J., 'The Place of Practical Reasoning in Judicial Decisions' in Friedrich, *Rational Decision*.

Lamont, W. D., *Law and the Moral Order*, Aberdeen, 1981.

Landis, J. M., *The Administrative Process*, New Haven, 1938.

Lazarus, S. and Onek, J., 'The Regulators and the People' (1971) 57 *VaLR* 1069.

Levinson, S., 'Taking Rights Seriously: Reflections on "Thinking Like a Lawyer"' (1977–8) 30 *StanLR* 1071.

Leys, W. A. R., 'Ethics and Administrative Discretion' 1943 *PAdR* 10.

Lindblom, C., 'The Science of Muddling Through' (1959) 19 *PAdR* 79.

—— *The Intelligence of Democracy: Decision Making Through Mutual Adjustment*, New York, 1965.

Lively, J., *Democracy*, Oxford, 1975.

Lloyd, D., *Introduction to Jurisprudence*, London, 4th edn., 1979.

Lovegrove, Austin, 'The Listing of Criminal Cases in the Crown Court as an Administrative Discretion' 1984 *CrimLR* 738.

Lucas, J. R., *On Justice*, Oxford UP, 1978.

Luhmann, Niklas, *Trust and Power*, London, 1969.

—— 'Differentiation of Society' (1977) 11 *CanJSoc* 29.

—— 'Generalized Media and the Problem of Contingency' in J. Loubser *et al.* (eds.), *Explorations in General Theory in the Social Sciences: Essays in Honour of Talcott Parsons*, New York, 1978.

Lustick,. I., 'Explaining the Variable Utility of Disjointed Incrementalism' (1980) 74 *AmPolSciR* 342.

Lyons, David, *Ethics and the Rule of Law*, Cambridge UP, 1984.

MacCallum, G., 'Legislative Intent' in Summers, *Essays in Legal Philosophy*.

—— 'Dworkin on Judicial Discretion' (1963) 60 *JPhil* 638.

MacCormick, Neil, *Legal Reasoning and Legal Theory*, Oxford UP, 1978.

—— 'Rights in Legislation' in Hacker and Raz, *Law, Morality and Society*.

Macdonald, R. A., 'Judicial Review and Procedural Fairness in Administrative Law' (1979) 25 *McGill LJ* and (1980) 26 *McGill LJ*.

MacNeil, M., 'Property in the Welfare State' (1984) 7 *DalLR* 343.

Macpherson, C. B., 'Capitalism and the Changing Concept of Property' in Kamenka and Neale, *Feudalism, Capitalism and Beyond*.

—— 'The Meaning of Property' in Macpherson, *Property*.

—— (ed.), *Property*, Oxford, 1978.

Madison, James and Jay, John, *The Federalist*, London, 1970 edn.

Magat, W. A., and Estomin, S., 'The Behaviour of Regulatory Agencies' in Ferguson, *Attacking Regulatory Problems*.

Manning, P. K., *Police Work: The Social Organization of Policing*, Massachusetts, 1977.

Marini, F., *Toward a New Public Administration*, New Jersey, 1971.

Markovits, I., 'Socialist vs Bourgeois Rights' 1 (1978) 45 *UChicLR* 612.

Marshall, G., *Constitutional Theory*, Oxford UP, 1968.

—— 'Justiciability' in Guest, *Oxford Essays in Jurisprudence*.

Marshall, T. H., *The Right to Welfare*, London, 1981.

Martin, R. C. (ed.), *Public Administation and Democracy*, Syracuse UP, 1965.

Mashaw, J. L., 'The Supreme Court's Due Process Calculus for Administrative Adjudication in *Mathews* v. *Eldridge*: Three Factors in Search of a Theory of Value' (1976) 44 *UChicLR* 28.

—— 'Conflict and Compromise Among Models of Administrative Justice' (1981) *DukeLJ*.

—— *Bureaucratic Justice*, Yale UP, 1983.

—— ' "Rights" in the Federal Administrative State' (1983) 92 *YLJ* 1129.

—— 'Mirrored Ambivalence: a Sometimes Curmudgeonly Comment on the Relationship Between Organization Theory and Law' 1983 *JLegEd* 24.

Merrill, R. R., 'Regulating Carcinogens in Food' (1978) 77 *MichLR* 171.

Merton, R. K. (ed.), *Reader in Bureaucracy*, New York, 1952.

Michelman, F., 'Welfare Rights in a Constitutional Democracy' 1979 *WashULQ* 659.

—— 'Process and Property in Constitutional Theory' (1981) 30 *ClevStLR* 577.

Mill, J. S., *Considerations on Representative Government*, London, 1964 edn.

Mommsen, W., *The Age of Bureaucracy*, Oxford UP, 1974.

Montesquieu, L., *The Spirit of the Laws*, New York, 1949 edn.

Munzer, P., 'Right Answer, Pre-existing Rights and Fairness' (1977) 11 *GaLR* 1055.

Mureinik, E., 'The Application of Rules: Law or Fact?' (1982) 98 *LQR* 587.

Murphy, W. T., 'Modern Times: Niklas Luhmann on Law, Politics and Social Theory' (1984) 47 *MLR* 603.

Nelson, W. N., 'The Very Idea of Procedural Justice' (1980) 90 *Ethics* 502.

—— *On Justifying Democracy*, London, 1980.

Neuborne, Bert, 'Judicial Review and Separation of Powers in France and the United States' (1982) 57 *NYULR* 363.

Newman, Otto, *The Challenge of Corporatism*, London, 1981.

Noble, David, 'From Rules to Discretion? The Housing Corporation' in Alder and Asquith, *Discretion and Welfare*.

Nonet, P., 'Taking Purpose Seriously' in Gray Dorsey, *Proceedings of the International Conference on Legal and Social Philosophy*.

Nonet, P. and Selznick, D., *Law and Society in Transition*, Berkeley, 1978.

Nozick, Robert, *Anarchy, State and Utopia*, Oxford, 1974.

Offe, C., *Contradictions of the Welfare State*, London, 1984.

Ogus, A. I., 'Quantitative Rules and Judicial Decision-Making' in Burrows and Veljanovski, *The Economic Approach to Law*.

Panitch, Leo, 'The Development of Corporatism in Liberal Democracies' (1977) 10 *CompPolStud*.

—— 'Recent Theorizations of Corporatism: Reflections on a Growth Industry' (1980) 31 *BJSoc* 159.

Parliamentary Commissioner for Administration, Annual Report, 1983.

Pashukanis, E., *General Theory of Marxism and Law*, C. Arthur ed., London, 1978.

Passmore, J. A., 'Civil Justice and Its Rivals' In Kamenka and Tay, *Justice*.

Pateman, C., *Participation and Democratic Theory*, Cambridge UP, 1970.

Paterson, Alan, *The Law Lords*, Oxford UP, 1982.

Pattenden, R. M., *The Judge, Discretion and the Criminal Trial*, Oxford UP, 1982.

Pearce, D., 'Courts, Tribunals and Government Policy' (1980) 11 *FLR* 203.

Pennock, J. R., *Democratic Political Theory*, Princeton UP, 1975.

—— and Chapman, J. W. (eds.), *Due Process*, Nomos XVIII, New York UP, 1977.

—— —— (eds.), *Participation in Politics*, Nomos XVI, New York UP, 1975.

—— —— (eds.), *Representation*, New York, 1968.

Perelman, Ch., *Justice, Law, and Argument*, Netherlands, 1980.

Pettit, Philip, *Judging Justice: an Introduction to Contemporary Political Philosophy*, London, 1980.

Pike, F. B. and Stritch, T. (eds.), *The New Corporatism*, Notre Dame UP, 1975.

Plamenatz, J., *Man and Society*, London, 1963.

Plant, R., Lesser, H. and Taylor-Goodby, P., *Political Philosophy and Social Welfare*, London, 1980.

Poggi, G., *The Development of the Modern State*, London, 1980.

—— Introduction to Luhmann, Niklas, *Trust and Power*.

—— 'Two Themes from N. Luhmann's Contribution to the Sociology of Law' 1981 *BASLP*.

Posner, R., 'The Behaviour of Administrative Agencies' (1972) 1 *JLegStud* 305.

—— 'An Economic Approach to Legal Procedure and Judicial Administration' (1972–3) 2 *JLegStud* 399.

Pound, Roscoe, 'Discretion, Dispensation, and Mitigation: The Problem of the Individual Special Case'(1960) 35 *NYULR* 925.

—— *Contemporary Juristic Theory*, California, 1940.

—— *Jurisprudence*, St Paul, 1959.

Prosser, Tony, 'The Politics of Discretion: Aspects of Discretionary Power in the Supplementary Benefits Scheme' in Adler and Asquith, *Discretion and Welfare*.

Rabin, R. L., 'Legitimacy, Discretion, and the Concept of Rights' (1983) 92 *YLJ* 1174.

—— 'Job Security and Due Process: Monitoring Administrative Discretion Through a Reasons Requirement' (1976–7) *UChicLR* 60.

Rawls, John, *A Theory of Justice*, Oxford UP, 1972.

Raz, Joseph, 'Legal Principles and the Limits of Law' (1972) 81 *YLJ* 823.

—— 'On the Functions of Law' in Simpson, *Oxford Essays in Jurisprudence*.

—— (ed.), *Practical Reasoning*, Oxford UP, 1978.

—— *The Authority of Law*, Oxford UP, 1979.

—— 'On the Nature of Rights' (1984) xciii *Mind* 194.

—— 'Legal Rights' (1984) 4 *OJLS*.

Redford, E. S., *Democracy in the Administrative State*, Oxford UP, 1969.

Reich, Charles, 'The New Property' (1964) 73 *YLJ* 733 and in Macpherson, *Property*.

—— 'Individual Rights and Social Welfare: the Emerging Legal Issues' (1965) 74 *YLJ* 1245.

Reiss, A. J., Book Review of Discretionary Justice (1970) 69 *MichLR* 794.

Resnick, David, 'Due Process and Procedural Justice' in Pennock and Chapman, *Due Process*.

Richardson, Genevra with Ogus, A., and Burrows, P., *Policing Pollution: A Study of Regulation and Enforcement*, Oxford UP, 1982.

Robinson, G. O., 'The Making of Administrative Policy: Another Look at Rulemaking and Adjudication and Administrative Procedure Reform' (1970) 118 *UPaLR* 485.

Rourke, F. E. (ed.), *Bureaucratic Power in National Politics*, Boston, 1965.

Sackville, Ronald, 'Property Rights and Social Security' (1973–8) 2 *UNSWLR* 246.

Sartorious, R., 'The Justification of the Judicial Decision' (1968) 78 *Ethics* 171.

—— 'Social Policy and Judicial Legislation' (1971) 8 *AmPhilQ* 151.

—— 'Bayes' Theorem, Hard Cases, and Judicial Discretion' (1977) 11 *GaLR* 1269.

Scanlon, T. M., 'Due Process' in Pennock and Chapman, *Due Process*.

Schmitter, P. C., 'Still the Century of Corporatism' in Pike and Stritch, *The New Corporatism*.

Schuck, P. H., 'Organization Theory and the Teaching of Administrative Law' 1983 *JLegEd* 13.

—— 'When the Exception Becomes the Rule: Regulatory Equity and the Formulation of Energy Policy Through an Exception Process' 1984 *DukeLJ* 163.

Schutz, Alfred, 'The Problem of Rationality to the Social World' (1943) 10 *Economica* 134.

Schwartz, B., *Administrative Law*, New York, 1976.

Schwartz, B. and Wade, H. W. R., *Legal Control of Government: Administrative Law in Britain and the United States*, Oxford UP, 1972.

Self, P., *Administrative Theories and Politics*, Toronto UP, 1973.

Sellers, J. M., 'Regulatory Values and the Exceptions Process' (1984) 93 *YLJ* 938.

Selznick, P., *Law, Society and Industrial Justice*, New York, 1969.

—— 'A Theory of Organizational Commitments' in Merton, *Reader in Bureaucracy*.

Shapiro, M., *The Supreme Court and Administrative Agencies*, New York, 1968.

—— 'Administrative Discretion: the Next Stage' (1983) 92 *YLJ* 1487.

Shulman, D. R., 'Nonincremental Policymaking: Notes Towards an Alternative Paradigm' (1975) 69 *AmPolSciR* 1354.

Simon, Herbert, *Administrative Behaviour*, New York, 1945.

Simpson, A. W. B. (ed.), *Oxford Essays in Jurisprudence*, Oxford UP, 1973.

Skelly Wright, J., 'Beyond Discretionary Justice' (1971–2) 81 *YLJ* 575.

—— 'The Courts and the Rulemaking Process: the Limits of Judicial Review' (1974) 59 *CornLR* 375.

Skolnick, J. H., *Justice Without Trial: Law Enforcement in Democratic Society*, London, 1966.

Slogobin, C., 'Dangerousness and Expertise' (1984) 133 *UPaLR* 97.

Staatsn, A. A. M. F., 'General Assistance in the Netherlands' in Davis, *Discretionary Justice in Europe and America*.

Stacey, P., *The British Ombudsman*, Oxford UP, 1971.

Stein, P. and Shand J., *Legal Values in Western Society*, Edinburgh UP, 1974.

Steiner, J. M., 'Judicial Discretion and the Concept of Law' (1976) 35 *CLJ* 135.

Stevens, R., 'Justiciability: The Restrictive Practices Court Re-Examined', 1964 *PL* 221.

—— *Law and Politics: the House of Lords as a Judicial Body 1800–1976*, London, 1979.

Stewart, R., 'The Reformation of Administrative Law' (1974–5) 88 *HarvLR* 1667.

—— '*Vermont Yankee* and the Evolution of Administrative Procedure' (1978) 91 *HarvLR* 1805.

—— 'Regulation, Innovation and Administrative Law: A Conceptual Framework' (1981) 69 *CalLR* 1259.

Stone, Julius, *Social Dimensions of Law and Justice*, Sydney, 1966.

—— 'From Principles to Principles' (1981) 97 *LQR* 224.

Summers, R. S., 'Justiciability' (1963) 26 *MLR* 530.

—— (ed.), *Essays in Legal Philosophy*, Oxford, 1970.

Swartzman, D., Liroff, R. A. and Croke, K. G., *Cost-Benefit Analysis and Environmental Regulations: Politics, Ethics and Methods*, United States, 1982.

Symposium on Sentencing (1978–9) 7 *HofstraLR* 1.

Tapper, C. F. H., 'A Note on Principles' (1971) 34 *MLR* 628.

—— (ed.), *Crime, Proof and Punishment: Essays in Memory of Rupert Cross*, London, 1981.

Taylor, F. W., *Principles and Methods of Scientific Management*, New York, 1911.

Taylor, G. D. S., 'The New Administrative Law' (1977) 51 *ALJ* 804.

Thomas, D. A., *Principles of Sentencing*, London, 2nd edn., 1979.

Thompson, D. F., *The Democratic Citizen*, Cambridge UP, 1970.

—— 'Bureaucracy and Democracy' in Duncan, *Democratic Theory and Practice*, Cambridge UP, 1983.

Thompson, E. P., *Whigs and Hunters*, London, 1977.

Timms, N. and Watson, D. (eds), *Philosophy in Social Work*, London, 1978.

Titmuss, R. M., 'Welfare "Rights", Law and Discretion' (1971) 42 *PolQ* 113.

—— *Essays on the Welfare State*, London, 3rd edn., 1976.

Tomasic, R., 'Preventative Detention and the High Court' (1981) 55 *ALJ* 259.

Toulmin, S., 'Equity and Principles' (1982) 20 *Osgoode HLJ* 1.

Treitel, G. H., *Doctrine and Discretion in the Law of Contract*, Oxford UP, 1981.

Tribe, Lawrence, *Constitutional Law*, New York, 1978.

—— 'The Puzzling Persistence of Process-Based Constitutional Theories' (1980) 89 *YLJ* 1063.

Trubek, D., 'Max Weber on Law and the Rise of Capitalism' (1972) 3 *WiscLR* 720.
Truman, D., *The Governmental Process*, United States, 1957.
Tuebner, G., 'Substantive and Reflexive Elements in Modern Law' (1983) 17 *LSR* 239.
Tushnet, M., 'Darkness on the Edge of Town' (1980) 89 *YLJ* 1037.

Unger, R. M., *Law in Modern Society*, New York, 1976.

Verkuil, P., 'Judicial Review of Informal Rule Making'(1974) 60 *VaLR* 185.
—— 'The Emerging Concept of Administrative Procedure' (1978) 78 *ColLR* 258.
Vile, J. M. C., *Constitutionalism and the Separation of Powers*, Oxford 1967.
Vining, Joseph, *Legal Identity: The Coming of Age of Public Law*, Yale UP, 1978.
Von Hirsch, A., *Doing Justice*, New York, 1976.

Wade, H. W. R., *Administrative Law*, Oxford UP, 4th edn., 1977.
Waldo, D., *The Administrative State: a Study of the Political theory of American Public Administration*, New York, 1948.
Waldron, J., (ed.), *Theories of Rights*, Oxford UP, 1984.
Weber, Max, *The Protestant Ethic and the Spirit of Capitalism*, London, 1930.
—— *Methodology in the Social Sciences*, New York, 1949.
—— *Economy and Society*, G. Roth and C. Wittick eds., California UP, 1978.
Weiler, P., 'Two Models of Judicial Decision-making' (1968) 46 *CanBR* 406.
Wellman, Carl, *Welfare Rights*, New York, 1982.
Wells, R. S. and Grossman, J. B., 'The Concept of Judicial Policy-Making' (1965) 15 *JPL* 286.
Westen, Peter, 'The Empty Idea of Equality' (1982) 95 *HarvLR* 537.
White, A. R., *Rights*, Oxford UP, 1984.
Wilson, Bryan (ed.), *Rationality*, Oxford, 1970.
Wilson, H. T., '"Discretion" in the Analysis of Administrative Process' (1972) 10 *OsgoodeHLJ* 117.
Wilson, J., 'The Rise of the Bureaucratic State' (1975) 41 *PubInt* 77.
Winkler, J., 'Law, State, and Economy' (1975) 2 *BJLS* 103.
—— 'The Political Economy of Administrative Discretion' in Adler and Asquith, *Discretion and Welfare*.
Witherspoon, J. P., 'The Bureaucracy as Representatives' in Pennock and Chapman, *Representation*.
Woodford, Howard J., 'Adjudication Considered as a Process of Conflict Resolution: a Variation on Separation of Powers' (1969) 18 *JPL* 339.

Yellin, J., 'High Technology and the Courts: Nuclear Power and the Need for Institutional Reform' (1981) 94 *HarvLR* 489.
Young, O. R., *Natural Resources and the State*, California UP, 1981.

Index

Printed in Great Britain
by Amazon